TEST ANXIETY:

Theory, Research, and Applications

EDITED BY

IRWIN G. SARASON
University of Washington

LEA LAWRENCE ERLBAUM ASSOCIATES, PUBLISHERS
1980 Hillsdale, New Jersey

Lawrence Erlbaum Associates, Inc., Publishers
365 Broadway
Hillsdale, New Jersey 07642

Library of Congress Cataloging in Publication Data

Main entry under title:

Test anxiety.

   Bibliography: p.
   Includes index.
   1. Test anxiety.   I. Sarason, Irwin G.
BF575.A6T47   152.4   79-28344
ISBN 0-89859-022-1

Printed in the United States of America

Contents

257152

PART II: THEORY AND RESEARCH

Preface

Because I had heard many comments about the unfortunate lack of a book reviewing research on test anxiety, I invited a group of major contributors to the field to join me in writing one. The collaboration was unusual because of the many animated exchanges among contributors. Although we never met as a group, we circulated the chapters and added our constructive comments. More often than not, the comments stimulated authors' thinking and led to broader-gauged articles.

A book like this has not heretofore been available because test anxiety seems to cover a restricted domain. Because of that fact, however, research on the topic is burgeoning. It permits study of important aspects of the general problem of anxiety in a relatively well-defined situational context. Even older persons who no longer attend school frequently face situations in which they are evaluated in some way. The chapters in this book convey the richness of human processes involved in taking tests and being evaluated.

In a sense, test anxiety is a "sleeper," possessing more than meets the eye. At times, even workers in the field underestimate its scope. When I invited Don Meichenbaum to contribute a chapter, he said he would try, but he wasn't sure there was either enough material or that he had that much to say. In my most recent conversation with Don, I tactfully pointed out that his chapter was a bit longer than we had agreed it would be. He replied that he had barely been able to boil down all the material into the pages he had sent me. He then uttered a refrain familiar to editors: "I can't cut out anything. If I do, the whole thing won't make sense."

Marty Lindley was a great help in preparing the final manuscript before it was sent to the publisher. Laura Kalb made several incisive comments concerning one chapter. Most of all, I want to thank the contributors, who are both scholars and nice people.

Seattle, Washington   IRWIN G. SARASON

INTRODUCTION

1 Introduction to the Study of Test Anxiety

Irwin G. Sarason
University of Washington

Why has interest in test anxiety not only persisted but actually intensified over the years? There are at least two reasons. First, all researchers know how difficult it is to come to grips with such global concepts as anxiety, aggression, and dependence. Concepts that are rooted in specific classes of situations are more manageable. People experience anxiety in situations or in anticipating them. The anxious football player may not be the anxious public speaker or the anxious parent. Testing situations are relatively specific and are experienced by everyone. Their universality makes them significant educational, social, and clinical problems; they are also scientifically convenient. For the researcher, they are empirically valuable because they provide a path to the study of stress and how people cope with it.

Second, research on test anxiety has prospered because testing situations have high salience and face validity for people. This is particularly true for those who go to school or may be subjected to evaluations of intellectual skills and performance. Anyone who has ever taught the Introductory Psychology course in a college or university is well aware of the question all too often asked by students when they serve as subjects in the experiments that usually go along with that course: "What in the world does that experiment have to do with real life?" People, at least in Western industrial societies, know from personal experience that performance evaluations take place all the time and that these evaluations can be of great personal importance. It is not surprising, therefore, that many researchers find the performance evaluation situation a useful one for studying the effects of anxiety. It is also not surprising that the clinical and educational aspects of test anxiety have received widespread attention.

For many years, theories of anxiety were rooted primarily in the experiences of the clinical worker and the insights of the sensitive observer of people as they go about their day-to-day activities. Important scientific papers appeared during the 1930s and 1940s when increasing efforts were made to study the problem of anxiety from an experimental perspective. Psychologists were in the forefront of these efforts that often took the shape of analogues of psychoanalytic concepts. During the 1950s, researchers took another step forward in their attempts to assess anxiety quantitatively. Although some work along these lines had been done earlier, the 1950s saw a flowering of anxiety scales, questionnaires, and measures (I. Sarason, 1960). (A few observers of the psychological scene noted this flowering of indexes of anxiety with more than a little alarm, arguing that the garden was infested with too many weeds.)

Soon after its publication, the Manifest Anxiety Scale (MAS), became the most widely used measure of anxiety (Taylor, 1951, 1953). Both the construction and use of this instrument were somewhat anomalous. Although the word "anxiety" appeared in its title, the MAS was constructed as a measure of drive—Hull's D, to be specific. However, the 50 true–false statements of the MAS were selected by asking clinical psychologists to judge which items of the Minnesota Multiphasic Personality Inventory (MMPI) reflected Norman Cameron's definition of anxiety. Despite the perhaps too subtle or fuzzy logic of this procedure (what does Cameron's definition of anxiety have to do with Hull's D?), the fact that the MAS's items appeared to deal with anxieties, worries, and reactions to stressful situations led to its incorporation into many research designs and even into clinical batteries.

Because of the desirability of rooting the study of anxiety in a definable situational context, some researchers turned their attention to specific sources of anxiety, such as social anxiety, anxiety over public speaking, and test anxiety. Test anxiety has become the most widely studied of these specific anxieties, and there are now available a number of indexes of persons' anxieties about being examined and having their performances evaluated. The Test Anxiety Scale for Children, constructed by Seymour Sarason and his associates (S. Sarason, Davidson, Lighthall, Waite, & Ruebush, 1960), was the first index of test anxiety to be used widely by researchers. It continues to be a popular and valued instrument. Seymour Sarason's research highlighted the usefulness of defining as explicitly as possible the situational domain within which theoretical issues are explored.

THE AIMS OF THIS BOOK

Despite the hundreds of studies on the topic, a source book dealing with research, theory, and applications concerning test anxiety has not been available. This book is intended to fill that gap.

Although not designed to be encyclopedic, most of the topics in the area are mentioned, discussed, and, where possible, interrelated. The authors of the chapters have surveyed the literature relevant to their contributions but have not stopped there. Perhaps the greatest need in research on test anxiety is not more studies, but rather an analysis of where we are now and where we should be going. The contributors were encouraged to be analytical. As a consequence, the chapters are both objective and subjective. They are objective in that they survey available knowledge. They are subjective because the contributors have also put their idiosyncratic stamps on the chapters. They express their opinions about important issues and give the background for those opinions. In this way, treatments of theoretical issue permeate the entire book.

Research on test anxiety falls into two overlapping domains: (1) hypothesis-testing, laboratory, field, and developmental studies of persons differing in test anxiety; and (2) applied studies, most of which are directed toward reducing test anxiety and its undesirable effects. Although the cognitive point of view seems currently to be the most influential theoretical force in research in test anxiety, a variety of theories have influenced work in the field. The diversity of these perspectives will be evident to readers of the book.

Following the two chapters in Part I, the introductory section, Part II deals with several research areas whose main locus is the laboratory. These chapters deal with basic methodological and theoretical issues. Part III analyzes interventive strategies, ranging from clinical treatment studies to comparisons of different educational approaches. As will be seen, these strategies grow out of and contribute to theory. Jeri Wine's concluding chapter in Part IV overviews the preceding chapters, identifies consistencies and inconsistencies in our current knowledge, makes integrative observations, and offers suggestions for future study.

Test anxiety has been a little like the weather: "Everybody talks about it, but no one does anything about it." I will not attempt to review the current status of research on weather and its modification (such an effort by the writer would surely be his wildest—and least informed—contribution to human literature), but I do know that a lot of people are now trying to do something about test anxiety. I hope that this book will provide worthwhile perspectives for continuation of this effort.

STRESS AND TEST ANXIETY

People come to situations with their distinctive sets of personal characteristics, including assumptions, concerns, and expectations. One useful starting point in analyzing anxiety begins with the objective properties of problematic situations and individuals' interpretations of them. Regardless of the objective situation, it is personal interpretation or cognitive appraisal of the situation that leads to behavior. Someone who has failed a test, but isn't aware of it, will not become upset. Students who feel they have performed creditably on a test will relax and anticipate recognition for their achievements. Students who feel they have performed poorly will experience stress; that is, they will see a problem to be solved.

When stress is experienced, the individual feels on the spot: "What will I do now? It's up to me, I guess." There are several types of response to stress. The most adaptive one is a task-oriented attitude that leads the individual to take specific steps toward successfully coping with the stress-arousing situation. Seeking a conference with the teacher and studying harder are two adaptive responses to failing a test. An example of a maladaptive response is denying its importance: "So what if I got a low grade? I can't have such bad luck next time. It was a dumb test." The anxious response to failure and its anticipation is to stew about the problem and engage in self-derogation.

Whereas stress inheres in one's interpretation of a situation, anxiety is a response to perceived danger and inability to handle a challenge or unfinished business in a satisfactory manner. Among the characteristics of anxiety are:

1. The situation is seen as difficult, challenging, and threatening.
2. The individual sees himself as ineffective, or inadequate, in handling the task at hand.
3. The individual focuses on undesirable consequences of personal inadequacy.
4. Self-deprecatory preoccupations are strong and interfere or compete with task-relevant cognitive activity.
5. The individual expects and anticipates failure and loss of regard by others.

These characteristics can become linked to situations through experience. Anxiety might be associated with any or all of the following: anticipating a situation, experiencing it, and "recovering" from it. There are varied, often quite idiosyncratic, physiological concomitants of anxiety. Both the quantity of anxiety and the mix of situations in which it is experienced vary from person to person:

1. Anxiety can be experienced in well-defined situations commonly seen as stressful to which the individual feels unable to respond adequately.
2. It can be experienced in ambiguous situations where the individual must structure task requirements and personal expectations.
3. It might be linked to classes of situations defined in idiosyncratic ways (interpersonal relationships with certain groups of peers, family members, female authority figures, members of the opposite sex; situations requiring verbal, mathematical, spatial, or motoric skills).

This view is similar to Freud's in that anxiety is described as a state marked by heightened self-awareness and perceived helplessness. This helplessness can arise from inability to cope with a situational demand in a satisfactory manner, perceived inability to understand situational demands, or uncertainty about the consequences of inadequacy in coping. The self-preoccupations of the anxious person, even in apparently neutral or even pleasant situations, may be due to a history of experiences marked by a relative paucity of signals indicating that a safe haven from danger has been reached.

The reasons for the perception of danger are various, including the stimulus properties of situations and unrealistically high standards. Every teacher knows students who, although quite able and bright, are virtually terror stricken at exam time. In these cases, a student often expresses concern about the consequences of not performing at a satisfactory level and embarrassment at what is regarded as "failure."

Stress then is a call for action determined by the properties of situations and personal dispositions. The anxious person feels unable to respond to that call.

EXPERIMENTAL APPROACH TO TEST ANXIETY

The view of test anxiety taken in this chapter is a cognitive one because it directs attention to what the individual is thinking about when confronted with evaluative stressors. Through cognitive appraisal, individuals define for themselves the opportunities and dangers connected with tests. They also appraise their abilities. For the test anxiety researcher, the challenge is to relate individual difference in cognitive appraisals of tests, self, and outcomes to objective elements of testing situations. From this perspective, individual differences in test anxiety are important factors in how persons process information.

Laboratory experiments carried out by many researchers have added to our knowledge about the deleterious influence of high levels of test anxiety on information processing and performance (see Chapters 3 and 4). There is considerable evidence that the performance of highly test-anxious persons on complex tasks is deleteriously affected by evaluational stressors. The less complex, less demanding the task, the weaker this effect is. An example of an evaluational stressor is achievement-orienting instructions that either inform subjects that some kind of evaluation of their performances will be made or provide some other rationale for the importance of performing well. When persons are reassured that a negative evaluation of their performance will not be made, highly test-anxious persons often perform as well or better than those who are typically less worried.

An experiment carried out by Sarason and Stoops (1978) illustrates the experimental approach to test anxiety. The index was the Test Anxiety Scale (TAS) (Sarason, 1978). Table 1.1 contains its 37 items.

Sarason and Stoops (1978) used the TAS in testing hypotheses about both performance and cognitive processes. The investigation comprised a series of three experiments concerning subjective judgments of the passage of time. After being given either achievement-orienting or neutral instructions, subjects waited for an undesignated period of time before performing an intellective task. The achievement-orienting manipulation involved telling the subject that the task was a measure of intelligence. The dependent measures were subjects' estimates of the duration of the waiting and performance periods and their scores on the assigned task.

The experiments were aimed at providing information about the way individuals differing in anxiety fill time. It was predicted that, in the presence of achievement-orienting cues, time would pass more slowly for high than for middle and low TAS scorers. When these cues are not present, there should not be a significant gap in estimates of time duration among groups differing in test anxiety. Furthermore, it was felt that the effects of an achievement orientation should be as noticeable while the individual is waiting to perform as during performance itself.

The findings of the first two experiments supported the conclusion that not only is the performance of TAS subjects deleteriously affected by achievement-orienting instructions, but the subjects also tend to overestimate both the duration of the test period and the period during which they wait to have their ability evaluated. This appears analogous to the tendency to exaggerate time spent in the dentist's waiting room and office. Anticipating and going through unpleasant, frightening, or threatening experiences seem to take up a lot of time. If this interpretation is correct, the question arises: Do individuals differing in anxiety fill time periods in similar or dissimilar ways? The third experiment dealt with this question.

In the experiment, college students worked on a digit-symbol task prior to a waiting period and then were asked to solve a series of difficult anagrams. Following this, the subjects responded to a questionnaire dealing with their cognitive activity during the anagrams task. The subjects were 60 female

TABLE 1.1
Test Anxiety Scale (TAS) Items
(Keyed answers are in parentheses.)

(T) 1. While taking an important exam, I find myself thinking of how much brighter the other students are than I am.

(T) 2. If I were to take an intelligence test, I would worry a great deal before taking it.

(F) 3. If I knew I was going to take an intelligence test, I would feel confident and relaxed, beforehand.

(T) 4. While taking an important examination, I perspire a great deal.

(T) 5. During course examinations, I find myself thinking of things unrelated to the actual course material.

(T) 6. I get to feel very panicky when I have to take a surprise exam.

(T) 7. During tests, I find myself thinking of the consequences of failing.

(T) 8. After important tests, I am frequently so tense that my stomach gets upset.

(T) 9. I freeze up on things like intelligence tests and final exams.

(T) 10. Getting a good grade on one test doesn't seem to increase my confidence on the second.

(T) 11. I sometimes feel my heart beating very fast during important exams.

(T) 12. After taking a test, I always feel I could have done better than I actually did.

(T) 13. I usually get depressed after taking a test.

(T) 14. I have an uneasy, upset feeling before taking a final examination.

(F) 15. When taking a test, my emotional feelings do not interfere with my performance.

(T) 16. During a course examination, I frequently get so nervous that I forget facts I really know.

(T) 17. I seem to defeat myself while working on important tests.

(T) 18. The harder I work at taking a test or studying for one, the more confused I get.

(T) 19. As soon as an exam is over, I try to stop worrying about it, but I just can't.

(T) 20. During exams, I sometimes wonder if I'll ever get through college.

(T) 21. I would rather write a paper than take an examination for my grade in a course.

(T) 22. I wish examinations did not bother me so much.

(T) 23. I think I could do much better on tests if I could take them alone and not feel pressured by a time limit.

(T) 24. Thinking about the grade I may get in a course interferes with my studying and my performance on tests.

(T) 25. If examinations could be done away with, I think I would actually learn more.

(F) 26. On exams I take the attitude, "If I don't know it now, there's no point worrying about it."

(F) 27. I really don't see why some people get so upset about tests.

(T) 28. Thoughts of doing poorly interfere with my performance on tests.

(F) 29. I don't study any harder for final exams than for the rest of my course work.

(F) 30. Even when I'm well prepared for a test, I feel very anxious about it.

(T) 31. I don't enjoy eating before an important test.

(T) 32. Before an important examination, I find my hands or arms trembling.

(F) 33. I seldom feel the need for "cramming" before an exam.

(T) 34. The university should recognize that some students are more nervous than others about tests and that this affects their performance.

(T) 35. It seems to me that examination periods should not be made such tense situations.

(T) 36. I start feeling very uneasy just before getting a test paper back.

(T) 37. I dread courses where the professor has the habit of giving "pop" quizzes.

undergraduates. The experimental design encompassed two factors: (1) high, middle, and low TAS scores; and (2) achievement-orienting and neutral instructions. Each subject worked on the digit-symbol task for 4 minutes. This was followed by a 4-minute period. At the end of the waiting period, subjects performed for 18 minutes on the anagrams. The experiment concluded with subjects responding to the Cognitive Interference Questionnaire (see Table 1.2).

There were two significant factors in an analysis of variance performed on waiting-period time estimates, those for Test Anxiety ($p < .002$) and those for Test Anxiety × Conditions ($p < .05$). The means for time estimates by the high, middle, and low TAS groups were 321.8, 270.4, and 266.3 seconds, respectively. The significant interaction was attributable to the higher time estimates mean obtained by the high TAS group receiving achievement-orienting instructions. The mean for that group was 357.0 seconds, whereas the high TAS control group mean was 286.5 seconds. Table 1.3 presents the means of the four dependent measures for all groups in the experiment.

TABLE 1.2
Cognitive Interference Questionnarie

I. We are interested in learning about the kinds of thoughts that go through people's heads while they are working on a task. The following list includes some thoughts you might have had *while doing the task that you just completed.* Please indicate approximately how often each thought occurred to you while working on this task by placing the appropriate number in the blank provided to the left of each question.

Example: 1. = never
           2. = once
           3. = a few times
           4. = often
           5. = very often

____ 1. I thought about how poorly I was doing.
____ 2. I wondered what the experimenter would think of me.
____ 3. I thought about how I should work more carefully.
____ 4. I thought about how much time I had left.
____ 5. I thought about how others have done on this task.
____ 6. I thought about the difficulty of the problems.
____ 7. I thought about my level of ability.
____ 8. I thought about the purpose of the experiment.
____ 9. I thought about how I would feel if I were told how I performed.
____10. I thought about how often I got confused.
____11. I thought about things completely unrelated to the experiment.

II. Please circle the number on the following scale which best represents the degree to which you felt your mind wandered *during the task you have just completed.*

Not at all   1. : 2. : 3. : 4. : 5. : 6. : 7.   very much

TABLE 1.3
Mean Waiting Time & Task Times Estimates, Anagram Performance Scores, &
Cognitive Interference Scores (Sarason & Stoops, 1978)

	Waiting Time (sec)	Task Time (sec)	Anagrams Score	Cognitive Interference Score
H–E	357.0	1354.1	3.3	33.2
H–C	286.5	1114.0	4.8	24.6
M–E	266.3	1031.5	5.5	18.2
M–C	274.4	1103.5	5.7	21.6
L–E	266.5	1172.0	5.0	19.8
L–C	265.0	1140.5	5.0	21.4

Note: H, M, and L refer to levels of test anxiety; E and C refer to experimental (achievement-orientation) and control conditions.

The analysis of estimates of duration of the anagrams task also yielded two significant factors, for Test Anxiety and for Test Anxiety × Conditions (each at the .05 level). Again, the significant results were explicable largely in terms of the relatively large estimates given by the high TAS achievement-orientation group (see Table 1.3). The mean for that group was 1354.1 seconds, whereas the mean for all other groups combined was 1112.3 seconds.

When the analysis was performed on the number of correct responses to the anagrams task, only the Test Anxiety factor was statistically significant. As the means in the third column of Table 1.3 show, this effect was due mainly to the relatively poor performance of the high TAS group receiving the achievement-orienting instructions.

There were two significant results in the analysis of Cognitive Interference Questionnaire scores obtained by summing subjects' responses to the questionnaire's 11 items. These were the factors for Test Anxiety ($p < .0001$) and for Test Anxiety × Conditions ($p < .05$). As column four of Table 1.3 shows, most of the interaction effects were due to the high scores obtained by the high TAS achievement-orientation group, whose mean was 33.2. The mean for the high TAS control group was 24.6, and the combined mean for the middle and low TAS group was 20.3. Results for separate analyses of individual items were, in every case, in the same direction as the results presented for the questionnaire as a whole.

An item appended to the questionnaire asked the subject to indicate on a 7-point scale the degree to which her mind wandered while working on the anagrams task. An analysis of variance of these scores yielded significant factors for Test Anxiety ($p < .05$) and for Test Anxiety × Conditions ($p < .05$); the directions of these results resembled those in the other analyses.

Individuals for whom tests are noxious experiences (high TAS subjects) apparently tend to overestimate, to a greater degree than do others, both the duration of their performance evaluation period and the time spent waiting for the evaluation to take place. In addition, highly test-anxious subjects performed at significantly lower levels than did low and middle scorers when emphasis was placed on the evaluational implications of performance. The evidence concerning cognitive interference is enlightening from the standpoint of what people think about while working on a task. Highly test-anxious scorers, more so than low and middle scorers, are preoccupied with how poorly they are doing, how other people are faring, and what the examiner will think about the subject. It is difficult not to interpret these preoccupations as appreciably complicating the task at hand. Although a measure of cognitive interference during the waiting period was not obtained, it seems likely that similar preoccupations would also have characterized highly test-anxious subjects during that period.

TEST ANXIETY AND SELF-EFFICACY

One of the most promising recent developments in the areas of stress and test anciety is research aimed at strengthening persons' abilities to handle tensions and problematic situations. Whereas the research focus for many years had been on what stress and test anxiety "do" to people, building competencies is now also a major concern. An example of this latter approach is Sarason's (1973) study using an anagrams task similar to the one employed in the experiment just described. In the 1973 study, subjects differing in test anxiety were given the opportunity to observe a model who demonstrated effective ways of performing the task. Using a talk-out-loud technique, the model displayed several facilitative thoughts and cognitions. The major finding was that high TAS subjects benefited more from the opportunity to observe a cognitive model than did low TAS scorers.

People come to terms with their anxieties in different ways. Some highly test-anxious individuals are helped by learning to be less demanding of themselves. Others benefit when they revise their expectations about the consequences of failure. They view with alarm less and attend to the task more. Still others need to strengthen their behavioral repertory in specific ways such as strengthening study skills. Worry and emotionality seem to be the major components of test anxiety, and researchers have made progress in helping people gain more self-control over both of them (see Chapters 6, 8, 9, and 10).

When interventions are successful in reducing test anxiety, there is a commensurate increase in self-efficacy. Bandura (1977) has described persons high in self-efficacy as seeing themselves personally effective and able. These positive self-appraisals presumably result from personal successes and reinforcements following the successes. Persons experience increments of self-efficacy when they observe connections between their behavior and tasks that are successfully completed. One reason why highly test-anxious persons are low in self-efficacy is that they are so preoccupied with fear of failure and self-blame. In other words, they attend too often to what is going on within themselves and become diverted from the step-by-step approach needed in solving problems. This self-preoccupation is at the core of test anxiety. As Part III shows, there have been some exciting developments in the area of reducing the intensity of self-preoccupation.

A GLIMPSE INTO THE FUTURE

The person who attempts to predict the future either has the confidence that goes with self-efficacy or is foolhardy. In either case, the odds for successful prognostications are not favorable. There are too many unknowns, especially new methods and information in other fields that may come to intersect with the study of test anxiety. It may even be, as Jeri Wine suggests (Chapter 16), that test anxiety is a misleading term. We can, nevertheless, be certain that the referents for that term (the internal processes that interfere with attention to tasks and plans to deal with them) will still be around.

The safest prediction is that much of what happens in the future will surprise us. Some of it, however, seems predicatble on the basis of the unfinished business of the present. We need to know more about where test anxiety comes from. Which factors within the family (parents' characteristics, birth order) play roles in its acquisition? How important are extra-family relationships, such as those that contribute to comparisons with peers? What are the mechanisms by which test anxiety is acquired (modeling, reinforcement)? We also need to explicate more fully the role test anxiety plays in information processing. In the area of intervention, studies comparing different treatments are needed. To do this, it will be necessary to achieve a better understanding of the ingredients of therapies.

No book can provide a clear blueprint for the future. If this book provides information and ideas that stimulate the creative thought of readers, it will have achieved its goal.

REFERENCES

Bandura, A. Self-efficacy: Toward a unifying theory of behavioral change. *Psychological Review*, 1977, *2*, 191–215.

Sarason, I. G. Empirical findings and theoretical problems in the use of anxiety scales. *Psychological Bulletin*, 1960, *57*, 403–415.

Sarason, I. G. Test anxiety and cognitive modeling. *Journal of Personality and Social Psychology*, 1973, *28*, 58–61.

Sarason, I. G. The Test Anxiety Scale: Concept and research. In C. D. Spielberger & I. G. Sarason (Eds.), *Stress and anxiety* (Vol. 5). Washington, D.C.: Hemisphere Publishing Corp., 1978.

Sarason, I. G., & Stoops, R. Test anxiety and the passage of time. *Journal of Consulting and Clinical Psychology,* 1978, *1,* 102–109.

Sarason, S. B., Davidson, K. S., Lighthall, F. F., Waite, R. R., & Ruebush, B. K. *Anxiety in elementary school children.* New York: Wiley, 1960.

Taylor, J. A. The relationship of anxiety to the conditioned eyelid response. *Journal of Experimental Psychology,* 1951, *41,* 81–92.

Taylor, J. A. A personality scale of manifest anxiety. *Journal of Abnormal and Social Psychology,* 1953, *48,* 285–290.

2 Defining Test Anxiety: Problems and Approaches

Joan E. Sieber
California State University, Hayward

Overview. Within the framework of current behavioral models of test anxiety, a broad set of definitions is offered and evaluated. The difficulty of arriving at a comprehensive definition of test anxiety, using current behavioral models, is discussed. Emphasis is placed on the scientific and ethical problems that accompany behavioral research on test anxiety rather than on the many noteworthy achievements of this approach. Because anxiety has important *experiential* components, the need for nonbehavioral models is raised. To illustrate ways in which nonbehavioral models might be used in research on test anxiety, to stimulate debate, and to challenge investigators to consider other perspectives, some concepts from transpersonal psychology and neurolinguistic programming are discussed briefly in relation to test anxiety.

INTRODUCTION

Test anxiety has proven difficult for behavioral scientists to define adequately. The difficulty of defining test anxiety arises, in part, because test anxiety has many facets, and no theory has yet been formulated that describes it adequately. A second major source of difficulty arises out of the nature of behavioral science, which is literally a science of behavior and not a science of mind. In contrast, anxiety is an emotion—a phenomenon both of behavior and of mind; and removing the behavioral manifestations of anxiety does not necessarily remove the anxiety one has in one's mind (Solomon & Wynne, 1954). However, most behavioral scientists are not trained to investigate phenomena of the mind, nor do they feel that it is something that is appropriate or possible to do.

The view that it is inappropriate for scientists to examine mental phenomena gained prominence in the 1940s, when logical positivism began to dominate the philosophy of science. Carl Hempel, a leading proponent of logical positivism in the philosophy of science, asserted (1965) that there cannot be a science of mind. He holds that in scientific investigation and explanation, that which is to be explained must have empirical content; i.e., it must be observable or open to the senses. Clearly, the thoughts and feelings associated with anxiety are not observable, and in psychologists' attempts to meet positivist standards for scientific activity, they have not given serious attention to the possibility of exploring and experimenting with their own experience or to developing methods of exploring others' experience of anxiety.

The mental phenomena of anxiety are not alone in their failure to meet the criterion of observability. For example, many important phenomena of physics have turned out to be unobservable; e.g., force is not open to the senses or independently definable, nor are quarks. The physical sciences have now largely abandoned positivism because it would not permit precisely those theoretical approaches that have turned out to be most fruitful in recent years. In contrast to the physical sciences, the behavioral sciences have continued to pay lip service to positivism, while delving apologetically into various phenomena, such as anxiety, which fail to meet Hempel's criterion. For example, psychologists have "observed" and measured anxiety using objectified measures of unobservable processes (e.g., self-report scales). Mechanistic theories have been created that ignore the properties of subjective experience that underlie the behavioral phenomena of anxiety. Indeed, the overwhelming dominance of behavioral approaches has made it difficult for contemporary psychologists to imagine creative theoretical approaches to the study of the mental phenomena of test anxiety.

Thus, the link between thoughts and actions is not well understood, perhaps because it actually is a very complex link or perhaps because the conceptual and experiential tools needed to grasp that link have not been developed. In any case, present-day behavioral and neuropsychological measures reveal little or nothing about what it means to have emotions such as anxiety. Investigators tend to employ behavioral models that include self-report, behavioral, and physiological definitions of anxiety as well as descriptions of stimuli which evoke anxiety and to probe first one and then another of these components in order to explore the interrelationships among them. Anxiety is thus reified—converted into a complex of concrete parts and processes. When reliable (i.e., replicable) evidence indicates that certain parts of the model obey certain principles, it is claimed that the understanding of anxiety has been increased. In our zeal to understand anxiety phenomena, we run a danger of overlooking the fact that we are dealing with an extremely complex matter. An analogy from the history of medicine will illustrate the need for skepticism regarding the current state of knowledge about test anxiety: Bloodletting was long considered an excellent treatment for many ailments. Indeed, it gave relief to those with hypertension. However, subsequent theory and research in physiology and disease showed that better treatments could be devised!

What Is Test Anxiety?

Test anxiety is a special case of general anxiety. It refers to those phenomenological, physiological, and behavioral responses that accompany concern about possible failure. Yet, this does not restrict the concept much; the stimuli, experiences, and responses of test anxiety are almost as varied as those of general anxiety. Therefore, we shall consider the nature of general anxiety before discussing and defining test anxiety.

The experience of general anxiety pervades our lives; its impact can be traced in literature, politics, philosophy, theology, and other human affairs (e.g., see May, 1977, pp. 3–86). It is a vital adaptive mechanism that forewarns man and higher animals of possible danger and triggers innate and learned coping responses. It is, thus, a cause of our survival and development as a species and of our individual survival and personal development.

The relation between anxiety and the learning of coping responses is crucial to the way anxiety is experienced and to the adaptiveness of anxiety in the individual case. The anxiety response may vary depending on the past experience and constitutional qualities of the individual, the nature of the problem to be solved, the context of the problem, and the level of anxiety evoked. The individual may respond to anxiety with effective problem solving and thus experience the anxiety as part of a positive experience. Or he may respond with ineffective problem solving and experience the anxiety as distress, confusion, fear, physical malaise, worry, or failure. This does not exhaust the possibilities, however, for one may also respond with effective problem solving and simultaneously experience anxiety that is based on fears learned in association with previous evaluation. Or, one may mask one's anxiety by responding with irrational anger while otherwise handling the problem effectively or ineffectively.

Whichever way the process unfolds for an individual, it will tend to generalize, as a conditioned response, to new situations which may evoke anxiety. That is, for one individual, anxiety may become a stimulus for effective problem solving, whereas for another it may become a confounding stimulus in problem solving. Anxiety that does not lead to effective problem solving reduces further the chances of developing effective problem-solving habits. The individual's attention is occupied by specific conditioned emotional responses of panic, illness, worry, anger, resignation, shame, or the desire to escape physically or mentally through defensive acts of repression or rationalization. None of these responses leads to effective problem solving.

Thus, anxiety does not serve only as a fail-safe mechanism for promoting survival, healthy adaptation and development. In its nonadaptive modes, it can promote incompetence and extreme and lasting misery. Consequently, it offers an important challenge to applied as well as basic scientists to discover how anxiety functions and how maladaptive anxiety can be transformed to more adaptive modes of coping.

To meet this challenge, a comprehensive definition of anxiety is needed—a definition that coherently takes into account the range of mental, physiological, and behavioral events that characterize anxiety. Since anxiety is a complex of behaviors, perceptions, and experiences that are somehow acquired and that may be transformed or extinguished, definitions of isolated observable phenomena of anxiety do not define anxiety, per se. To define anxiety, per se, definitions of its components need to be placed into the context of a theory that accounts for acquisition, functioning, and transformation of the entire complex.

CONTEMPORARY APPROACHES TO DEFINING TEST ANXIETY

Test anxiety is usually defined as a set of responses to a class of stimuli that have been associated in the individual's experience of evaluation or testing. The character and components of this process have been described by many (e.g., Mandler & Watson, 1966; S. Sarason, 1966; Spence & Spence, 1966; Wine, 1971; Wolpe, 1966). Most models or descriptions of anxiety have focused on a limited set of conditions under which anxiety may occur, e.g., on a particular class of demands, feedback, available resources, or prior learning. In contrast, the concept of anxiety refers to a general system of conditions that may function in a variety of ways, depending on the nature of the associated demands, feedback, prior learning, and so on. Therefore, a broad, general model of anxiety—the state–trait model (Spielberger, 1966— is introduced here, and then definitions of possible conditions are presented within this model.

The State-Trait Model

According to the state–trait model of test anxiety (Spielberger, 1966,) the components of anxiety may be diagrammed as shown in Fig. 2.1.

1. *Test stimuli* are those which the individual associates with evaluation. These may be immediate events, such as a teacher's remark "We will have a

Test Stimuli	⇒	Interpretation of Test Stimuli	⇒	A-State Reactions	⇒	Cognitive Reappraisal	⇒	Coping, Avoidance, and Defensiveness

FIG. 2.1.   The state–trait model of test anxiety.

quiz today", or "John, how would you answer that?" Or, they may be related to the future, such as the decision to major in a premedical program with the knowledge that 4 years later one will be faced with MCAT exams and with personal interviews at the medical schools to which one applies. Test stimuli are conditioned stimuli. Their meaning to the individual depends on prior experience. Thus, what is a stimulus of test anxiety for one person may be a neutral event for another.

2. *Interpretation of test stimuli* depends on the nature of one's prior experience with these stimuli; they may be perceived as having interesting or positive meaning, as threatening, or as neutral. Some individuals can approach evaluation as a positive event. For example, one may approach a test with the mature view that "I will either succeed or not in meeting my expectations in this instance, and I will learn and grow from whatever happens." This is in marked contrast to those whose fear of failure causes them never to set out to achieve, to focus narrowly and intently on one area of achievement at the expense of failing to develop in other areas, or to bungle through challenging tasks. It is important to remember that the interpretation of test stimuli is, by definition, an interpretation based on one's own past history. Thus, fear of failure and other negative interpretations of test stimuli are not fear of failing to carry out the operations *required at the time*. Rather, these negative interpretations involve "plugging in" to old ideas, such as "If I fail at this, my life will be less worthwhile.", or "I will have fulfilled my father's views that I am not worth anything.", or "No one will respect me." Unfortunately, the interpretation of stimuli by test-anxious persons tends to be unexamined—to be accepted as the basic reality of the situation rather than simply as one of many possible interpretations.

3. *A-state reactions* vary depending on persons' interpretations of their prior experience and on the nature of the test stimulus. The A-state reaction may consist of heightened arousal, vigilence, and a sense of enthusiasm, or it may include fear and worry, confusion, illness, anger, lowering of self-esteem and other negative events.

4. *Cognitive reappraisal* refers to the way in which an individual responds to his or her A-state. These responses may be constructive, defensive, avoidant, or a combination of these kinds of responses.

5. *Coping, avoidance, and defensiveness* refers to the nature of the feelings, approaches, and actions in which one engages. A wide range of approaches and outcomes may occur; e.g., the task may be successfully or unsuccessfully completed. It may be consciously and confidently addressed,

fearfully approached, avoided, or blundered through. The nature of one's performance may be fully acknowledged, denied, or blamed on someone else. The individual may feel good, bad, unaware, or indifferent about the task and the performance.

As this general model suggests, there are adaptive test anxiety processes that healthy people experience every day, and there are maladaptive processes to which we refer when we speak of *high anxiety*. People who experience high anxiety in test situations are very sensitive to cues that suggest the imminence of testing and interpret testing situations as a serious threat to their well-being. The resulting A-state response is quite a powerful, unpleasant, and disruptive emotional reaction. The cognitive reappraisal typically involves considering a number of unconstructive ways to deal with the test and with the anxiety. The coping behaviors which follow are less constructive and effective than is desirable and may be accomplished by defensive and avoidant behavior.

Thus, we must distinguish between two meanings of the term *test anxiety: anxiety as a state* and *anxiety as trait* (Spielberger, 1966). *State anxiety* is a transitory state of anxiety that occurs when the individual perceives stimuli of a (real or imagined) test and responds with certain emotions and behavior. *Trait anxiety* refers to a relatively stable personality characteristic—the disposition to perceive as threatening a wide range of the stimuli that are associated with tests and the tendency to respond to these with extreme A-state reactions.

The state–trait model of anxiety, set forth by Spielberger (1972), describes the properties of state and trait anxiety as follows:

> State anxiety (A-State) may be conceptualized as a transitory emotional state or condition of the human organism that varies in intensity and fluctuates over time. This condition is characterized by subjective, consciously perceived feelings of tension and apprehension, and activation of the autonomic nervous system ... Trait anxiety (A-Trait) refers to relatively stable individual differences in anxiety proneness, that is, to differences in the disposition to perceive a wide range of stimulus situations as dangerous or threatening, and in the tendency to respond to such threats with A-State reactions. A-Trait may also be regarded as reflecting individual differences in the frequency and the intensity with which A-States have been manifested in the past, and in the possibility that such states will be experienced in the future [p. 39].

The state–trait model further describes the relationship between the variables diagrammed in Figure 2.1. Evaluation situations that threaten self-esteem evoke higher levels of A-state response in high A-trait individuals than in persons low in A-trait. Differential level of A-state reaction is related to level of performance in intellectual tasks (e.g., Denney, 1966; Hodges, 1968). In contrast, physical danger does not evoke such differential A-state responses; rather, it evokes a similar increase in A-state for high and low A-trait persons (Lamb, 1969).

The performance decrement in high A-trait persons is attributed to two factors; the emotionality or high drive level associated with the elevated A-state (see subsequent discussion of drive theory and anxiety) and the worrying and other self-centered interfering responses that are cued by the A-state reaction. The worrying responses and their interference with task orientation have been examined extensively by Liebert and Morris (1967) and I. G. Sarason (1972).

Problems of Defining Components of the State–Trait Model

Some of the components of the model diagramed in Figure 2.1 have been used as conceptual or operational definitions of test anxiety. The following are some definitional problems that arise from the various components of this model:

1. *The external stimuli of anxiety.* Test anxiety may be operationally defined in terms of its stimuli, but this is a crude approach in three respects. First, individuals differ with regard to those stimuli that are conditioned stimuli of test anxiety. Second, this approach overlooks individual differences in level of trait anxiety, in reappraisal, and in coping responses. And, this definition is circular; anxiety is defined as that which is evoked by the stimuli of anxiety. Nevertheless, this may prove to be an important approach to defining anxiety; identification of classes of stimuli that evoke anxiety may lead to a more basic understanding of the way in which anxiety may be aroused and extinguished in natural settings.

The external stimuli of anxiety are, as yet, poorly understood. Little is known about the ecology of the stimuli of anxiety—the structural aspects of settings and of entire cultures in relation to the capacity to create, develop, or reduce destructive test anxiety. Practical, ethical, and scientific problems make it difficult to study the ecology of the stimuli of test anxiety. Ecological research, such as that of Phillips et al. (Chapter 15), has only begun to yield information regarding the environments and interpersonal factors that affect test anxiety.

2. *The interpretation of test stimuli.* Perhaps if we understood how distal and proximal stimuli are associated, it would be obvious how persons interpret test stimuli. There may be surprises in store for us, however, when we attempt to generalize what has been learned from the in-depth study of a few individuals. Garmezy (1975) has undertaken an impressive study of "invulnerables"—children whose background would suggest that they stand no chance of developing into competent, self-respecting individuals but who somehow are able to regard as stimuli for personal growth those conditions

which for most others are stimuli for distress, anxiety, incompetence, and poor mental health. Gestalt theory and attribution theory have served to remind psychologists that meaning is entirely a function of the context in which the individual holds events or ideas. Stimuli and mental contents have no meaning in and of themselves. However, little is understood presently about the creation of the personal contexts in which individuals interpret test stimuli. What enables some to perceive evaluation from a position of self-respect and willingness to experiment? Why do others perceive evaluation from a position of low self-esteem and allow themselves to be ruled by fear and brandishments of coercive power and to pursue symbols of success that do not produce satisfaction? Other, largely nonbehavioral approaches to understanding the structure of experience, such as neurolinguistic programming that is described in the last part of this chapter, may provide answers that purely behavioral approaches do not offer.

3. *A-state reaction.* The A-state reaction is a diffuse set of physiological, emotional, perceptual, cognitive, and motivational responses that has not been defined, measured, or interrelated in a satisfactory way.

The *physiological* component of the A-state reaction has been defined operationally as change in galvanic skin response (Endler & Hunt, 1966), systolic blood pressure (O'Neil, Spielberger, & Hansen, 1969), heart rate (Hodges, 1968), and other indicators of physiological arousal. The relation between physiological arousal and other components of the anxiety response is unclear and has been the subject of much speculation.

Selye (1976) speculated that the widespread bodily changes that accompany anxiety are mediated by the release of ACTH, which regulates the secretion of various corticoids. Berlyne (1961) has theorized that physiological arousal mediates postural, perceptual, and cognitive responses—that arousal leads to heightened vigilence and greater information processing, except at extremely high levels of arousal, where confusion, avoidance, and defensiveness (blocking out of relevant stimuli) occur. Berlyne's theory is consistent with the older and more general Yerkes–Dodson Law, which states that an increase in arousal results in improved performance up to a point and that further increases in arousal result in decrements in performance. However, as our understanding of the relationship between anxiety and performance broadens, it becomes evident that the Yerkes–Dodson Law and Berlyne's arousal theory are inadequate to predict the effects of anxiety arousal on performance (e.g., McKeachie, 1977). Spence and Spence (1966) have shown that high-anxious persons have many of the characteristics of persons in a high drive state, including greater difficulty learning complex tasks and great facility learning simple tasks, relative to low-anxious persons. They have equated the heightening of physiological arousal with increased motivation and used Hullian drive theory to explain some effects of anxiety on learning and performance.

According to Hullian drive theory, behavior is determined by several factors. The most important are habit strength and drive, and it is proposed that drive level multiplies habit strength to produce the strength of the tendency to respond with a given habit. Thus, a particular response tendency is at zero when there is no drive and no habit. At any given level of habit strength above zero, an increase in drive increases the tendency to respond with that habit. In the early stages of learning, the habit being learned is at a relatively low level in the response hierarchy compared with other responses to the (to-be-conditioned) stimulus. When drive increases and the correct habit is weak, one of the incorrect responses is likely to occur. This analysis of anxiety and performance turns out, unfortunately, to be greatly oversimplified when we examine cognitive components of the A-state reaction, for there we find many possibilities that this analysis does not explain.

The *cognitive* components of the A-state reaction are usuallly examined through the use of questionnaires that ask how the individual feels when test-anxious. Research of this kind has differentiated between worry responses and arousal responses. Those who tend to respond to anxiety with arousal responses suffer less decrement of performance than those who respond by worrying (Sarason & Stoops, 1976). However, worry and arousal are not unitary constructs, and much remains to be learned about styles of worrying and of responding to arousal. For example, it is difficult to reconcile the findings of Sarason and Stoops (1976) with the finding of Janis (1958) that some styles of worrying are a step toward dealing effectively with threatening situations. Similarly, the factors that influence cognitive responses to arousal remain poorly understood. For example, Schachter and Singer (1962) have shown that persons use contextual cues to label their physiological arousal (e.g., as excitement or as fear), but it is not known how this is mediated or how it may be altered in the case of test anxiety.

Other concepts and definitions of the A-state response are *experimental* or *treatment-related* in character. For example, desensitization, or deep muscle relaxation procedures have been developed to help persons reduce the magnitude of their A-state reaction. This approach is only partially effective in reducing test anxiety, which has less the character of a phobia than of a warranted fear. To date, no method of treatment aimed directly at altering the A-state reaction has proven highly effective. Treatments such as those noted under *cognitive reappraisal* have been more successful.

4. *Cognitive reappraisal.* The notion that persons respond to their felt sense of anxiety by deciding what to do has suggested various lines of research and operational definitions of anxiety. Particularly promising lines of research are those which employ, as treatment, instruction in cognitive reappraisal that is designed to promote more constructive problem solving. Some of these approaches are described in detail in subsequent chapters by Denney (Chapter 10), Rosenthal (Chapter 11), Richardson and Woolfolk

(Chapter 12), and Wine (Chapter 16). This creative approach to understanding and modifying the dynamics of anxiety is, unfortunately, still without a comprehensive theory that would enable us to evaluate cognitive reappraisal strategies or to understand what factors affect the compatibility of reappraisal and coping skills.

5. *Coping, avoidance, or defensiveness.* The action an individual takes differs from the cognitive reappraisal that informs the action. What one does is dictated not only by what one plans to do, but also by the actual characteristics of the task, the emotional state of the individual, and the *actual* abilities and heuristics that one can bring to bear on the task. Initial failure at a task can result in subsequent avoidance of the task and in defensiveness. Defensiveness—the denial of feelings of anxiety, the denial of components of the problem, or the denial of need for skills that one does not have—can arise quickly and subtly in subsequent tasks, depending on the characteristics of the task at hand, the characteristics of the environment, the problem solver, and the mode and success of the problem solving. Unfortunately, behavioral theories offer little that can indicate how to control defensiveness or planning and coping processes. The low degree of success of programs for cognitive reappraisal may be due, in part, to our lack of understanding of what enables anxious individuals to turn good intentions into competent problem solving..

Problems of Defining Test Anxiety Operationally

As the prior discussion is intended to convey, a staggering, but incomplete, array of definitions and concepts pertaining to test anxiety has been developed. Another way to consider what has been done to define anxiety is to organize the definitions and measures of it according to the nature of the operational definition. Four major operational approaches have been taken in defining anxiety. These are described in detail in Sieber, O'Neil, and Tobias (1977) and are summarized here:

1. *The phenomenology of anxiety* refers to the content of the individual's consciousness at each stage of the anxiety process. Phenomenological measures typically have taken the form of self-report questionnaires, the most notable of which are the Worry–Anxiety Scale (Liebert & Morris, 1967), the State–Trait Anxiety Scale (Spielberger, Gorsuch, & Lushene, 1970), the Facilitating–Debilitating Anxiety Scale (Alpert & Haber, 1960), and the Defensiveness or Lie Scale (Sarason, Hill, & Zimbardo, 1964). Self-report scales have proved to be the most valid predictors of other anxiety phenomena. However, they are not without their problems, as pointed out by McKeachie (1977) and others. Most notable among these problems is the difficulty of measuring transitory changes in level of A-state and defensiveness, the difficulty of separating anxiety and defensiveness (denial of anxiety), and the failure of questionnaires to differentiate among the classes

of situations that evoke anxiety and among the styles of responding to anxiety.

2. *The physiological responses of anxiety* refer to the physiological changes that occur as a function of anxiety. Measures such as galvanic skin response, pupil dilation, systolic blood pressure, and heart rate have proven unreliable. A variety of possible patterns of physiological activity may accompany the phenomenological and behavioral components of anxiety. Whether anxiety is manifested in physiological changes depends, in part, on the eliciting stimuli (Endler & Hunt, 1966). Moreover, there are many interesting individual differences that remain to be understood; for example, it appears that persons who experience a lack of emotionality (e.g., "cool" psychopaths) tend to have extremely high levels of physiological reactivity (Schachter, 1971). In summary, the role of physiological arousal in mediating anxiety is not well understood. This, in addition to the cost and technical difficulty of obtaining physiological measurement, makes physiological measures poor candidates for operational definitions of anxiety.

3. *Performance of tasks.* Various cognitive and behavioral measures of performance may be obtained during test taking. This approach is limited in that it focuses only superficially, at most, on the experience of anxiety. However, the study of problem-solving variables, such as attention, memory, response time, and learning speed, in relation to anxiety, has yielded useful knowledge about the effects of anxiety on cognitive processes. In turn, the use of these variables has led to the use of theories of learning, motivation, and cognition (such as Hullian drive theory) to generate new hypotheses about the nature and role of anxiety in the performance of intellectual tasks. This focus on performance of tasks has led naturally to a fourth approach.

4. *Modification of anxiety and its undesirable effects.* A major motive for studying test anxiety is to find ways of helping anxious persons to be more effective and satisfied in their education and work activities. Thus, an implicit set of conceptual and operational definitions are those having to do with treatment. Three major approaches to treatment include: change of social interaction, change of perceptions, and change of instructional setting.

Therapeutic change of social interaction typically involves some procedure for allowing anxious persons to express their dependency and to receive positive reinforcement. Highly anxious children tend to be extremely dependent and to receive punishment from their parents and teachers for their dependency. Because unreasonable demands for performance are made on the young child and no emotional support or help is given, the child has no chance to outgrow dependency (S. Sarason, 1972). The only defense the child has is to deny fear of failure and to withdraw from close interaction with others. The result is a rather dehumanized and incompetent individual. Phillips, Martin, and Meyers (1972) indicate the effectiveness of accepting the anxious child's dependency and giving help until competence is developed and dependency is outgrown. Sarason and Harmatz (1965) and Sarason and Glanzer (1963) have shown that positive reinforcement, especially in the form of warm, accepting verbal and nonverbal responses, is the most effective reinforcer of behavior in anxious children.

Changing an individual's perception of those events that provoke anxiety can enable highly anxious persons to perform like persons who have a lower level of anxiety. Highly anxious persons regard a relatively large number of cues as evaluative ones; they disrupt their performance by dwelling on these cues and the worries that these cues evoke. Various approaches have been used to reorient attention and to alter the interpretation of cues. For example, S. Sarason (1972) has experimented with instructions to tasks and found ways to help students redefine their tasks, goals, and feelings so that test anxiety is not evoked. In contrast, Wine (Chapter 8) has developed a training program based on the assumption that test-anxious persons will seek to focus on cues that evoke A-state responses; her program provides training in the recognition of destructive patterns of attention and in disengagement from these patterns during problem solving.

Changes in instructional setting, to date, have been partial and remedial in character, rather than holistic. That is, attempts have been made to alter the way the individual performs without changing the ecology of the entire setting. For example, instructional materials and settings have been altered so that the cognitive skills needed for successful performance are shaped and reinforced (e.g., Wine, 1971) or supplemented by external aids (Sieber, Kameya, & Paulson, 1970; Lehrissey, O'Neil, & Hansen, 1971), but the anxious person is not given a more general ability to perform effectively. One suspects that failure to alter the overall situation in certain critical (and yet-to-be-discovered) ways may account for the low impact of instructional changes on level of anxiety and performance.

Summary

In an attempt to define anxiety, psychologists have drawn operational definitions from the spectrum of methods of general experimental psychology. Unfortunately, each definition tells us little about what anxiety is; it does offer a toehold from which to try to glimpse some of the phenomena of anxiety. Whether this array of definitions should be regarded as a sign of progress or of confusion is difficult to say. Perhaps it is both. It has taught us that a procrustean approach seems not to work well; we must also seek broad strategies for dealing with our environments and ourselves. In the final section of this chapter, concepts from transpersonal psychology and neurolinguistic programming are introduced, which may enable us to understand more than we do at present about the creator of anxiety—the mind.

ETHICAL DILEMMAS IN DEFINING AND
STUDYING TEST ANXIETY

Reading between the lines of the preceding discussion, it is apparent that these definitional approaches may engender ethical dilemmas for the investigator. Each of the four approaches raises special ethical problems.

Self-report measures indicating anxiety or defensiveness yield highly private sensitive data. Under what conditions is it justified to obtain private information about whether persons are unduly fearful or lie and deny experiences of anxiety? How are these data kept confidential? To whom do the data belong? Are they shown to parents or to the institutional authorities (e.g., school personnel) who authorized the research?

Physiological measures yield data that the naive subject is likely to misinterpret or overinterpret. How are the data ultimately interpreted to the subject, given that such data are generally uninterpretable by the scientist?

Task performance measures may be obtained either through the investigator's presence and intervention in some truly important evaluation of the individual or through deception in which the individual is caused to believe that an important evaluation is occurring. How are either of these kinds of intervention justified?

If *anxiety is modified* through an experimental treatment, how is the purported program justified to subjects and to the institution that offers it? How are control subjects selected so that expectancy effects do not contaminate results and so that there is random assignment to experimental and control groups? Are controls enticed to take the treatment but then are not given it? Are reactive effects prevented by lying to subjects about the purposes of the research? If not, are the results valid? These and numerous other ethical questions can be raised in connection with behavioral research on test anxiety.

Behavioral research on test anxiety or on any other psychological event that is painful, negatively regarded, or deeply personal is fraught with ethical problems. Depending on which operational definitions are chosen, the research is likely to create painfully high levels of anxiety, to invade privacy, to deceive, to produce damaging information about persons' lives, or to create stress or humiliation. When procedures for reducing anxiety are employed, scientific rigor requires control groups, the members of which expect, but do not receive, the treatment. Can such treatment of research subjects be justified? Can these kinds of activities be employed with captive populations, such as school children and members of university subject pools? The purpose of this section is to explore some of the ethical dilemmas associated with behavioral research on the text anxiety and to indicate some techniques that enable one to meet ethical and scientific requirements simultaneously. First, it is appropriate to define what is meant by an ethical dilemma.

An ethical dilemma arises when unintended harmful outcomes seem likely to arise in the course of taking actions that are intended to do good. In behavioral research, a typical kind of ethical dilemma is as follows: A scientist selects an important goal, such as reducing test anxiety, and pursues it using scientifically valid means which happen to have undesirable effects on subjects. These effects may include invading their privacy, inducing unpleasant feelings, or leaving subjects wondering about their adequacy.

Ethical Problems Associated with Laboratory Research. Laboratory research offers advantages of control and convenience. However, the effects of test anxiety cannot be studied unless anxiety is evoked, and objectionably massive deception is sometimes required to evoke a high level of test anxiety in persons who are not actually taking a legitimate rest. For all of the pain and resentment that this causes, the results may be of dubious validity for several reasons.

1. *Informational background of subjects.* To arouse test anxiety, the difficulty and complexity of the test material must be appropriate; it should be neither too simple nor too difficult to motivate subjects to take it seriously. Curriculum materials and tests that are part of a student's academic work usually are more valid stimuli than are contrived laboratory tasks.

2. *Reactive effects.* When persons sense that experimental materials are not a valid part of their academic curriculum, they are unlikely to respond spontaneously. They are more likely to fake responses or to do what they think the experimenter wishes them to do.

3. *Sequential effects.* Levels of anxiety and modes of coping change over time; adaptation occurs, defenses develop, new coping skills are learned, and new sources of anxiety begin to affect the student. Investigation of this process can best be done by longitudinal methods in an actual academic setting.

4. *Generalizability of results.* Contrived laboratory tasks are likely to differ in important ways from the classroom settings to which the researcher wishes to generalize. The way to discover what characterizes testing in the classroom setting is to do research in that setting.

Ethical Problems Associated With Field Research. Not surprisingly, the field setting also presents some ethical problems. In order to obtain and deserve the trust of those in control of field settings where research on test anxiety might be performed, the investigator must demonstrate a sensitivity, willingness, and ability to protect the rights and well-being of the subjects, their families, and the institution where the research is performed. A comprehensive account of what this might involve may be found elsewhere (e.g., Sieber, in press; Mirvis & Seashore, in preparation). A few of the major ethical issues associated with field research on test anxiety are considered here.

1.   *Informed consent* within an organization (such as a school) is a complex process. Each level of the organization must give its informed consent, beginning at the top. The higher levels of the hierarchy will want to know what the research is about, how to "sell" it to those lower in the hierarchy, and what benefits the research and the investigator will provide in return. After many iterations of this process, the research finally begins. The informing goes on at a new level because people's curiosity has been piqued, and new problems arise. As Mirvis and Seashore (in prep.) assert, to be ethical when doing research in an organization, one needs to do more than follow the usual ethical principles of research. One needs to sensitively anticipate the conflicts of interest that inevitably arise; and one needs to have established effective role relationships and communication channels so that problems can be detected, discussed, and resolved at the earliest point possible. Investigators lack the power to respond unilaterally to ethical dilemmas in research in organizations. They must be prepared to alter their procedures or curtail their research as required by the authorities within the organization.

In order to continue to carry out daily research within an organization, the investigators must be prepared to give continuing friendly explanations of what is going on and what is being done to respect and protect those who are participating. Investigators must walk a narrow line between being too closed versus giving out too much personal information about individuals who have been observed. They must strive to help improve the organization in the ways that were promised, without harming specific individuals in the process; they must bear in mind that power and interest groups within the organization may use information against one another in harmful ways. For example, an investigator may be called upon by a school administrator to discuss the anxiety-arousing behavior of a particular teacher. The investigator needs to have a clear policy, communicated in advance, about how such cases will be handled. To the extent that the researcher discloses confidential information about subjects to parents and school personnel, or is suspected of doing so, it is difficult to obtain valid data. However, unilateral or on-the-spot decisions to withhold information may result in the eviction of the research team.

Informing must be done candidly and freely. If the researcher is less than candid about the methods and reasons for the research, the research program will evoke a high level of speculation that will create more harmful reactive effects than would the truth. Therefore, the researcher must take seriously the need to inform all persons connected with the research of its purposes and methods *in terms that they are sure to understand.* Most researchers tell subjects what *the researcher* thinks the subject ought to know. This is inappropriate in view of what is known about perceptual and motivational differences among people. Much can be learned about what persons want or need to know by simply explaining to peers of the subjects what the procedure is about and then asking them what they would want to know before deciding whether to participate. After a number of such conversations, it will become clear which facts most persons would like to know in order to be in a position to give informed consent.

2. *Privacy and confidentiality* are salient concerns in research on test anxiety. The investigator observes events that should not be disclosed to others. There are questions the investigator has no right to ask persons directly. There are kinds of data that should not be stored with names or other unique identifiers attached. There are facts about students, parents, and school administrators that should not be published in such a way that readers can learn where the research was performed. Three aspects of privacy and confidentiality merit particular attention: subpoena, secret matters, and handling of data.

a. *Subpoena of data.* Most researchers are unaware that research data may be subpoenaed. A variety of circumstances, ranging from drug abuse by students to unauthorized punishing of students by teachers, could bring about a subpoena of data believed relevant. When data are subpoenaed, the researcher essentially is faced with the choice of giving the data to the law enforcement agency or going to jail. In actuality, there are many steps that can be taken to stop the subpoena. Some of the most important are to obtain competent legal counsel the moment one suspects that a subpoena will be issued and to be prepared to demonstrate that the data do not bear on the matter in question and that revealing the data would do considerable harm to the research and to subjects. For a detailed discussion of what to do before and after a subpoena arrives, see Knerr (in preparation).

b. *Secret matters.* The researcher who interviews teachers, parents, and students about conditions pertaining to their anxiety may find it necessary to inquire about very private matters, such as whether parents or teachers belittle or physically punish the students. This raises three distinct ethical questions: Does the researcher have the right to ask such a private question? Will the respondent tell the truth, in any case? And, might not such data be subject to subpoena? There are various ways of obtaining such data so that there is no record of who has answered questions in a given way. These methods are discussed in detail in Boruch and Cecil (1979). Two examples are given here to illustrate some possible solutions to this ethical problem.

Code name method. Research subjects can give themselves code names. Questionnaires can thus be filled out on various occasions, using only the code name for identification. The researcher cannot match code names with subjects' names but can match sequential sets of responses to obtain longitudinal data.

Randomized response method. This device enables the researcher to obtain data without knowing which question a given subject answered. There are many variations of the randomized response method; these are described in detail in Boruch and Cecil (1979). The present example is given for illustrative purposes only.

Suppose that the researcher wishes to know what proportion of parents have physically punished their child in the last week for failure to do a task well. The researcher plans to base the proportion on a sample of 400 parents. The researcher selects 600 persons to interview and creates a jar containing 600 beads, 400 of which are red, 100 white, and 100 blue. The researcher asks each subject to draw a bead, privately determine its color, and replace it. If the bead is red, the subject is to answer the question honestly: "Have you physically punished your child for poor performance this week?" If the bead is white, the subject is to say "yes" arbitrarily, and if blue, to say "no" arbitrarily. Thus, there will be 400 true answers, and 100 irrelevant "yes" responses. To compute the percent of parents who have punished their child in the last week for poor performance, the researcher subtracts 100 from the total number of "yes" responses, and divides by 400. Because the validity of this method depends on whether the subject *believes* that it is straightforward and valid (and not a trick to invade privacy), it is necessary to find ingenious ways to explain the method to subjects. In schools, this is readily done in group settings, such as PTA meetings. There, the method can be demonstrated and discussed, and those who understand how it works can easily show those who do not understand it that it is indeed a straightforward, valid method, and not a trick.

c. *Handling of data.* Data pertaining to test anxiety are inevitably somewhat sensitive. No one would want his or her test anxiety data to become a public matter. It is essential that the researcher devise, ahead of time, a system for removing names and other unique identifiers from all data and assigning numbers in place of names. The key linking numbers and names should be stored in a separate place, such as a safe deposit box, and should not be available to persons who have no research-related need for the data. As soon as the data have been analyzed and there is no longer a need for names, the list of names should be destroyed. Data such as school records of grades, IQ scores, and attendance, often are unavailable to researchers for reasons of privacy. There are, however, methods of merging data files so that individual data are never made available to the researcher or to other "outsiders." These methods are discussed in Campbell, Boruch, Schwartz, and Steinberg (1977).

3. *Treatment and control-group* requirements sometimes create ethical dilemmas; when an experimental treatment is given, there inevitably arises a conflict between the scientific requirement of valid control and the ethical requirement of providing equitable treatment for control-group members. A useful way to resolve this problem is through the *wait-list control procedure*: Subjects are pretested and those who would be appropriate for participation in the experiment are contacted and asked if they would wish to receive the

treatment. When enough volunteers have been obtained to fill both the treatment and control groups, they are randomly assigned to each. Control-group subjects are treated like treatment-group subjects, except that they do not receive treatment prior to performing the criterion tasks. They are told that they are on a list to receive the treatment later. The required criterion measures are obtained from them. Then, to fulfill the researcher's agreement, the control (wait-list) subjects are given the treatment after the experiment is completed. (See Sieber, O'Neil, & Tobias, 1977, pp. 55 and 195 for further discussion and examples.)

4. *Providing benefits* to those in the field setting in return for research privileges requires forethought and planning. It is desirable to discuss in advance the kinds of benefits the institution and its members would like to receive from the investigator and what kinds of benefits the investigator is prepared to offer. Undue inducement would violate the requirement that research participation be voluntary. An appropriate and useful benefit would be talks with individuals and groups about the nature of test anxiety and ways to recognize and reduce it. These may be supplemented with written material that is clear, positive and does not "blame the victim" (Ryan, 1971). It should be sympathetic to the individuals involved and should offer constructive and understandable advice. Some readable materials that might be appropriate include Dyer (1977), Woolfolk and Richardson (1978), and Sieber and Crockenberg (1970).

5. *Discussing cases* is an important part of communicating about research. Cases are discussed among members of the research team and with subjects and administrative personnel in the research setting, and in other research-related activities. Case studies are informative and interesting, and it is not reasonable to create rules prohibiting their discussion; yet discussion of case studies can jeopardize the privacy of individuals unless identity is cloaked.

One rule for cloaking identity is to select names from a list of common names. Another workable rule is to assign meaningful pseudonyms to people. Thus, the name becomes a heuristic part of the case, and a new identity is created that is dissociated from the actual case.

Summary

In summary, the ethical investigator of test anxiety does valid research, causing minimal additional burden to subjects. This often indicates choosing field research over laboratory research. Within the field setting, the ethical investigator conducts research, stores and analyzes data, and communicates with all persons concerned so that there is minimal disturbance to the setting, all concerned are given an opportunity to improve on their ability to cope with test anxiety, and private information remains confidential. The investigator's aims and the way in which these are communicated must be such that all persons connected with the research understand it is a constructive endeavor aimed primarily at understanding and helping. Assurance must be given that the privacy and needs of the individuals involved will be respected by all members of the research staff. In keeping with this attitude, it is important that all members of the staff examine the definitions and terminology they employ and make sure their language reflects a collaborative, respectful relationship with subjects. Above all, labeling people with diagnostic terms and using terms that ascribe blame to the victim should be avoided.

ALTERNATIVE APPROACHES: TRANSPERSONAL PSYCHOLOGY AND NEUROLINGUISTIC PROGRAMMING

As noted in the introduction, the concept of anxiety is plagued or blessed (depending on the level of challenge we choose to enjoy) with the same epistemological problems as other concepts of emotion. Anxiety is both something we have in our mind and something that materializes in our behavior; and the having of it in our mind can exist apart from our behaving anxiously (Solomon & Wynne,, 1954). Despite the inroads of cognitive psychology, present-day experimental psychology remains more a science of behavior than of mind. Nonbehavioral approaches also need to be employed if the nature of test anxiety is to be more fully understood. To illustrate other possible concepts and methods for examining test anxiety, traditional behavioral approaches are contrasted with possible transpersonal and neurolinguistic approaches. Transpersonal psychology is concerned with optimal psychological well-being, and takes consciousness, rather than behavior, as its central concern (Walsh & Shapiro, 1978). Neurolinguistic programming is a form of psychotherapy that is based on principles of neurology, psychophysiology, linguistics, cybernetics, and communication theory, developed out of the work of Bateson, Perls, Satir, Erickson, Bandler, and Grinder.

Transpersonal Psychology

Within the last decade, transpersonal psychology has become the fourth distinct school of Western psychology (the first three being behaviorism, psychoanalysis, and humanistic psychology). Transpersonal psychotherapy includes traditional areas and techniques of psychotherapy as well as concepts and tools for facilitating growth and awareness beyond usual levels. Walsh and Shapiro (1978) provide excellent sources of information on transpersonal psychology and psychotherapy. This chapter offers only a few summary statements about the transpersonal model of the person and some indication of how transpersonal psychology might be of value in examining and transforming anxiety. According to Walsh and Vaughn (1978):

> A transpersonal model views "normal" consciousness as a defensively contracted state. This "normal" state is filled to a remarkable and unrecognized extent with a continuous and largely uncontrollable flow of fantasies which exert an extraordinarily powerful but once again largely unappreciated influence on perception, cognition and behavior. Prolonged self-observation inevitably reveals that "normal" experience is perceptually distorted by the continuous, automatic, and unconscious blending of inputs from reality and fantasy in accordance with our needs and defenses (p. 3).
>
> With regard to conditioning, the transpersonal perspective holds that "normal man" is vastly more ensnared and trapped in his conditioning than he appreciates, but that freedom from this conditioning is possible, at least experientially (Goleman, 1977). The aim of transpersonal psychotherapy is essentially the extraction of awareness from this conditioned tyranny (Ram Dass, 1977) [p. 4].

As these remarks suggest, reading *about* transpersonal psychology can do little more than pique one's curiosity. The psychologist wishing to acquire some training in techniques of transpersonal psychology might, for example, undertake insight meditation (Walsh, 1977) or the *est* training (Erhard & Fadiman, 1977).

The psychological properties of the mind that cannot be understood through behavioral or positivist approaches can be observed, described, and defined through use of techniques of transpersonal psychology (e.g., Walsh, 1977). Discovery of the dynamics of one's defensiveness and anxiety, of ways to observe and describe these dynamics, and of ways to alter and reduce one's defensiveness and to promote well-being is accomplished largely through meditative techniques that enable one to access and integrate information in new ways. It is difficult to describe these methods here, because they involve transforming one's ability to be conscious of one's experience. Generally, persons know their experience only through multiple layers and filters of thoughts and do not know the difference between their direct *experiences* and their *beliefs about those experiences*. Further, persons generally do not know that they do not know this. That is, they are out of touch with their direct experience and unaware of being so.

To give but a very limited sense of what some techniques of transpersonal psychology can offer, I will describe a technique that one can use to transform mental events such as anxiety, headaches, and guilt in various ways, including making them disappear. This involves sensing (typically with mind alert and open, eyes closed, and body relaxed) what is being experienced and taking a nonevaluative approach to what is being experienced, resisting the urge to repress. The next step somewhat eludes description because it is a mental attitude that does not have external reference and is generally unknown to the uninitiated. It involves an intensified attitude (though the word *intensified* gives the wrong impression of much effort) of nonevaluation in which the person puts aside all reasons for rejecting the experience, for being at fault or for not being at fault, for being victimized or unfortunate, or for being superior. The person sees that the events (e.g., the anxiety and its stimuli) are all a part of the self. The person expands his awareness and identity so that the experience of anxiety (not the rationalized, partially repressed idea of it) is perceived as an intrinsic part of the self; the full experience of it is to be recreated without defensiveness and so that the person feels larger than it. The nondefensive recreation of the experience causes the experience to vanish along with its unpleasant side effects. In terms of Fritz Perls (1973), this perspective is called *taking responsibility*. In the rest of this discussion, we will use the term "taking responsibility," using quotes to remind us that this does not mean being at fault in a legal or moral sense, or taking the blame, guilt, or burden. "Taking responsibility" will mean taking the perspective described earlier; its exact meaning is not very understandable to persons who have not received training in "taking responsibility."

Note that "taking responsibility" for one's anxiety is quite the opposite of denial or rationalization. It feels very different also! At first, it can cause a heightened awareness of the very thing one want to make go away, flooding one with the feelings one has been resisting all along. This may seem frightening to the uninitiated. (Indeed, "taking responsibility" in new areas may be resisted greatly even by those who have become adept at "taking responsibility" in other areas of their life.) There is always a sense of risk attached with taking what you get when you "take responsibility." However, after experiencing fully the feelings one normally defends against, one later experiences a heightened energy level, clearer and more creative thinking, greater calmness, and a tendency not to blame or punish oneself. (What could be better treatment for a test-anxious person?)

There is a paradox about "taking responsibility." It involves choosing to explore one's feelings rather than denying them, and to the uninitiated, this would seem like accepting a dismal state of affairs. However, this is not so; within the mind, we get what we resist. By "taking responsibility" for one's experience rather than resisting it, one radically transforms the situation so that one's perception of the situation can change. In Spielberger's Model (Fig. 2.1), this can be said to occur largely at Steps 2, 3, and 4. That is, one ceases to respond to evaluative stimuli with destructive fantasies. In turn, the A-state reaction is no longer automatic, and (4) a broad range of perceptual and behavioral alternatives becomes apparent and the individual finds it interesting to experiment with these. By *choosing* one's anxiety, experiencing it fully as it is, and "taking responsibility" for it, one lets go of it, and it transforms and may disappear.

Another paradoxical aspect of "taking responsibility" is that it is noninstrumental. If one "takes responsibility" for something in order to make it go away, what one gets is the awareness that one has gone through a ritual to get away from something that has not gone away. Thus, one must "take responsibility" as an end in itself and take what one gets. The exact form of the transformation cannot be anticipated. For example, as a result of "taking responsibility" for one's test anxiety, one might have the startling realization of having failed to make a commitment to be a good student and then make that commitment. Or, a student might find that his program of study is unrelated to intrinsic values and change educational plans so that intrinsic values are promoted.

The transpersonal approach holds that the mind is capable of much greater mediation between stimuli and responses than previously recognized in Western psychology and that the character of the mediation is greatly influenced by the level and nature of consciousness and defensiveness. It holds that undefensive mediation can change the original relationship between stimuli and responses. Let us see what a technique such as "taking responsibility" can contribute to development of the model shown in Fig. 2.1.

1. *Stimuli of anxiety.* "Taking responsibility" reduces defensiveness so that one becomes aware of stimuli of anxiety that previously were repressed. Not only can one become aware of additional proximal cues that are "charged" with threat, but one can also grasp that certain prior events, long forgotten, are the distal stimuli that keep the anxiety occurring in irrational ways. One can then "take responsibility" for all of these perceptions and feelings and do some additional exercises involving successive changes in the evaluation one places on each cue (see next part on neurolinguistic programming). Consequently, the emotional responses originally associated with each cue are transformed and may disappear entirely.

2. *Interpretation of test stimuli.* "Taking responsibility" involves looking in an undefensive way at the stimuli of anxiety and at one's own responses. What one then sees is more complete and disentangled from rationalization, distortion, and denial. One suspects that the perception of "anxiety stimuli" consists partly of the perception of incomplete and distorted images and ideas. In much the sense that Ellis and Harper (1975) speak of correcting wrong ideas, "taking responsibility" serves, in part, to correct wrong perceptions and thoughts.

3. *A-state reaction.* Behaviorists hold that the character of the A-state reaction is tied in a lawful way to the character of the distal conditioned stimuli. Transpersonal psychologists would agree. Moreover, the transpersonal approach offers ways of learning more about these processes. For example, "taking responsibility" helps persons to perceive with greater

accuracy the stimuli to which they are responding and, as a consequence, to transform their perceptions and responses. Those perceptions may include the distal stimuli and the way in which distal and proximal stimuli are associated with feelings of anxiety. A collection of case-history material about the observation and transformation of one's perceptions and responses would offer important new generalizations about the nature of the A-state reaction.

   4. *Cognitive reappraisal.* This is the process of deciding what to do to cope with anxiety and the demands of a task. A better understanding of possible forms and methods of responding is needed. "Taking responsibility" results in a cognitive reappraisal of the situation in which powerful mediating and transforming processes of the mind come into play. "Taking responsibility" frees the person from established habits and impulses of fight or flight, or the narrow forcing of oneself to concentrate on an unpleasant task. Awareness and constructive thought are expanded so that new ways to accomplish one's goals become apparent, and the appropriate behavior is set into motion. Case studies of this process would provide useful insight about strategies for overcoming anxiety and poor performance.

Neurolinguistic Programming

Neurolinguistic programming is a new therapeutic approach to understanding and altering patterns of experience and behavior. It is behavioristic in the sense that its major concern is in understanding and using the establishment, interruption, and change of conditioned programs of behavior. However, it does not deal with the conditioning of specific behaviors, but with the reorganization of persons' learning sets—the way persons process information, the modality in which it is stored, and the ways in which it is accessed from memory. A basic assumption of this model is that humans receive and represent information through sight, hearing, smell, taste, and body sensations but are often not consciously aware either of what information has been accessed or how it is being represented.

   Therapeutic techniques of neurolinguistic programming are intimately related to techniques of transpersonal psychology. They enable the individual to access their experience in unaccustomed ways, to acquire a fuller sense of their experience (a relatively unrepressed sense of what is in their experience), and to alter the way that experience is represented so that negative and disruptive feelings are eliminated—e.g., feelings of hopelessness, anxiety, inadequacy, or inability to try and succeed at new endeavors. These techniques may be used on oneself (in the case of healthy individuals tackling minor or well-understood problems) or by a therapist with a client. The techniques are described in Bandler and Grinder (1975a, 1975b), Grinder and Bandler (1976), and Grinder, DeLozier, and Bandler (1977).

Summary

Definitions and theories of test anxiety will be incomplete until they take into account the experiential component of anxiety. Transpersonal psychology and neurolinguistic programming offer promising avenues for exploring the experience of anxiety. It is hoped that the reader will be empiricist enough to seek instruction in these techniques in order to competently evaluate them and perhaps incorporate them in future research on test anxiety. Those investigators who do so may discover personally the role of defensiveness and attachment to old habits in maintaining anxiety and may find new approaches to the definition, theory, and treatment of test anxiety.

Irrespective of whether transpersonal psychology or neurolinguistic programming is adopted as an approach to the study of test anxiety, it seems safe to predict that in the course of the next 20 years of research on test anxiety, investigators will turn more and more to approaches that enable them to study the *experience* of anxiety, how it arises, and how it can be transformed. It would be naive to assume that an experiential orientation will solve the scientific and ethical problems that are currently unresolved without raising new dilemmas. No matter how intricately an experiential or phenomenal model of anxiety is developed, the model ultimately will need to be tested in terms of its impact on behavior. Challenging problems of privacy and scientific validity will continue to arise. However, a basically experiential or phenomenal orientation would provide important new perspectives and advance the art of transforming anxiety into a useful form of energy.

ACKNOWLEDGMENTS

This chapter was written while the author was Senior Visiting Research Scholar at the Kennedy Institute of Ethics, Georgetown University. Valuable criticism of an earlier draft was received from Wilbert J. McKeachie, Frank Richardson, Steven Sabat, Irwin Sarason, and Roger Walsh and is gratefully acknowledged.

REFERENCES

Alpert, R., & Haber, R.N. Anxiety in academic achievement situations. *Journal of Abnormal and Social Psychology,* 1960, *61,* 207–215.

Bandler, R., & Grinder, J. *The structure of magic: I.* Palo Alto, Calif.: Science and Behavior Books, 1975.

Bandler, R., & Grinder, J. *Patterns of the hypnotic techniques of Milton Erickson, M.D.* (Vol. 1). Cupertino, Calif.: Meta Publications, 1975.

Berlyne, D.E. *Conflict, arousal and curiosity.* New York: McGraw Hill, 1961.

Boruch, R.F., & Cecil, J.S. *Methods of assuring the confidentiality of social research data.* Philadelphia: University of Pennsylvania Press, 1979.

Campbell, D.T., Boruch, R.F., Schwartz, R.D., & Steinberg, J. Confidentiality-preserving modes of access to files and to interfile exchange for useful statistical analysis. *Evaluation Quarterly,* 1977, *1,* 269–300.

Denney, J.P. Effects of anxiety and intelligence on concept formation. *Journal of Experimental Psychology,* 1966, *72,* 496–602.

Dyer, W. *Your erroneous zones.* New York: Avon Books, 1977.

Ellis, A., & Harper, R.A. *A new guide to rational living.* Englewood Cliffs, N.J.: Prentice Hall, 1975.

Endler, N., & Hunt, J. McV. Sources of behavioral variance as measured by the S-R inventory of anxiousness. *Psychological Bulletin,* 1966, *65,* 336–346.

Erhard, W., & Fadiman, J. Some aspects of *est* training and transpersonal psychology. *Journal of Transpersonal Psychology,* 1977, *9,* 27–42.

Garmezy, N. *Vulnerable and invulnerable children: Theory, research and intervention.* APA: Master Lecture in Developmental Psychology, No. 1115, 1975.

Goleman, D. *The varieties of the meditative experience.* New York: Dutton, 1977.

Grinder, J., & Bandler, R. *The structure of magic: II.* Palo Alto, Calif.: Science and Behavior Books, 1976.

Grinder, J., DeLozier, J., & Bandler, R. *Patterns of the hypnotic techniques of Milton H. Erickson, M.D.: II.* Cupertino, Calif.: Meta Publications, 1977.

Hempel, C.G. *Aspects of scientific explanation.* New York: Free Press, 1965.

Hodges, W.F. The effects of success, threat of shock and failure on anxiety. *Dissertation Abstracts,* 1968, *28*(10-B), 4296. Order No. 68-5388.

Janis, I.L. *Psychological stress.* New York: Wiley, 1958.

Knerr, Jr., C. What to do before and after a subpoena arrives. In J.E. Sieber (Ed.), *Ethical decision making in social science research.* N.Y.: Cambridge University Press, in preparation.

Lamb, D.H. *The effects of public speaking on self-report, physiological and behavioral measures of anxiety.* Doctoral Dissertation, Florida State University, 1969.

Lehrissy, B.L., O'Neil, H.F., & Hansen, D.N. Effects of memory support upon anxiety and performance in computer-assisted learning. *Journal of Educational Psychology,* 1971, *62,* 413–420.

Liebert, R.M., & Morris, L.W. Cognitive and emotional components of test anxiety: A distinction and some initial data. *Psychological Reports,* 1967, *20,* 975–978.

Mandler, G., & Watson, D.L. Anxiety and the interruption of behavior. In C.D. Spielberger (Ed.), *Anxiety and behavior.* New York: Academic Press, 1966.

May, R. *The meaning of anxiety.* New York: Norton, 1977.

McKeachie, W.L. Overview and critique. In Sieber, J.E., O'Neil, H.F., & Tobias, S. *Anxiety, learning and instruction.* Hillsdale, N.J.: Lawrence Erlbaum Associates, 1977.

Mirvis, P.H., & Seashore, S.E. Being ethical in organizational research. In J.E. Sieber (Ed.), *Ethical decision making in social science research.* N.Y.: Cambridge University Press, in preparation.

O'Neil, H.F., Spielberger, C.D., & Hansen, D.N. The effects of state anxiety and task difficulty on computer-assisted learning. *Journal of Educational Psychology,* 1969, *60,* 343–350.

Perls, F. *The gestalt approach: Eyewitness to therapy.* Palo Alto, Calif.: Science and Behavior Books, 1973.

Phillips, B.N., Martin, R.P., & Meyers, J. Interventions in relation to anxiety in school. In C.D. Spielberger (Ed.), *Anxiety: Current trends in theory and research* (Vol. 2). New York: Academic Press, 1972.

Ram Dass, B. Preface. In D. Goleman (Ed.), *The varieties of meditative experience.* New York: Dutton, 1977.

Ryan, W. *Blaming the victim.* New York: Pantheon, 1971.

Sarason, I.G. Experimental approaches to test anxiety: Attention and the uses of information. In C.D. Spielberger (Ed.), *Anxiety: Current trends in theory and research* (Vol. 2). New York: Academic Press, 1972.

Sarason, I. G., & Glanzer, V. J. Effects of test anxiety and reinforcement history on verbal behavior. *Journal of Abnormal and Social Psychology,* 1963, *67,* 87–91.

Sarason, I. G., & Harmatx, M. G. Test anxiety and experimental conditions. *Journal of Personality and Social Psychology,* 1965, *1,* 499–505.

Sarason, I.G., & Stoops, R. *Test anxiety and the passage of time.* Unpublished manuscript, 1976.

Sarason, S. B. The measurement of anxiety in children: Some questions and problems. In C.D. Spielberger (Ed.), *Anxiety and behavior.* New York: Academic Press, 1966.

Sarason, S.B. Anxiety, intervention and the culture of the school. In C.D. Spielberger (Ed.), *Anxiety: Current trends in theory and research.* (Vol. 2). New York: Academic Press, 1972.

Sarason, S.B., Hill, K.T., & Zimbardo, P.G. A longitudinal study of the relation of test anxiety to performance on intelligence and achievement tests. *Monographs of the Society for Research in Child Development,* 1964, *29,* (2, Serial No. 7).

Schachter, S. *Emotion, obesity and crime.* New York: Academic Press, 1971.

Schachter, S., & Singer, J.E. Cognitive, social and physiological determinants of emotional state. *Psychological Review,* 1962, *69,* 379–399.

Selye, H. *Stress without distress.* Philadelphia: J.B. Lippincott, 1976.

Sieber, J.E. *Methods and values in behavioral research.* In J.E. Sieber (Ed.) *Ethical decision making in social science research.* N.Y.: Cambridge University Press, in preparation.

Sieber, J.E., & Crockenburg, S.B. The teacher and the anxious child. *Today's Education,* 1970, *59,* 76–77.

Sieber, J.E., Kameya, L.I., & Paulson, F.L. Effects of memory support on the problem solving abilities of test-anxious children. *Journal of Educational Psychology,* 1970, *61,* 159–168.

Sieber, J.E., O'Neil, H.F., & Tobias, S. *Anxiety, learning and instruction.* Hillsdale, N.J.: Lawrence Erlbaum Associates, 1977.

Solomon, R.L., & Wynne, L.C. Traumatic avoidance learning: The principle of anxiety conservation and partial irreversibility. *Psychological Review,* 1954, *61,* 353–385.

Spence, J.T., & Spence, K.W. The motivational components of manifest anxiety: Drive and drive stimuli. In C.D. Spielberger (Ed.), *Anxiety and behavior.* New York: Academic Press, 1966.

Spielberger, C.D. Theory and research on anxiety. In C.D. Spielberger (Ed.), *Anxiety and behavior.* New York: Academic Press, 1966.

Spielberger, C.D. Anxiety as an emotional state. In C.D. Spielberger (Ed.), *Anxiety: Current trends in theory and research.* Vol. 1. N.Y.: Academic Press, 1972.

Spielberger, C.D., Gorsuch, R.L., & Lushene, R.E. *Manual for the state-trait anxiety inventory.* Palo Alto, Calif.: Consulting Psychologists Press, 1970.

Walsh, R.N. Initial meditative experiences: Part I. *Journal of Transpersonal Psychology,* 1977, *9,* 151–191.

Walsh, R.N., & Shapiro, D. *Beyond health and normality.* New York: Van Nostrand, 1978.

Walsh, R.N., & Vaughn, R.E. Transpersonal models of the person and psychotherapy. Unpublished manuscript, 1978.

Wine, J.D. Test anxiety and the direction of attention. *Psychological Bulletin,* 1971, *76,* 92–104.

Wolpe, J. The conditioning and deconditioning of neurotic anxiety. In C.D. Spielberger (Ed.), *Anxiety and behavior.* New York: Academic Press, 1966.

Woolfolk, R.L., & Richardson, F.C. *Stress, sanity and survival.* New York: Sovereign Books, 1978.

II

THEORY AND RESEARCH

3 Test Anxiety and Cue Utilization

Russell G. Geen
University of Missouri-Columbia

Most current conceptualizations of anxiety stress the importance of cognition as an intervening variable that mediates effects of anxiety on performance. Consistent with this emphasis, many investigators define test anxiety as a variable related to individual differences in such cognitive activities as attention, appraisal, and the storage and retrieval of information. Such an approach assumes a transactional relationship between individuals and their environments. Although people are required to perform under the situational constraints of tests and evaluations, they are not merely passive participants in the process. Instead, they search the environment for cues, they attend to events selectively, they appraise informational inputs, and they evaluate feedback of both their performance and their emotional reactions. In all of these processes, test anxiety is considered to be an important variable (e.g., I. Sarason, 1972; Sieber, O'Neil, & Tobias, 1977). This chapter reviews research and theory on the influence that test anxiety has on three specific processes whereby information is utilized in test situations. These processes are: (1) the utilization of stimuli related to, and necessary for performance of, the task; (2) reactions to cues related to performance on the task; and (3) interpretation of cues arising from body states that occur during performance. Although these processes probably interact during the course of prolem solving, each will be reviewed separately.

ANXIETY AND RANGE OF CUE UTILIZATION

Obviously, quality of performance on a task depends to a large degree on the efficiency with which task-related stimuli are attended to and utilized. The influence of motivation on cue utilization has been recognized for many years. Tolman (1948), dealing with the phenomenon in the context of his theory of learning, listed "strongly motivational conditions" as one of several causes of the formation of narrow cognitive maps in animals and humans. The study of motivational effects on responses to peripheral stimuli was the subject of an important early paper by Bahrick, Fitts, and Rankin (1952), whereas Bartlett (1950) introduced to the literature the concept of "range of cues utilized." By the late 1950s, a number of studies had been reported in which an assumption of motivational influences on range of cue utilization was upheld (e.g., Bahrick, 1954; Bruner, Matter, & Papanek, 1955; Callaway & Dembo, 1958; Callaway & Thompson, 1953). The early research culminated in, and was summarized by, an influential paper by Easterbrook (1959).

The point of the Easterbrook (1959) paper, which was extended slightly in the following year by Kausler and Trapp (1960), was the empirical generalization that " . . . when the direction of behavior is constant, increase in drive is associated with a reduction in the range of cue use.[p. 183]." Drive was defined as "a dimension of emotional arousal or general covert excitement, the innate response to a state of biological deprivation or noxious stimulation, which underlies or occurs simultaneously with, overt action and affects its strength and course [p. 184]." Clearly, Easterbrook considered the process by which the range of cue utilization is reduced to be one produced by physiological activation. One implication of Easterbrook's analysis is that drive may either facilitate or inhibit performance, depending on the importance of peripheral cues for performance. Increasing drive up to a point will lead to the elimination of noncentral stimuli that are unimportant and possibly distracting, but further increase will narrow the focus to the point that necessary central cues are being eliminated. Furthermore, the level of drive at which the transition occurs should be lower for complex tasks than for relatively simple ones because, in the former case, a wider range of cues may be necessary for good performance. This set of hypothetical drive-related effects is, of course, a theoretical explication of the Yerkes–Dodson Law. Support for the hypothesis has been fairly strong, coming from experiments employing a wide range of independent variables with both human subjects (Agnew & Agnew, 1963; Bruning, Capage, Kozuh, Young, & Young, 1968; Hockey, 1970; 1973; McNamara & Fisch, 1964; O'Malley & Poplawsky, 1971) and rats (Telegdy & Cohen, 1971).

Of particular interest for purposes of this review have been experiments that show restriction of range of cue utilization as a function of trait anxiety (Korchin, 1964; Mendelsohn & Griswold, 1967; Solso, 1968; Solso, Johnson, & Schatz, 1968; Zaffy & Bruning, 1966). Test anxiety has been shown to be an antecedent of narrowed cue utilization in several experimental studies designed to test Easterbrook's hypothesis. Wachtel (1968) found a significant negative correlation between TAS scores and speed of reaction to signals occurring on the periphery of a central tracking task, provided that the situation was structured as one involving evaluation of the subject's performance. West, Lee, and Anderson (1969) tested children who had scored relatively high or low on the Test Anxiety Scale for Children (Sarason, Davidson, Lighthall, Waite, & Ruebush, 1960) with 40 arithmetic "story" problems constructed in such a way that some contained only information necessary to solution and others contained additional irrelevant information. Whereas subjects low in TA performed more efficiently on the unembellished items than on the ones containing irrelevant cues, the highly test-anxious subjects did not. Although the highly test-anxious subjects showed a slightly poorer level of performance overall than their less anxious counterparts, their performance was not hindered by the addition of useless information.

Geen (1976) found further evidence of test anxiety as a source of restricted cue utilization in an experiment involving serial learning. The task required the subject to remember which of a set of several stimuli was the one designated correct on each of 15 trials. In two conditions, numerical subscripts were added to the stimuli; in one, the subscript was consistent with the ordinal position of the correct one within the set, and in the other, it was selected randomly. Subjects also performed under social conditions designated to induce relatively strong or weak feelings of evaluation apprehension. The results indicated that under conditions of strong evaluation apprehension subjects who had scored high on the TAS prior to the experiment were helped less by the addition of the relevant information thant those who had scored low, but they were also hindered in their recall less by the insertion of irrelevant and potentially distracting information. In both cases, subjects high in TA behaved as if they were less affected by the additional cues than those low in TA, a finding consistent with an assumption of a restricted range of cue utilization. The data, therefore, affirmed the implication of Easterbrook's hypothesis that arousal will have either a facilitating or inhibiting effect on performance, depending on whether peripheral cues contribute to or detract from efficiency of performance.

Various theoretical explanations have been offered for the narrowing of range of cue utilization under high arousal. Broadbent (1971) considers the effect to be due to the influence of arousal on filtering. The aroused attentional system is selective in acceptance of inputs, so that it "devotes a higher proportion of its time to the intake of information from dominant sources and less from relatively minor ones [p. 433]." A similar argument is that of Kahneman (1973), who suggests that arousal reduces the amount of spare attentional capacity in the system, i.e., capacity beyond what is required for the primary task. Thus, both Broadbent and Kahneman propose the same narrowing function described by Easterbrook. In addition, both also suggest another effect of arousal upon attention. Kahneman notes that whereas high arousal does produce an increased tendency to focus on a small number of relevant cues, this selection process often involves a discrimination between the relevant cues and other less relevant ones. A high state of arousal has been shown (Broadbent, 1971) to impair the process of discrimination and consequent ability to focus on relevant stimuli. Kahneman concludes (1973):

> Thus, although subjects spontaneously become more selective when highly aroused, the effectiveness of their selections is likely to deteriorate, if the selection requires a fine discrimination... High arousal restricts the range of cues among which attention may be divided, and also disrupts the control of selective attention. In terms of a capacity model, the allocation of capacity becomes both more uneven and less precise when arousal is high [pp. 38, 40].

The possibility of a dual function of arousal in cue utilization, with one result being restricted range and the other being increased lability (cf. Wachtel, 1967), is discussed later at greater length.

A possible physiological mechanism underlying cue utilization is suggested in the argument of Walley and Weiden (1973) that when simultaneous inputs are processed the encoding of one interferes with the encoding of the others, an effect described as "cognitive masking." These investigators have further proposed that masking is produced by lateral inhibition at the cortical level. The relevance of this notion for Easterbrook's hypothesis lies in the contention that the degree of inhibition that occurs in cognitive masking is directly related to arousal. Arousal may, in this case, be either phasic or tonic so that individual differences in propensities to experience anxiety can be thought of as one possible antecedent. Thus, while parallel processing of multiple inputs may be possible at relatively low levels of arousal, it would become increasingly less likely as arousal increased. The result would be the restriction in range of processing described by Easterbrook.

Whatever the underlying mechanism, most investigators agree that restriction in the range of cue utilization represents a shifting in attentional bias or priorities toward a primary task and away from a secondary one. Wine (1971) has taken a similar point of view, describing the phenomenon in terms of diversion of attention away from the task and toward the self under conditions of high test anxiety. Her position is derived from I. Sarason's (1972) definition of test anxiety, whereby the person scoring high on that variable is thought to be "self-oriented":

> There is considerable evidence that the test-anxious person is strongly self-depreciative and ruminative.... Cues that suggest his behavior will be evaluated according to some norm or standard of excellence seem to constrict his focus.... He either (1) neglects or misinterprets informational cues that may be readily available to him or (2) experiences attentional blocks. [p. 393].

Wine (1971) has elaborated upon this idea by proposing that the self-centered responses of the highly test-anxious person during test situations interfere with attention to task-relevant stimuli necessary to good performance. Physiological arousal is involved in the process only insofar as it serves as a stimulus for diversion of attention (Wine, 1973, p. 11). Thus, according to Wine (1971): "highly evaluative conditions cause the highly test-anxious person to direct his attention internally rather than to the task [p. 96]," with the result that "the high-test-anxious person attends to fewer task cues than does the low-test-anxious person [p. 97]."

Concentration of attention inwardly toward the self therefore draws attention away from task-related stimuli. The underlying implication of this position is that there exists in the organism some finite capacity for attention and that attention must be allocated among the various stimuli in the field that demand it. This notion has much in common with the analyses of attention proposed by Kahneman (1973) and with other findings from studies of arousal and cue utilization (Hockey & Hamilton, 1970; Bacon, 1974). Hamilton (1975) has proposed an interesting model of attention that is related to Wine's hypothesis, one which makes use of the constructs of allocation and spare capacity. According to this model, whenever a person's priorities in allocation of attention (from the available limited store) give precedence to the demands of "enduring dispositions," less spare capacity is left over for demands of the task. Hamilton (1975) states that the person may respond by paying less attention to external, task-related inputs, either by "narrowing the area focussed for selective attention or by restricting attention to a small number of foci [pp. 54–55]." An important variable in this analysis is the basis on which demand priorities are ordered. Possibly a trait variable such as test anxiety constitutes one such basis. The person who is high in TA may, as I. Sarason (1972) has argued, be relatively likely to respond to a test situation by giving attention to internal reactions rather than to task-relevant stimuli.

The notion that anxiety reduces the range of cues utilized fails to account for some other findings in the literature. Anxiety, for example, has been found to be associated with a broadened range of perception of stimuli by both Schmidt (1964) and Solso, Johnson, and Schatz (1968). In both of these studies, subjects were given instructions that maximized the importance of the peripheral cues to good performance: Schmidt's was a study of visual angle, in which subjects were set to report stimuli as soon as they became discernible on the periphery, whereas the Solso et al. experiment required subjects to report as many stimuli as possible from a wide stimulus layout. In both cases, subjects scoring high on the Taylor MAS manifested broader reporting of stimuli than those scoring low. A related finding is Cornsweet's (1969) observation that when peripheral cues are relevant to the central task the threat of a highly arousing shock increases the extent to which they are utilized. Mendelsohn and Griswold (1967) have also reported the unusual finding of a curvilinear relationship between a measure of trait anxiety and range of task-relevant peripheral cues utilized, with moderately anxious males showing the greatest amount of restriction. Their explanation is that up to a point increasing anxiety produces narrowing of the range but that at higher anxiety levels there is a tendency to broaden the scope, provided that the peripheral cues are task related. Their reasoning thus proposes a two-process model incorporating elements from Easterbrook's hypothesis as well as empirical generalizations similar to those of Cornsweet and others. Additional evidence that anxiety may promote broadened cue utilization has been reported by Nottelmann and Hill (1977), who found that children high in test anxiety showed greater performance decrements and more off-task behavior in the classroom than less anxious ones. They proposed that anxious children are more sensitive to, and reliant on, feedback and evaluation from others. It might be suggested that the others in this case represent sources of information that are, to the child, quite important for performance, even though attention to them has a harmful overall effect.

The assumption that under certain conditions anxiety may produce a broadened range of cue utilization also helps clarify an otherwise confusing state of the data on the relationship between anxiety and incidental learning. Taking into account the Easterbrook hypothesis only, one would have to predict that high levels of anxiety would be associated with relatively poor incidental learning, because utilization of the cues necessary to such learning would be hampered. Such an expectation is implicit in Wine's (1971) attentional analysis of cue utilization, as Sieber et al. (1977, p. 36–37) have explicitly argued. However, this is exactly opposite what has been reported in two studies of the influence of TA on intentional and incidental learning in children by Dusek and his associates (Dusek, Kermis, & Mergler, 1975; Dusek, Mergler, & Kermis, 1976). In both studies, it was found that children who had scored low on the Test Anxiety Scale for Children showed superior learning of the central task when compared to those who had scored high, but poorer learning of incidental stimuli. The finding of poor central learning in highly test-anxious children is consistent with the assumption that anxiety produces task-irrelevant responses that compete with attention to the task, but the finding of improved incidental learning is not.

One key to understanding the findings of Dusek and his colleagues is a hypothesis offered by Wachtel (1967) in which arousal has two effects on attention and cue utilization. One is the now-familiar effect described by Easterbrook. Wachtel decribes this as analogous to the width of a beam of light that figuratively plays across the stimulus field. The "beam" may be relatively narrow and focused, ot it may be relatively broad and diffuse; this width is assumed to be a negative function of the individual's level of arousal. The other characteristic of the attentional "beam" is the extent to which it scans the available cues in the field. It may range widely over the field, or it may be restricted to a small range of focal points. This range of latitude in scanning is presumably independent of the narrowness of focus at any one point. Arousal is assumed to increase the range of stimuli scanned even while it narrows the focus of attention within any given area searched.

With this double function of arousal in mind, it is important to consider the methodology used by Dusek and his associates. Test stimuli consisted of eight cards, with each containing a line drawing of an animal and a common household object. Each card was placed in a given position in a layout with a 2-sec interval between placements until all eight were in place, at which time the layout was covered. The procedure was repeated five times, and then the child was asked to recall the proper position of each animal (the central task) and the household object paired with each animal (the incidental task). It seems possible that this procedure, in which a progressively larger number of stimuli are placed in the subject's visual field on each trial, enhances the importance of scanning so that subjects with a tendency toward a broad range of such visual activity would apprehend and encode more stimuli, central and peripheral, than subjects disposed toward a narrower search. Breadth of scanning may be what led the highly test-anxious subjects to perform better on the incidental task than the less test-anxious. The poorer central learning of the highly test-anxious may have resulted in part from superior incidental performance: Allocation of attention toward peripheral stimuli may have detracted from attention available for processing central cues.

The role of attentional processes in cue utilization is further shown in studies of attention training as a means of reducing the potentially harmful effect of test anxiety of task performance. As Wine (Chapter 16) points out, training highly test-anxious subjects to attend to task-related stimuli effectively reduces the differential in performance between those subjects and their less test-anxious counterparts. In the aforementioned studies, Dusek and his associates found that verbal labeling of the stimuli facilitated the performance on the intentional learning task for children high in test anxiety but did not affect the performance of those low in test anxiety. This is consistent with the argument that verbal labeling promotes attention to central stimuli and offsets the antagonistic effects of anxiety.

In addition to influencing the breadth of cues processed and the general level of activity involved in encoding, anxiety may also affect the particular type of processing in which the person engages. This point of view has recently been articulated by Mueller (1976), who has proposed that anxious (or otherwise aroused) subjects utilize fewer of the available attributes of stimuli in encoding for memory. Mueller's hypothesis is important in the discussion of cue utilization if we consider the total set of stimulus attributes to be cues, and anxiety to be a variable that restricts or limits the utilization of these cues in the encoding process. In testing his point of view, Mueller (1976) showed that test anxiety has particular influence on organization processes that occur during free recall. Subjects high in test anxiety clustered less than those low in test anxiety for taxonomic categories, acoustic categories, and associative categories. They also showed less subjective organization of formally unrelated terms and gave less priority in output to previously unrecalled items. The difference in clustering tended to be attenuated with practice, however, and was not accompanied by differences in total recall.

Recently, Mueller (1978) has suggested that test anxiety affects encoding by influencing the level at which information is processed (Craik & Lockhart, 1972). He has hypothesized that, compared to subjects low in test anxiety, those that are high on the same variable either do not process as deeply, do not process deeply with the same speed, or do not process as thoroughly at deep levels. Encoding is shallow when it is based on physical characteristics, such as the acoustic properties of words, whereas it is deep when it is based on semantic properties. Mueller studied free recall of items from an "ambiguous" list arranged so that encoding of deep and shallow attributes would presumably be equally likely. In two experiments, he found that subjects high in test anxiety tended to do less clustering and to show poorer recall than subjects low in test anxiety. The highly test-anxious subjects were also less likely to utilize subtle alphabetic cues that mediated the transfer from one stimulus category to another. However, no evidence was found for test anxiety differences in depth of processing; highly test-anxious subjects did not show a superiority in clustering of physically similar items. In part, this may have been due to differential potency in the two attributes of the list. In general, the semantic characteristics of the items seemed to be more salient than the physical in both experiments.

Mueller also inserted into his design a variable that has relevance for the attentional training procedures already reviewed. In both experiments, some subjects were given, before exposure to the list, an orienting task calculated to focus attention on one or the other of the attributes of the items. Subjects given instructions that oriented them to the semantic features of the words generally recalled more items than those oriented toward the physical characteristics, and this difference was greater for subjects scoring high in test anxiety than those scoring low. Mueller has noted that his orienting task for semantic features is analogous to Wine's treatment, already cited, of selective direction of attention toward task-relevant matters and possibly also to I. Sarason's (1973) use of a model as an attention-focusing technique. A comparable finding has been reported by Edmunson and Nelson (1976). In their study, subjects attempted to learn either a difficult or a relatively simple paired-associates list under instructions either to rehearse the words or to form a mental image relating the two words of each pair to each other. Under instructions to rehearse, subjects who had scored high on the A-trait scale of the STAI made more errors than those low in A-trait, especially on the relatively difficult list. The use of instructions that induced interaction imagery eliminated the effects of anxiety, suggesting again that direction of attention toward certain features of the test stimuli may produce attenuation of performance decrements that would otherwise occur in highly test-anxious subjects.

ANXIETY AND REACTIONS TO SUCCESS AND FAILURE

Compared to the amount of research that has been conducted on the effects of anxiety on cue utilization, little has been reported on anxiety influences on responses to success and failure. The problem would seem to be an important one, however, in light of the possibility that feedback cues regarding success or failure on a task contribute to the number and intensity of self-deprecatory responses the person makes and to the ongoing self-instructional process that may occur in states of anxiety (Mandler, 1972). It is especially probable that the person who is confronted with a difficult task under stressful evaluative conditions will experience some failure, at least initially, and that this failure could affect highly test-anxious people differently.

The relation of trait anxiety to behavior following success and failure has been recognized for many years. I. Sarason (1957) gave subjects the task of learning a list following failure on a digit-cancellation task and found that subjects who had scored high on the Taylor Manifest Anxiety Scale performed more poorly after failure than did a group of highly anxious controls that had not previously failed. Among subjects low in manifest anxiety, however, performance of subjects who had undergone prior failure was superior to that of nonfailing controls. Sarason ascribed the findings, in part, to a greater sensitivity evidenced by highly anxious subjects to situations that might lead to success or failure. A similar line of reasoning was applied by Katchmar, Ross, and Andrews (1958) to their finding that failure-stress decreased efficiency on a subsequent task for subject high in anxiety but facilitated performance among the less anxious.

The emphasis in these early interpretations was on the debilitating effects of failure for highly anxious subjects. Reasons for enhancement of performance following failure for less anxious subjects were not as obvious. Recently, Weiner has investigated the interaction of anxiety with success–failure experiences and has sought to explain the subsequent behavior of both highly anxious and less anxious subjects. In his first study, Weiner (1966) showed that performance differences on difficult and easy tasks by subjects high and low in anxiety (e.g., Spence, Farber, & McFann, 1956) are a function of perceived success and failure, not of task difficulty. Task difficulty, he has argued, is important for performance only because success is the likely outcome on a simple task and failure the probable result on a difficult one. Subjects classified as high or low in anxiety were given either a difficult or an easy paired-associates list to learn. Those given the easy list were given false feedback concerning their performance by being informed that they were performing at a level inferior to that of most of their age-mates. By contrast, other subjects were given a difficult list but were informed that their performance was superior to that of their peers. The results indicated that among subjects learning the difficult list with feedback of successful performance, the ones that were high in anxiety required fewer trials to criterion than the ones low in anxiety. Subjects working on the easy task, with bogus feedback of failure, showed an opposite pattern of results: Those high in anxiety required more trials to criterion than did their less anxious colleagues. Similar findings have been reported by Weiner and Schneider (1971), who found that subjects high in resultant achievement motivation (defined as the net motivational difference between need for achievement and fear of failure) performed at a level superior to that of subjects low in the same variable following perceived failure, but worse following perceived success. A high level of resulting achievement motivation is roughly comparable to a low level of test anxiety, because the latter contributes to the former. The Weiner and Schneider (1971) findings therefore support Weiner's (1966) earlier ones.

Two theoretical explanations for these data have been offered. At first, Weiner discussed them in terms of inertial motivation (Atkinson, 1964; Weiner, 1970). It was assumed that failure at a task leaves a residue of unfulfilled approach and avoidance tendencies evoked by expectancies of the goal. The strength and persistence of each tendency depends on whether the individual is primarily motivated by need to achieve or by fear of failure. According to Weiner (1972):

> If the previously aroused approach motivation exceeds that of avoidance motivation, as among individuals...(high in resultant achievement motivation)..., then the persisting tendency augments future performance. That is, prior failure increases achievement strivings. Conversely, if the aroused avoidance motivation exceeds that of the approach tendency, as among individuals...(low in resultant achievement motivation)..., then the persisting tendency dampens future performance. That is, prior failure further inhibits achievement strivings [p. 239].

Weiner now (1972; Weiner & Schneider, 1971; Weiner, Frieze, Kukla, Reed, Rest, & Rosenbaum, 1971) has modified his approach to the study of success and failure by emphasizing the attributions of causality that the person makes after the success or the failure experience. These attributions serve as the cognitive link between past task-related experiences and future motivation and attention. It is argued that individuals who are high in resultant achievement motivation attribute failure to a lack of effort expended on the task. When they perform poorly but still have a motive to succeed, they react to their poor performance with increased effort and attention to the task. Persons low in resultant achievement motivation, on the other hand, attribute failure to lack of ability. Their response to this attribution is one of giving up at the task, with consequent inattention, disengagement, and poor performance.

Reactions to the experience of success have not been spelled out by attribution theorists as satisfactorily as have been reactions to failure. One attempt has been made by Heckhausen (1975), who uses the terms "hope of success" and "fear of failure" to refer to, respectively, the categories of high and low resultant achievement motivation. He cites data indicating that persons high in fear of failure tend to attribute success to good fortune, relative to persons high in hope of success. Heckhausen agrees with Weiner, as cited earlier, on the differential attributions of cause of failure made by persons varying in resultant achievement motivation. Heckhausen concludes (1975):

> In summary, there is a pervading asymmetry in the motive-linked patterns of causal attribution bias. Under comparable conditions, . . . (persons high in hope of success) . . . credit themselves more for their success than for their failures, and . . . (persons high in fear of failure) . . . credit themselves more for their failures than for their successes [p. 122].

We might conclude from this analysis that persons high in resultant achievement motivation will manifest behavior consistent with attributions of personal causation. Unfortunatley, Heckhausen does not specify whether these are attributions of ability or of effort, but in either case, we might expect success to be followed by increased motivation and attention, with good performance as a consequence. In the same way, people low in resultant achievement motivation might be expected to respond to success by attributing their outcomes to such external causes as good luck or relative ease of the task. Given such attributions, such people might be expected to try less hard on succeeding tasks and to show a relative decrement in performance. Such predictions, however, are not consistent with the data reported by Weiner (1966), who found results generally opposite to those predicted here in the case of subjects given false feedback of success at the task. Obviously, more theoretical refinements of the attributional analysis of reactions to success are required. Weiner and Schneider concluded, in 1971, that an attributional analysis of responses to success parallel to that already made of responses to failure had yet to be formulated, and that conclusion appears still to be justified today.

Another line of evidence somewhat different from the one described previously may be relevant to the present discussion. Success and failure at tasks derive their affective value for the subject, to a great extent, from the general context of social evaluation in which they occur. The subject in such a situation is usually evaluated, or is expected to be evaluated later, by an experimenter or other judges. In two recent reviews of the literature on the effects of observers upon performance (Geen, 1979; Geen & Gange, 1977), it has been concluded that the evaluation apprehension that occurs in evaluative social settings is fear of failure and not a more positive incentive motivation.In fact, evidence has been presented (Geen, 1979) that if the evaluative testing session is preceded by a success experience for the subject on a task related to the main one, the presence of an observer is associated with enhancement of performance and not with a decrement.

The significance of this research for our discussion lies in the finding that text anxiety interacts with audience and coactor variables to influence performance on complex tasks. In general, the debilitating effect of potentially evaluative social settings is greater for people high in test anxiety or related types of evaluation anxiety than it is for people who score low on the same traits (Ganzer, 1968; Paivio, 1965; Pederson, 1970). Furthermore, Geen (1977) has shown that subjects high in test anxiety are not only hurt more than those low in test anxiety by the presence of an observer during performance, but also helped more by a reappraisal of the observation that renders it less threatening. Subjects in this study were females who worked at an anagrams task, either alone or in the presence of an observing female experimenter. In one of the conditions, the experimenter ostentatiously watched the subject and made notes of her performance, with no other information given. In another condition, the experimenter played the same observer role, but explained beforehand that she was observing only so that she could give the subject information on how to improve her performance on a later anagrams task. The redefinition of the evaluation as potentially helpful led to a significantly more efficient performance in that condition than was found when no such explanation of the observation had been given. Moreover, the superiority of performance in the "helpful" evaluation condition over that in the "evaluation only" condition was significantly greater for subjects who were high in test anxiety than for those who were low. Therefore, this study suggests that highly test-anxious subjects are more sensitive to audience cues in evaluative situations than less test-anxious ones.

ANXIETY AND RESPONSES TO INTERNAL CUES

Contemporary investigators of test anxiety have devoted considerable attention to individual differences in reactions to internal arousal states. In general, they have differentiated between the somatic–emotional aspects of arousal and the cognitive–ideational aspects. Although the distinction has sometimes been phrased in terms of physiological versus nonphysiological reactions, with emotional arousal equated with autonomic activation and cognitive arousal with emotions such as worry, it now seems that the two aspects of arousal are both accompanied by distinct physiological states.

Several studies have suggested, for example, that emotional arousal occurring during states of stress is associated with elevation in tonic skin conductance, whereas arousal induced through cognitive activity is associated with elevated levels of phasic conductance (Katkin, 1965; Kilpatrick, 1972; Miller, 1968). In addition, Davidson, Davison, and Freedland (1977) have recently contrasted cardiovascular and electrodermal activity under conditions of emotional and cognitive arousal. Subjects in this study were asked to imagine various situations that had been found through pretesting to vary in their capacity to evoke cognitive and/or somatic arousal. Measures of autonomic activity gathered during this imaginal behavior revealed that subjects imagining events high in somatic and low in cognitive arousal showed higher levels of heart rate than subjects in the low-somatic–high-cognitive condition. The highest heart rate overall was manifested by subjects imagining situations judged to be high in somatic arousal potential. Higher levels of skin conductance were shown by subjects in the high-cognitive–low-somatic condition than in the high-somatic–low-cognitive. Moreover, the highest levels of conductance were found in subjects imagining events high in cognitive arousal.

If cognitive and somatic arousal are revealed by different patterns of physiological activity, then cognitive arousal such as worry may be thought of as either a response to an underlying change in bodily activity or as a correlate of such change. In either case, cognitive arousal appears to have influences on behavior that are different from those of somatic or emotional arousal. In particular, worry tends to be fairly constant within individuals across time, whereas emotionality is more confined to the situation in which the person is evaluated, peaking just before a test and falling off rapidly thereafter (Doctor & Altman, 1969; Liebert & Morris, 1967; Morris & Liebert, 1970). In addition, worry has generally been shown to be more highly correlated with performance in test situations than emotionality (e.g., Deffenbacher, 1977; Morris & Liebert, 1970).

Worry and emotionality are possibly related in a way that has as yet received little attention from students of test anxiety. Broadly construed, the cognitive-physiological theory of emotion advocated by Schachter and Singer (1962) would define worry as a label attached to an underlying state of increased physiological activation. It has been suggested (e.g., Mandler & Watson, 1966) that this approach may be a satisfactory one for defining anxiety as a particular label attached to arousal emanating from diffuse states of excitement, such as occur in the interruption of behavior. Possibly somatic arousal is, as argued by some, a relatively transient response to situational stressors and worry is a more enduring cognitive reaction to those same stressors. It is further possible that the cognition of "being anxious" becomes the label attached to the physiological condition by reference to the cognition of worry. This label may then come to define the arousal state for the person. In this way, persons who are disposed toward strong emotional arousal in the presence of stressors and are also likely to worry in such a situation (i.e., highly test-anxious people) should be especially likely to experience those symptoms of self-deprecation that I. Sarason (1972) has described as the primary source of performance deficits. The self-informing process of such a person is likely to be: "I am highly excited because I am worried about my performance on this test."

We may speculate on how such a model of labeling of internal states would predict behavior of less test-anxious persons and behavior in less threatening situations. Fig. 3.1 outlines a suggested approach to this problem. It rests on three assumptions. The first, already discussed, is that the label attached to behavior is a joint function of emotional arousal and available cues. The second is that in the test situation a powerful source of cues is the person's repertoire of cognitions elicited by situational stimuli. As we have seen, for highly test-anxious people in test situations one such dominant cognition is worry. The third assumption, consistent with the foregoing discussion, is that strong physiological reactions such as phasic skin conductance and heart rate change are associated mainly with situational stressors, whereas variations in cognitive response to the situation are mainly a function of more enduring variables, such as test anxiety.

From this set of assumptions, it may be predicted that when a task is described to the subject as one that is evaluative, ego-involving, and

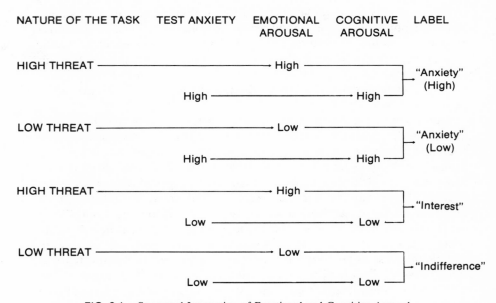

FIG. 3.1.   Suggested Interaction of Emotional and Cognitive Arousal.

potentially threatening, it will elicit a high level of somatic arousal. As we have already supposed, the highly test-anxious person should label somatic arousal in terms of the worry also elicited by the test, with the result being a condition that we might term "state anxiety." If, by contrast, the task is structured in a way that attenuates its threat potential, such as through the provision of reassurances to the subject (I. Sarason, 1972), it is proposed here that the result will be primarily a lower level of somatic arousal. The highly test-anxious subject will, under these conditions, still experience worry but will attach that label to a lower overall level of arousal and, hence, experience less state anxiety. The result in performance would be that mitigating the threat inherent in the task will produce improved performance in high-test-anxious subjects, a common finding in Sarason's research. Threatening and less threatening tasks will produce strong and weak somatic arousal, respectively, in subjects low in test anxiety. However, these subjects will react to high arousal not with state anxiety, but with some other reaction appropriate to whatever label they attach to the arousal state. This labeling cannot be specified, although we may assume that it will be based less on a cognition of "worry" than would be the case in high-test-anxious subjects. The combination of high arousal from a potentially threatening task and a relative tendency to label arousal in terms other than worry could produce a strong positive emotion, such as curiosity or interest, and a consequent approach tendency. The low-test-anxious subject who is given a test that is basically nonthreatening will, on the other hand, experience both low arousal and cognitions unrelated to worry. The result might be an emotional state of indifference and disinterest. The result in performance of such tasks would likely be that the subject who is high in test anxiety will do better than the one who is low: this prediction is consistent with research evidence.

To date, there is little evidence available pertaining to the theoretical paradigm outlined here. One published study does have some bearing on it, however. Weiner and Samuel (1975) manipulated the labeling of arousal supposedly occurring in the course of a difficult anagrams task by means of a misattribution procedure. Their experiment consisted of a treatment whereby some subjects were encouraged to attribute task-induced arousal to the ingestion of a pill. Such a treatment would, in terms of the model proposed here, have the effect of supplying an obvious cue by which arousal could be labeled. The tendency of subjects in this condition, therefore, might be to label arousal in terms of the supposed effects of the pill and not in terms of cognitions elicited by dispositions toward anxiety. The result should be that, compared to the condition in which arousal was not attributed to the pill, high-test-anxious subjects in the pill-attribution condition would perform at a superior rate, whereas low-test-anxious subjects in the pill-attribution condition would do worse. The data tended to support this notion. When arousal was not attributed to the pill, high-test-anxious subjects solved fewer anagrams than did those low in test anxiety. Attributing arousal to the pill had no appreciable effect on the performance of low-test-anxious subjects, but it resulted in sufficient improvement among the highly test-anxious that they did not differ from those low in test anxiety. Thus, breaking the link between worry and arousal through misattribution of arousal to another source had an effect that might be thought of as due to reduced state anxiety.

The cognitive labeling paradigm proposed in the present discussion represents an attempt to establish a syntactic link between constructs related to characteristics of the task and others relating to individual differences in test anxiety. The proposed link is a process of interpretation and appraisal involving two hypothesized arousal reactions to the perception of threat arising from the testing situation. The labels that are semantically tied to the constructs in this case represent the heart of the model, because they define the various "states" that ultimately bring about the effects on performance attributable to test anxiety. We have proposed that the state of anxiety, defined as a high level of emotional arousal interpreted and understood as worry, should have a particularly debilitating effect on performance, whereas the state of emotionality not labeled as worry could have a facilitating influence. In part, this facilitation or enhancement of performance could involve other processes of information-utilization suggested in this chapter. Possibly, therefore, what one does with information concerning one's emotional state is the most fundamental case of cue utilization, and one that affects the way in which information is processed at other points in the task, as in attention, encoding, retrieval, and responding to success–failure cues.

REFERENCES

Agnew, N., & Agnew, M. Drive level effects on tasks of narrow and broad attention. *Quarterly Journal of Experimental Psychology,* 1963, *15,* 58–62.

Atkinson, J. W. *An introduction to motivation.* New York: Van Nostrand, 1964.

Bacon, S. J. Arousal and the range of cue utilization. *Journal of Experimental Psychology,* 1974, *102,* 81–87.

Bahrick, H. P. Incidental learning under two incentive conditions. *Journal of Experimental Psychology,* 1954, *47,* 170–172.

Bahrick, H. P., Fitts, P. M., & Rankin, R. E. Effects of incentives upon reactions to peripheral stimuli. *Journal of Experimental Psychology,* 1952, *44,* 400–406.

Bartlett, F. Program for experiments on thinking. *Quarterly Journal of Experimental Psychology,* 1950, *2,* 145–152.

Broadbent, D. W. *Decision and stress.* New York: Academic Press, 1971.

Bruner, J. P., Matter, J., & Papanek, M. L. Breadth of learning as a function of drive level and mechanization. *Psychological Review,* 1955, *62,* 1–10.

Bruning, J. L., Capage, J. E., Kozuh, G. F., Young, P. F., & Young, W. E. Socially induced drive and range of cue utilization. *Journal of Personality and Social Psychology,* 1968, *9,* 242–244.

Callaway, E., & Dembo, E. Narrowed attention: A psychological phenomenon that accompanies a certain physiological change. *Archives of Neurology and Psychiatry,* 1958, *79,* 74–90.

Callaway, E., & Thompson, S. V. Sympathetic activity and perception. *Psychosomatic Medicine,* 1953, *15,* 443–455.

Cornsweet, D. M. Use of cues in the visual periphery under conditions of arousal. *Journal of Experimental Psychology,* 1969, *80,* 14–18.

Craik, F. I. M., & Lockhart, R. S. Levels of processing: A framework for memory research. *Journal of Verbal Learning and Verbal Behavior,* 1972, *11,* 671–684.

Davidson, R. J., Davison, G. C., & Freedland, E. S. *Cardiac and electrodermal patterning during cognitive and somatic anxiety.* Paper read at annual meeting of Society for Psychophysiological Research, Philadelphia, October 1977.

Deffenbacher, J. L. Relationship of worry and emotionality to performance on the Miller Analogies Test. *Journal of Educational Psychology,* 1977, *69,* 191–195.

Doctor, R. M., & Altman, F. Worry and emotionality as components of test anxiety: Replication and further data. *Psychological Reports,* 1969, *24,* 563–568.

Dusek, J. B., Kermis, M. D., & Mergler, N. L. Information processing in low- and high-test anxious children as a function of grade level and verbal labelling. *Developmental Psychology,* 1975, *11,* 651–652.

Dusek, J. B., Mergler, N. L., & Kermis, M. D. Attention, encoding, and information processing in low- and high-test anxious children. *Child Development,* 1976, *47,* 201–207.

Easterbrook, J. A. The effect of emotion on cue utilization and the organization of behavior. *Psychological Review,* 1959, *66,* 183–201.

Edmunson, E. D., & Nelson, D. L. Anxiety, imagery, and sensory interference. *Bulletin of the Psychonomic Society,* 1976, *8,* 319–322.

Ganzer, V. J. The effects of audience presence and test anxiety on learning and retention in a serial learning situation. *Journal of Personality and Social Psychology,* 1968, *8,* 194–199.

Geen, R. G. Test anxiety, observation, and range of cue utilization. *British Journal of Social and Clinical Psychology,* 1976, *15,* 253–259.

Geen, R. G. The effects of anticipation of positive and negative outcomes on audience anxiety. *Journal of Consulting and Clinical Psychology,* 1977, *45,* 715–716.

Geen, R. G. The influence of passive audiences on performance. In P. Paulus (Ed.), *The Psychology of Group Influence.* Hillsdale, N.J.: Lawrence Erlbaum Associates, 1979.

Geen, R. G., & Gange, J. J. Drive theory of social facilitation: Twelve years of theory and research. *Psychological Bulletin,* 1977, *84,* 1267–1288.

Hamilton, V. Socialization anxiety and information processing: A capacity model of anxiety-induced performance. In I. G. Sarason & C. D. Spielberger (Eds.), *Stress and anxiety* (Vol. 2). Washington: Hemisphere, 1975.

Heckhausen, H. Fear of failure as a self-reinforcing motive. In I. G. Sarason & C. D. Spielberger (Eds.), *Stress and anxiety* (Vol. 2). Washington: Hemisphere, 1975.

Hockey, G. R. J. Signal probability and spatial location as possible bases for increased selectivity in noise. *Quarterly Journal of Experimental Psychology,* 1970, *22,* 37–42.

Hockey, G. R. J. Changes in information-selection patterns in multi-source monitoring as a function of induced arousal shifts. *Journal of Experimental Psychology,* 1973, *101,* 35–42.

Hockey, G. R. J., & Hamilton, P. Arousal and information selection in short-term memory. *Nature,* 1970, *226,* 866–867.

Kahneman, D. *Attention and effort.* Englewood Cliffs, N.J.: Prentice-Hall, 1973.

Katchmar, L. T., Ross, S., & Andrews, T. G. Effects of stress and anxiety on performance of a complex verbal-coding task. *Journal of Experimental Psychology,* 1958, *55,* 599–563.

Katkin, E. S. Relationship between manifest anxiety and two indices of autonomic response to stress. *Journal of Personality and Social Psychology,* 1965, *2,* 324–333.

Kausler, D. H., & Trapp, E. P. Motivation and cue utilization in intentional and incidental learning. *Psychological Review,* 1960, *67,* 373–379.

Kilpatrick, D. G. Differential responsiveness of two electrodermal indices to psychological stress and performance of a complex cognitive task. *Psychophysiology,* 1972, *9,* 218–226.

Korchin, S. J. Anxiety and cognition. In C. Scheerer (Ed.), *Cognition: Theory, research, promise.* New York: Harper & Row, 1964.

Liebert, R. M., & Morris, L. W. Cognitive and emotional components of test anxiety: A distinction and some initial data. *Psychological Reports,* 1967, *20,* 975–978.

Mandler, G. Comments on Dr. Sarason's paper. In C. D. Spielberger (Ed.), *Anxiety: Current trends in theory and research.* New York: Academic Press, 1972.

Mandler, G., & Watson, D. L. Anxiety and the interruption of behavior. In C. D. Spielberger (Ed.), *Anxiety and behavior.* New York: Academic Press, 1966.

McNamara, H. J., & Fisch, R. I. Effect of high and low motivation on two aspects of attention. *Perceptual and Motor Skills,* 1964, *19,* 571–578.

Mendelsohn, G. A., & Griswold, B. B. Anxiety and repression as predictors of the use of incidental cues in problem solving. *Journal of Personality and Social Psychology,* 1967, *6,* 353–359.

Miller, L. H. *The bidimensional nature of the galvanic skin response.* Unpublished doctoral dissertation, Duke University, 1968.

Morris, L. W., & Liebert, R. M. Relationship of cognitive and emotional components of test anxiety to physiological arousal and academic performance. *Journal of Consulting and Clinical Psychology,* 1970, *35,* 332–337.

Mueller, J. H. Anxiety and cue utilization in human learning and memory. In M. Zuckerman & C. D. Spielberger (Eds.), *Emotions and anxiety: New concepts, methods, and applications.* Hillsdale, N. J.: Lawrence Erlbaum Associates, 1976.

Mueller, J. H. The effects of individual differences in test anxiety and type of orienting task on levels of organization in free recall. *Journal of Research in Personality,* 1978, *12,* 100–116.

Nottelmann, E. D., & Hill, K. T. Test anxiety and off-task behavior in evaluative situations. *Child Development,* 1977, *48,* 225–231.

O'Malley, J. J., & Poplawsky, A. Noise-induced arousal and breadth of attention. *Perceptual and Motor Skills,* 1971, *33,* 887–890.

Paivio, A. Personality and audience influence. In B. Maher (Ed.), *Progress in experimental personality research* (Vol. 2). New York: Academic Press, 1965.

Pederson, A. M. Effects of test anxiety and coacting groups on learning and performance. *Perceptual and Motor Skills,* 1970, *30,* 55–62.

Sarason, I. G. The effect of anxiety and two kinds of failure on serial learning. *Journal of Personality,* 1957, *25,* 282–392.

Sarason, I. G. Experimental approaches to test anxiety: attention and the uses of information. In C. D. Spielberger (Ed.), *Anxiety: Current trends in theory and research.* New York: Academic Press, 1972.

Sarason, I. G. Test anxiety and cognitive modeling. *Journal of Personality and Social Psychology,* 1973, *28,* 58–61.

Sarason, S. B., Davidson, K. S., Lighthall, F. F., Waite, R. R., & Ruebush, B. K. *Anxiety in elementary school children.* New York: Wiley, 1960.

Schachter, S., & Singer, J. E. Cognitive, social and physiological determinants of emotional state. *Psychological Review,* 1962, *69,* 379–399.

Schmidt, H. E. Relation of the narrowing of the visual field with an increase in distance to manifest anxiety. *Journal of Experimental Psychology,* 1964, *68,* 334–336.

Sieber, J. E., O'Neil, H. F., & Tobias, S. *Anxiety, learning, and instruction.* Hillsdale, N.J.: Lawrence Erlbaum Associates, 1977.

Solso, R. L. The effect of anxiety on cue selection in the A-Br paradigm. *Psychonomic Science,* 1968, *13,* 105–106.

Solso, R. L., Johnson, J. E., & Schatz, G. C. Perceptual perimeters and generalized drive. *Psychonomic Science*, 1968, *13*, 71–72.

Spence, K. W., Farber, I. E., & McFann, H. H. The relation of anxiety (drive) level of performance in competitional and noncompetitional paired-associates learning. *Journal of Experimental Psychology*, 1956, *52*, 296–305.

Telegdy, G. A., & Cohen, J. S. Cue utilization and drive level in albino rats. *Journal of Comparative and Physiological Psychology*, 1971, *75*, 248–253.

Tolman, E. C. Cognitive maps in rats and men. *Psychological Review*, 1948, *55*, 189–208.

Wachtel, P. L. Conceptions of broad and narrow attention. *Psychological Bulletin*, 1967, *68*, 417–429.

Wachtel, P. L. Anxiety, attention, and coping with threat. *Journal of Abnormal Psychology*, 1968, *73*, 137–143.

Walley, R. E., & Weiden, T. D. Lateral inhibition and cognitive masking: A neuropsychological theory of attention. *Psychological Review*, 1973, *80*, 284–302.

West, C. K., Lee, J. F., & Anderson, T. H. The influence of test anxiety on the selection of relevant from irrelevant information. *Journal of Educational Research*, 1969, *63*, 51–52.

Weiner, B. The role of success and failure in the learning of easy and complex tasks. *Journal of Personality and Social Psychology*, 1966, *3*, 339–344.

Weiner, B. New conceptions in the study of achievement motivation. In B. Maher (Ed.), *Progress in experimental personality research* (Vol. 5). New York: Academic Press, 1970.

Weiner, B. *Theories of motivation*. Chicago: Markham, 1972.

Weiner, B., Frieze, I., Kukla, A., Reed, L., Rest, S., & Rosenbaum, R. M. *Perceiving the causes of success and failure*. New York: General Learning Press, 1971.

Weiner, B., & Schneider, K. Drive versus cognitive theory: A reply to Boor and Harmon. *Journal of Personality and Social Psychology*, 1971, *18*, 258–262.

Weiner, M. J., & Samuels, W. The effect of attributing internal arousal to an external source upon test anxiety and performance. *Journal of Social Psychology*, 1975, *96*, 255–265.

Wine, J. D. Test anxiety and direction of attention. *Psychological Bulletin*, 1971, *76*, 92–104.

Wine, J. D. *Cognitive-attentional approaches to test anxiety modification*. Paper presented at annual convention of APA, Montreal, August 1973.

Zaffy, D. J., & Bruning, J. L. Drive and the range of cue utilization. *Journal of Experimental Psychology*, 1966, *71*, 382–384.

4 Test Anxiety and the Encoding and Retrieval of Information

John H. Mueller
University of Missouri, Columbia

The present chapter examines the effect of test anxiety on memory. The primary emphasis is on how anxiety affects attention and rehearsal during encoding. This perspective derives from the analysis by Easterbrook (1959) and Kausler and Trapp (1960), which was reviewed by Geen in Chapter 3. It is argued that differences in the type of feature encoded and the type of rehearsal strategy employed are involved in the commonly observed performance deficit for anxious subjects. Current models in general memory research seem quite compatible with this attentional analysis. Specifically, the breadth-of-processing model proposed by Craik and Lockhart (1972) is considered as an explanation for the anxiety deficit. Research related to a breadth-of-processing explanation of anxiety differences in encoding is examined first. Anxiety effects on retrieval are then considered briefly. The emphasis is on areas of general memory work that seem of potential interest for anxiety research, because definitive data are often unavailable.

Test Anxiety and Memory Research

Research on individual differences and memory often has been erratic, and it typically has not involved much interaction between memory and personality theorists. Although there may be additional reasons for this state of affairs, one factor has been the absence of common concepts in the theories of each domain. Because attention has been implicated in test anxiety theory and therapy (e.g., I. Sarason, 1972, 1975a, 1975b; Wine, 1971), this construct can serve as a valuable theoretical link to memory research.

However, this emphasis on variation in attention need not exclude other mechanisms that have been used to explain anxiety-arousal effects in learning (cf. Eysenck, 1977). One prominent research tradition derives from classical drive theory (Goulet, 1968; Spence & Spence, 1966) and has concerned the manner in which alternative responses are energized by increments in anxiety. This analysis seems more pertinent to *retrieval* differences and thus need not conflict with an encoding analysis. Another major research tradition has concerned the effect of physiological arousal on consolidation of memories. Much of this research has been conducted as a test of Walker's (1958) action-decrement theory. The major hypothesis in this work has been that, compared to low arousal, high arousal during learning leads to poor short-term memory but superior long-term retention (Levonian, 1972; Uehling, 1972). This view also seems compatible with the attention interpretation. In fact, the attention component is perhaps best considered as a *supplement* to the drive theory and consolidation views rather than a replacement. While this may appear unparsimonious, a multiprocess framework could be required to explain the complicated and sometimes apparently contradictory results in anxiety-memory research.

Whereas other indices of anxiety and arousal have been used, test anxiety seems an especially appropriate index for memory research. First, subjects (i.e., college students) approach participation in learning studies as an evaluation, especially if ego-involving statements are included in the general instructions.[1] Second, recent theoretical and psychometric developments in test anxiety research have identified two components of test anxiety, worry and emotionality, that may have different effects on learning (Spielberger, Gonzalez, Taylor, Algaze, & Anton, 1978). This distinction could help resolve contradictory findings in anxiety-memory research. Finally, principles based on experimental findings may be more readily and more successfully applied beyond the laboratory, to the extent that test anxiety is a more specific analogue of classroom examination tensions than other indices. However, surprisingly few of the many studies of anxiety in laboratory research on memory have involved test anxiety. The present chapter examines some of the research that has been done and offers some suggestions about possible directions for further work.

ENCODING PROCESSES AND TEST ANXIETY

Most research on test anxiety and memory has concentrated on the encoding or storage of information. this is understandable in terms of test anxiety theory, and it also reflects much of the current zeitgeist in memory research.

---

[1]Ideally this would be further verified by the use of some state anxiety (e.g., Spielberger, Gorsuch, & Lushene, 1970) or arousal (e.g., Thayer, 1967) measure. Needless to say, appropriate experimental debriefing should also be used.

Test anxiety theory has traditionally (Mandler & Sarason, 1952) argued that high-anxiety subjects spend relatively more time attending to task-irrelevant events (e.g., negative self-evaluations) than low-anxiety subjects; thus acquisition is hindered. The concern with processing activities provides a useful link to memory theories which postulate a limited-capacity short-term store. Anxious subjects could encode differently because task-irrelevant events take up processing space, with the result that less task-relevant information can be accomodated (e.g., Hamilton, 1975). Given a distinction between structural and control processes in memory (Atkinson & Shiffrin, 1968), two questions can be posed. First, do anxious subjects have reduced immediate memory capacity, and second, do they utilize immediate memory differently?

Structural Differences

Digit-span tests have consistently shown that anxious subjects recall fewer digits than low-anxiety subjects (e.g., Mueller, 1977). The difference is not always statistically significant, and there are some apparent exceptions for certain indices of anxiety (Haynes & Gormly, 1977). But, the general finding appears to be so reliable that increasing digit span performance is even used as an index of the progress of test anxiety therapy (Parish, Buntman, & Buntman, 1976). However, digit-span tests may measure more than just short-term store capacity (Watkins, 1977), so other assessments seem desirable.

An alternative index of the capacity of immediate memory was introduced by Tulving and Colotla (1970), and it is computed directly from the recall protocols (Watkins, 1974). An item is classified as recalled from short-term store if fewer than some fixed number of input–output events intervene between presentation and recall, e.g., seven items. Two studies have found high- and low-anxiety subjects equivalent on this measure (Brower & Mueller, 1978; Mueller, 1976, Exp. 3), whereas one found anxious subjects had greater recall from short-term store (Mueller, & Overcast, 1976). Daee and Wilding (1977) reported no effects due to white noise on recall from short-term store using this measure.

The short-term store measure is not a pure index of capacity. That is, it is a measure of the strategy of early recall for last-presented items as well as a measure of capacity. This is shown in the results of Mueller and Overcast (1976), where high-anxiety subjects had smaller digit spans than low-anxiety subjects, yet in fact recalled more from short-term store. Short-term recall is also distinguishable from recency recall because low- and high-anxiety subjects recalled a comparable number of last-presented items, but low-anxiety subjects recalled them later in output. One would not consider excessive reliance on short-term store recall to be a good strategy. Thus, high-anxiety subjects may be using a strategy for which they are ill-equipped structurally, and which is not beneficial in the long run for other reasons.

Although the high-anxiety deficit in working-memory capacity is not large in absolute terms, it is more substantial when viewed as a proportion of the size of working memory. For example, if primary memory capacity is estimated as roughly six or seven items, a difference of just one item between high- and low-anxiety subjects means a loss of about 15%. From the data at hand, a deficit in this component is not always accompanied by a deficit in total recall or organization, or vice versa. One reason for this may be that the span seems to correlate more with order information than item information (Martin, 1978), and most of our research has used free recall. Perhaps verbatim recall (Schwartz, 1975) would show greater covariation for span and recall as a function of anxiety. Another factor may be that various recall measures often do not show very high intercorrelations in general. However, the discrepancy between a span deficit and a general recall deficit may also indicate that more is involved in the overall performance deficit than a structural limit on capacity.

Consolidation

There have not been any test anxiety experiments directed solely to the action-decrement predictions, but a delayed test has been incorporated as a secondary phase in some studies more directly concerned with immediate free recall. The results are quite consistent in failing to show superior performance for high-anxiety subjects on a delayed test, at intervals up to a week (e.g., Brower & Mueller, 1978; Mueller, 1976; Mueller, 1978; Mueller, Carlomusto, & Marler, 1977; Mueller, Carlomusto, & Marler, 1978). Similar evidence was apparently obtained in a serial learning study by Ganzer (1968). It may be that test anxiety during the immediate test phase dissipates during the retention interval, after the initial evaluation threat is removed or as a result of practice and adaptation to the task. Ganzer (1968) reported just such a reduction in task-irrelevant comments between sessions. Presumably, it would be the worry component that declines, rather than emotionality, or perhaps both.

Some methodological difference between the test anxiety and arousal studies may be responsible for the discrepancy. For example, the test anxiety studies typically involved several learning trials, which perhaps reduced consolidation differences. However, the problem may be more basic because free recall experiments generally fail to support the action-decrement hypothesis (Eysenck, 1977), and there are failures to replicate the main results under the original conditions (Saufley & LaCava, 1977).

A more detailed analysis of short-term storage functioning may prove helpful in clarifying anxiety effects. For example, Baddeley and Hitch (1974) distinguished between an "articulatory loop" and a "work space." Covert verbalizations of an irrelevant nature would likely interfere with an articulatory loop, whether or not anxiety involves a difference in the *size* of the work space. In addition, more consideration needs to be given to the interaction between short- and long-term stores. Broadbent (1971) has proposed an "address register" component, intermediate to short- and long-term storage, which holds information *about* the contents of short-term storage but not the events per se. This information may include features such as category labels that could function as retrieval cues in the interaction between working and permanent memories. Conceivably, high- and low-anxiety subjects differ in terms of the contents of the address register or its utilization rather than the size of working memory itself. The next section concerns other possible differences in feature utilization.

Depth of Processing

Recent developments in memory theory reflect an interest in the interaction between perceptual processing and retention, notably the levels-of-processing analysis proposed by Craik and Lockhart (1972). This model argues that retention is determined by two factors, either or both of which might vary as a function of test anxiety. First, verbal stimuli are concepualized in terms of a hierarchy of features, ranging from shallow (sensory) attributes (e.g., orthographic or phonemic) to deep (semantic) content. The subject processes attributes as a function of time and task demands, with more durable memory traces presumably resulting when stimuli are processed to "deeper" levels. In addition to *depth* of processing, different *types of rehearsal* also influence retention. One type of rehearsal merely "maintains" stimulus processing at the same level, whereas another "elaborates" processing by relating attributes at one level to features at another level or to other features at the same level. Elaboration is said to improve retention (Craik & Tulving, 1975).

There are several strategies that can be used to study processing depth, but only three have been used with test anxiety: (1) inspection of recall protocols to determine the bases of organization used by a subject: (2) analysis of serial position effects in recall: and (3) provision of a study task which orients attention to specific attributes. The outcomes are not conclusive with regard to an extension of the depth analysis to the anxiety deficit. The reasons for this may relate either to shortcomings in the memory model itself or its extension to anxiety research, and it is not always possible to determine which is the source of the problem. The breadth analysis is still evolving; it has received its fair share of criticism, but it has been a useful starting point in the generation of hypotheses.

Clustering.   In free recall, subjects are required to reproduce a set of study words in any order. Since there are no experimenter-imposed constraints on recall order, it seems likely that subjects try to maximize performance by recalling in an order that reflects the manner of storage. Related words are typically clustered together in output, and such utilization of intralist relationships is generally accompanied by corresponding increments in recall. However, clustering is less apparent for anxious and aroused subjects (cf. Eysenck, 1977). The clustering deficit is not always accompanied by a significant difference in the number of words recalled, perhaps due to the insensitivity of clustering as a measure of *total* organizational activity.[2]

Aroused subjects have been found to be more likely to process the physical attributes of stimuli and neglect semantic content (e.g., Schwartz, 1975). If anxiety is analogous to arousal, it may be that anxious subjects are less attentive to the deep attributes required for durable memory traces. This could occur because anxious subjects are more self-preoccupied and thus at least need relatively more time for deep processing than low-anxiety subjects. In fact, as a result of their learning history (under high arousal), anxious subjects may have learned to attend to physical rather than semantic cues. (If this is so, then younger high-anxiety subjects would seem less likely to show the hypothesized sensory-semantic attribute difference.)

Whatever the mechanism, a reasonable empirical question is whether anxious subjects are less proficient only for deep processing or whether they fail to process as well as low-anxiety subjects at all levels. A clustering test of this question requires multiple bases for organization so that clustering is possible utilizing either a shallow or a deep feature. Although other arrangements are possible, lists can be constructed with both levels presented by using triads such as TABLE-CHAIR-SHARE. The relative amounts of deep (associative) and shallow (rhyme) clustering would reflect the depth of cue utilization.

Such lists were used in a series of recent studies. Mueller (1977) found that anxious subjects recalled fewer clusters of both rhymes and associates, as if the encoding deficit was general instead of qualitatively different. This clearly indicates a deficit for deep processing, but the rhyme results present an interpretative problem, due to the difficulty of equating the potency of semantic and nonsemantic dimensions. If the rhymes were just less obvious, then these results could mean that anxious subjects encode fewer deep attributes and fewer *weak* nonsemantic features. In this sense, the high-anxiety cue-utilization deficit could be either a problem of discovery or a true utilization deficit. An interesting question would be what would happen with potent or "obvious" nonsemantic features.

---

[2]Clustering has the advantage of experimenter control over likely bases for organization and thus ready identification of such utilization, but it does not preclude other strategies. High-anxiety subjects could be more adept at some of these strategies than low-anxiety subjects.

One procedure that would increase the salience of the rhymes would be to present all words simultaneously rather than using conventional single-item presentation. Related words can be grouped together in a whole-list display, rendering both bases of organization as obvious as possible; any remaining anxiety deficit could be attributed to encoding activity rather than discovery per se. A recent study by Mueller, Carlomusto, and Marler (1977) using whole-list displays found no anxiety differences for either type of clustering, though anxious subjects still recalled fewer words than low-anxiety subjects.

The two studies involved slightly different procedures, but the major difference was method of presentation.[3] Although comparisons must be made cautiously, these two studies suggest that the high-anxiety deficit will be reduced when the discovery of intralist relationships is facilitated. However, both the results of Mueller (1977), with a deficit for semantic *and* nonsemantic clustering, and those of Mueller, Carlomusto, and Marler (1977), with no significant deficit for either type of clustering, seem at variance with the expectation that high- and low-anxiety subjects differ only in terms of how they utilize deep attributes.

Another factor that might be involved in the high-anxiety deficit is the apparent fact that deep processing requires more time than shallow processing (Craik & Tulving, 1975). This differential might be greater for anxious subjects than for low-anxiety subjects if short-term storage is already overloaded. This could create a biased impression with regard to the utilization of deep cues, because time pressures seem to cause aroused subjects to attend more to typically nondominant (i.e., physical) features of words (Eysenck, 1977). A recent experiment in our laboratory (Mueller, Carlomusto, & Marler, 1978) used the triad list construction and varied the rate of presentation, either 1 sec or 6 sec per word. Some of the results of this study are shown in Table 4.1.

The critical result was the Anxiety X Rate interaction for rhyme clusters. Whereas a slower rate of presentation led to greater utilization of the nonsemantic attribute by low-anxiety subjects, this was not true for high-anxiety subjects. This may mean that anxious subjects perseverate on nonsemantic features without processing to deeper levels in spite of additional time, whereas low-anxiety subjects will progress to deeper levels unless fast rates limit them to nondominant information. In other words, low-anxiety subjects engage in processing of peripheral information when given extra time, but anxious subjects do not. In any event, the results are not

---

[3]Mueller (1977) utilized triads separated by an unrelated filler word, whereas Mueller, Carlomusto, and Marler (1977) did not include unrelated items. The presence of unrelated words may generate some confusion if subjects persist in trying to find relationships between them and the other members of the triad, but that is uncertain.

TABLE 4.1
Average Recall and Organization in Free Recall as a Function of Test
Anxiety and Presentation Rate

	High		Low	
	1-Sec	6-Sec	1-Sec	6-Sec
Total Recall	20.07	23.61	20.13	25.42
Associative Clusters	5.29	6.94	5.75	6.69
Rhyme Clusters	3.29	3.15	3.10	5.27
Consecutive Triads	.32	.37	.42	.49

consistent with the simple expectations that the high-anxiety deficit is restricted to either fast rates (within the range of values manipulated here) or semantic relationships. In passing, it may be noted that drive theory would have predicted superior associative recall and clustering for high-anxiety subjects here, because high-strength associates were used, but that was not found in the studies with triad lists.

Serial Position Analyses. The depth analysis has been used to explain variation in the probability of recall as a function of input position. On immediate tests with unrelated words, the last-presented (recency) items have a higher probability of recall than items from earlier positions. If a final test for all items is given after several unrelated lists, however, the last-presented items in each list are not recalled as well as earlier items. The depth analysis explains this pattern of results by arguing that subjects learn that even superficial processing of the recency items will suffice for an immediate test. Unfortunately, these shallow traces dissipate by the time of the unexpected delayed test.

If recency items are not processed as deeply as earlier items, and if the anxiety deficit is limited to deep processing, then the high-anxiety deficit should be more apparent for primacy and middle items than for recency items. Also, if high-anxiety subjects initially encode more shallowly in general than low-anxiety subjects, then anxious subjects should show a greater loss between an immediate and a delayed test (contrary to the action-decrement view). To examine these predictions, a recent experiment in our laboratory (Brower & Mueller, 1978) gave high- and low-anxiety subjects a single free recall test on each of eight lists composed of 12 unrelated high-frequency concrete nouns. After the eighth list, they were given an unannounced final test for all 96 items.

Some of the results are shown in Table 4.2. Primacy recall was computed by collapsing over the first two positions, recency recall was defined as the last two items, and middle recall was positions 5–8. There were no anxiety main effects, but the Anxiety X Sex interaction was significant for all immediate-

TABLE 4.2
Average Probability of Recall for Each Input Segment by Test Anxiety
and Sex, Pooled over Eight Lists

	High		Low	
	Male	*Female*	*Male*	*Female*
Immediate Recall				
Primacy	.63	.76	.69	.64
Middle	.43	.62	.51	.48
Recency	.62	.68	.71	.56
Short-Term Store	2.59	2.50	2.81	2.20
Final Recall				
Primacy	.38	.51	.44	.47
Middle	.24	.44	.35	.34
Recency	.20	.20	.17	.15

test measures except short-term storage recall (Tulving & Colotla, 1970); it was significant only for middle items on the final test. In short, high anxiety hindered males, while it led to better performance by females. (In 1973, Mandelson found similar sex-anxiety effects in a study of foreign-language learning.)

We have not often found Anxiety X Sex interactions and have only speculations to offer by way of explanation. Males may be higher on the worry component of test anxiety; thus their performance is hindered. Females may have higher emotionality scores, with beneficial effects. However, separate subscale scores were not available for these subjects. Another post hoc explanation would allege greater verbal fluency for females, so this outcome would be the high-anxiety–easy-task result from drive theory. Or perhaps a sex difference in achievement motivation or persistence is involved. The possible difference in test anxiety effects by sex makes it desirable to continue to control for sex in subject selection. In any event, these results are not consistent with a depth analysis of the high-anxiety deficit, because, even when the deficit occurred (i.e., for males), it was not limited to the first-presented items in immediate recall, though it was most apparent for middle items in final recall.

Orienting Tasks: Recall.   One technique used to achieve more direct control over encoding requires subjects to make a decision about each word during study, followed by a memory test. Retention is typically better when the decision requires attention to semantic content as opposed to nonsemantic features (e.g., Hyde & Jenkins, 1973). Test anxiety therapy has focused on redirecting attention (e.g., Wine, 1971). While orienting decisions are not designed to direct attention *from* task-irrelevant events, such tasks could be used to direct attention *to* the more productive features or strategies which anxious subjects might overlook.

Semantic and nonsemantic orienting tasks were examined in a recent free recall experiment where the word list could be organized by conceptual (deep) or first-letter (shallow) categories (Mueller, 1978, Exp. 1). During study, subjects were required to decide for each word whether it was pleasant or unpleasant, began with a vowel or a consonant, or had no task. Orienting tasks had minimal effects for low-anxiety subjects, as if they encode deeply whenever they expect a test. However, the deep task seemed to help and the shallow task to hinder anxious subjects, relative to the no-task condition, more in accord with the depth analysis of anxiety effects. This pattern of results was partially replicated using the triad lists discussed previously (Mueller, 1978, Exp. 2).

Orienting Tasks: Recognition.   Some recent experiments have found that facial photographs are better recognized when subjects have made an abstract decision about the person, such as honesty, than when they have made a decision about some physical features, such as sex (Bower & Karlin, 1974). Mueller, Bailis, and Goldstein (1979) examined whether this would vary as a function of anxiety level and whether self-reference would have an effect on recognition performance. For example, a shallow-self reference decision would be "Is the person taller than you," whereas a shallow-absolute criterion decision would be "Is the person more than 5'6" tall," with a similar breakdown for deep tasks. Rogers, Kuiper, and Kirker (1977) found that self-reference led to especially deep processing. However, in view of the test anxiety theory of self-preoccupation, it seemed that the effect of a self-reference criterion would vary as a function of anxiety level.

Subjects were shown photographs of male and female faces, making a decision for each under the guise of a reaction-time study. The unannounced[4] recognition test was given immediately, with the items shown one at a time mixed with distractor faces. The results are summarized in Table 4.3. Low-anxiety subjects made fewer false alarms and generally displayed greater sensitivity (d'). However, the most interesting result was an Anxiety X Reference interaction for d', as the high-anxiety deficit was present only when the orienting task used an absolute standard. Low-anxiety subjects were hindered when using a personal reference point for decisions, perhaps because they do not normally engage in self-preoccupied behavior. Although deep tasks generally led to better performance, there were no Anxiety X Depth interactions.

---

[4]An unannounced test may seem at odds with inducing test anxiety but the anxiety subsets did differ here in state anxiety, and the incidental study task has many desirable features for a study of storage effects.

TABLE 4.3

Mean Recognition Performance by Orienting Task, Reference Point, and Test Anxiety

	Deep				Shallow			
	Absolute		Self		Absolute		Self	
	High	Low	High	Low	High	Low	High	Low
Hit Rate	.68	.69	.66	.63	.63	.63	.64	.63
False Alarm Rate	.19	.10	.17	.15	.27	.17	.25	.19
d'	1.46	1.93	1.45	1.43	1.04	1.41	1.10	1.29
B	1.66	3.73	2.52	1.87	1.32	2.34	1.22	1.98

Evaluating the Depth Analysis

Overall, the preceding results are not very supportive of a *simple* depth explanation of the high-anxiety memory deficit. The apparent discrepancy with the arousal literature (e.g., Schwartz, 1975) may have to do with differences in what test anxiety and arousal indices measure or the relative suitability of the procedures used to examine deep and shallow processing. In retrospect, the experiments described earlier illustrate the problems in adequately defining deep and shallow processing. For example, the evolving depth analysis of the serial position curve has become quite complicated, so primacy-recency curves may not offer the best testing grounds. For another thing, there is some question as to whether the use of rhymes in recall reflects a *shallow* feature or merely a *peripheral* attribute. Furthermore, if rhyming functions as a generative retrieval rule it seems less suitable as a test of encoding differences. The results of the orienting task studies may be somewhat more in line with the levels hypothesis, but it also seems likely that an analysis in terms of a semantic-nonsemantic feature dichotomy is an incomplete explanation of the anxiety deficit.

Breadth of Processing

Just as deeper processing presumably improves retention, so does *elaborative* rehearsal that relates features within or across levels (Craik & Tulving, 1975), relative to maintenance rehearsal. Although intuitively appealing and often invoked post hoc, this distinction has only recently been subjected to experimental test. One recent study provides a promising procedure. Battig and Einstein (1977) had subjects rate the same words on either correlated or uncorrelated attributes. Their contention was that responding to correlated dimensions (concreteness, imageability, and categorizeability) during study would lead to "narrower" processing than uncorrelated dimensions (concreteness, pleasantness, and number of features). Battig and Einstein found some evidence for better retention in the latter condition, as the breadth model predicts.

The breadth analysis seems promising for anxiety research. Even if high anxiety limits processing capacity, subsequent encoding may go as deep as with low anxiety but not incorporate *as many* features. The Anxiety X Rate interaction previously discussed (Table 4.1) can be interpreted as an elaboration deficit. Furthermore, anxious subjects are less likely to recall entire triads consecutively in output (Table 4.1). Because this would entail using both deep and shallow features together, this aspect of the deficit may be viewed as a problem in elaborative encoding. Limited capacity combined with time pressures may induce anxious subjects to repetitively process central features, with little opportunity to elaboratively encode peripheral features or to invoke complex strategies. Of course, it is possible that the anxiety deficit extends to maintenance encoding as well, especially if anxiety interferes with the articulatory loop (Baddeley & Hitch, 1974).

Strategy Differences

There is evidence to indirectly suggest the use of more limited strategies by anxious subjects. In most cases, this research was conducted independently of the elaboration-maintenance distinction. Poor strategies may be a part of the anxiety deficit, and they may be accompanied by reduced deep processing or less elaboration as a byproduct.

Short-Term Recall. One instance of a strategy difference is the tendency for anxious subjects to emphasize recall from the short-term store (Mueller & Overcast, 1976). If such items are not thoroughly processed, then anxious subjects wold be expected to do worse on a delayed test. The evidence generally reveals that high-anxiety subjects recall less than low-anxiety subjects would be expected to do worse on a delayed test. The evidence carryover of acquisition differences). The meager effect probably reflects the fact that differences in short-term store recall are small in absolute terms, and such recall accounts for only a small proportion of total recall.

Priority in Recall. A related phenomenon involves output order, where a class of items is recalled earlier in output than other items. Early recall of weak items should maximize overall performance, because it would reduce output interference and minimize decay. It has been observed that high-anxiety subjects are more likely to give output priority to previously unrecalled items than low-anxiety subjects (Mueller & Overcast, 1976), which suggests either a differential awareness of this strategy *or* a different assessment of its efficacy. That is, anxious subjects may perceive its value, but then use it to the exclusion of other performance-optimizing strategies.

Inflexibility. The subject's output order in free recall sometimes simply repeats the input order. This rote pattern in recall has been found to be more typical of aroused subjects (e.g., Schwartz, 1975). Such behavior may be conceptualized as attention to a physical property of the list, or it may reflect an overestimate of the utility of seriation as a strategy. Serial recall is, after all, one option in "free" recall, but it may be incompatible with other more useful strategies.

One research strategy then would be to examine the effects of anxiety on *serial* learning, because in that case position is a relevant attribute. Daee and Wilding (1977) found that white noise improved memory for position when learning position was an incidental part of the task, but not when serial learning was intentional. This is consistent with the notion that aroused subjects attend to sequential information more than unaroused subjects. However, in a test anxiety study, Ganzer (1968) found high anxiety led to slightly worse serial learning than low anxiety, a result that seems fairly typical.

Rigidity in recall and inflexibility in strategy selection seem unlikely to maximize performance, and both may be another aspect of generally poor cue utilization by anxious subjects. This rigidity has a counterpart in the problem-solving literature, i.e., functional fixedness, and it may be involved in the anxiety deficit in anagram solution (e.g., I. Sarason, 1973). Studies of *learning-to-learn* would be useful. Subjects could be given several tasks which use the same strategies, such as a succession of free (serial) recall tasks, and then compared to subjects who are given a series which requires strategy changes from one list to another, such as alternating free and serial recall tasks.

Another interesting procedure that seems pertinent involves giving several successive tests following a single study phase (Tulving, 1967). Some items may be recalled on all tests, others on just some of the tests, and others not at all. The relative stability in the content of recall as a function of test anxiety seems of interest. In addition, this technique may be adapted so that the subsequent study phase involves the presentation of only certain subsets identified on the successive tests, e.g., present only unrecalled items. Mandler, Worden, and Graesser (1974) used the latter technique to identify the items which were most important in subjective organization, and this method seems potentially useful in anxiety-memory research.

Multilevel Organization.   Hierarchical list constructions (e.g., Bower, Clark, Lesgold, & Winzenz, 1969) have not been used in test anxiety research, but they offer an interesting way to test cue utilization and higher-order strategy differences. Just as recall is improved when items can be grouped into categories, performance is facilitated when the categories themselves can be organized into yet higher-level categories. There is evidence to suggest anxiety differences when the list involves multiple bases for organization. Mueller (1978, Exp. 1) found that anxious subjects were less likely to use common first letters to bridge transitions between conceptual categories. Another strategy which involves multiple relationships in the same list has been observed with the triad lists noted earlier. In addition to rhyme and associate clusters, subjects could recall the whole triad unit (base-rhyme-associate) consecutively, using both organizational dimensions together. This is a strategy in accord with the elaboration conceptualization, and anxious subjects usually show fewer triad groupings (see Table 4.1). ˙

Mnemonic Instructions. The inducement to utilize special mnemonic instructions is relevant in that high-anxiety tendencies toward rumination, maintenance rehearsal, and shallow encoding might be offset. Such instructions could take many forms, but imagery is one of the few mnemonics to have been studied in conjunction with test anxiety. In general, instructions to form interacting images facilitate recall of concrete words, relative to various alternative mnemonics. Presumably this occurs because recall of part of the image redintegrates the whole scene. In addition, concrete words generally are recalled better than abstract words, perhaps because concrete words can be processed by both a visual and verbal coding system, whereas abstract words can be processed only by the latter system. Thus, there may be an anxiety deficit in using imagery as a *strategy,* separate from a deficit in imagery per se.

Mueller and Overcast (1976) found no anxiety differences in the recall of concrete and abstract words, nor in the effect of the imagery strategy; unfortunately, the (somewhat) anomalous failure to find any differences between imagery, verbal, and control groups renders the latter finding equivocal. In a paired-associate test, however, Edmunson and Nelson (1976) found that interactive image instructions substantially reduced the (trait) anxiety deficit, relative to a repetition strategy. In an effort to extend this result, Scott and Nelson (1979) found that high test anxiety impaired performance under the imagery strategy, though not with repetition, as if anxiety hinders elaborative processing but not maintenance rehearsal. The results are hardly conclusive at this point, but mnemonic instructions, including orienting tasks, would seem to be promising areas for further work.

Additional Encoding Analyses

Two other procedures that seem of value in the study of encoding differences can be briefly noted here. Neither one has been used in test anxiety research.

Release from Proactive Inhibition. A number of studies have examined encoding by observing interference in short-term memory. The procedure requires the presentation of a subspan amount of material, followed by a brief distractor task, then recall. As this continues for additional sets of items of the same general type, performance slowly deteriorates, presumably due to the accumulation of proactive inhibition. On a critical test trial, the type of material is switched for the experimental group, for example, from male names to female names. Such changes generally yield a recovery to near initial levels of performance, as if the subject had been "released" from the inhibition. Although other interpretations are possible, it can be argued that such release occurs because proactive inhibition accumulated to a specific dimension (Wickens, 1972). Thus, the dimensions that yield release can identify the attributes encoded.

This procedure seems a potentially useful method for the assessment of test anxiety effects. From the levels viewpoint, if high-anxiety subjects are not encoding deeply, switches among deep attributes should not produce much release; if low-anxiety subjects are processing only at deep levels, then they would show little release when the change involved a shallow attribute. In other words, high-anxiety subjects might show release only for variations involving shallow features, whereas low-anxiety subjects would show release for variations in deep features.

Rehearsal Monitoring.   Finally, one methodology that would have direct applicability would require subjects to "think out loud." This procedure requires subjects to rehearse overtly, with rate of rehearsal then compared to, for example, probability of recall over serial positions (Rundus, 1971). In a test anxiety study, this could reveal both the extent of task-irrelevant responding, though this is often done covertly (Ganzer, 1968; Nottlemann & Hill, 1977), and the nature of task-relevant processing. For example, it should be possible to assess the relative extent of elaboration and maintenance rehearsing as well as the level of the attributes being processed and to determine whether these differ as a function of anxiety level. This would require a qualitative analysis of rehearsal, not just the rate of rehearsal, though rate alone might yield useful preliminary data. However, there is some question as to just how "natural" this method is because it seems disposed toward mere verbal repetition (i.e., maintenance rehearsal).

On an applied note, it is entirely possible that overt rehearsal would help identify poor strategies for anxious subjects and even clarify alternatives, thus speeding the course of any therapy. This use of rehearsal monitoring seems directly related to the use of models in therapy (e.g., I. Sarason, 1973).

To summarize, there is ample evidence to document an anxiety effect on storage, but the precise characterization remains to be determined. The levels-of-processing view has served a very useful heuristic function, but a simple deep-shallow feature dichotomy seems incomplete as an explanation. It seems level per se must be supplemented by a consideration of the type of rehearsal. Consideration of other factors which may interact with attention and anxiety could be helpful, such as the extent to which "effort" is involved in encoding (Kahneman, 1973).

RETRIEVAL PROCESSES

Retrieval differences have seldom been directly examined in regard to test anxiety. This is disappointing in terms of the everyday reports by students that they "knew more than could be recalled for the test" and in view of the name of the construct itself—*test* anxiety, not study (storage) anxiety. The experiments originally conducted as tests of drive theory were concerned with output effects. Those results might be extrapolated to the case of test anxiety if Hullian theory could be integrated with modern memory views of retrieval and the assumption of self-preoccupation in test-anxiety research. Perhaps self-oriented response could be viewed as the dominant responses for high-anxiety subjects, who thus always start retrieval with an incorrect response most likely to be energized. There really are no pertinent test anxiety studies, however, so the following discussion is more of a prospectus than a summary.

Encoding Specificity

The encoding-specificity view of retrieval (Tulving & Thomson, 1973) seems compatible with the breadth analysis of the anxiety deficit. Encoding specificity assumes that a retrieval cue is effective only when the cue is the one that was developed by the subject during storage: An associatively "equivalent" cue will not be effective. The rationale underlying the cued recall technique can be found in Tulving and Bower (1974).

Zubrzycki and Borkowski (1973) used cueing in a study of the effect of manifest anxiety on short-term memory (though since they did not provide the cues during study, it cannot be construed as a direct test of encoding specificity). Using either weak or strong cues and large or small categories, they found low-anxiety subjects recalled more on both uncued and prompted tests, as if anxiety had a greater effect on storage than retrieval. The anxiety difference was more apparent for large categories, as if high anxiety led to restricted encoding during study.

It may be that self-preoccupation leads high-anxiety subjects to encode fewer attributes than low-anxiety subjects. On the test then, anxious subjects would have fewer cues to use spontaneously for retrieval and would be able to respond to fewer experimenter-provided cues. In addition, self-monitoring during a test may hinder attending to the relevant cue or executing the retrieval "plan." In general, anxious subjects should show less recall on a cued test (unless we can be sure that they attended to that specific cue at input, in which case high anxiety should then energize the dominant response). Furthermore, it would be possible to test the depth analysis by providing either a deep or a shallow cue (Fisher & Craik, 1977), to determine whether high- and low-anxiety subjects were differentially responsive to them.

Although not a direct test of encoding specificity, such cued tests were used by Mueller (1978, Exp. 1). The list was composed of words that could be clustered conceptually or by first letters. Subjects made decisions during study about pleasantness or whether the first letter was a vowel, with an immediate uncued test each trial. The subjects returned after 48 hours for an uncued test, a test with first letters as cues, and a test with category labels as cues. Performance on the delayed tests is summarized in Table 4.4. Assuming the orienting tasks produced deep and shallow encoding, the diagonal entries

TABLE 4.4

Mean Recall on Delayed Tests as a Function of Test Anxiety, Orienting Task, and Type of Retrieval Cue

	High			Low		
Cue	*Control*	*Vowel*	*Pleasant*	*Control*	*Vowel*	*Pleasant*
Uncued	17.00	16.60	18.25	19.20	18.30	19.00
Letter	14.35	13.20	15.45	15.20	15.40	16.20
Category	19.75	18.40	20.15	20.65	21.20	21.20

provide evidence about the effectiveness of cues of differential depth. Compared to no cues, shallow (letters) cues hindered recall for both high- and low-anxiety subjects, as if those cues had not been used (or were not useful after 48 hours), whereas semantic cues improved recall more for high-anxiety subjects than for low-anxiety subjects. This may indicate that low-anxiety subjects routinely encoded more deep cues.

The encoding specificity view can function as a retrieval analysis of storage differences, and there are a number of relevant questions. One interesting aspect concerns restoration of the arousal state. For example, are high-anxiety subjects more likely to vary in arousal from study to test, thus being hindered at retrieval due to a contextual cue (i.e., emotion) mismatch? Although it might not be feasible to vary test anxiety per se, evaluative threat could be systematically varied between study and test. Qualitative differences in such instructions have been examined (e.g., I. Sarason, 1975b), but the timing of administration should be considered as well. In fact, the best procedure to separate storage and retrieval effects would be to factorially vary instructions at study and test (Eysenck, 1976b). One interesting project related to this question was recently reported by I. Sarason (1978), where students were allowed to retake classroom exams under less stressful (no-loss) conditions. High-anxiety students showed considerably greater gains than low-anxiety students, as if arousal at the original test did interfere with retrieval (assuming equal rehearsal during the interim).

There are other procedures that are used to examine retrieval differences. However, no test anxiety studies have utilized these procedures, so this discussion will take the form of suggested lines of investigation.

Other Approaches to Retrieval

Recognition Versus Recall.   Storage and retrieval have often been distinguished by comparing recognition and recall data. Although there is some room for question, the presumption is that recall involves both processes, whereas recognition virtually eliminates retrieval. This strategy has proven useful in studying arousal effects on retrieval (e.g., Eysenck, 1975). There have been no systematic comparisons involving test anxiety, but an anxiety deficit seems fairly well established for both types of tests, indicating that the anxiety difference involved at least storage processes. A comparison of existing studies is complicated by other differences; for example, the free recall and recognition studies previously described that used orienting tasks also differed in terms of test expectancy, type of materials, and so forth.

Short-Term Memory.   Another method that could be used in an anxiety-retrieval analysis would compare short-term and long-term recall. It is possible to view recall from immediate consciousness as a "direct readout," involving minimal retrieval. A systematic comparison of short- and long-term recall as a function of test anxiety has not been done. There may be considerable benefits to be derived from giving more attention to short-term memory, as such retention intervals seem compatible with the assumption of *ongoing* interference due to self-monitoring, and continuous testing should maintain test anxiety differences.

Reaction Time.   Response latencies seem of interest, even if only as a supplemental measure because the functional relationships obtained for test anxiety level might be different than for probability of recall. The latency measure seems quite compatible with the drive theory characterization of response dominance, but it also seems plausible that self-monitoring would slow search and retrieval as well. Drive theory predicts that high anxiety would speed the retrieval of dominant responses while hindering nondominant responses (Eysenck, 1975). Test anxiety theory would seem to require that both types of responses would be hindered, although dominant responses might not suffer as much.

Latencies are of central importance in some tasks. One of these concerns the distinction between episodic and semantic memory (Tulving, 1972). Recall of personal experiences seems to reflect both storage and retrieval, whereas utilization of stored semantic information may reflect primarily retrieval processes. *Semantic memory* was examined in a study by Eysenck (1975), where subjects were required to name an instance of a category beginning with a particular letter. Response dominance was varied by choosing instances of varying associative strength in taxonomic category norms and then using those first letter constraints. High arousal led to better recall for dominant instances and worse performance for weak instances, but neither arousal nor response dominance had much effect on recognition.

Another task requires subjects to rapidly specify whether two items match on some dimension. For example, are two letters the same semantically (i.e., ignore upper- and lower-case type variations), versus are two letters identical physically. A recent study by Goldberg, Schwartz, and Stewart (1977) revealed some interesting differences related to level of verbal ability, and this seems a useful paradigm for studying test anxiety differences. In fact, it seems particularly well suited to an investigation of the breadth analysis of the anxiety deficit.

Another procedure that utilizes reaction time is the memory-set paradigm (cf. Sternberg, 1975). This technique presents a limited number of items to the subject; then a probe is given and the subject's task is to decide whether that item was in the target set. This method could be quite informative with regard to differences in search processes due to test anxiety.

Constructive Processes.   Another untapped procedure involves the concept of reconstructive memory (Bartlett, 1932). According to this view, subjects abstract a *schema* during study, composed of the essential aspects of the experience but not all of the details. Remembering then does not involve the elicitation of a fully fleshed static memory, but rather the reconstruction of the original event by embellishing the schema. This can be studied in several ways, including recall of textual passages and sentence recognition (e.g., Bransford & Franks, 1971; Cofer, 1973).

This view suggests anxiety effects in schema formation (storage) and reconstruction. Eysenck (1976a) has shown the utility of this procedure in a study of prose recall by introverts and extraverts, with moderate levels of arousal associated with better recall than either low or high arousal. No research has been done examining test anxiety, but self-preoccupation seems a relevant factor in shaping the schema as well as in regenerating the original details. One possibility is that the schemas of chronically high-anxiety subjects would involve considerable personal material, i.e., negative self-reference; because this would be a common part of many schemas, valuable distinctive content would be missing and differential reconstruction would be hindered. Furthermore, such self-reference content might intrude during reconstruction, hindering recall of other details.

The prose tasks used here have an obvious compatibility with classroom learning. Furthermore, this view seems to relate rather directly to the case of eyewitness testimony, in that such reports clearly involve an element of reconstruction, either at the lineup or for the police artist. Since the original observation was often made under stressful circumstances (viz. armed robbery), an analysis of anxiety effects on reconstruction could be helpful. Failure to consider this aspect may be involved in the cases of low reliability reported here, but the analog of self-preoccupation, i.e., self preservation, may well be an irrelevant response—at least in terms of later identification!

ACKNOWLEDGMENTS

The author would like to acknowledge the helpful comments on an earlier draft by Donald Kausler, Matt Marler, and Steve Schwartz.

REFERENCES

Atkinson, R. C., & Shiffrin, R. M. Human memory: A proposed system and its control processes. In K. W. Spence and J. T. Spence (Eds.), *The psychology of learning and motivation* (Vol. 2). New York: Academic Press, 1968.

Baddeley, A. D., & Hitch, G. Working memory. In G. H. Bower (Ed.), *The psychology of learning and motivation* (Vol. 2). New York: Academic Press, 1974.

Bartlett, F. C. *Remembering: A study in experimental and social psychology.* New York: Macmillan, 1932.

Battig, W. F., & Einstein, G. O. Evidence that broader processing facilitates delayed retention. *Bulletin of the Psychonomic Society*, 1977, *10*, 28–30.

Bower, G. H., Clark, M. C., Lesgold, A. M., & Winzenz, D. Hierarchical retrieval schemes in recall of categorized word lists. *Journal of Verbal Learning and Verbal Behavior*, 1969, *8*, 323–343.

Bower, G. H., & Karlin, M. B. Depth of processing pictures of faces and recognition memory. *Journal of Experimental Psychology*, 1974, *103*, 751–757.

Bransford, J. D., & Franks, J. J. The abstraction of linguistic ideas. *Cognitive Psychology*, 1971, *2*, 331–350.

Broadbent, D. E. *Decision and stress*. London: Academic Press, 1971.

Brower, P. E., & Mueller, J. H. Serial position effects in immediate and final free recall as a function of test anxiety and sex. *Bulletin of the Psychonomic Society*, 1978, *12*, 61–63.

Cofer, C. N. Constructive processes in memory. *American Scientist*, 1973, *61*, 537–543.

Craik, F. I. M., & Lockhart, R. S. Levels of processing: A framework for memory research. *Journal of Verbal Learning and Verbal Behavior*, 1972, *11*, 671–684.

Craik, F. I. M., & Tulving, E. Depth of processing and the retention of words in episodic memory. *Journal of Experimental Psychology: General*, 1975, *1*, 268–294.

Daee, S., & Wilding, J. M. Effects of high intensity white noise on short-term memory for position in a list and sequence. *British Journal of Psychology*, 1977, *68*, 335–349.

Easterbrook, J. A. The effect of emotion on cue utilization and the organization of behavior. *Psychological Review*, 1959, *66*, 183–201.

Edmunson, E. D., & Nelson, D. L. Anxiety, imagery, and sensory interference. *Bulletin of the Psychonomic Society*, 1976, *8*, 319–322.

Eysenck, M. W. Effects of noise, activation level, and response dominance on retrieval from semantic memory. *Journal of Experimental Psychology: Human Learning and Memory*, 1975, *1*, 143–148.

Eysenck, M. W. Extraversion, activation, and the recall of prose. *British Journal of Psychology*, 1976, *67*, 53–61. (a)

Eysenck, M. W. Arousal, learning, and memory. *Psychological Bulletin*, 1976, *83*, 389–404. (b)

Eysenck, M. W. *Human memory: Theory, research and individual differences*. Oxford: Pergamon Press, 1977.

Fisher, R. P., & Craik, F. I. M. Interaction between encoding and retrieval operations in cued recall. *Journal of Experimental Psychology: Human Learning and Memory*, 1977, *3*, 701–711.

Ganzer, V. J. Effects of audience presence and test anxiety on learning and retention in a serial learning situation. *Journal of Personality and Social Psychology*, 1968, *8*, 194–199.

Goldberg, R. A., Schwartz, S., & Stewart, M. Individual differences in cognitive processes. *Journal of Educational Psychology*, 1977, *69*, 9–14.

Goulet, L. R. Anxiety (drive) and verbal learning: Implications for research and some methodological considerations. *Psychological Bulletin*, 1968, *69*, 235–247.

Hamilton, V. Socialization anxiety and information processing: A capacity model of anxiety-induced performance deficits. In I. G. Sarason and C. D. Spielberger (Eds.), *Stress and anxiety* (Vol. 2). New York: Hemisphere/Wiley, 1975.

Haynes, J., & Gormly, J. Anxiety and memory. *Bulletin of the Psychonomic Society*, 1977, *9*, 191–192.

Hyde, T. S., & Jenkins, J. J. Recall for words as a function of semantic, graphic, and syntactic orienting tasks. *Journal of Verbal Learning and Verbal Behavior*, 1973, *12*, 471–480.

Kahneman, D. *Attention and effort*. Englewood Cliffs, N.J.: Prentice-Hall, 1973.

Kausler, D. H., & Trapp, E. P. Motivation and cue utilization in intentional and incidental learning. *Psychological Review*, 1960, *67*, 373–379.

Levonian, E. Retention over time in relation to arousal during learning: An explanation of discrepant results. *Acta Psychologica*, 1972, *36*, 290–321.

Mandelson, L. R. Test performance on a verbal learning task as a function of anxiety-arousing testing instructions. *Journal of Educational Research,* 1973, *67,* 37–40.

Mandler, G., & Sarason, S. B. A study of anxiety and learning. *Journal of Abnormal and Social Psychology,* 1952, *47,* 166–173.

Mandler, G., Worden, P. E., & Graesser, A. C. Subjective disorganization: Search for the locus of list organization. *Journal of Verbal Learning and Verbal Behavior,* 1974, *13,* 220–235.

Martin, M. Memory span as a measure of individual differences in memory capacity. *Memory & Cognition,* 1978, *6,* 194–198.

Mueller, J. H. Anxiety and cue utilization in human learning and memory. In M. Zuckerman and C. D. Spielberger (Eds.), *Emotions and anxiety: New concepts, methods and applications.* Hillsdale, N.J.: Lawrence Erlbaum & Associates, 1976.

Mueller, J. H. Test anxiety, input modality, and levels of organization in free recall. *Bulletin of the Psychonomic Society,* 1977, *9,* 67–69.

Mueller, J. H. The effects of individual differences in test anxiety and type of orienting task on levels of organization in free recall. *Journal of Research in Personality,* 1978, *12,* 100–116.

Mueller, J. H., Bailis, K. L., & Goldstein, A. G. Depth of processing and anxiety in facial recognition. *British Journal of Psychology,* 1979, *70,* in press.

Mueller, J. H., Carlomusto, M., & Marler, M. Recall as a function of method of presentation and individual differences in test anxiety. *Bulletin of the Psychonomic Society,* 1977, *10,* 447–450.

Mueller, J. H., Carlomusto, M., & Marler, M. Recall and organization in memory as a function of rate of presentation and individual differences in test anxiety. *Bulletin of the Psychonomic Society,* 1978, *12,* 133–136.

Mueller, J. H., & Overcast, T. D. Free recall as a fucntion of test anxiety, concreteness, and instructions. *Bulletin of the Psychonomic Society,* 1976, *8,* 194–196.

Nottelmann, E. D., & Hill, K. T. Test anxiety and off-task behavior in evaluative situations. *Child Development,* 1977, *48,* 225–231.

Parish, T. S., Buntman, A. D., & Buntman, S. R. Effect of counterconditioning on test anxiety as indicated by digit span performance. *Journal of Educational Psychology,* 1976, *68,* 297–299.

Rogers, T. B., Kuiper, N. A., & Kirker, W. S. Self-reference and the encoding of personal information. *Journal of Personality and Social Psychology,* 1977, *35,* 677–688.

Rundus, D. Analysis of rehearsal processes in free recall. *Journal of Experimental Psychology,* 1971, *89,* 63–77.

Sarason, I. G. Experimental approaches to test anxiety: Attention and the uses of information. In C. D. Spielberger (Ed.), *Anxiety: Current trends in theory and research* (Vol. 2). New York: Academic Press, 1972.

Sarason, I. G. Test anxiety and cognitive modeling. *Journal of Personality and Social Psychology,* 1973, *28,* 58–61.

Sarason, I. G. Test anxiety, attention, and the general problem of anxiety. In C. D. Spielberger and I. G. Sarason (Eds.), *Stress and anxiety* (Vol. 1). New York: Hemisphere/Halstead, 1975. (a)

Sarason, I. G. Anxiety and self-preoccupation. In I. G. Sarason and C. D. Spielberger (Eds.), *Stress and anxiety* (Vol. 2). New York: Hemisphere/Halstead, 1975. (b)

Sarason, I. G. The Test Anxiety Scale: Concept and Research. In C. D. Spielberger and I. G. Sarason (Eds.), *Anxiety and stress* (Vol. 5). Washington, D.C.: Hemisphere, 1978.

Saufley, W. H., & LaCava, S. C. Reminiscence and arousal: Replications and the matter of establishing a phenomenon. *Bulletin of the Psychonomic Society,* 1977, *9,* 155–158.

Schwartz, S. Individual differences in cognition: Some relationships between personality and memory. *Journal of Research in Personality,* 1975, *9,* 217–225.

Scott, J. C., & Nelson, D. L. Anxiety and encoding strategy. *Bulletin of the Psychonomic Society,* 1979, *13,* 297–299.

Spence, J. T., & Spence, K. W. The motivational components of manifest anxiety: Drive and drive stimuli. In C. D. Spielberger (Ed.), *Anxiety and behavior*. New York: Academic press, 1966.

Spielberger, C. D., Gonzalez, H. P., Taylor, C. J., Algaze, B., & Anton, W. D. Examination stress and test anxiety. In C. D. Spielberger and I. G. Sarason (Eds.), *Anxiety and stress* (Vol. 5). New York: Hemisphere/Wiley, 1978.

Spielberger, C. D., Gorsuch, R. L., & Lushene, R. E. *Manual for the state-trait anxiety inventory*. Palo Alto, Calif.: Consulting Psychologists Press, 1970.

Sternberg, S. Memory scanning: New findings and current controversies. *Quarterly Journal of Experimental Psychology*, 1975, *27*, 1–32.

Thayer, R. E. Measurement of activation through self-report. *Psychological Reports*, 1967, *20*, 663–678.

Tulving, E. The effects of presentation and recall of material in free-recall learning. *Journal of Verbal Learning and Verbal Behavior*, 1967, *6*, 175–184.

Tulving, E. Episodic and semantic memory. In E. Tulving and W. Donaldson (Eds.), *Organization of memory*. New York: Academic Press, 1972.

Tulving, E., & Bower, G. H. The logic of memory representations. In G. H. Bower (Ed.), *The psychology of learning and motivation* (Vol. 8). New York: Academic Press, 1974.

Tulving, E., & Colotla, V. A. Free recall of trilingual lists. *Cognitive Psychology*, 1970, *1*, 86–98.

Tulving, E., & Thomson, D. M. Encoding specificity and retrieval processes in episodic memory. *Psychological Review*, 1973, *80*, 352–373.

Uehling, B. S. Arousal in verbal learning. In C. P. Duncan, L. Sechrest, and A. W. Melton (Eds.), *Human memory: Festschrift in honor of Benton J. Underwood*. New York: Appleton-Century-Crofts, 1972.

Walker, E. L. Action decrement and its relation to learning. *Psychological Review*, 1958, *65*, 129–142.

Watkins, M. J. Concept and measurement of primary memory. *Psychological Bulletin*, 1974, *81*, 695–711.

Watkins, M. J. The intricacy of memory span. *Memory & Cognition*, 1977, *5*, 529–543.

Wickens, D. D. Characteristics of word encoding. In A. W. Melton and E. Martin (Eds.), *Coding processes in memory*. Washington, D.C.: Winston, 1972.

Wine, J. Test anxiety and the direction of attention. *Psychological Bulletin*, 1971, *76*, 92–104.

Zubrzycki, C. R., & Borkowski, J. G. Effects of anxiety on storage and retrieval processes in short-term memory. *Psychological Reports*, 1973, *33*, 315–320.

5 The Development of Test Anxiety in Children

Jerome B. Dusek
Syracuse University

As the title indicates, this chapter is concerned with the development of test anxiety during the childhood years. Research on the effects of test anxiety on children's learning and performance was spurred by the work of Seymour Sarason and his colleagues at Yale University (e.g., Hill & S.B. Sarason, 1966; S. B. Sarason, Hill, & Zimbardo, 1964; S. B. Sarason, Davidson, Lighthall, Waite & Ruebush, 1960). The negative relationships they found between test anxiety and children's IQ and achievement test performance led a number of other researchers to investigate the cognitive and motivational aspects of the deleterious effects of test anxiety during the childhood years. It is this literature that is reviewed later.

Because of space considerations, several limitations have been imposed on the material discussed in this chapter. First, no attempt is made to present an exhaustive review of the pertinent literature. Rather, the focus is on representative studies of more contemporaneous concern in the field. Ruebush (1963), S. B. Sarason et al. (1960), and Hill (1972) provide excellent sources for those wishing a more complete historical review. Second, there is no discussion of research on physiological reactions to stress and test anxiety. This work has been conducted almost exclusively with adults and is reviewed by Holroyd and Appel (Chapter 7 in this volume).

A brief discussion of definitional issues in the study of text anxiety during the childhood years is followed by a summary of the major theories guiding research on the influence of test anxiety on children's learning and performance. The review continues with a description of the Test Anxiety Scale for Children (TASC), the scale used most frequently in research with children. Included is a discussion of the multidimensionality of the TASC and developmental trends in scores on the TASC. The next topic considered is the relation of test anxiety to attentional processes. We then move to a consideration of the relation between test anxiety and children's IQ and school achievement test performance.

TEXT ANXIETY IN CHILDREN

Test anxiety is an unpleasant feeling or emotional state that has physiological and behavioral concomitants and that is experienced in formal testing or other evaluative situations (Ruebush, 1963; I. G. Sarason, 1975, 1978; Spielberger, 1966; Wine, 1971; cf. Sieber, Chapter 2 of this volume, for a discussion of issues in defining test anxiety). When test anxiety is experienced, a variety of cognitive and attentional processes are called into play that interfere with effective and successful task performance (Hill, 1972; I.G. Sarason, 1972a, 1978; Wine, 1971). Current theoretical formulations are focused on explaining the nature and functioning of these cognitive and attentional variables.

Theories of Test Anxiety in Children

Theories of the development of test anxiety have been formulated to describe: (1) how children become test-anxious: and (2) the cognitive and behavioral factors that mediate the deleterious effects of test anxiety.

The Etiology of Test Anxiety.   Researchers generally agree that test anxiety results from the child's reactions to evaluative experiences during the preschool and early school years (Hill, 1972; S. B. Sarason et al., 1960). S. B. Sarason and his colleagues view test anxiety as a personality characteristic that develops during the child's interactions with the parents during the preschool years and that slowly stabilizes during the school years. High levels of evaluation anxiety result when the child's performance and achievement do not live up to the parents' (usually unrealistically high) expectations. As a result, the parental judgments of the child's performance are often negative, and the child may be subject to derogation of other sorts from the parents. As the child internalizes these negative parental feelings, a hostile view of the rejecting parent develops. These hostile feelings produce guilt in the child, who then begins to engage in self-derogation and repression of the negative feelings toward the parents. In addition, the child fantasizes about parental retaliation for the child's hostile feelings. This threat, in turn, leads the child to engage in behaviors aimed at satisfying parental wishes and at pleasing the parents. The high-test-anxious child, then, may develop great dependence upon adult direction and support in evaluative situations. Of course, using this strategy may result in the child avoiding evaluative situations unless adult support is present.

Some evidence supports the suppositions of Sarason et al. (1960) about the etiology of test anxiety. The parents of 32 pairs of low- and high-anxious children, matched for grade level, sex, and IQ, were interviewed, and they also completed a rating scale of their children's personalities. All 64 mothers but only 21 of the fathers participated. The interview schedule assessed parental judgments about the child's anxiety reactions toward school, parental strictness of punishment, handling of aggression, development of dependence and independence, and the like. On the rating scale, the parents indicated the degree to which 25 traits (e.g., mature-immature) described their children. Mothers' ratings did not distinguish between the two groups of children. In other words, the mothers of both low- and high-anxious children rated their children as nonanxious even though the high-anxious children had indicated they were anxious. The fathers' ratings did distinguish between the low- and high-anxious children. Fathers rated the low-anxious children as more mature, responsible, optimistic, and the like, and as less generous and less affectionate than the high-anxious children.

S. B. Sarason et al. (1960) offer two explanations for the discrepancy between the results from the maternal and parental interviews. First, they suggest that fathers may see their children in a more objective light than mothers. We would add that the 21 fathers interviewed may have been a very select sample. Second, they suggest that mothers and fathers may base their judgments on different samples of their children's behavior resulting from interactions with their children in qualitatively different situations. (Recent research (e.g., Lamb, 1976a, 1976b, 1976c, 1977) indicating that as early as infancy and very early childhood parents interact with children in identifiably different situations supports this interpretation.) The mother is more salient in attachment situations and the father in play and affiliative situations. These differing interactions may cause mothers and fathers to have different impressions of their children's reactions to stress and evaluations. Other evidence indicates a tendency for the mothers of high-anxious children to be more defensive than the mothers of low-anxious children (S. B. Sarason et al., 1960), which may contribute to the discrepancy between maternal and paternal ratings of high- and low-anxious children.

Others (e.g., Hermans, ter Laak & Maes, 1972) have also examined parent–child relations pertaining to the development of test anxiety. In problem-solving situations, parents of high-anxious children tend to be aversive toward their children. They ignore their children's bids for security, do not offer constructive help in problem solving, and may teach their children to engage in task-irrelevant and even task-inappropriate behaviors in problem-solving or evaluative situations. The children, then, come to rely on external supports from their parents or other adults to effectively deal with evaluation and problem solving and to avoid criticism. Parents of low-anxious children, in contrast, offer effective problem-solving strategies without completely taking over the problem solving. They teach their children to rely on their own resources and may help them learn task-oriented responses, thereby increasing their effectiveness as problem solvers.

Clearly, data linking child-rearing techniques to the emergence of test anxiety are very scarce. This has made it difficult to test, evaluate, and refine S. B. Sarason's theory or to develop alternatives. Much more successful theoretical formulations exist to describe the effects of test anxiety on children's learning and achievement.

Theories of the Effects of Test Anxiety. The generally accepted current explanation of the negative effects of test anxiety is that they result from ineffective cognitive strategies and attentional deficits that cause poor task performance in evaluative situations. Low-anxious children appear to become deeply involved in evaluative tasks but high-anxious children do not. High-anxious children seem to experience attentional blocks, extreme concern with autonomic and emotional self-cues, and cognitive deficits such as misinterpretation of information (cf. I. G. Sarason, 1972a, 1978; Wine, 1971). The high-anxious child's attentional and cognitive deficits are likely to interfere with both learning and responding in evaluative situations and result in lowered performance.

The aforementioned conceptualizations suggest the importance of cognitive factors as mediating influences in the effects of test anxiety on children's learning and performance. It is these cognitive factors that influence the perception of a situation as evaluative or not (I. G. Sarason, 1978). The cognitive activities considered important in the mediation of test anxiety are generally conceptualized as attentional in nature (e.g., I. G. Sarason, 1972a, 1975, 1978; Wine, 1971). These mechanisms influence stimulus reception and interpretation as well as overt behavior (I. G. Sarason, 1975, 1978). The mechanisms that have been examined most frequently are those that relate to searching the environment for cues. Hence, a theoretical and empirical emphasis on selective attention deficits in high-anxious individuals has been a major concern.

Some researchers (e.g., Liebert & Morris, 1967; Morris & Liebert, 1970) have examined the high-anxious person's attention to self-stimuli as opposed to task stimuli. Worry (*W*) is conceptualized as cognitive concern over performance in a task; emotionality (*E*) is viewed as an autonomic arousal aspect of test anxiety. The adverse effects of test anxiety are presumed to be due to a division of attention between concern over task performance, on the one hand, and the physiological aspects of arousal, on the other hand. The high-anxious person attends more to the autonomic aspects of arousal and less to the task than does the low-anxious person. This division of attention results in poorer task performance by high- than low-test-anxious persons. The primary concept from this perspective is worry because it results in a cognitive concern about one's ability relative to others and about the consequences of failure. This concern replaces attending to and working at the task at hand. (See Wine, Chapter 16 of this volume for a more complete description of this point of view).

According to attentional theory, it should be possible to negate the deleterious effects of test anxiety by helping the child focus attention more directly on the task (Dusek, Kermis, & Mergler, 1975; Dusek, Mergler, & Kermis, 1976; Wine, 1971; I. G. Sarason, 1972b). Research reviewed later (see Test Anxiety and Attending Processes) indicates that providing task-relevant strategies helps high-anxious children better attend to evaluative tasks and increases their performance. Other research (see I. G. Sarason, 1972a, 1972b and material reviewed by others in this volume) indicates that providing task-oriented instructions, cues about expected performance, task-effective models, and memory supports facilitate the performance of high-anxious performance of high-anxious persons in evaluative situations.

As noted previously, the cognitive and attentional deficits associated with high test anxiety are partly the result of parental and other adult reactions to the child's success and failure in evaluative situations. Hill (1972; Hill & Eaton, 1977) has placed special emphasis on the developing child's success and failure experience in explaining why some children become highly test-anxious. Low-anxious children generally have a history of success in school and other evaluative situations and experience generally positive interactions with adults in evaluative settings. As a result, they develop a relatively higher motive to approach success than avoid failure (Hill, 1972) and learn to rely on their own evaluations of their performance for guidance in problem solving. Since high-anxious children have a generally poorer history of success in school and other evaluative situations and have experienced somewhat more punitive interactions with evaluative adults— both parents and teachers—they develop problem-solving strategies indicative of a generally higher motive to avoid failure and criticism than to approach success. High-anxious children, then, are prone to developing a high dependence on adults for evaluation of their performance and for direction in problem solving. Understanding children's evaluations of success and failure based on adult feedback, then, is critical to theoretically describing the effects of anxiety on children's performance (see Dweck (1976) for a review of this concept).

The relation between success and failure experiences and scores on the TASC was directly measured by Bradshaw and Gaudry (1968). The ninth-grade children were divided into three groups: a control group, a group that experienced success on a multiple choice vocabulary test, and a group that experienced failure on a multiple choice vocabulary test. Success and failure were manipulated by making the test easy or hard. The test for the control group included both easy and hard items. Each test contained 40 questions which were to be answered in 5 minutes. After taking the test, the students marked it, compared their scores to a standard (30 or more was very good, 20 or less was poor), and then took the TASC. The finding of direct relevance is that children who experienced failure on the vocabulary test scored higher on the TASC than those who experienced success. This was especially pronounced for children in the lower stream. The results of this study lend credence to the view that histories of success and failure are important determinants in the development of test anxiety. The results also suggest that by structuring school-related tasks to lessen the obvious evaluative components (e.g., increasing available time or ensuring a degree of success) the performance of high-anxious children may be improved.

Further evidence in support of Hill's theory of the relation between success and failure experiences and test anxiety comes from a study of children's performance on mathematics problems (Hill & Eaton, 1977). Sixty fifth- and sixth-grade children were divided into high-, middle-, and low-anxious groups on the basis of their TASC scores. Half the children were given a series of arithmetic problems that were easy to do, and the children experienced success doing them. Half the children were in a mixed success/failure condition in which one-third of the problems were fairly difficult and two-thirds were easy. One-third of the problems in each set were identical to allow comparisons of the performance of the low-, middle-, and high-test-anxious children. All children were told that if a bell rang while they were working on a problem they were to put it aside and start on a new problem. For subjects in the mixed success/failure condition, the experimenter rang the bell on the difficult problems, causing the children to fail to complete approximately one-third of the problems they attempted. Children in the success condition completed all the problems they attempted. The dependent variables were: (1) average time to complete a problem: (2) accuracy (errors): and (3) cheating (working after the bell had rung, skipping a problem, or returning to a previous problem).

In support of Hill's (1972, 1976) theory, the high-anxious children in the success/failure condition took somewhat longer to complete the problems, were less accurate, and cheated somewhat more than low-anxious children (see Fig. 5.1). In the success condition, however, the performance of the high-anxious children nearly matched that of their low-anxious counterparts. These results indicate not only that failure experiences are related to the high-anxious child's poorer performance in evaluative situations, but also that providing high-anxious children with success and nonevaluative testing conditions can increase their performance, presumably because it allows their achievement motive to operate more strongly than their failure motive (Hill & Eaton, 1977). The data also indicate that the relatively poorer performance of

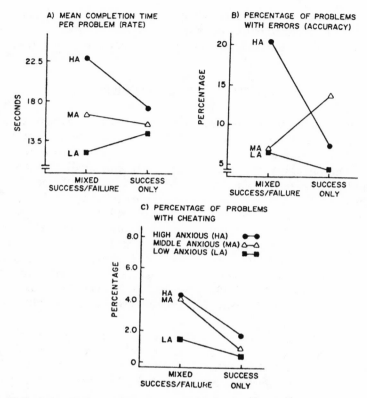

FIG. 5.1. Performance means as a function of test anxiety and success–failure experience. Different subjects determine each point. (Source: Hill, K. T., & Eaton, W. O. The interaction of test anxiety and success-experiences in determining children's arithmetic performance. *Developmental Psychology*, 1977, *13*, 205–211.)

high-anxious children does not represent a learning ability deficit relative to their low-anxious peers. In the success condition, the high-anxious children went as fast and were as accurate as the low-anxious children. Differences in the performance of low- and high-anxious children in the failure situation, then, were due to motivational factors (Hill & Eaton, 1977). By altering situational characteristics—for example, providing success experiences, nonevaluative instructions and procedures, and the like—one can obtain a more accurate estimate of the learning and achievement of high-anxious children.

Current research and theory point to test anxiety resulting from a developmental history of success/failure experiences in evaluative situations. The high-anxious child's history of failure leads the child to rely on external supports in evaluative situations. When these supports are lacking, the high-anxious child suffers cognitive and attentional deficits that result in poorer task performance than would be obtained in nonevaluative situations.

MEASURING TEST ANXIETY

A number of questionnaires have been developed to measure test anxiety. The Test Anxiety Questionnaire (Mandler & S. B. Sarason, 1952), Test Anxiety Scale (I. G. Sarason & Ganzer, 1962; I. G. Sarason, Pederson, & Nyman, 1968)., Achievement Anxiety Test (Alpert & Haber, 1960), the State–Trait Anxiety Inventory (e.g., Spielberger & Gorsuch, 1966; Spielberger, Gorsuch, & Lushene, 1970), and Liebert and Morris's (1967; Morris & Liebert, 1970; cf. also Doctor & Altman, 1969; Spiegler, Morris, & Liebert, 1968) scales that measure the Worry and Emotionality components of anxiety all have been used nearly exclusively with adults. Since these have been thoroughly reviewed elsewhere (e.g., Ruebush, 1963; S. B. Sarason, 1966; S. B. Sarason, Davidson, Lighthall, Waite, & Ruebush, 1960; Spielberger, 1972; Spielberger, Anton, & Bedell, 1975), we shall focus on the Test Anxiety Scale for Children (TASC), the most widely used scale to assess children's test anxiety.

The TASC is a group-administered paper and pencil test consisting of 30 items to which the child responds "yes" or "no" by circling the appropriate response on an answer sheet as the questions are read by an examiner. Twelve of the items specifically mention the word "test." Others ask about "worry" over classroom performance. The anxiety score is the number of "yes" responses. The TASC has been demonstrated to have suitable reliability (Ruebush, 1963) and validity (Hill, 1972; Ruebush, 1963).

In order to deal with the problem of defensiveness against admitting to anxiety, S. B. Sarason and his colleagues developed two scales. The Lie Scale for Children, LSC (S. B. Sarason et al., 1960), is composed of 11 items that ask questions to which nearly every child reasonably answers "yes." These questions, e.g., "Have you ever been afraid of getting hurt?" and "Do you ever worry?," relate to feeings of anxiety presumably experienced by most children. The score on the LSC is the number of times the child says "No." The Defensiveness Scale for Children, DSC (S. B. Sarason et al., 1964), is composed of 27 items that measure the child's willingness to admit to a wide range of feelings and emotions. Example questions are: "Do you sometimes feel like hurting someone?" and "Are there some people that you don't like?" Again, it is assumed that virtually every child has experienced these feelings and emotions. The child's defensiveness score is the sum of the "No" responses. The LSC and DSC are highly correlated and are usually given jointly: the child's total defensiveness score is the sum of "No" responses on the set of 38 questions.

The correlation between the TASC and total defensiveness scores is about −.5 (Hill & Sarason, 1966). Highly defensive chidren tend to admit to less anxiety. As a result, the TASC scores of highly defensive children are questionable (S. B. Sarason et al., 1969). By eliminating from the sample those children whose defensiveness scores fall in the upper 10% of the distribution of defensiveness scores, the experimenter gains some control, albeit imperfect, over the validity of the scores of the group of low-anxious subjects included in the research.

Multidimensionality of the TASC

Evidence from factor analytic studies of the TASC indicates that it is not a unidimensional instrument. The initial factor analytic studies of the TASC apparently were reported by Dunn (1964, 1965). In the earlier of these studies, the TASC was completed by 633 middle-class children in grades four, five, and six. Four factors emerged from the analyses: Text Anxiety, Generalized School Anxiety, Recitation Anxiety, and Physiological Arousal in Anticipated Recitation Situations. The sample (N = 866) in the later study consisted of 223 boys and 191 girls from grades four and five and 226 boys and 226 girls from grades seven and nine of an upper-middle-class school. The data from each sex–grade-level subgroup were analyzed separately. In each of the four analyses, a Test Anxiety factor emerged as well as a factor labeled Manifest Dream Anxiety. The remaining factors from each analysis were not consistent across the four subgroups. Dunn (1964, 1965) concluded that, in general, children's concerns and worries over being tested are different from their broader concerns about school; each of these sets of concerns is measured to a degree by the TASC, suggesting it may be a measure of school anxiety when all the items are considered. Consistent with this view, Phillips (1966) reported a correlation of .82 (corrected r = .61, Phillips, 1978) between the TASC and a test of school anxiety for elementary school children. (See Phillips et al., 1978 and Chapter 15 in this volume for a discussion of school anxiety.)

More recent research supports Dunn's conclusion tht the TASC is a multidimensional instrument. Feld and Lewis (1967, 1969) factor analyzed TASC data from 7551 primarily middle-class second-grade children. Four factors emerged from the principal component analysis. The Test Anxiety component measured children's reactions and feelings about school tests. Nearly all the items with the word "test" in them loaded on this factor (e.g., "Do you worry a lot while you are taking a test?"). The Somatic Signs of Anxiety component was defined by items asking about physiological reactions (e.g., "When you are taking a test, does the hand you write with shake a little?"). The items defining the third component, Comparative Poor Self-Evaluation, involved primarily children's derogation of themselves relative to other children (e.g., "When the teacher is teaching you about arithmetic, do you feel that other children in the class understand her better than you?"). The fourth component, Remote School Concern, was defined by items assessing the child's worries about school while at home. All the TASC items mentioning dreams (e.g., "Do you sometimes dream at night that the teacher is angry because you do not know your work?") and most of the items dealing with thinking about school while at home loaded on this component.

Comparison of these four components with the four factors reported by Dunn revealed a high degree of similarity (Feld & Lewis, 1969). In both instances, the Text Anxiety factor accounted for more variance than any other factor. Hence, it appears that there is some stability to the factor structure of the TASC across grade and sex.

Feld and Lewis (1969) suggest that these four factors indicate individual differences in the way children express anxiety. Anxious children differ in the types of school situations that elicit anxiety and in the reactions they show to their own anxiety. For example, some children may react primarily to avoid failure (e.g., Atkinson & Litwin, 1960), which seems to be at the heart of test anxiety and is assessed by the Test Anxiety factor. Other children express anxiety by comparing themselves to their peers and may score high on items defining the Comparative Poor Self-Evaluation factor. Still others may score high on the item sets defining one of the remaining factors because of individual differences in situational characteristics eliciting anxiety.

The research reviewed thus far in this section rests on the TASC responses of middle-class children. Rhine and Spaner (1973) compared the TASC factor structure derived from their lower-class sample of 287 boys and 266 girls in the third grade to the structure reported by Feld and Lewis (1967). Separate factor analyses were conducted for sex–social-class subgroup. The four factors identified by Feld and Lewis for middle-class subjects also emerged in the analyses from the lower-class sample. However, measures of factor structure similarilty revealed a sex-social class interaction. The factor similarity coefficients for the middle-class boys and girls for like factors were all .99 in absolute value. The coefficients for dissimilar factors ranged from |.03| to |.08|. In the lower-class sample, the evidence indicated less cross-sex factor similarlity. Like-factor coefficients ranged from |.82| to |.92|, the latter for the Test Anxiety factor, and dissimilar factor coefficients ranged from |.07| to |.55|. The comparisons across social class revealed very similar factor structures between middle-class boys and girls and lower-class girls, and middle-class boys and lower-class boys. But, with the exception of the Test Anxiety factor, the factor similarity for lower-class boys and middle-class girls was only moderate. Summarizing their results, Rhine and Spaner (1973) suggest that lower-class boys may be in greater conflict in the school situation because it suppresses their needs for independence and autonomy. They also receive more punishment in school and are more likely to be disciplined. These qualitatively poorer interactions with teachers apparently alter the lower-class boys' views of school, which in turn alters the meaning of the TASC items for them relative to their peers.

Although it is clear that the TASC is not a unidimensional instrument, researchers interested in test anxiety and its influence on children's learning and performance have not attempted to identify the correlates of the individual differences associated with the items defining the foregoing factors. Generally speaking, high-test-anxious children are identified by their responses to the entire 30-item instrument. It would seem a worthwhile endeavor to examine the effects of test anxiety by identifying high-test-anxious subjects on the basis of responses to those items that load on the Test Anxiety factor identified in all of the factor analytic studies cited earlier. Dividing subjects into high- and low-test-anxious groups on this basis may provide more adequate tests of the theories of test anxiety in children. This seems especially important in investigating the view that test anxiety represents a tendency to avoid failure, an aspect of the items defining the Test Anxiety factor. It may also prove beneficial to examine the effects of test anxiety for the various forms of anxiety indicated by high versus low performance on the items loading on the other various factors. Such research may contribute to our understanding of the meaning of test anxiety and its effects on performance in tasks and situations with diverse characteristics. It would also seem beneficial from the standpoint of schooling and its relationship to fostering test anxiety (Hill, 1972; Phillips, 1966).

Developmental Trends in Test Anxiety

The most extensive longitudinal study of developmental trends in TASC scores was carried out by S. B. Sarason and his colleagues (Hill & S. B. Sarason 1966; S. B. Sarason et al., 1964). A sample of 670 predominantly white middle- and working-class children were studied over a 5-year period. The subjects were in the first and second grades at the start of the study. The TASC, LSC, and DSC were administered during the 1st, 3rd, and 5th years of the study. Hence, test–retest correlations could be computed for 2-year intervals and, for the initial first-grade sample only, for a 4-year interval (the initial second-grade data were destroyed by fire). Over the 2-year intervals, the test–retest correlations were of a moderate magnitude (.3 to .4) for each of the scales: the TASC correlations were somewhat higher for girls than boys and for the second and third testing (grades four to six). The 4-year test–retest correlations for the inital first-grade sample were quite low, indicating little stability in any of the measures. Children's first-grade text anxiety scores, then, do not allow accurate prediction of fifth-grade test anxiety level. The correlations indicate that test anxiety begins to stabilize during the later elementary school years, perhaps because of the contribution schooling makes to children's evaluation of their competencies in evaluative situations.

Some research (e.g., Manley & Rosemier, 1972) indicates that TASC scores stabilize even further in the middle- and high-school years.

Hill and S. B. Sarason (1966) and others (Manley & Rosemier, 1972) have reported sex and age differences in the TASC (and defensiveness) test–retest correlations. During the later elementary school years, girls have higher TASC scores and somewhat lower defensiveness scores than boys. Initially, however, there were no sex differences in the mean scores of these measures. Mean TASC scores for boys in the longitudinal sample (Hill & S. B Sarason, 1966; S. B. Sarason et al., 1964) described earlier were 7.52, 8.71, and 9.44 in the first, third, and fifth grades, respectively. The corresponding mean TASC scores for the girls were 7.72, 10.57, and 12.71. Similar findings occurred for the boys and girls in the initial second-grade sample. In the fourth and sixth grades, the mean TASC scores were 10.2 and 9.31 for the boys and 11.47 and 12.84 for the girls. In general, with increases in the grade level, girls admit to more anxiety than boys, and this trend increases in strength across the elementary school years. In turn, boys tend to become more defensive *relative to girls,* although both groups decrease in defensiveness across the elementary school years. Some evidence (Manley & Rosemier, 1972) shows that these developmental trends and sex differences continue in grades seven through twelve.

These trends have several implications for the researcher interested in studying test anxiety during the childhood years. At the experimental design level, in cross-sectional studies involving the age variable it may be difficult to cross level of test anxiety in the experimental design because of different medians for the age levels involved in the design. In such instances, the use of multiple regression (e.g., Cohen, 1968) analytic techniques may prove useful and may be more informative than a simple high versus low or high versus medium versus low split on test anxiety. At a more substantive level, the developmental trends for TASC and defensiveness scores suggest that the scales may measure different psychological processes at the different age levels and, perhaps, for the two sexes. The interpretation of these developmental trends (see Hill & Sarason, 1966) is far from straightforward, however. Older children may admit to more anxiety because they are actually more anxious, because of a true reduction in defensiveness, or because they view the extreme questions as being unrealistic. Increased exposure to the school situation may put increasing numbers of children, or the same child to an increasing degree, in the position of experiencing increases in school-related anxiety.

The sex differences in test anxiety seem best explained by reference to sex-role socialization. Girls are allowed, and may be encouraged, to admit to anxiety because it is a feminine trait in our culture. Because boys in our culture are taught that they should not exhibit feminine traits, they may admit to less anxiety although they may experience it as much as girls do (Hill & S.

B. Sarason, 1966). Maccoby and Jacklin (1974) doubt that the reported sex differences in anxiety questionnaire responses reflect real sex differences in anxiety. They suggest that a number of items on anxiety scales, and specifically 10 of the 45 items on the General Anxiety Scale for Children, tap fears that are directly or indirectly taught to girls—e.g., "Do you get scared when you have to walk home alone at night?" In turn, few items relate to fears specifically taught to boys—e.g., appearing cowardly or fearing public failure. Maccoby and Jacklin suggest the sex differences in self-reported anxiety could be reversed, or eliminated, by changing the items to reflect fears resulting from the socialization experiences of boys.

Because the specific reasons for sex differences in response to the TASC are elusive, it seems wise to exercise caution in interpreting their meaning. Until more definitive data become available, it appears best to consider the sex differences on the TASC and defensiveness scales as reflecting different ways of coping with anxiety that is experienced equally by each sex. Both boys and girls experience test anxiety at similar levels as they progress through the schools, but boys become relatively more defensive about it. In effect, girls may cope with anxiety by admitting to it; boys may defend against it (Hill, 1972).

TEXT ANXIETY AND ATTENDING PROCESSES

In recent research, the nature and effect of attention focusing as a mediating influence in performance differences of low- and high-test-anxious children have been investigated. One hypothesis based on attentional and information-processing theories of test anxiety (e.g., Wine, 1971; I. G. Sarason, 1972a, 1978), is that in evaluative situations high-test-anxious children direct their attention less toward task-relevant and more toward task-irrelevant information to a greater extent than do low-test-anxious children. A second hypothesis is that manipulations forcing attention to task-relevant aspects of the situation should improve high-test-anxious children's performance in evaluative situations.

To investigate these hypotheses, Dusek, Kermis, and Mergler (1975) tested 144 high- and low-test-anxious second-, fourth- and sixth-grade children, half males and half females, in an incidental learning task developed by Maccoby and Hagen (1965) and Hagen (1967). In this task, the child faces a cardboard panel on which are drawn eight boxes. The experimenter places eight stimulus cards into the boxes, one at a time. Each card contains a line drawing of an animal (the central stimuls) centered above a line drawing of a household object (the incidental stimulus). The child is instructed to learn the positions of the eight animals in the stimulus array. After several exposure trials in which the cards are placed on the panel with each animal occupying the same position on each trial, the array remains covered by a second, identical panel and the child's learning is assessed. Central learning is measured by holding up a card showing a line drawing of one of the animals and asking the child to point to the position in the covered array occupied by that animal. Incidental learning is assessed by asking the child to match cards containing individual pictures of the central and incidental stimuli. In this study, half the children in each subgroup performed under game instructions and half under test instructions. Half labeled (named) the central stimuli as the cards were placed on the panel and half did not.

The results most relevant to the current discussion were the significant anxiety-level main effect and the triple interaction between anxiety level, instruction condition, and labeling condition in the analysis of the central learning scores, and the significant anxiety-level main effect in the analysis of the incidental learning scores. The low-test-anxious subjects had higher central learning scores and lower incidental learning scores than the high-test-anxious subjects. The means for the significant triple interaction are presented in Table 5.1. Under game instructions, the mean scores were significantly higher in the label than no-label condition for both the low- and high-test-anxious children. Under test instructions, the mean scores of the low-test-anxious children did not differ as a function of labeling condition. But, the high-test-anxious children in the labeling condition had a higher mean score than the high-test-anxious children in the no-label condition. Under test instructions, the mean scores for the low- and high-test-anxious subjects were not different in the labeling condition, but the low-anxious children had a higher mean score than the high-anxious children in the no-

TABLE 5.1
Mean Central Learning for the Anxiety Level X
Instruction Condition X Labeling Condition
Interaction

| | Condition | |
Group	Label	No Label
Game Instructions		
Low-Anxious	6.39	4.89
High-Anxious	5.33	4.56
Test Instructions		
Low-Anxious	6.11	5.89
High-Anxious	6.17	4.44

[a]From Dusek, J. B., Kermis, M. D., & Mergler, N. L. Information processing in low- and high-test-anxious children as a function of grade level and verbal labeling. *Developmental Psychology,* 1975, *11,* 651–652.

label condition. Labeling equalized the scores of the low- and high-test-anxious children tested under test instructions.

These results support the hypothesis that high-anxious children attend to task-irrelevant stimuli to a greater extent than low-test-anxious children and this detracts from their task performance. The data suggest that the high-anxious children have a more globally oriented attention than the low-anxious children. Under game instructions, there were no differences between low- and high-test-anxious children. These findings replicate earlier research (e.g., Lekarczyk & Hill, 1969; McCoy, 1965) and indicate only limited performance differences between low- and high-test-anxious children under nonevaluative conditions. As suggested by Hill (1972; Hill & Eaton, 1977; Nottelmann & Hill, 1977), the test-anxious child is motivated to avoid failure in evaluative situations such as those presented by the test instructions. Differences in performance between low- and high-test-anxious children appear to be due to these motivational differences rather than learning differences. If one measures total learning in the preceding incidental learning experiment, the mean scores for low- and high-anxious children are equivalent. What is learned comes from different sources of information in the experimental situation.

Components of evaluative situations apparently act as attention attractors for low-test-anxious children but as attention diffusers for high-test-anxious children (I. G. Sarason, 1972b). Providing high-test-anxious children with an effective task strategy, however, eliminates performance decrements. Labeling reduced performance differences in the above experiment for one of two reasons: it focused attention on the central stimuli or it aided encoding of the to-be-learned material, or both (Dusek, 1978; Wheeler & Dusek, 1973). With regard to the latter alternative, it may be that the labeling manipulation resulted in a restructuring of the subjects' cognitive strategies, thus leading to improved task performance (I. G. Sarason, 1972b).

In order to clarify the effect of labeling on the high-test-anxious child's learning, Dusek, Mergler, and Kermis (1976) employed the same task with another group of second, fourth, and sixth graders, half of whom were high- and half low-anxious. Only test instructions were used in this study. Half the children labeled the central stimuli as they were placed down and half did not. For half the children, the central and incidental stimuli were spatially separated on the stimulus cards—the central stimulus appearing in the upper third and the incidental stimulus in the lower third of the card. Previous research (e.g., Wheeler & Dusek, 1973) has shown that spatially separating the stimuli results in lowered incidental learning, presumably because the incidental stimuli are less distracting and do not detract attention from the central stimuli. Therefore, it was expected that separating the central and incidental stimuli would facilitate the central learning of the high-test-anxious children but would probably have no effect on the central learning of the low-test-anxious children. By incuding both labeling and spatial separation of the central and incidental stimuli, it was possible to compare the facilitative effects of each and begin to determine the nature of the facilitative influence of the labeling procedure. If labeling acts to increase central learning primarily through its attention-focusing properties, the two manipulations should produce similar effects. If labeling acts primarily to aid encoding of to-be-remembered material, it should prove more effective than the separation of stimuli as assessed by measures of central learning (Dusek, 1978). In turn, such comparisons provide insight into the nature of cognitive process differences in the performance of high- and low-test-anxious children in evaluative situations.

The low-test-anxious children had higher central learning and lower incidental learning scores than the high-anxious children, replicating the findings of the earlier study. Spatially separating the central and incidental stimuli had no effect on central learning scores but resulted in lowered incidental learning for both low- and high-test-anxious children, suggesting that the performance deficit of the high-anxious children is more than simple attention-focusing phenomenon. The significant interaction between anxiety level and labeling condition in the analysis of the central learning scores (see Table 5.2) supports this assertion. Labeling exerted no effect on the performance of the low-test-anxious children but significantly facilitated the performance of the high-test-anxious children, making it equal to that of the low-test-anxious children. These data suggest that the lower performance of the high-test-anxious child is a result of failure to either generate or use efficient cognitive strategies in evaluative situations. Labeling facilitates high-test-anxious children's performance by aiding encoding, a highly task-relevant strategy that these children do not normally employ or that is more efficient than the strategies they do employ.

Nottelmann and Hill (1977) have shown that high-test-anxious children's attention is distracted not only by task stimuli but also by stimuli outside of the to-be-done task. They investigated the relation between performance and

TABLE 5.2
Mean Central Learning Scores for the Anxiety
Level X Labeling Condition Interaction

Anxiety Level	Labeling Condition	
	Label	No Label
Low	6.36	6.36
High	6.31	4.44

[a]From Dusek, J. B., Mergler, N. L., & Kermis, M. D. Attention, encoding and information processing in low- and high-test anxious children. *Child Development*, 1976, *47*, 201–207.)

off-task behavior in low-, middle-, and high-test-anxious fourth- and fifth-grade children while the children worked at an anagram task. The child was instructed to make as many words as possible out of the word "generation." While the child was working on this task, the experimenter took a second set of materials and made words out of the word "inoperable." After 5 minutes, the experimenter asked the child to make words out of the word "inoperable" and the experimenter worked on a third word. Off-task behavior was indexed by: (1) glances at the experimenter and what he was doing: (2) glances directed at the experimenter's task: and (3) other off-task glances. The high-test-anxious children made fewer words than the low- or middle-anxious children and glanced away from the task more frequently than the low- or middle-anxious children (see Fig. 5.2). Similar effects occurred for the other two

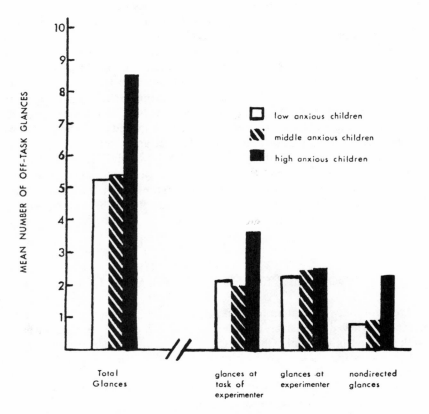

FIG. 5.2. Mean number of total off-task glances, glances directed at the experimenter's task, glances directed at the experimenter, and nondirected glances for children at each level of low, middle, and high anxiety. (Source: Nottelmann, E. D., & Hill, K. T. Test anxiety and off-task behavior in evaluative situations. *Child Development,* 1977, *489,* 225–231.)

measures, glances at the experimenter's task and other off-task glances. The high-anxious children, then, had the lowest performance levels and also the highest levels of inattention to the task.

The finding that the high-anxious children avoided working at the task by glancing away from it is consistent with Hill's (1972, 1976) conceptualization of the effects of test anxiety. Nottelmann and Hill (1977) interpret the high-anxious child's off-task behavior within the framework of these children's high dependency needs. They propose that the early child-rearing patterns experienced by these children teach them to depend on others for help in problem-solving situations. Low-anxious children are reared by parents who provide support in times of insecurity and offer appropriate problem-solving strategies, thereby teaching their children to become self-reliant. High-anxious children, on the other hand, are reliant on others' evaluations of their performance and on external cues. This analysis may help us understand the etiology of attentional differences between high- and low-anxious children.

The distracting effects of task-irrelevant information, the presence of others in the situation, and self-stimuli are not confined to laboratory tasks. West, Lee and Anderson (1969), for example, demonstrated that irrelevant information on achievement-type tests interfered with the performance of high-anxious children. Considerations of attentional mechanisms in mediating the negative influences of anxiety in evaluative situations suggests that on school tests, or papers that are done in class and are to be graded by the teacher, the high-anxious child may be distracted by self-stimuli (e.g., Doctor & Altman, 1969; Liebert & Morris, 1967; Morris & Liebert, 1970) or by irrelevant task characteristics or non-task-related stimuli, such as the other children in the room and what they are doing. If they are distracted, they may divide their attention between task-relevant and off-task behaviors, thereby lowering their performance.

TEST ANXIETY AND IQ
AND ACHIEVEMENT TEST PERFORMANCE

The relation between test anxiety and IQ and achievement test performance has been reviewed extensively elsewhere (Hill, 1972, 1976; S. B. Sarason et al., 1969; cf. also Phillips et al., Chapter 15 in this volume). Therefore, we are only briefly discussing these relationships in order to fill in the picture of text anxiety effects on children.

Measures of test anxiety and IQ are negatively correlated (Ruebush, 1963; S. B. Sarason et al., 1960). However, there are developmental trends in this relationship (Hill & S. B. Sarason, 1966; S. B. Sarason et al., 1964). At the first-grade level there is no significant relationship between TASC scores and IQ test performance. By the middle of the elementary school years, the correlation is significant but low (approximately –.2 in the third and fourth grades for both boys and girls). By the fifth to sixth grade, however, the magnitude of the correlation increases to –.3 to –.4.

Of some interest are data (Hill & S. B. Sarason, 1966; S. B. Sarason et al., 1964) indicating that change in TASC scores is related to change in IQ scores. Although complex, the results of the foregoing longitudinal study indicate that initially (first grade) high-anxious students who subsequently (third grade) have reduced test anxiety scores show increased IQ scores. That is, reductions in test anxiety are related to increased performance on IQ measures.

Similar trends were observed for the relation between TASC scores and achievement test measures. There is a negative correlation between TASC scores and achievement test performance, and the size of this correlation increases during the elementary school years. In general, these negative correlations are of approximately the same magnitude for boys and girls.

Two important issues may be raised with respect to that data. The first is the direction of cause–effect relationships. The second deals with teacher reactions to high- and low-anxious students as a function of the students' IQ and achievement test scores.

The direction of cause–effect relations in correlational research is never a simple one to answer. It is very tempting to suggest that high levels of test anxiety lead the child to perform at relatively low levels on IQ or achievement tests for the reasons outlined previously. Specifically, high anxious children are presumed to utilize less efficient problem-solving strategies, attend less well to the tasks presented, and to be more distractible than their low-anxious counterparts. As a result, their performance on evaluative tests is poorer. However, it may be that experiencing greater success on evaluative tasks leads the high-anxious child to experience less anxiety and, as a result, to score lower on tests of anxiety. Hill (1972) has convincingly argued that the most utilitarian view is to consider the influences reciprocal in nature. Increasing levels of anxiety may hinder task performance to greater degrees, and this may in turn increase anxiety over evaluation. The reverse, too, is likely to be true. As we noted, there is a direct relationship between failure and TASC scores, and there seems no reason to doubt a relation between success and reduction in TASC scores. Research reviewed earlier suggests that providing attentional aids and task-relevant strategies increases the high-anxious child's task performance. If similar procedures could be used in a variety of common "testing" situations, as in school testing, it might be possible to program more successful testing experiences for high-anxious children. This might result in a lowering of their TASC scores because they learn more appropriate cognitive and attentional strategies relevant to evaluative situations.

The second problem is equally if not more complex and is likely more important in understanding the child's behavior in the classroom. It is well known that teachers form expectancies for children's academic competencies (Brophy & Good, 1974; Dusek, 1975; Rist, 1970). Recent research into the bases teachers use to form expectancies indicates that during the early elementary school years "hard test" data are the primary source of information (Dusek & O'Connell, 1977). Since teachers behave differently toward students for whom they have high versus low expectancies (Brophy & Good, 1974), it seems likely that students who are high-anxious will be rated lower by their teachers (because of their lower IQ and achievement test scores) in terms of expected academic competencies and will experience a qualitatively different form of classroom interaction with their teachers than low-anxious students. Although no data speak directly to this question, it may be that teachers reinforce the generally inadequate feelings high-anxious children have about problem solving and learning. Therefore, they continue trends, started by parents' interactions with these children, of poor problem-solving strategies and high dependence on adults in evaluative, problem-solving situations. (See Phillips et al., Chapter 15 for a more complete treatment of this issue).

CONCLUSIONS

Test anxiety is a construct that can be measured reliably in children. It indexes an individual difference characteristic related to the quality of children's performance in evaluative situations. Although research on the etiology of test anxiety is sparse, it has been associated with a constellation of parental child-rearing techniques, including a failure of parents to provide emotional support to the child in problem-solving situations while teaching the child to rely on outside aid and evaluation of performance in achievement situations. Children who learn this mode of behaving in evaluative situations score lower on tests of achievement and IQ than do students who rely more on their own resources and students who are more highly task-oriented. With increasing grade levels, high-anxious children become relatively more anxious, and the negative correlations between test anxiety and measures of school achievement become stronger.

One mechanism that has recently been shown to be important in this conceptualization is the child's attention to task-relevant versus task-irrelevant information. High-anxious children spend more time attending to task-irrelevant material, including irrelevant behavior of others, than do low-test-anxious children. This division of attention results in lowered task performance. Providing test-anxious children with appropriate task-relevant strategies reduces this difference. In our highly competetive and achievement-oriented society, it is important that we have a more firm understanding of the mechanisms that underlie test anxiety and that we devise ways to attenuate its influences so that all children will be able to achieve to the best of their ability.

In order to accomplish this goal, research is needed on a number of questions that remain, at best, incompletely answered. To clarify the nature of the mechanisms mediating the effects of test anxiety on children's performance, it would seem wise to take into account the multidimensionality of the TASC. Research with adults amply demonstrates the importance of considering separately the various components of test anxiety when relating it to performance in evaluative situations. Such research strategies in studies of children's test anxiety would help clarify relationships, aid theoretical developments, and suggest ways in which the negative influence of test anxiety can be ameliorated. In a similar vein, considerably more research is needed on the etiology of test anxiety in children and on its long-term consequences, i.e., longitudinal studies of the degree of relationship between test anxiety measures in the elementary school years and its relationship to later school performance. By researching parental child-rearing techniques related to test anxiety, and child–teacher interactions with low- and high-anxious children, we should be better able to identify those factors that initially promote an avoidance approach to evaluative situations as well as those school encounters that reinforce this approach in academic situations. Of most important and generally lacking in the literature on the effects of test anxiety on children's learning and performance, are studies aimed at assessing techniques that reduce test anxiety. Although research suggests the prior success (vs. failure), game (vs. test) instructions, and provision of task-relevant strategies, for example, aid the performance of high-test-anxious children, little systematic research has been done to investigate various treatment effects or assess their long-term consequences.

ACKNOWLEDGMENTS

Thanks are expressed to Dr. Daniel Kaye, Dr. William J. Meyer, Dr. Beeman N. Phillips, and Dr. Irwin Sarason for reading and commenting on an earler version of this paper. Thanks are also due Edward Blatt, Susan Kaplan, and Dana Plude for their help in searching the literature.

REFERENCES

Alpert, R., & Haber, R. N. Anxiety in academic achievement situations. *Journal of Abnormal and Social Psychology,* 1960, *61,* 207–215.

Atkinson, J. W., & Litwin, G. H. Achievement motive and test anxiety conceived as motive to approach success and motive to avoid failure. *Journal of Abnormal and Social Psychology.* 1960, *60,* 52–63.

Bradshaw, G. D., & Gaudry, E. The effect of a single experience of success or failure on test anxiety. *Australian Journal of Psychology,* 1968, *20,* 219–223.

Brophy, J. E., & Good, T. L. *Teacher-student relationships: Causes and consequences.* New York: Holt, Rinehart & Winston, 1974.

Cohen, J. Multiple regression as a general data-analytic system. *Psychological Bulletin,* 1968, *70,* 426–443.

Doctor, B., & Altman, F. Worry and emotionality as components of test anxiety: Replication and further data. *Psychological Reports,* 1969, *24,* 563–568.

Dunn, J. A. Factor structure of the test anxiety scale for children. *Journal of Consulting Psychology,* 1964, *28,* 92.

Dunn, J. A. Stability of the factor structure of the test anxiety scale for children across age and sex groups. *Journal of Consulting Psychology,* 1965, *29,* 1897.

Dusek, J. B. Do teachers bias children's learning? *Review of Educational Research,* 1975, *45,* 661–684.

Dusek, J. B. The effects of labeling and pointing on children's selective attention. *Developmental Psychology,* 1978, *14,* 115–116.

Dusek, J. B., & O'Connell, E. *The bases of teacher's expectancies for student's performance.* Unpublished manuscript, Syracuse University, 1977.

Dusek, J. B., Kermis, M. D., & Mergler, N. L. Information processing in low- and high-test anxious children as a function of grade level and verbal labeling. *Developmental Psychology,* 1975, *11,* 651–652.

Dusek, J. B., Mergler, N. L., & Kermis, M. D. Attention, encoding, and information processing in low- and high-test-anxious children. *Child Development,* 1976, *47,* 201–207.

Dweck, C. S. Children's interpretation of evaluative feedback: The effect of social cues on learned helplessness. *Merrill-Palmer Quarterly,* 1976, *22,* 105–109.

Feld, S., & Lewis, J. Further evidence on the stability of the factor structure of the text anxiety scale for children. *Journal of Consulting Psychology,* 1967, *31,* 434.

Feld, S. C., & Lewis, J. The assessment of achievement anxieties in children. In C. P. Smith (Ed.), *Achievement-related motives in children.* New York: Russell-Sage, 1969.

Hagen, J. W. The effect of distraction on selective attention. *Child Development,* 1967, *38,* 685–694.

Hermans, H. J. M., ter Laak, J. J. F., & Maes, P. C. J. M. Achievement motivation and fear of failure in family and school. *Developmental Psychology,* 1972, *6,* 520–528.

Hill, K. T. Anxiety in the evaluative context. In W. Hartup (Ed.), *The young child* (Vol. 2). Washington, D.C.: National Association for the Education of Young Children, 1972.

Hill, K. T. Individual differences in children's response to adult presence and evaluative reactions. *Merrill-Palmer Quarterly,* 1976, *22,* 99–104.

Hill, K. T., & Eaton, W. O. The interaction of test anxiety and success–failure experiences in determining children's arithmetic performance. *Developmental Psychology,* 1977, *13,* 205–211.

Hill, K. T., & Sarason, S. B. The relation of test anxiety and defensiveness to test and school performance over the elementary school years: A further longitudinal study. *Monographs of the Society for Research in Child Development,* 1966, *31,* (2, Serial No. 104).

Lamb, M. E. Effects of stress and cohort on mother- and father-infant interaction. *Developmental Psychology,* 1976, *12,* 435–443. (a)

Lamb, M. E. *The role of the father in child development.* New York: Wiley, 1976. (b)

Lamb, M. E. Twelve-month-olds and their parents: Interaction in a laboratory playroom. *Developmental Psychology,* 1976, *12,* 237–244. (c)

Lamb, M. E. Father-infant and mother-infant interaction in the first year of life. *Child Development,* 1977, *48,* 167–181.

Lekarczyk, D. T., & Hill, K. T. Self-esteem, test anxiety, stress, and verbal learning. *Developmental Psychology,* 1969, *1,* 147–154.

Liebert, R., & Morris, L. W. Cognitive and emotional components of test-anxiety: A distinction and some initial data. *Psychological Reports,* 1967, *20,* 975–978.

McCoy, N. Effects of test anxiety on children's performance as a function of instructions and type of task. *Journal of Personality and Social Psychology,* 1965, *2,* 634–641.

Maccoby, E. E., & Hagen, J. W. Effects of distraction upon central versus incidental recall: Developmental trends. *Journal of Experimental Child Psychology,* 1965, *2,* 280–289.

Maccoby, E. E., & Jacklin, D. *The psychology of sex differences.* Stanford, Calif.: Stanford University Press, 1974.

Mandler, G., & Sarason, S. G. A study of anxiety and learning. *Journal of Abnormal and Social Psychology,* 1952, *47,* 166–173.

Manley, M. J., & Rosemier, R. A. Developmental trends in general and test anxiety among junior and senior high school students. *Journal of Genetic Psychology,* 1972, *120*(2), 219–226.

Morris, L. W., & Liebert, R. M. The relationship of cognitive and emotional components of test anxiety to physiological arousal and academic performance. *Journal of Consulting and Clinical Psychology,* 1970, *35,* 332–337.

Nottelmann, E. D., & Hill, K. T. Test anxiety and off-task behavior in evaluative situations. *Child Development,* 1977, *48,* 225–231.

Phillips, B. N. An analysis of causes of anxiety among children in school. Final report submitted to U.S.O.E. (Contract No. OE-5-10-012), 1966.

Phillips, B. N. *School stress and anxiety: Theory, research and intervention.* New York: Human Sciences Press, 1978.

Rhine, W. R., & Spaner, S. D. A comparison of the factor structure of the test anxiety scale for children among lower- and middle-class children. *Developmental Psychology,* 1973, *9,* 421–423.

Ruebush, B. K. Anxiety. In H. W. Stevenson, J. Kagan, & C. Spiker (Eds.), *NSSE sixty-second yearbook, Part I: Child psychology.* Chicago: University of Chicago Press, 1963.

Rist, R. G. Student social class and teacher expectations: The self-fulfilling prophecy in ghetto education. *Harvard Educational Review,* 1970, *40,* 411–451.

Sarason, I. G. Experimental approaches to test anxiety: Attention and the uses of information. In C. D. Spielberger (Ed.), *Anxiety: Current trends in theory and research* (Vol. 2). New York: Academic Press, 1972. (a)

Sarason, I. G. Test anxiety and the model who fails. *Journal of Personality and Social Psychology,* 1972, *28,* 410–413. (b)

Sarason, I. G. Anxiety and self-preoccupation. In I. G. Sarason & C. D. Spielberger (Eds.), *Stress and anxiety* (Vol. 2). Washington, D. C.: Hemisphere Publishing Company, 1975.

Sarason, I. G. The test anxiety scale: Concept and research. In C. D. Spielberger & I. G. Sarason (Eds.), *Stress and anxiety* (Vol. 5). Washington, D. C.: Hemisphere Publishing Company, 1978.

Sarason, I. G., & Ganzer, V. J. Anxiety, reinforcement and experimental instructions in a free verbal situation. *Journal of Abnormal and Social Psychology,* 1962, *65,* 300–307.

Sarason, I. G., Pederson, A. M., & Nyman, B. A. Test anxiety and the observation of models. *Journal of Personality,* 1968, *36,* 493–511.

Sarason, S. B. The measurement of anxiety in children: Some questions and problems. In C. D. Spielberger (Ed.), *Anxiety and behavior.* New York: Academic Press, 1966.

Sarason, S. B., Davidson, K. S., Lighthall, F. F., Waite, R. R., & Ruebush, B. K. *Anxiety in elementary school children.* New York: Wiley, 1960.

Sarason, S. B., Hill, K. T., & Zimbardo, P. G. A longitudinal study of the relation of test anxiety to performance on intelligence and achievement tests. *Monographs of the Society for Research in Child Development,* 1964, *29,* (7, Serial No. 98).

Spiegler, M. D., Morris, L. W., & Liebert, R. M. Cognitive and emotional components of test anxiety: Temporal factors. *Psychological Reports,* 1968, *22,* 451–456.

Spielberger, C. D. Theory and research on anxiety. In C. D. Spielberger (Ed.), *Anxiety and behavior.* New York: Academic Press, 1966.

Spielberger, C. D. Anxiety as an emotional state. In C. D. Spielberger (Ed.), *Anxiety: Current trends in theory and research* (Vol. 1). New York: Academic Press, 1972.

Spielberger, C. D., Anton, W. D., & Bedell, J. The nature and treatment of test anxiety. In M. Zuckerman & C. D. Spielberger (Eds.), *Emotions and anxiety: New concepts, methods, and applications.* New York: LEA-Wiley, 1975.

Spielberger, C. D., & Gorsuch, R. L. *Mediating processes in verbal conditioning.* Report to National Institute of Mental Health, 1966.

Spielberger, C. D., Gorsuch, R. L., & Lushene, R. E. *Manual for the State-Trait anxiety inventory.* Palo Alto, Calif.: Consulting Psychologist Press, 1970.

West, C. K., Lee, J. F., & Anderson, T. H. The influence of test anxiety on the selection of relevant from irrelevant information. *The Journal of Educational Research,* 1969, *63,* 51-52.

Wheeler, R. J., & Dusek, J. B. The effects of attentional and cognitive factors on children's incidental learning. *Child Development,* 1973, *44,* 253-258.

Wine, J. Test anxiety and direction of attention. *Psychological Bulletin,* 1971, *76,* 92-104.

6 Worry and Emotionality in Test Anxiety

Jerry L. Deffenbacher, Ph.D.
Colorado State University

Early research demonstrated that test performance of individuals reporting high levels of test anxiety is inferior to that of persons reporting low levels of test anxiety. For example, highly test-anxious persons score lower on classroom and intellectual aptitude tests (Alpert & Haber, 1960; Mandler & Sarason, 1952; I. Sarason, 1957, 1959a, 1963; Zweibelson, 1956) and have reduced reading comprehension (Lunneborg, 1964; Standford, Dember, & Standford, 1963). Experimental studies (e.g., I. Sarason, 1959b, 1961a, 1961b; Sarason, Mandler, & Craighill, 1952; Sarason & Palola, 1960) show that the performance of the highly test-anxious varies as a function of evaluative stress. When evaluative stress is low, the highly anxious perform as well as the less anxious. However, when evaluative stress is high, the highly anxious perform at levels lower than the low-anxious or than themselves when stress is low. The observed performance deterioration under evaluative stress, therefore, is not a simple artifact of ability because the highly anxious are not demonstrably less capable. Evaluative stress appears to elicit some type of "state anxiety" which interferes with the performance of the highly anxious. But what, specifically, is the nature of this anxiety. What is (are) the source(s) of interference? What do the highly anxious do under evaluative stress that they do not do when stress is reduced?

I. Sarason (1960) postulated that for highly test-anxious individuals evaluative stress elicits heightened atonomic arousal and a tendency to ruminate about possible failure. As the highly anxious respond with personalized, self-oriented responses, attention is directed away from the task, and performance suffers because a lower proportion of time and energy is devoted to the task itself.

Little of the early research, however, assessed or validated the nature of interfering anxiety as suggested by I. Sarason (1960). Instead, research mapped basic parameters which influenced the performance of subjects high and low in test anxiety, and performance differences among groups were attributed to elevations or reductions in state anxiety level. State test anxiety thus took on the part of an important intervening variable. It was treated as a univariate condition that interfered with performance as it increased. Rarely, however, was it operationally defined and measured concurrently with the performance differences for which it was to account.

Liebert and Morris (1967) countered both the trend toward lack of operationalism and treatment of state anxiety as a uniform state. They described a 10-item measure of state test anxiety and suggested that state test anxiety consisted of two conceptually different components—worry and emotionality. Worry refers to focusing of attention on concerns about performance, consequences of failure, negative self-evaluation, evaluation of one's ability relative to others, and the like. Emotionality, on the other hand, refers to the affective-physiological experience generated from increased autonomic arousal. Thus, for Liebert and Morris, interfering anxiety takes the form of heightened worry and/or emotionality, a distinction not unlike I. Sarason's (1960) differentiation between preoccupation with failure and autonomic arousal.

MEASUREMENT OF WORRY AND EMOTIONALITY

Two separate self-report scales have been developed to measure the worry and emotionality components of test anxiety. One is the 10-item Worry–Emotionality Inventory (Liebert & Morris, 1967). The other is the 16-item Inventory of Test Anxiety (Osterhouse, 1972).

The exact five items for each component of the Liebert–Morris scale may be found in Morris and Fulmer (1976). Worry items include: (1) not feeling confident about performance (2) worrying a great deal; (3) thinking how much brighter others are; (4) thinking about the consequencs of failure; and (5) feeling not as prepared as possible. Emotionality items include: (1) so nervous cannot remember facts; (2) heart beating fast; (3) upset stomach; (4) uneasy, upset feeling; and (5) feeling panicky. These items were developed from items on the Sarason–Mandler Test Anxiety Questionnaire. They were chosen on the basis of their general factor loadings (Gorsuch, 1966; Sassenrath, 1964) and further selected on the basis of 100% interjudge agreement regarding the dimension involved (Liebert & Morris, 1967). Items are rated on a 1–5 scale indicating how much the feeling, state, or condition applies to the person. The range of scores on each subscale thus varies from 5–25 with increasing scores indicating more worry or emotionality.

The Inventory of Test Anxiety was constructed in a manner similar to that of the Liebert–Morris Scale. The 10 items from the Liebert–Morris Scale were pooled with 11 others drawn from various test anxiety scales. Osterhouse then employed a similar interjudge procedure and eliminated five items, resulting in eight items each for worry and emotionality. This new worry scale contains, in addition to the five worry items from the Liebert–Morris Scale, items referring to worry about having enough time to complete the test, letting self and others down, and feeling the person could have done better. The emotionality scale is minus the uneasy, upset feeling item from the Liebert–Morris Scale and includes items referring to dryness of mouth, mind going blank, headache, and hands perspiring. These items are rated on the same 1–5 scale so that scores range from 8–40 with larger scores indicating greater worry or emotionality. A copy of the Inventory of Test Anxiety may be found in Osterhouse (1976).

The two short scales appear to have moderately high reliability. For the Inventory of Test Anxiety, split-half reliability was .92 (Osterhouse, 1972), and test–retest reliabilities over a 7-week period in a college classroom were .68 for emotionality and .72 for worry (Osipow & Kreinbring, 1971). Alpha coefficients for the Liebert–Morris Scale were .83 and .76 for emotionality and .68 and .69 for worry (Morris & Liebert, 1970) and were in the .79–.88 range for both scales in another study (Morris & Fulmer, 1976). Although no reported test–retest reliabilities were found for the Liebert–Morris Scale, the author has found reliabilities of .43 and .48 for worry and .49 and .52 for emotionality over 6-week intervals in the college classroom. These reliabilities may not seem high, but it should be remembered that they reflect measures of momentary "state" anxiety and are expected to fluctuate with the conditions related to any given exam.

CORRELATES OF WORRY AND EMOTIONALITY

It should be noted from the outset that the worry–emotionality distinction is a relative one because the two are intercorrelated. Table 6.1 summarizes studies reporting worry–emotionality correlations. Inspection of this table shows that worry and emotionality are positively correlated and that the correlations range from .55 to .76 when the situation involves evaluative stress. However, as is shown later, this degree of intercorrelation does not invalidate the distinction between the two factors.

Several studies (Doctor & Altman, 1969; Liebert & Morris, 1967; Morris & Liebert, 1970; Spiegler, Morris, & Liebert, 1968) have shown that worry was inversely related to performance expectations of high school and college students taking classroom exams. Emotionality, on the other hand, was negatively related to performance expectations in some samples (Doctor &

TABLE 6.1
Worry–Emotionality Correlations

Study	Situation	Worry–Emotionality r
Morris & Liebert (1973)	Experimental study involving threat of shock and ego-involving instructions	.23
Morris & Liebert (1970)	High school and college classroom examinations	.55 & .62
Morris & Perez (1972)	Experimental study involving performance on a reading test	.64
Deffenbacher (1978)	Experimental study involving high- and low-stress instructions and performance on difficult anagrams	.66
Deffenbacher (1977)	College students taking the Miller Analogies Test	.69
Deffenbacher (unpub-lished—see Table 6.2)	Five college classroom exams	.66-.76

Altman, 1969; Morris & Liebert, 1970; Spiegler, Morris, & Liebert, 1968) but unrelated in others (Liebert & Morris, 1967; Morris & Liebert, 1970; Spiegler, Morris, & Liebert, 1968). In all but one of the two samples in the Morris and Liebert (1970) study, worry correlated more negatively with performance expectations than emotionality.

A similar pattern of correlations has been found for the relationships of worry and emotionality to performance. For example, Morris and Liebert (1970) reported these relationships for high school and college students taking classroom exams. In the college sample, worry, but not emotionality, formed an inverse relationship with test performance, and the worry–performance relationship was stronger than the emotionality–performance relationship. In the high school sample, however, both worry and emotionality were inversely related to performance, and the strengths of the relationships did not differ. In both samples, worry and emotionality were significantly correlated with each other and consequently shared considerable variance. Partial correlation analyses on both samples revealed that when the common variance between worry and emotionality was controlled, worry was negatively correlated with test grades, but emotionality was no longer significantly related to test grades.

In five unpublished studies involving college students taking psychology exams, the author found results similar to those of the Morris and Liebert (1970) college sample (see Table 6.2 for a summary of correlations and partial correlations). As shown in the table, worry consistently correlated negatively with exam performance, whereas emotionality did on some occasions and not on others. Partial correlations demonstrated that when the effects of emotionality were partialed out, worry continued to form a significant negative correlation with performance. However, when worry was partialed out, emotionality was not significantly correlated with performance. This suggests that when the common variance is controlled, worry, but not emotionality, is significantly and negatively correlated with performance in college exams.

Doctor and Altman (1969) also found that students high on worry scored significantly lower on a college psychology final than did students low on worry. The relationship of emotionality and test performance, however, was more complex. At high levels of worry, emotionality was unrelated to test score, but at low levels of worry, low-emotionality subjects scored better than high-emotionality subjects.

Classroom examinations provide the opportunity for preparation and overlearning that may attenuate the effects of worry and emotionality on performance. Deffenbacher (1977), therefore, investigated the relationship of worry and emotionality to performance on the Miller Analogies Test, a test which is important because it is used for graduate admissions, but for which little preparation is possible. He found that both worry and emotionality were

TABLE 6.2
Correlations and Partial Correlations For Classroom Exams

Sample	Correlations			Partial Correlations	
	Performance–Worry	Performance–Emotionality	Worry–Emotionality	Performance–Worry Partialing Emotionality	Performance–Emotionality Partialing Worry
I ($n = 86$)	-.29**	-.07	.66***	-.33***	+.18
II ($n = 87$)	-.35***	-.18*	.75***	-.33***	+.13
III ($n = 83$)	-.26**	-.12	.75***	-.26*	+.11
IV ($n = 86$)	-.35***	-.26**	.76***	-.25*	+.02
V ($n = 77$)	-.36***	-.26*	.69***	-.25*	-.02

*$p < .05$ **$p < .01$ ***$p < .001$

negatively correlated with performance. However, when partial correlations were calculated, only worry continued to form a significant, negative relationship with performance on the Miller Analogies Test. Further analysis revealed a complex relationship among worry, emotionality, and performance. Worry was broadly related to performance; subjects high on worry solved fewer analogies than subjects low on worry (defined by a median split on the worry distribution). The effects of emotionality, however, varied with worry level. At low levels of worry (below the·median on the worry distribution), emotionality was unrelated to performance, but at high levels of worry (above the median on the worry distribution), high emotionality was debilitative. That is, the negative effects of emotionality were nested within the upper range of worry, whereas worry contributed more pervasively to the relationship of state test anxiety and performance.

Two other studies explored the relationships of worry and emotionality to performance. Morris and Perez (1972) found that worry, but not emotionality, was negatively correlated with reading test performance and that worry was correlated stronger with performance than emotionality. The author performed partial correlational analyses on their data and found that the partial correlation between worry and performance was negative (-.29) and was significant, z (74) = 2.62, $p < .01$, whereas the partial correlation between emotionality and performance was positive (.03) and not significant, z (74) = .26. In the other study (Morris & Liebert, 1969), worry and emotionality were employed in a design that manipulated level of stress through obvious and nonobvious timing and difficulty of items for the timed subtests for the Wechsler Adult Intelligence Scale (WAIS). Subject worry level was found to interact with timing and difficulty, e.g., subjects high on worry performed better in the untimed (lower stress) than in the timed condition (higher stress). The reverse was true for subjects low on worry; they performed better in the obvious timing condition than in the nonobvious timing condition. Emotionality level did not interact with difficulty or timing conditions and was unrelated to performance in this study.

The following consistent pattern of results emerges from the research reviewed in this section:

1. Worry and emotionality are significantly correlated.
2. Worry consistently forms a negative or inverse relationship with performance expectations and actual test performance.
3. The findings for emotionality are much more inconsistent and mixed. Emotionality was unrelated to performance expectations in three samples but related negatively in three other samples. Emotionality was either unrelated, related only within certain strata of worry, or negatively related to performance measures. Thus whether exploring the correlations with

performance or performance expectations, emotionality is not as consistently related to these as is worry.

4. Worry is the more important variable of the two, accounting for more variance in relationships with performance or performance expectations. Furthermore, studies controlling the common variance show that worry forms a negative correlation with performance, whereas emotionality no longer correlates significantly with performance.

This research exploring the correlates of worry and emotionality provides support for the distinction between the two. Although most anxiety scales include items of both a worry and emotionality nature, only worry consistently correlates negatively with test performance and performance expectations. This suggests that worry alone or at least most strongly is associated with deteriorated performance.

CUES ELICITING WORRY AND EMOTIONALITY

Morris and his colleagues (Morris & Fulmer, 1976; Spiegler, Morris, & Liebert, 1968) have postulated that worry and emotionality are two separate response classes. Although some stimuli would be expected to elicit both worry and emotionality, the two are thought to be elicited by different cues. Emotionality is postulated to be a classically conditioned autonomic-affective reaction to the cues associated with the start of a testing or evaluative situation. Emotionality would be elicited only by the actual presence of exam cues. Therefore, it would be expected to be at its greatest level just prior to and at the beginning of an exam and to dissipate over the course of the exam as attention was turned to the test itself. Emotionality should show its most marked elevations at the beginning of an exam and should drop off rather rapidly in a temporal gradient before and after the beginning of the exam. Worry, on the other hand, is conceived to be a cognitive-attentional response to cues of evaluation and possible failure. Worry, therefore, would be expected to remain at a relatively stable level in relation to a test or evaluative situation as long as the evaluative cues remained salient and no other information or experience altered the estimated degree of possible failure. Changes in evaluative input, either manipulated in the experimental design or inferred from changes in performance expectations, would be expected to increase or decrease worry level. Thus, worry should co-vary with external and/or internal cues relating to evaluation and possible failure, whereas emotionality should co-vary with the beginning of a test or with situations which refocus attention on these cues. Data which confirm these predictions would provide additional support for the worry–emotionality distinction.

Emotionality has been shown to vary as a function of temporal proximity to exams. For example, emotionality significantly increased from 5 days before an exam to the beginning of the examination (Spiegler, Morris, & Liebert, 1968) and decreased significantly over the course of the exam (Doctor & Altman,1969; Morris & Fulmer, 1976; Smith & Morris; 1976; Spiegler, Morris, & Liebert, 1968). Spiegler, Morris, and Liebert (1968) found that worry remained at a relatively stable level in relation to temporal distance from classroom exams. Doctor and Altman (1969) found that when very high levels of worry were included in the sample, small decreases in worry were found following the exam. In both of these studies (Doctor & Altman, 1969; Spiegler, Morris, & Liebert, 1968), however, changes in worry appeared to be primarily a function of changes in expectancy rather than merely the passage of time, as was the case for emotionality. That is, worry appeared to change as a function of the individual's cognitive reappraisal of the situation, whereas emotionality co-varied with temporal proximity to exams and peaked at the beginning.

Studies involving experimental manipulation of conditions have shown worry and emotionality to be responsive to different cue conditions. For example, Morris and Liebert (1969) demonstrated that worry increased as the difficulty of WAIS items increased but that emotionality was not affected. Morris and Liebert (1973) found that emotionality was somewhat responsive to threat of shock but not to verbal suggestions of failure. The reverse was true for worry. Worry was very susceptible to failure suggestions but not to threat of shock. In this study, had the two subscales been summed together (which is typical for many anxiety scales), the differential responsiveness of each would have been masked. Morris and Fulmer (1976) reported two studies which investigated the effects of item-by-item feedback regarding the correctness of response on worry and emotionality levels in college exams. In study 1, worry decreased with feedback, and emotionality was unaffected. In study 2, however, both worry and emotionality increased with feedback and with increased test importance (manipulated by having the test count as usual, only be able to help a student's grade, or have no impact on grade). Deffenbacher (1978) also found that both worry and emotionality varied with evaluative stress. High- and low-test-anxious subjects worked difficult anagrams under either high- or low-stress instructions. The high-anxiety–high-stress group reported significantly greater worry and emotionality than other groups.

These studies showed that worry level rose with conditions which increased the saliency of evaluation and possible failure, e.g., increased task difficulty (Morris & Liebert, 1969), item-by-item feedback on a very difficult test (Morris & Fulmer, 1976, study 2), suggestions of failure (Morris & Liebert, 1973), ego-involving instructions (Deffenbacher, 1978), and increased test importance (Morris & Fulmer, 1976, study 2). The only apparent exception to this pattern was the reduction of worry as a function of feedback in study 1 reported by Morris and Fulmer (1976). On closer inspection, however, this test was relatively easy. The feedback told subjects they were doing relatively better than expected and thereby reduced the perceived possibility of failure. This interpretation is supported by the fact that performance expectations improved significantly in this test. That is, worry decreased as the feedback experience reduced the uncertainty and saliency of evaluation. All of these studies, therefore, support the predictions that worry varies with cues signaling possible failure.

On the surface, the results regarding emotionality appear confusing. In three studies (Morris & Fulmer, 1976, study 1; Morris & Liebert, 1969, 1973), emotionality was not influenced by cues related to possible failure. In two others (Deffenbacher, 1978; Morris & Fulmer, 1976, study 2), emotionality increased with such cues. The explanation for these differing findings may lie in the nature of the tasks. Both studies in which significant elevations of emotionality were found involved very difficult tasks with clear feedback that the subjects were not doing well. In such situations, subjects may not remain absorbed in the task and may, therefore, periodically refocus on the test circumstances. This would reelicit emotionality and explain the elevation of emotionality in these studies. That is, when relatively poor performance is clear and certain, subject attention may occasionally shift to cues of the evaluative setting, rearousing emotionality.

In summary, to a considerable degree worry and emotionality are elicited by different conditions. Emotionality appears to be elicited by cues signaling the beginning of an exam or by situations which refocus attention on the cues of the examination setting. Worry appears to be a function of conditions which increase or decrease cues of possible failure.

WORRY AND EMOTIONALITY AS SOURCES OF INTERFERENCE

In the previous section, it was shown that worry is elicited by evaluative stressors and remains elevated throughout the exam unless cues of possible failure are removed or reduced. Emotionality, on the other hand, tends to decrease over the course of the test. It seems logical that a factor that remains elevated over time will have a greater probability of disrupting performance than one that dissipates with time on task. In order to outweigh the influence of worry, emotionality will have to have a greater, more debilitative impact at the beginning of the exam. This, however, does not appear to be the case.

A similar logic applies for the effects of worry and emotionality on preexam preparation. Because worry is significantly elevated prior to exams and emotionality is not, it is more likely that worry would interfere with preparation. Worry about possible failure would distract attention from learning and rehearsal and decrease performance as information and skills were not encoded and rehearsed appropriately.

Further evidence suggestive of greater interference due to worry comes from the correlational and partial correlational patterns described previously. Worry was consistently negatively correlated with performance, whereas emotionality was not. Furthermore, the partial correlations demonstrated that only worry was inversely related to performance when the common variance between worry and emotionality was controlled. It is unlikely that emotionality interferes significantly with performance because it fails to correlate with that with which it is supposed to interfere. Only worry consistently and negatively correlates with performance, suggesting it is a greater source of interference in the anxiety–performance relationship.

To this point, the arguments have been logical and inferential in nature. Greater supporting evidence would be found in direct statistical comparisons in the levels of worry and emotionality. Because the scales used to measure worry and emotionality contain the same number of items and are rated on the same rating scales, then the scale showing the greater elevation is likely to be measuring the factor contributing greater interference. In all studies reviewed, the means for worry have been larger than those for emotionality except for the condition employing threat of electric shock (Morris & Liebert, 1973) where emotionality was higher. Although none of the reported studies contained information sufficient to perform t tests for differences between correlated means, the author's research has shown worry level to be significantly greater than emotionality level. For example, in one college class of 55 students the mean for worry (10.53) was significantly greater than the mean for emotionality, (9.45), t (54) = 2.30, $p < .05$. Worry was also significantly higher than emotionality ($p < .001$) for students taking the Miller Analogies Test (Deffenbacher, 1977). Recently, Deffenbacher and Deitz (1978) found that on three separate college exams students high on test anxiety reported significantly more worry than emotionality ($ps < .001$). Deffenbacher (1978) also found that high-anxious subjects working under stressful, evaluative conditions experienced significantly greater worry and task-generated interference (a response category derived from drive theory measuring intrusive, task-produced competing responses) than emotionality ($ps < .001$). Thus, not only does worry appear to contribute greater interference than emotionality, but direct statistical comparisons show that worry is at significantly higher levels than emotionality and, more specifically, that highly anxious subjects facing evaluative stress experience more worry than emotionality. These results suggest that worry acts as a greater source of anxiety-related interference.[1]

OTHER EVIDENCE ON THE
IMPORTANCE OF WORRY

Several studies that do not employ the worry–emotionality distinction further point to worry as an important factor in test anxiety. For example, Feather (1963) found that self-rated worry was negatively related to performance on a problem-solving task. Highly anxious subjects also reported worrying more about how well they and others were doing while engaged in a digit symbol task (Mandler & Watson, 1966; Neale & Katahn, 1968). In addition, reports of thinking about other's performance correlated negatively with performance. Marlett and Watson (1968) found that highly anxious subjects spent more time worrying about their performance in a test-like avoidance task. More recently, Sarason and Stoops (1978) found that high-anxious subjects under achievement-oriented instructions tended to overestimate pretest waiting time and experience more cognitive distraction and drift of attention than high-anxious subjects under neutral conditions. Ganzer (1968) also found that highly anxious subjects working on a verbal learning task involving high-stress instructions emitted significantly more self-devaluative, apologetic statements than low-anxious subjects. Once again, we find that worry-like factors are elevated under evaluative stress and are inversely related to performance, suggesting that they may interfere with performance.

CONCLUSIONS AND CAUTIONS

Worry and emotionality are significantly correlated but should not be considered synonymous or equivalent constructs. They appear to be different response classes elicited by somewhat different conditions. Emotionality is elicited primarily by cues associated with the beginning of evaluation and peaks at the initiation of evaluation. Worry, on the other hand, is elicited by

---

[1]These comparisons raise an important logical issue which is sometimes overlooked in anxiety research. Sometimes it is assumed that if two scales are significantly intercorrelated, as are worry and emotionality, then they are measuring the same thing. For interference theories of anxiety, it is important to remember that correlation only implies increased predictability from knowledge of one variable to the other. It is the relative levels of the variables that have implication for the amount of interference due to those variables. Two scales might correlate .90 with each other, yet if the mean interference rating on the first is five times that of the second, then the factor measured by the first scale is much more likely to be a significant source of interference.

cues which make evaluation and possible failure salient and co-varies with input or feedback related to possible failure. In addition, worry and emotionality differ as sources of anxiety-related interference. In all studies involving evaluative stress, worry is at higher levels than emotionality. More specifically, highly trait-test-anxious individuals report significantly more worry than emotionality. That is, evaluative stress appears to elicit a tendency for the highly test-anxious to become preoccupied with worrisome cognitions and only secondarily with self-perceived affective-autonomic arousal. Of the two, worry is the greater, more important source of anxiety-related interference that in turn may account for the consistent finding that only worry correlates negatively with performance when the common variance between worry and emotionality is controlled.

Although there is considerable support for the validity of the worry–emotionality distinction, several cautions are in order.

1. Emotionality and physiological arousal should not be taken as the same thing. For example, Morris and Liebert (1970) found emotionality significantly related to physiological arousal, as measured by heart rate, in only one of two samples, and then the correlation was only .34. Furthermore, the heart-rate item from the emotionality scale was significantly correlated with heart rate in only one of the two samples. In both cases, self-report of emotionality was not highly correlated with at least this measure of physiological arousal. Some of the lack of relationship might be explained in terms of methodological problems and individual differences in physiological response patterns to stress, but it is unlikely that these factors alone would account for the low degree of interrelationship. Emotionality may relate more to the degree of awareness or attention paid to affective-autonomic arousal rather than to the level of arousal per se. Physiological arousal and emotionality may relate separately to experience and performance in evaluative settings. At some level, heightened physiological arousal may interfere directly with performance. Attention to physiological arousal (emotionality) may also interfere with performance as attention is directed to the arousal and away from the task.

2. Although this review has supported the validity of worry and emotionality as separate components of state test anxiety, they should not be considered the only ones. Physiological arousal has just been considered another possible factor. In addition, Deffenbacher (1978) suggested another factor, task-generated interference, defined as the tendency to become preoccupied with inefficient or irrelevant task-produced competing responses. It was found that worry, emotionality, and task-generated interference were all intercorrelated, but the highly anxious experiencing evaluative stress reported significantly more task-generated interference and worry than emotionality. Thus state anxiety appears anything but a uniform

state or condition. Worry, emotionality, task-generated interference, and physiological arousal may all be elements of state anxiety, and there may be more. One of the challenges of research in the area will be to map the factors, their interrelationships, their eliciting conditions, and their relative levels as sources of interference.

3. We should be very careful in generalizing findings from one situation to another. The levels of worry and emotionality, the strengths of correlations, and the form of worry–emotionality relationships have varied from study to study. For example, Deffenbacher (1977) found that both the absolute levels of worry and emotionality and the form of the worry–emotionality relationship for students taking the Miller Analogies Test as part of graduate admissions differed from those found for classroom exams (Doctor & Altman, 1969; Spiegler, Morris, & Liebert, 1968). For classroom tests, high levels of emotionality were detrimental within low but not high levels of worry (Doctor & Altman, 1969), whereas the reverse was true for students taking the Miller Analogies Test; emotionality was most debilitative within high levels of worry. Also, somewhat unexpectedly, students taking the Miller Analogies Test were significantly less worried and emotional than college students taking classroom exams. Therefore, conclusions about worry and emotionality must be based on a very careful empirical mapping of factors such as population, exam content, format and difficulty, test implications and importance, and the like.

4. Worry and emotionality should not automatically be considered separate elements of trait test anxiety. For example, Richardson, O'Neil, Whitmore, and Judd (1977) factor analyzed the Test Anxiety Scale and found that worry and emotionality items, except for the heart-rate item, factored together. This factor appeared to represent worry about oneself and one's performance and the physical–emotional consequences of such worry. The second factor appeared to reflect emotional distress but without worry for individuals who are noncompetitive and not highly achievement motivated. Thus, although worry and emotionality separate out as elements of state anxiety, they may cluster together as elements of trait test anxiety.

IMPLICATIONS OF WORRY AND EMOTIONALITY FOR THE TREATMENT OF TEST ANXIETY

In order to minimize overlap with other chapters, the material in this section is limited strictly to implications derived from the worry–emotionality distinction. Although the majority of studies reviewed were correlational in nature, they offer the following suggestions for the design of anxiety-reduction interventions:

1. Worry is elicited by evaluative stress, is a greater source of interference for the highly test-anxious, and accounts for more variance in the anxiety–performance relationship. This suggests that programs containing cognitive restructuring of worrisome thoughts and training in task-oriented self-instruction (e.g., Deffenbacher & Hahnloser, 1978; Goldfried, Linehan, & Smith, 1978; Holroyd, 1976) may hold considerable promise for the reduction of test anxiety.

2. Because worry is elevated several days prior to examinations, cognitive restructuring programs should be tailored to the preexamination period as well as the test-taking period itself. That is, cognitive restructuring interventions should give clients cognitive coping skills for both preparation and test-taking phases. This should lead to improved performance in two ways. First, intrusive worry would be reduced or removed during the preparation period, reducing avoidance behavior and improving the learning and rehearsal of material. Second, worry would be reduced during the exam so that worry does not interfere with the orderly recall and organization of skills and information.

3. Because emotionality interacts with worry level and proves debilitative at some worry levels (Deffenbacher, 1977; Doctor & Altman, 1969), interventions which add self-managed relaxation to cognitive restructuring (e.g., Deffenbacher & Hahnloser, 1978; Little & Jackson, 1974; Meichenbaum, 1972) may improve treatment effectiveness as skills for the reduction of heightened emotionality and/or physiological arousal are added.

4. Emotionality is most prevalent at the start of a test, suggesting that applied relaxation components might be cued most productively near the beginning of an exam. For example, students might apply self-managed relaxation while waiting for exams to be passed out rather than becoming preoccupied with worry about the exam.

In all, this review suggests that cognitive restructuring programs with applied relaxation components should hold substantial promise for reducing worry and emotionality that, in turn, should reduce affective discomfort and give the individual the greatest opportunity to demonstrate his/her skills and abilities.

Several treatment studies have tested differential predictions derived from the worry–emotionality literature. For example, Goldfried, Linehan, and Smith (1978) found that a cognitively oriented program reduced worry but not emotionality in a stressful analogue testing situation. The majority of the studies, however, fail to confirm the seemingly logical predictions of the worry–emotionality model. For example, Osterhouse (1972) predicted that high worry subjects would be more responsive to study skills intervention, whereas high emotionality subjects would be more affected by systematic desensitization. His data, however, did not support these predictions; both types of subjects responded more favorably to desensitization. Finger and Galassi (1977) reasoned that covert reinforcement of relaxation or cognitive coping skills would reduce emotionality and worry respectively but found that covert reinforcement of either skill reduced both worry and emotionality equally well. In our studies (Deffenbacher & Parks, 1979; Snyder & Deffenbacher, 1977), we found that relaxation as self-control, self-control desensitization, and traditional desensitization all reduced worry rather than emotionality in an evaluative analogue. In a more recent study (Deffenbacher, Mathis, & Michaels, 1979), however, we found both relaxation as self-control and a self-control variant of desensitization to reduce worry and emotionality. In one further study (Deffenbacher & Hahnloser, 1978), we compared a cognitively oriented, a relaxation-oriented, and a combined intervention, and again all three treatments reduced both worry and emotionality and did not differ significantly from one another. That is, across our studies and those of others, cognitively oriented and relaxation-oriented treatments do not reliably reduce worry and emotionality respectively as they theoretically should.

Because worry and emotionality are not differentially responsive to treatments theoretically designed to reduce them, Finger and Galassi (1977) suggested that the results fail to support and thereby weaken the worry–emotionality distinction. An alternative which is equally plausible is that the worry–emotionality distinction is valid, as suggested by this review, but that our treatment interventions are successful for reasons other than those derived from our theoretical models. It may be that relaxation-based interventions reduce worrisome cognitions and that cognitive restructuring reduces physiological arousal or, at least, the preoccupation with it. In other words, according to Lazarus and Davison (1971) "techniques may, in fact, prove effective for reasons that do not remotely relate to the theoretical ideas that gave birth to them [p. 199]."

REFERENCES

Alpert, R., & Haber, R. N. Anxiety in academic achievement situations. *Journal of Abnormal and Social Psychology*, 1960, *61*, 207–215.

Deffenbacher, J. L. Relationship of worry and emotionality to performance on the Miller Analogies Test. *Journal of Educational Psychology*, 1977, *69*, 191–195.

Deffenbacher, J. L. Worry, emotionality and task-generated interference in test anxiety: An empirical test of attentional theory. *Journal of Educational Psychology*, 1978, *70*, 248–254.

Deffenbacher, J. L., & Deitz, S. R. Effects of test anxiety on performance, worry, and emotionality in naturally occurring exams. *Psychology in the Schools*, 1978, *15*, 446–450.

Deffenbacher, J. L., & Hahnloser, R. M. *A comparison of cognitive restructuring and progressive relaxation in test anxiety reduction.* Unpublished manuscript, Colorado State University, 1978.

Deffenbacher, J. L., & Parks, D. H. A comparison of traditional and self-control systematic desensitization. *Journal of Counseling Psychology,* 1979, *26,* 93–97.

Deffenbacher, J. L., Mathis, H., & Michaels, A. C. Self-control procedures in the reduction of targeted and nontargeted anxieties. *Journal of Counseling Psychology,* 1979, *26,* 120–127.

Doctor, R. M., & Altman, F. Worry and emotionality as components of test anxiety: Replication and further data. *Psychological Reports,* 1969, *24,* 563–568.

Feather, N. T. The effect of differential failure on expectation of success, reported anxiety, and response uncertainty. *Journal of Personality,* 1963, *31,* 389–412.

Finger, R., & Galassi, J. P. Effects of modifying cognitive versus emotionality responses in the treatment of test anxiety. *Journal of Consulting and Clinical Psychology,* 1977, *45,* 280–287.

Ganzer, V. J. Effects of audience presence and test anxiety on learning and retention in a serial learning situation. *Journal of Personality and Social Psychology,* 1968, *8,* 194–199.

Goldfried, M. R., Linehan, M. M., & Smith, J. L. Reduction of test anxiety through cognitive restructuring. *Journal of Consulting and Clinical Psychology,* 1978, *46,* 32–39.

Gorsuch, R. L. The general factor in the text anxiety questionnaire. *Psychological Reports,* 1966, *19,* 308.

Holroyd, K. A. Cognition and desensitization in the group treatment of test anxiety. *Journal of Consulting and Clinical Psychology,* 1976, *44,* 991–1001.

Lazarus, A. A., & Davison, G. C. Clinical innovation in research and practice. In A. E. Bergin & S. L. Garfield (Eds.), *Handbook of psychotherapy and behavior change: An empirical analysis.* New York: John Wiley & Sons, 1971.

Liebert, R. M., & Morris, L. W. Cognitive and emotional components of test anxiety: A distinction and some initial data. *Psychological Reports,* 1967, *20,* 975–978.

Little, S., & Jackson, B. The treatment of test anxiety through attentional and relaxation training. *Psychotherapy: Theory, Research, and Practice,* 1974, *11,* 175–178.

Lunneborg, P. W. Relations among social desirability, achievement, and anxiety measures in children. *Child Development,* 1964, *35,* 169–182.

Mandler, G., & Sarason, S. B. A study of anxiety and learning. *Journal of Abnormal and Social Psychology,* 1952, *47,* 166–173.

Mandler, G., & Watson, D. L. Anxiety and the interruption of behavior. In C. D. Spielberger (Ed.), *Anxiety and behavior.* New York: Academic Press, 1966.

Marlett, N. J., & Watson, D. Test anxiety and immediate or delayed feedback in a test-like avoidance task. *Journal of Personality and Social Psychology,* 1968, *8,* 200–203.

Meichenbaum, D. H. Cognitive modification of test anxious college students. *Journal of Consulting and Clinical Psychology,* 1972, *39,* 370–380.

Morris, L. W., & Fulmer, R. S. Test anxiety (worry and emotionality) changes during academic testing as a function of feedback and test importance. *Journal of Educational Psychology,* 1976, *68,* 817–824.

Morris, L. W., & Liebert, R. M. Effects of anxiety on timed and untimed intelligence tests. *Journal of Consulting and Clinical Psychology,* 1969, *33,* 240–244.

Morris, L. W., & Liebert, R. M. Relationship of cognitive and emotional components of test anxiety to physiological arousal and academic performance. *Journal of Consulting and Clinical Psychology,* 1970, *35,* 332–337.

Morris, L. W., & Liebert, R. M. Effects of negative feedback, threat of shock, and level of trait anxiety on the arousal of two components of anxiety. *Journal of Counseling Psychology,* 1973, *20,* 321–326.

Morris, L. W., & Perez, T. L. Effects of test-interruption on emotional arousal and performance. *Psychological Reports,* 1972, *31,* 559–564.

Neale, J. M., & Katahn, M. Anxiety choice and stimulus uncertainty. *Journal of Personality,* 1968, *36,* 235–245.

Osipow, S. H., & Kreinbring, I. Temporal stability of an inventory to measure test anxiety. *Journal of Counseling Psychology,* 1971, *18,* 152–154.

Osterhouse, R. A. Desensitization and study-skills training as treatment for two types of test-anxious students. *Journal of Counseling Psychology,* 1972, *19,* 301–307.

Osterhouse, R. A. Group systematic desensitization of test anxiety. In J. D. Krumboltz & C. E. Thoresen (Eds.), *Counseling Methods.* New York: Holt, Rinehart & Winston, 1976.

Richardson, F. C., O'Neil, H., Whitmore, S., & Judd, W. A. Factor analysis of the Test Anxiety Scale. *Journal of Consulting and Clinical Psychology,* 1977, *45,* 704–705.

Sarason, I. G. Test anxiety, general anxiety and intellectual performance. *Journal of Consulting Psychology,* 1957, *21,* 485–490.

Sarason, I. G. Intellectual and personality correlates of test anxiety. *Journal of Abnormal and Social Psychology,* 1959, *59,* 272–275. (a)

Sarason, I. G. Relationship of measures of anxiety and experimental instructions to word association test performance. *Journal of Abnormal and Social Psychology,* 1959, *59,* 37–42. (b)

Sarason, I. G. Empirical findings and theoretical problems in the use of anxiety scales. *Psychological Bulletin,* 1960, *57,* 403–415.

Sarason, I. G. A note on anxiety, instructions, and word association performance. *Journal of Abnormal and Social Psychology,* 1961, *62,* 153–154. (a)

Sarason, I. G. The effects of anxiety and threat on the solution of a difficult task. *Journal of Abnormal and Social Psychology,* 1961, *62,* 165–168. (b)

Sarason, I. G. Test anxiety and intellectual performance. *Journal of Abnormal and Social Psychology,* 1963, *66,* 73–75.

Sarason, I. G., & Palola, E. G. The relationship of test and general anxiety, difficulty of task, and experimental instructions to performance. *Journal of Experimental Psychology,* 1960, *59,* 185–191.

Sarason, I. G., & Stoops, R. Test anxiety and the passage of time. *Journal of Consulting and Clinical Psychology,* 1978, *46,* 102–109.

Sarason, S. B., Mandler, G., & Craighill, P. G. The effect of differential instructions on anxiety and learning. *Journal of Abnormal and Social Psychology,* 1952, *47,* 561–565.

Sassenrath, J. M. A factor analysis of rating-scale items on the test anxiety questionnaire. *Journal of Consulting Psychology,* 1964, *28,* 371–377.

Smith, C. A., & Morris, L. W. Effects of stimulative and sedative music on cognitive and emotional components of anxiety. *Psychological Reports,* 1976, *38,* 1187–1193.

Snyder, A. L., & Deffenbacher, J. L. Comparison of relaxation as self-control and systematic desensitization in the treatment of test anxiety. *Journal of Consulting and Clinical Psychology,* 1977, *45,* 1202–1203.

Spiegler, M. D., Morris, L. W., & Liebert, R. M. Cognitive and emotional components of test anxiety: Temporal factors. *Psychological Reports,* 1968, *22,* 451–456.

Standford, D., Dember, W. N., & Standford, L. B. A children's forms of the Alpert-Haber achievement anxiety scale. *Child Development,* 1963, *34,* 1027–1032.

Zweibelson, I. Test anxiety and intelligence test performance. *Journal of Consulting Psychology,* 1956, *20,* 479–481.

7 Test Anxiety and Physiological Responding

Kenneth A. Holroyd
Margret A. Appel
Ohio University

Physiological arousal is regarded as one of the main components of anxiety together with cognitive and behavioral manifestations. Common sense suggests a strong and straightforward relationship between these components of anxiety. However, research indicates that the response components are poorly correlated with each other, contradicting commonly held notions that they are concordant. This finding has raised fundamental problems for research on anxiety. These problems have been discussed in reviews by Borkovec, Weerts, and Bernstein (1977), Hodges (1976), Lader and Marks (1971), Lang (1978), and Lang, Rice, and Sternbach (1972).

The present chapter focuses specifically on the physiological concomitants of test anxiety and the relationship of physiological measures to behavior and self-report in testing situations. In the first section of the chapter, empirical evidence associating test anxiety with physiological arousal in testing situations is evaluated. In the second section of the chapter, task requirements and the individual's coping activity are emphasized as determinants of physiological responding.

THE ROLE OF PHYSIOLOGICAL AROUSAL IN TEST ANXIETY

Theory

In the first attempt to differentiate test anxiety theory from general anxiety theory, Mandler and S. Sarason (1952) hypothesized that test anxiety consisted of both cognitive (e.g., feelings of inadequacy and helplessness, anticipation of punishment or loss of esteem) and physiological (autonomic arousal) components. They further suggested that these two types of responses are linked together as coeffects of a "learned anxiety drive." It was hypothesized that evaluative examination situations elicited higher levels of this anxiety drive from test-anxious individuals than from non-test-anxious individuals, and, as a result, higher levels of autonomic arousal and worry. Poor test performance was thought to result because the cognitive and autonomic responses elicited by the anxiety drive were incompatible with responses necessary for effective test performance.

Subsequent formulations have retained the consideration of both the autonomic and cognitive components of test anxiety. However, different theorists have made different assumptions about the role of these two types of responses. In particular, two different hypotheses about the relationship of physiological responding to test anxiety appear explicitly or implicitly in most of the theorizing in this area.

It is frequently assumed that massive and diffuse sympathetic arousal energizes the overt behaviors associated with anxiety and determines the experience of anxiety. Cannon (1915) originally made this assumption when he conceptualized fear as an emergency reaction involving sympathetic arousal in preparation for overt motor responding. Although this relationship between physiological arousal and anxiety is implicitly assumed by many investigators, it has been most explicitly stated by activation theorists (e.g., Duffy, 1962, 1972; Malmo, 1966). For example, Epstein (1972) argues that "almost all the phenomena attributed to anxiety are actually consequences of arousal [pp. 307–308]." The phenomenology of anxiety is assumed to result from high levels of physiological arousal, and the relationship between physiological arousal and behavioral efficiency is depicted as an inverted U-shaped function. Thus, test anxiety and the associated performance deficits could be expected to occur whenever sufficiently high levels of physiological arousal are elicited in examination situations.

This direct relationship between physiological arousal and anxiety is generally not explicitly stated within test anxiety theory. However, it is often tacitly assumed. For example, Spielberger, Anton, and Bedell (1976) have suggested that high levels of autonomic activity and feelings of apprehension (i.e., state anxiety) "cue-off" cognitive ruminations and "activate" error tendencies that disrupt performance. Spielberger et al. thus assume that autonomic arousal plays a central role in test anxiety, contributing to both the performance deficits and cognitive rumination associated with this condition. Other theorists (e.g., Wolpe, 1973) also appear to assume that test anxiety is a consequence of high levels of autonomic arousal in examination situations.

Other formulations of test anxiety assume that individual differences in test anxiety bear little relationship to individual differences in autonomic arousal. These theories emphasize the cognitive responses and not the autonomic activity elicited by testing situations (Mandler, 1972, 1975; I. Sarason, 1975, 1978; Wine, 1971, 1978). I. Sarason (1975) regards test anxiety as primarily a cognitive response characterized by feelings of helplessness, inadequacy, self-doubt, and self-blame. Mandler (1975) argues that it is this self-critical cognitive response—and not individual differences in autonomic arousal—that distinguishes test-anxious individuals from non-test-anxious individuals. Presumably, all students are aroused physiologically by examination situations, but only the test-anxious student is preoccupied with self-critical rumination. In a similar fashion, it has been argued that the performance deficits associated with test anxiety result from the attentional demands of self-critical rumination and not from high levels of autonomic arousal (Wine, 1971, 1978). Of course, cognitive rumination itself might elicit autonomic arousal (cf. Candland, 1977; I. Sarason, 1975). Nevertheless, these formulations raise the possibility that test anxiety may be unrelated to individual differences in autonomic arousal in examination situations.

Measures of peripheral autonomic and somatic activity are generally used to assess the physiological component of anxiety. Increases in tonic levels of autonomic activity are typically interpreted as increased sympathetic activity. Unfortunately, there are often major problems with such straightforward interpretations of psychophysiological data. Before discussing these problems, the evidence associating test anxiety with elevated tonic levels of physiological activity is reviewed.

Empirical Findings

Individuals typically show substantial increments in tonic levels of physiological activity when they are exposed to testing situations. A variety of peripheral autonomic, neurohormonal, musculoskeletal, and electrocortical measures have been shown to change significantly in response to examination stress (Bliss, Migeon, Branch, & Samuels, 1956; Frankenhaeuser, 1976; Leitch, 1973; Naliboff, Rickles, Cohen, & Naimark, 1976; Powell, Eisdorfer, & Bogdonoff, 1964; Schnore, 1959; Smith & Wenger, 1965; Tucker, Antes, Stenslie, & Barnhardt, 1978; Bistline, Shanahan, & Jaremko, 1976; Papsdorf, Jamieson, & Ghannam, 1978).[1]

Unfortunately, individual differences in test anxiety are rarely assessed in studies where tonic physiological responses to examination situations are evaluated. Therefore, most of this research provides no information about the

---

[1] Readers who are relatively unfamiliar with psychophysiological measures will find Hassett's (1978) primer to be an informative and entertaining introduction to the field. More detailed information on psychophysiological techniques and their application may be obtained from Brown (1967), Venables and Martin (1967), Greenfield and Sternbach (1972), and the journal, *Psychophysiology*.

role of these physiological changes in test anxiety and in the performance of test-anxious individuals. Relatively few studies have actually compared the autonomic responses of test-anxious and non-test-anxious subjects in laboratory examination situations.

In two of these studies (Holroyd, Westbrook, Wolf, & Badhorn, 1978; Montgomery, 1977), college students scoring in the upper quartile in the Test Anxiety Scale were identified as text-anxious, and students scoring in the lower quartile were regarded as non-test-anxious. Montgomery (1977) monitored heart rate during eight-second "anticipation periods" that were signaled by a warning tone and immediately preceded the presentation of anagram problems. Although text-anxious students reported higher levels of state anxiety than non-test-anxious students in an evaluative testing condition, there was no significant difference in average heart rate between the groups. Anagram performance did not differentiate the two groups.

Holroyd et al. (1978) continuously monitored heart rate and skin resistance in female college students working on difficult anagrams in an analogue examination situation. Both self-report and performance measures indicated that the examination situation successfully evoked evaluative anxiety in the test-anxious women. Test-anxious women reported substantially higher levels of state anxiety and worry and performed more poorly on the anagram problems than non-test-anxious women. However, differences in reported anxiety and test performance were not accompanied by corresponding differences in autonomic activity.

The autonomic responses of both test-anxious and non-test-anxious subjects to the examination situation are reproduced in Figure 7.1. All three autonomic measures were highly sensitive to the stress created by the examination situation. However, text-anxious and non-test-anxious subjects showed virtually identical changes in skin conductance level, spontaneous skin resistance responses, and heart rate in response to the analogue examination. These findings have recently been replicated in a sample that included both male and female subjects. Thus, the results are consistent in showing that test-anxious students were no more physiologically aroused in these testing situations than non-test-anxious students.

Additional information about the role of physiological activity in test anxiety is provided by studies reporting correlations between physiological responses to examination situations and trait measures of test anxiety. Bistline et al. (1976) found that muscle tension recorded from the forearm extensor increased in response to examination stress. However, these increases were unrelated to subject's scores on the Test Anxiety Scale. Darley and Katz (1973) found that elementary-school children showed higher heart rate when a difficult counting task was presented as a test than when it was presented as a "guessing game." However, scores on the Test Anxiety Scale for Children were not significantly correlated with heart rate. Finally,

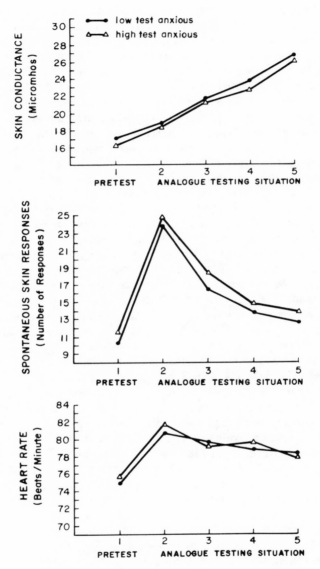

FIG. 7.1. Autonomic responding at pretest and during the analogue testing situation in 3-minute blocks (adapted from Holroyd et al., 1978).

Papsdorf et al. (1978) found that female college students receiving a desensitization-like treatment showed asymmetric reductions in skin temperature while imagining examination scenes. However, these temperature changes were unrelated to subjects' scores on the Test Anxiety Inventory. Although there are methodological factors in each of these studies that may account for the negative results, this research gives no indication that test anxiety is related to tonic changes in physiological activity.

When test anxiety has been assessed with state rather than trait measures, similar results have been obtained. In a well-known study, Morris and Liebert (1970) asked high school and college students to monitor their pulse rates and complete brief self-report measures of emotionality and worry immediately prior to an actual exam. Unfortunately, correlations between self-reported anxiety and pulse rate were influenced by the order in which these assessments were conducted. However, even when order was held constant, correlations tended to be small in magnitude and to vary across samples. When pulse rate was collected first, for example, the correlation between self-reported emotionality and pulse rate was .34 in one sample and −.03 in a second sample. Thus, no consistent relationship was observed between pulse rate and self-reported anxiety. Since pulse rate was also uncorrelated with test performance, Morris and Liebert suggested that actual autonomic activity is an independent dimension of test anxiety unrelated to self-report or performance measures. On the other hand, self-reports of both emotionality and worry were negatively correlated with test performance; this relationship appeared to be stronger for worry than for emotionality.

Results obtained by Holroyd et al. (1978) parallel those reported by Morris and Liebert. Tonic levels of electrodermal activity and heart rate during the analogue examination situation were not significantly correlated with self-reports of state anxiety, worry, or anagram performance. Furthermore, these correlations did not change noticeably when the three autonomic measures were combined to provide an overall index of autonomic activity nor when only the standard score for the most responsive measure was used for each subject in order to take individual response stereotypy into account (see, e.g., Engel, 1972; Hodges, 1976). Moreover, there was no evidence of a curvilinear relationship between autonomic response and anagram performance when subjects were categorized into high, medium, and low physiological responders on the basis of the z score of their most responsive autonomic measure.[2] However, self-reports of state anxiety and worry were negatively related to test performance and, consistent with Morris and Liebert's (1970)

---

[2]The notion that behavioral efficiency and tonic physiological activity are related in an inverted U-shaped fashion has intuitive appeal. However, there is little supporting evidence in the psychophysiological literature (see, e.g., Wilkinson, El-Beheri, & Gieseking, 1972).

findings, this relationship was stronger for worry than for state anxiety (e.g., $r = -.80$ and $r = -.27$, respectively, among high-test-anxious women).

The anxiety scales used in the foregoing studies contain items referring to both autonomic arousal and worry. When self-report measures containing only items referring to autonomic activity have been used, statistically significant (albeit weak) relationships have been obtained between self-reported autonomic activity and actual autonomic activity in examination situations. However, individual differences in test anxiety and test performance appear to be correlated only with the report of autonomic activity and to be unrelated to actual levels of autonomic activity.

Mandler (Mandler & Kremen, 1958; Mandler, Mandler, & Uviller, 1958) first examined the relationship between reports of autonomic activity (i.e., somatic anxiety) and actual autonomic activity in examination situations two decades ago. Perceptions of autonomic activity were assessed with the Autonomic Perception Questionnaire (APQ). This measure requires subjects to rate the extent to which their experience of anxiety is accompanied by perceptions of seven types of bodily changes: heart rate, perspiration, temperature, respiration, gastrointestinal sensations, muscle tension, and facial flushing. Actual autonomic response to the analogue examination situation was indexed with a composite measure combining five autonomic responses: heart rate, skin resistance, respiration, face temperature, and blood pressure.

Mandler et al. (1958) rank ordered college students scoring at the extremes of the APQ on the basis of their autonomic response to an analogue testing situation. The results suggested that differences in reported somatic anxiety were associated with differences in actual autonomic reactivity. However, the extent to which subjects accurately estimated their actual autonomic response was also assessed by comparing subjects' rank order on the APQ with their rank order on each of the five autonomic response measures. The results of this analysis suggested that subjects reporting high levels of somatic anxiety significantly overestimated their actual autonomic reactivity.

In a second study (Mandler & Kremen, 1958), self-reports of somatic activity and autonomic reactivity during the examination situation were found to be weakly correlated, both when perceptions of somatic activity were assessed with the APQ ($r = .22$) and when they were assessed during an interview immediately following the examination ($r = .25$ and $r = .26$). Reports of somatic anxiety were also associated with poor vocabulary test performance. However, the latter relationship appeared to result from the overestimation of autonomic activity and not from the effects of actual autonomic activity on performance. When the tendency to overestimate autonomic activity was assessed, overestimation was not only found to be associated with poor test performance ($r = -.27$), but the relationship was enhanced when actual autonomic activity was held constant ($r = -.45$). Actual autonomic activity was unrelated to test performance. In discussing these results, Mandler and Kremen (1958) suggested that preoccupation with autonomic activity interferes with effective test performance, but actual autonomic responsivity "is not a necessary antecedent to preoccupation with autonomic events [p. 395]."

Unpublished data from our laboratory are consistent with those of Mandler and his colleagues. Reports of both somatic and cognitive anxiety were collected during an analogue examination from students scoring in the top and bottom quartile of the Test Anxiety Scale. Somatic anxiety was assessed with a state form of the APQ. Cognitive anxiety was assessed with a similar measure requiring subjects to rate the extent to which they experienced worry and cognitive disruption during the anagram task. Heart rate and skin resistance were monitored continuously during the analogue testing situation. Test-anxious students reported substantially higher levels of both somatic and cognitive anxiety than non-test-anxious students, even though no actual differences in tonic autonomic activity were evident. Statistically significant, but small, correlations were obtained between reports of somatic anxiety and actual autonomic activity. Cognitive anxiety was not correlated with autonomic activity but was correlated with performance. Autonomic activity and performance were uncorrelated.

In contrast to the foregoing findings, Thayer (1967, 1970) has reported substantial corelations (r's up to .62) between a general self-report measure of activation-deactivation and tonic levels of autonomic activity during a laboratory testing situation. However, since Thayer's self-report measure of activation is not correlated with reports of text anxiety (Wittmaier, 1974), these findings provide no evidence of a relationship between test anxiety and autonomic arousal. To the contrary, they suggest that tonic levels of autonomic activity may be associated with some global self-report measures but not with reports of anxiety.

In the aforementioned studies, no relationship was observed between test anxiety and autonomic arousal. Test-anxious individuals consistently reported greater anxiety and more symptoms of autonomic arousal in testing situations than non-test-anxious individuals. However, when actual tonic levels of autonomic activity were monitored, test-anxious and non-test-anxious individuals could not be reliably distinguished on the basis of their physiological responses. Deficits in test performance were similarly associated with reports of worry, and, to a lesser extent, reports of arousal, but they were unrelated to actual autonomic arousal. Individual differences in test anxiety were thus unrelated to individual differences in autonomic arousal during examinations.

One way of interpreting these findings is to assume that the symptoms of test anxiety and associated performance deficits result more from the way autonomic feedback is perceived and appraised than from high levels of autonomic arousal per se. Cognitive processes that have been loosely conceptualized in terms of attention (Wine, 1971, 1978), labeling (Schachter, 1964), self-awareness (Liebling & Shaver, 1973), and self-preoccupation (I. Sarason, 1975) may mediate self-reports of anxiety. Performance differences may also be influenced by the individual's cognitive response to autonomic feedback. For example, test-anxious individuals may interpret symptoms of autonomic arousal as confirming their inability to cope with examination situations; consequently, they may not initiate or persist with coping efforts when they are confronted with signs of autonomic arousal. However, the same symptoms of autonomic activity may lead the non-test-anxious individual to mobilize active coping efforts (cf. Bandura, 1977). These information-processing differences and their consequences for performance deserve greater attention in future studies.

A recent study by Carver and Blaney (1977) is instructive in this regard. Using college students who were moderately fearful of snakes, they found that autonomic feedback signaling arousal elicited task-relevant coping activity from individuals who were confident of their ability to cope with a stressful task, and avoidance responses from individuals who doubted their ability to cope. For example, subjects who were confident of their ability to approach a snake reported that they paid more attention to their goal during an approach task when they heard false feedback indicating that they were aroused (heart rate increase) than when the feedback indicated that they were not aroused (heart rate constant). Doubtful subjects showed the opposite response: They reported paying less attention to their goal when feedback indicated that they were aroused than when it indicated that they were not aroused. Thus, the same feedback facilitated the coping efforts of confident subjects and debilitated the coping efforts of doubtful subjects.

PHYSIOLOGICAL EFFECTS OF
COPING AND TASK DEMANDS

The discussion up to this point has focused on the use of tonic physiological measures to index the individual's state of overall arousal. However, viewing autonomic measures as only indices of intensity of arousal or emotional reaction to stress ignores the physiological effects of other variables such as stimulus characteristics, task requirements, and the subject's efforts to cope with situational demands. All of these variables interact to produce the observed physiological outcome.

The Lacey Hypothesis

J. Lacey (1959, 1967) is one theorist who has proposed that the interpretation of physiological data take into consideration aspects of the situation other than those that relate to the intensity of reaction. In particular, he emphasizes that the intended aim of behavior affects physiological responding so that different stimulus situations produce different patterns of response. In some situations, measures will co-vary to some extent, producing what appears to be a general arousal pattern. In other arousing situations, physiological measures will dissociate or change in opposite directions.

The existence of specific physiological patterns associated with particular behavioral processes is demonstrated in the Laceys' (B. Lacey & J. Lacey, 1974; J. Lacey, 1967) work on environmental intake and rejection. Environmental intake refers to situations where the individual intends to pay attention to external events, such as looking at flashing lights, listening to auditory stimuli, or anticipating a signal. Environmental rejection refers to the individual's intention to ignore or reject environmental events during tasks involving mental work or cognitive elaboration, or when subjected to painful stimulation. The two situations are differentiated by heart rate and blood pressure changes. Phasic heart rate deceleration and blood pressure decreases are related to intake, whereas heart rate accelerates and blood pressure increases during rejection. On the other hand, skin conductance does not differentiate the two situations, showing an increase in both.

The intake–rejection patterns observed by the Laceys are congruent with Sokolov's (1963) description of the orienting reflex (OR) and the defensive reflex (DR) which are also differentiated by cardiovascular responses (Graham & Clifton, 1966). In addition to heart rate and blood pressure changes, intake or orienting is accompanied by cephalic vasodilation and digital and forearm vasoconstriction, whereas rejection or defense is associated with cephalic and digital vasoconstriction and forearm vasodilation (Frese & Kotses, 1975; Sokolov, 1963; Williams, Bittker, Buchsbaum, & Wynne, 1975).[3]

---

[3]There is a controversy concerning the relationship of somatic measures, such as respiration and muscle tension, to the cardiac decelerations observed in intake situations. Results have been variable, with studies showing increases, decreases, or no change in somatic measures concomitant with phasic cardiac deceleration. Readers who wish to pursue this topic are referred to Elliott (1972, 1974), J. Lacey and B. Lacey (1974), and Obrist, Howard, Lawler, Galosy, Meyers, & Gaebelein (1974).

The basic intake–rejection patterns have been replicated in numerous studies, and their interaction with stimulus parameters and task requirements has been investigated. Task difficulty and stimulus characteristics, such as intensity, novelty, and information value, affect the magnitude of the observed responses (Coles & Duncan-Johnson, 1975; Graham & Clifton, 1966; Higgins, 1971; B. Lacey & J. Lacey, 1974; Tursky, Schwartz, & Crider, 1970). In complex tasks, the physiological pattern observed depends on the specific nature of the stimulus and task demands. When the experimental situation evokes both decelerative and accelerative activity, the resulting physiological response may indicate summation of demands by showing no change or small and variable accelerations and decelerations (see examples in B. Lacey & J. Lacey, 1974), or it may lead to a polyphasic waveform with both accelerative and decelerative components.

A study by Kahneman, Tursky, Shapiro, & Crider (1969) illustrates the seemingly contradictory results that may occur when an experimental task evokes a divided response set by combining demands for external attention and internal problem solving. In the Kahneman et al. study, heart rate accelerated, rather than showing the expected deceleration, when subjects were ostensibly paying attention to the presentation of digits to be transformed. Tursky et al. (1970) explained this contradictory finding by suggesting that subjects were simultaneously attending to digits and performing the transformation because the transformation instructions preceded the digit series. When instructions were given after presentation of digits, Tursky et al. found the expected deceleration during intake and acceleration during cognitive processing.

Certain response requirements, such as verbalization or rating instructions, may lead to similar summation effects. Campos and Johnson (1966, 1967) and Edwards and Alsip (1969) found that when verbalization instructions were given, subjects showed cardiac acceleration while viewing visual stimuli. Hare (1972) found cardiac acceleration and cephalic and digital vasoconstriction when subjects were required to rate visual stimuli. When subjects merely looked at the stimuli or made a simple motor response to the stimuli, cardiac deceleration, cephalic vasodilation, and digital vasoconstriction were observed. Hare suggested that rating (and by analogy, verbalization) requirements led subjects to engage in analysis and appraisal of the stimuli while viewing them. This resulted in the physiological pattern associated with cognitive processing offsetting the attentional pattern.

A polyphasic waveform produced by combination of task demands is observed in reaction time tasks. The typical cardiac response in a signaled reaction time task is a triphasic one of acceleration after the warning stimulus, followed by deceleration prior to the respond signal, and acceleration during response (Obrist, Webb, & Sutterer, 1969). The acceleration during the response has been related to motor behavior or to homeostatic recovery (Jennings & Wood, 1977). The deceleration seems to be related to attentional demands and response requirements (Coles & Duncan-Johnson, 1975; Higgins, 1971; Jennings, Averill, Opton, & Lazarus, 1970; Jennings & Wood, 1977). The role of the initial acceleration is less clear and had been attributed to various factors including: anticipation of a motor response (Jennings et al., 1970); a reflection of the energy requirements of the anticipated task (Chase, Graham, & Graham, 1968); momentary increases in somatic activity, such as postural changes (Obrist, 1976); or a reflection of information-processing or decision-making activity related to the significance of the warning stimulus (Coles & Duncan-Johnson, 1975; Higgins, 1971).

The Laceys (J. Lacey & B. Lacey, 1974) suggest that cardiac deceleration has performance consequences for tasks requiring attention to the environment. They present data indicating significant, but low, positive correlations between the amount of foreperiod cardiac deceleration and speed of reaction time. The relationship had been frequently replicated (e.g., Connor & Lang, 1969; Jennings & Wood, 1977; Obrist et al., 1969). Also Schell and Catania (1975) found greater decelerations on hit trials than on miss trials for subjects performing a visual detection task.

The Laceys (J. Lacey & B. Lacey, 1974) suggest that cardiac acceleration also has implications for performance. In line with this suggestion, some investigators (e.g., Connor & Lang, 1969; Higgins, 1971) have found a relationship between foreperiod acceleration and reaction time. Jennings (1971) found that children's heart rates during cognitive tasks increased proportionally with higher levels of cognitive functioning, independently of level of arousal or motivation. Blatt (1961) demonstrated that efficient problem-solvers had higher and more variable cardiac rates than inefficient subjects while working on the John–Rimoldi Problem-Solving Apparatus. In addition, when cardiac rates were time-locked to problem-solving responses, the rates were found to be elevated at crucial points in the problem-solving process, that is, when sufficient information was available, when shifting from analysis to synthesis, and at solution.

Application to Test Anxiety. In a design based on the formulations of the Laceys, Montgomery (1977) tested the hypothesis that differences in attention deployment between high- and low-test-anxious subjects (e.g., Wine, 1971) would be reflected in the cardiac waveform. An anagram task was presented to the subjects in a format similar to a reaction time task. At the beginning of every trial, subjects heard a warning tone that signaled the start of an 8-sec anticipation period at the end of which an anagram problem was exposed visually for 500 msec. Subjects were tested under either a nonstress or an evaluation-stress condition.

Sec-by-sec cardiac responses during the anticipation period are presented in Figure 7.2. In the nonstress condition, there were no differences in the

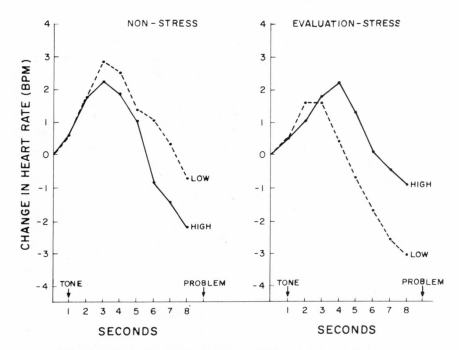

FIG. 7.2.   Phasic heart rate responses of high-test-anxious and low-test-anxious subjects in nonstress and evaluative-stress conditions (adapted from Montgomery, 1977).

waveform of the high- and low-anxiety groups. However, in the evaluation-stress condition, low-anxiety subjects showed less initial acceleration and more preproblem deceleration than high-anxiety subjects. Montgomery interpreted this finding as suggesting greater attentional control by low-anxiety subjects.

Cardiovascular Differentiation of Coping

Processes like intake and rejection may be viewed as coping responses, and, indeed, Montgomery suggested that the results of his experiment reflect differences in coping. Specifically, the attentional adjustment of the low-anxiety group in the stress condition was seen as a coping response to the discriminative stimuli provided by the cues of the anticipation period. High-anxiety subjects, on the other hand, did not show this differential adjustment to the stress condition as compared to the nonstress condition.

Coping processes may be reflected in both the amount and pattern of physiological responding. For example, Hare (1973) demonstrated that subjects with no fear of spiders showed an intake or orienting pattern of cardiac deceleration and cephalic vasodilation to pictures of spiders. In contrast, subjects who reported fear of spiders showed a defensive or rejection pattern of cardiac acceleration and cephalic vasoconstriction. There was a tendency for fearful subjects to give skin conductance responses which were larger and more resistant to habituation, but this result was not significant. Hare interpreted the cardiovascular responses as coping responses facilitating either attention to or tuning out of stimulation.

Hare (Hare, Frazelle, & Cox, 1978) has further suggested that different physiological response systems may reflect different aspects of the coping process. In anticipation of an aversive tone, high-psychopathy prison inmates showed larger increases in heart rate and smaller increases in skin conductance than did low-psychopathy inmates. Hare interpreted the anticipatory activity of the more psychopathic inmates as indicating the operation of an efficient coping mechanism (reflected in cardiac acceleration) and inhibition of fear arousal (reflected in electrodermal activity). The cardiac acceleration was assumed to be related to active attempts to cope with the aversive sensory input, whereas the electrodermal activity was seen as an index of how successful the coping attempts were. Similar results have been obtained by Averill and Rosenn (1972) and Averill, O'Brien, and DeWitt (1977) in comparisons of vigilant and nonvigilant college students.

Obrist (1976; Obrist, Gaebelein, Teller, Langer, Grignolo, Light, & McCubbin, 1978) has suggested that the degree of control subjects feel they have in coping with stressful events affects physiological reactivity. Obrist et al. (1978) evaluated the influence of several experimental conditions in which subjects had varying opportunities to control stressors. The cardiovascular measures of heart rate, slope of the carotid pulse wave, and systolic blood pressure showed greater change when subjects had some degree of control (or thought they did) than when they had no control over stressors or when they achieved easy mastery of experimental tasks.

Coping may change over time in stressful situations. Physiological responding can be expected to reflect the course of time changes in coping. For example, Williams, Poon, Thompson, and Marsh (1974) found that all subjects showed increases in forearm blood flow associated with internal cognitive processing in an easy learning task. On the other hand, subjects had varying degrees of success in learning a difficult task. Successful subjects showed increased forearm blood flow. However, subjects who failed showed continued forearm blood flow decrease.

The aforementioned studies indicate that cardiovascular responses are sensitive to coping processes. In addition, Hare et al.'s (1978) results suggest that the effectiveness of coping in some situations may be assessed physiologically by electrodermal activity. The different coping strategies which test-anxious and non-test-anxious individuals use in evaluative situations may be reflected in physiological responding. If these specific behavior-physiology relationships can be identified, our understanding of test anxiety would be enhanced.

Electrodermal Differentiation of Coping

Considerable psychophysiological research has been devoted to differentiation of psychological processes by means of cardiovascular measures. There is also a small body of data which suggests that electrodermal measures can be used in this manner. Two distinctions which are particularly relevant to anxiety research are those based on a differentiation between skin conductance level and conductance response frequency and between fast and slow recovery limbs of the skin conductance response.

Katkin (1965) hypothesized a differentiation based on electrodermal level and electrodermal frequency. In a study using threat of shock, Katkin noted that the experimental manipulations had different effects on skin resistance level and nonspecific skin resistance responses. Conductance increased and number of responses increased during the stressor. Responses decreased in a subsequent rest period, but conductance level continued to increase. Katkin suggested that the divergence of the two measures was related to an interview interposed between the shock threat and rest periods. He hypothesized that electrodermal response frequency reflects emotional processes, whereas level reflects nonemotional cognitive processes.

Kilpatrick (1972) tested Katkin's hypothesis in a study in which psychological stress (an evaluative testing situation) was used rather than physical threat (shock). After stress inductance, skin conductance response frequency increased, but conductance level was not affected. Conductance level increased during a cognitive task and remained high during a subsequent rest period. No response frequency data were presented for the task period, but they were at a low value in the subsequent rest period. Kilpatrick interpreted his data as supporting the hypothesis that electrodermal level reflects cognitive activity and electrodermal frequency reflects stress.

Drawing on this research, Davidson (1978; Davidson & Schwartz, 1976; Davidson, Davison, & Freedland, 1977) suggested that separate components of the electrodermal response might be sensitive to cognitive rumination or worry and to autonomic emotional arousal. He hypothesized that cognitive rumination would be primarily reflected in skin resistance level and autonomic arousal in skin resistance responses. If distinct physiological correlates of cognitive rumination and autonomic emotional arousal can, in fact, be identified, psychophysiological research may help clarify the role of cognitive processes in anxiety. In particular, this physiological distinction would provide a method for systematically investigating the relationship between cognitive and autonomic responding in test anxiety.

Edelberg (1970, 1972) has suggested that the recovery limb of the skin conductance response might also provide information about subjects' coping activity. He identified two recovery limb components: a slow one associated with sweating and a fast one associated with sweat reabsorption.

Faster recovery occurred during attentional and cognitive tasks. Slower recovery occurred during relaxation periods, during cold pressor exposure, and after shock threat. Edelberg interpreted steeper recovery limbs to reflect mobilization for goal-directed activity, whereas slower recovery rates were associated with defensive processes or the absence of goal orientation. Recovery limbs discriminated the two situations in the absence of differences in arousal as measured by skin conductance level, response frequency, or response amplitude. Thus, electrodermal recovery promised to be a sensitive measure of anxiety-related responses (cf. Borkovec et al., 1977).

Although there is no doubt that electrodermal activity is sensitive to stress, recent research suggests that interpretations of different electrodermal measures as indices of different psychological processes should be made with caution. Failure to take measurement problems into consideration may lead to spurious results. Bundy (1977; Bundy & Fitzgerald, 1975; Bundy & Mangan, 1979) suggests that different electrodermal responses reflect a single underlying process rather than different, independent processes. He argues that data suggesting independence occurs because of nonlinear time-dependent relationships based on skin hydration effects, not because the measures are associated with different psychological events. For example, increases in conductance level may be an artifact of having an electrolyte on the skin for a period of time or of frequent, closely spaced electrodermal responding. Both previous electrodermal activity and the electrolytic medium used for recording may increase the hydration of the skin. Bundy and Mangan (1979) demonstrated that the apparent dissociation of measures observed by Katkin (1965) was an artifact of high conductance levels due to the length of time the electrodes were on the skin: When new electrodes were applied, both conductance level and response frequency decreased in the final rest period.

In addition to effects on conductance level, increased skin hydration resulting from previous electrodermal activity also leads to increases in response recovery rate. Bundy and Fitzgerald (1975) demonstrated that the faster recovery observed by Edelberg (1970, 1972) in goal-oriented tasks could be explained by previous electrodermal activity rather than by the nature of the stimuli. Edelberg and Muller (1977) confirmed Bundy's suggestion that recovery is influenced by skin hydration and also noted that fast recovery occurred not with little sweat, but when there was considerable surface sweat. According to Edelberg, rather than qualitative differences in electrodermal measures, the basic variable to be measured to index sympathetic activity should be hydration of the skin or total sweat output.

Bundy and Edelberg's research has obvious significance for the interpretation of studies using electrodermal measures, especially when there is apparent dissociation of measures. Changes in one electrodermal measure cannot be interpreted independently of time effects and the effects of activity in other electrodermal measures. For example, increases in skin conductance level across a session may be due to the effects of the electrolyte rather than reflecting cognitive activity or worry. Similarly, rather than reflecting differences in psychological processes, differences between groups in conductance level may be due to more stimulus-elicited responding in one group than another if the time between stimuli is insufficient to allow for reabsorption of sweat.

An example of apparent dissociation of electrodermal measures is found in the Holroyd et al. 1978) data presented in Figure 7.1. Skin conductance level increased across the session, whereas nonspecific skin conductance response frequency decreased. Rather than reflecting an increase in cognitive activity and a decrease in emotional arousal, the dissociation is probably more parsimoniously interpreted as due to hydration effects on conductance level. Across trials, the subjects habituated to the situation, an effect demonstrated by decreases in both electrodermal response frequency and heart rate.

Other Response Systems

Research on the psychophysiology of anxiety has focused primarily on autonomic and somatic activity. Relatively little interest has been shown in electrocortical and neuroendocrine responses. Although these latter measures have yet to be used in test anxiety research, some related findings are noteworthy.

Recent interest in the patterning of cortical activity has been generated by the finding that specific cognitive tasks elicit identifiable patterns of cortical activation (e.g., Davidson, 1978). For example, it has been suggested that emotional responding may be mediated by the right hemisphere (e.g., Schwartz, Davidson, & Maer, 1975; Tucker et al., 1978) and verbal worry or rumination may be mediated by the left hemisphere (Davidson & Schwartz, 1976). It has also been suggested that "averaged" EEG measures such as contingent negative variation may provide methods for distinguishing cognitive activity and emotional responding (Cohen, 1974; Froehlich, 1978; Tecce, 1972). Although no definitive statements can be made about these measures at this point, initial results suggest that measures of cortical activation will play a larger role in future anxiety research.

Neurohormonal response profiles may also reflect coping activity in stressful situations (Mason, 1974, 1975). However, the findings in this area that appear of greatest relevance to test anxiety research have focused exclusively on sympathetic-adrenal medullary system activity as reflected in urinary adrenaline levels. Johansson, Frankenhaeuser, and Magnusson (1973) have reported that adrenaline secretion is positively correlated with intelligence test performance, academic achievement, and teacher ratings of adjustment in children. Adrenaline secretion has also been positively related to performance in laboratory testing situations (e.g., Frankenhaeuser & Anderson, 1974; Johansson & Frankenhaeuser, 1973). Although neuroticism scores appear to be associated with low levels of adrenaline secretion (Johansson & Frankenhaeuser, 1973), the relationship between adrenaline secretion and anxiety remains unclear. If relationships between adrenaline secretion, academic achievement, and test performance are replicable, the role of adrenaline secretion in test anxiety will deserve attention.

SUMMARY

This chapter focused on the physiological concomitants of test anxiety. Empirical evidence associating test anxiety with physiological arousal was reviewed first. It is often at least tacitly assumed that individual differences in test anxiety are associated with individual differences in tonic levels of autonomic and somatic activity during examinations. However, available evidence suggests that there may be no relationship between test anxiety and tonic physiological activity. Cognitive responses to autonomic feedback may play a more important role in text anxiety than individual differences in tonic autonomic activity.

In addition to providing indices of arousal, physiological measures are influenced by other aspects of the individual's interaction with the environment. Therefore, psychophysiological methods may provide unique information about the test-anxious individual's efforts to cope with examination stress. Selected relationships between physiological and psychological processes were illustrated for cardiovascular and electrodermal measures.

REFERENCES

Averill, J. R., O'Brien, L., & DeWitt, G. W. The influence of response effectiveness on the preference for warning and on psychophysiological stress reactions. *Journal of Personality*, 1977, *45*, 395-418.

Averill, J. R. & Rosenn, M. Vigilant and nonvigilant coping strategies and psychophysiological stress reactions during the anticipation of stress. *Journal of Personality and Social Psychology*, 1972, *23*, 128-141.

Bandura, A. Self-efficacy: Toward a unifying theory of behavioral change. *Psychological Review*, 1977, *84*, 191-215.

Bistline, J., Shanahan, F., & Jaremko, M. *An analogue study of the cognitive, physiological, and behavioral components of test anxiety.* Unpublished manuscript, University of Richmond, 1976.

Blatt, S. J. Patterns of cardiac arousal during complex mental activity. *Journal of Abnormal and Social Psychology*, 1961, *63*, 272-282.

Bliss, E. L., Migeon, C. J., Branch, C. H., & Samuels, L. T. Reaction of the adrenal cortex to emotional stress. *Psychosomatic Medicine*, 1956, *18*, 56-76.

Borkovec, T. D., Weerts, T. C., & Bernstein, D. A. Assessment of anxiety. In A. R. Ciminero, K. S. Calhoun, & H. E. Adams (Eds.), *Handbook of behavioral assessment*. New York: Wiley, 1977.

Brown, C. C. (Ed.). *Methods in psychophysiology*. Baltimore: Williams & Wilkins, 1967.

Bundy, R. S. *Electrodermal activity as a unitary phenomenon*. Paper presented at the meeting of the Society for Psychophysiological Research, Philadelphia, October 1977.

Bundy, R. S., & Fitzgerald, H. E. Stimulus specificity of electrodermal recovery time: An examination and reinterpretation of the evidence. *Psychophysiology*, 1975, *12*, 406–411.

Bundy, R. S., & Mangan, S. M. Electrodermal indices of stress and cognition: Possible hydration artifacts. *Psychophysiology*, 1979, *16*, 30-33.

Campos, J. J., & Johnson, H. J. The effects of verbalization instructions and visual attention on heart rate and skin conductance. *Psychophysiology*, 1966, *2*, 305-310.

Campos, J. J., & Johnson, H. J. The effect of affect and verbalization instructions on directional fractionation of autonomic response. *Psychophysiology*, 1967, *3*, 285-290.

Candland, D. K. The persistent problem of emotion. In D. K. Candland, J. P. Fell, E. Keen, A. I. Leshner, & R. M. Tarpy (Eds.), *Emotion*. Monterey, Calif.: Brooks/Cole, 1977.

Cannon, W. B. *Bodily changes in pain, hunger, fear, and rage*. New York: Appleton-Century-Crofts, 1915.

Carver, C. S., & Blaney, P. H. Avoidance behavior and perceived arousal. *Motivation and Emotion*, 1977, *1*, 61–73.

Chase, W. G., Graham, F. K., & Graham, D. T. Components of HR response in anticipation of reaction time and exercise tasks. *Journal of Experimental Psychology*, 1968, *76*, 642–648.

Cohen, J. Cerebral psychophysiology: The contingent negative variation. In R. F. Thompson & M. M. Patterson (Eds.), *Bioelectric recording techniques. Part B. Electroencephalography and human brain potentials*. New York: Academic Press, 1974.

Coles, M. G. H., & Duncan-Johnson, C. C. Cardiac activity and information processing: The effects of stimulus significance, and detection and response requirements. *Journal of Experimental Psychology: Human Perception and Performance*, 1975, *1*, 418–428.

Connor, W. H., & Lang, P. J. Cortical slow-wave and cardiac rate responses in stimulus orientation and reaction time conditions. *Journal of Experimental Psychology*, 1969, *82*, 310-320.

Darley, S. A., & Katz, I. Heart rate changes in children as a function of test versus game instructions and test anxiety. *Child Development*, 1973, *44*, 784–789.

Davidson, R. J. Specificity and patterning in biobehavioral systems: Implications for behavior change. *American Psychologist*, 1978, *33*, 430–436.

Davidson, R. J., Davison, G. C., & Freedland, E. *Psychophysiological specificity and the self-regulation of cognitive and somatic anxiety*. Paper presented at the International Conference on Biofeedback and Self-control, Tuebingen, Germany, November 1977.

Davidson, R. J., & Schwartz, G. E. The psychobiology of relaxation and related states: A multi-process theory. In D. I. Mostofsky (Ed.), *Behavior control and modification of physiological activity*. New York: Prentice-Hall, 1976.

Duffy, E. *Activation and behavior*. New York: Wiley, 1962.

Duffy, E. Activation. In N. S. Greenfield & R. A. Sternbach (Eds.), *Handbook of psychophysiology*. New York: Holt, Rinehart & Winston, 1972.

Edelberg, R. The information content of the recovery limb of the electrodermal response. *Psychophysiology*, 1970, *6*, 527–539.

Edelberg, R. Electrodermal recovery rate, goal-orientation, and aversion. *Psychophysiology*, 1972, *9*, 512–520.

Edelberg, R., & Muller, M. *The status of the electrodermal recovery measure: A caveat*. Paper presented at the meeting of the Society for Psychophysiological Research, Philadelphia, October 1977.

Edwards, D. C., & Alsip, J. E. Intake–rejection, verbalization, and affect: Effects on heart rate and skin conductance. *Psychophysiology*, 1969, *6*, 6–11.

Elliott, R. The significance of heart rate for behavior: A critique of Lacey's hypothesis. *Journal of Personality and Social Psychology,* 1972, *22,* 398–409.

Elliott, R. The motivational significance of heart rate. In P. A. Obrist, A. H. Black, J. Brener, & L. V. DiCara (Eds.), *Cardiovascular psychophysiology: Current issues in response mechanisms, biofeedback, and methodology.* Chicago: Aldine, 1974.

Engel, B. T. Response specificity. In N. S. Greenfield & R. A. Sternbach (Eds.), *Handbook of psychophysiology.* New York: Holt, Rinehart & Winston, 1972.

Epstein, E. The nature of anxiety with emphasis on its relationship to expectancy. In C. D. Spielberger (Ed.), *Anxiety: Current trends in theory and research* (Vol. 2). New York: Academic Press, 1972.

Frankenhaeuser, M. The role of peripheral catecholamines in adaption to understimulation and overstimulation. In G. Serban (Ed.), *Psychopathology of Human Adaption.* New York: Plenum Press, 1976.

Frankenhaeuser, M., & Anderson, K. Note on interaction between cognitive and endocrine functions. *Perceptual and Motor Skills,* 1974, *38,* 557–558.

Frese, F. K., & Kotses, H. Cardiovascular measures of mental effort. *Psychophysiology,* 1975, *12,* 226–227.

Froehlich, W. D. Stress, anxiety, and the control of attention: A psychophysiological approach. In C. D. Spielberger & I. G. Sarason (Eds.), *Stress and anxiety* (Vol. 5). Washington, D.C.: Hemisphere, 1978.

Graham, F. K., & Clifton, R. K. Heart-rate change as a component of the orienting response. *Psychological Bulletin,* 1966, *65,* 305–320.

Greenfield, N. S., & Sternbach, R. A. (Eds.). *Handbook of psychophysiology.* New York: Holt, Rinehart & Winston, 1972.

Hare, R. D. Response requirements and directional fractionation of autonomic responses. *Psychophysiology,* 1972, *9,* 419–427.

Hare, R. D. Orienting and defensive responses to visual stimuli. *Psychophysiology,* 1973, *10,* 453–464.

Hare, R. D., Frazelle, J., & Cox, D. N. Psychopathy and physiological responses to threat of an aversive stimulus. *Psychophysiology,* 1978, *15,* 165–172.

Hassett, J. *A primer of psychophysiology.* San Francisco: Freeman, 1978.

Higgins, J. D. Set and uncertainty as factors influencing anticipatory cardiovascular responding in humans. *Journal of Comparative and Physiological Psychology,* 1971, *74,* 272–283.

Hodges, W. F. The psychophysiology of anxiety. In M. Zuckerman & C. D. Spielberger (Eds.), *Emotions and anxiety: New concepts, methods, and applications.* Hillside, N.J.: Lawrence Erlbaum Associates, 1976.

Holroyd, K. Westbrook, T., Wolf, M., & Badhorn, E. Performance, cognition and physiological responding in test anxiety. *Journal of Abnormal Psychology,* 1978, *87,* 442–451.

Jennings, J. R. Cardiac reactions and different developmental levels of cognitive functioning. *Psychophysiology,* 1971, *8,* 433–450.

Jennings, J. R., Averill, J. R., Opton, E. M., & Lazarus, R. S. Some parameters of heart rate change: Perceptual versus motor task requirements, noxiousness, and uncertainty. *Psychophysiology,* 1970, *7,* 194–212.

Jennings, J. R., & Wood, C. C. Cardiac cycle time effects on performance, phasic cardiac responses and their intercorrelation in choice reaction time. *Psychophysiology,* 1977, *14,* 297–307.

Johansson, G., & Frankenhaeuser, M. Temporal factors in sympatho-adrenomedullary activity following acute behavioral activation. *Biological Psychology,* 1973, *1,* 63–73.

Johansson, G., Frankenhaeuser, M., & Magnusson, D. Catecholamine output in school children as related to performance and adjustment. *Scandinavian Journal of Psychology,* 1973, *14,* 20–28.

Kahneman, D., Tursky, B., Shapiro, D., & Crider, A. Pupillary, heart rate, and skin resistance changes during a mental task. *Journal of Experimental Psychology*, 1969, *79*, 164–167.

Katkin, E. S. Relationship between manifest anxiety and two indices of autonomic response to stress. *Journal of Personality and Social Psychology*, 1965, *2*, 324–333.

Kilpatrick, D. G. Differential responsiveness of two electrodermal indices to psychological stress and performance of a complex cognitive task. *Psychophysiology*, 1972, *9*, 218–226.

Lacey, B. C., & Lacey, J. I. Studies of heart rate and other bodily processes in sensorimotor behavior. In P. A. Obrist, A. H. Black, J. Brener, & L. V. DiCara (Eds.), *Cardiovascular psychophysiology: Current issues in response mechanisms, biofeedback, and methodology.* Chicago: Aldine, 1974.

Lacey, J. I. Psychophysiological approaches to the evaluation of psychotherapeutic process and outcome. In E. A. Rubinstein & M. P. Perloff (Eds.), *Research in psychotherapy.* Washington, D. C.: American Psychological Association, 1959.

Lacey, J. I. Somatic response patterning and stress: Some revisions of activation theory. In M. H. Apley & R. Trumbull (Eds.), *Psychological stress.* New York: Appleton-Century-Crofts, 1967.

Lacey, J. I., & Lacey, B. C. On heart rate responses and behavior: A reply to Elliott. *Journal of Personality and Social Psychology*, 1974, *30*, 1–18.

Lader, M., & Marks, I. *Clinical anxiety.* London: Heineman, 1971.

Lang, P. J. The psychophysiology of anxiety. In H. Akiskal (Ed.), *Psychiatric diagnosis: Exploration of biological criteria.* New York: Spectrum, 1978.

Lang, P. J., Rice, D. G., & Sternbach, R. A. The psychophysiology of emotion. In N. S. Greenfield & R. A. Sternbach (Eds.), *Handbook of psychophysiology.* New York: Holt, Rinehart & Winston, 1972.

Leitch, C. J. Effects of test anxiety on short term and long term recall under the Cr/ncr and A-F grade conditions and on potassium ion secretion (Doctoral dissertation, University of Utah, 1973). *Dissertation Abstracts International*, 1973, *34*, 1258B–1259B. (University Microfilms No. 73-20, 149).

Liebling, B. A., & Shaver, P. Evaluation, self-awareness and task performance. *Journal of Experimental Social Psychology*, 1973, *9*, 297–306.

Malmo, R. B. Studies of anxiety: Some clinical origins of the activation concept. In C. D. Spielberger (Ed.), *Anxiety and behavior.* New York: Academic Press, 1966.

Mandler, G. Comments on Dr. Sarason's paper. In C. D. Spielberger (Ed.), *Anxiety: Current trends in theory and research* (Vol. 2). New York: Academic Press, 1972.

Mandler, G. *Mind and emotion.* New York: Wiley, 1975.

Mandler, G., & Kremen, J. Autonomic feedback: A correlational study. *Journal of Personality*, 1958, *26*, 388–399.

Mandler, G., Mandler, J. M., & Uviller, E. T. Autonomic feedback: The perception of autonomic activity. *Journal of Abnormal and Social Psychology*, 1958, *56*, 367–373.

Mandler, G., & Sarason, S. B. A study of anxiety and learning. *Journal of Abnormal and Social Psychology*, 1952, *47*, 166–173.

Mason, J. W. Specificity in the organization of neuroendocrine response profiles. In P. Seeman & G. Brown (Eds.), *Frontiers of neurology and neuroscience research.* Toronto: University of Toronto Press, 1974.

Mason, J. W. Clinical psychophysiology: Psychoendocrine mechanisms. In M. Reiser (Ed.), *American handbook of psychiatry* (Vol. 4). New York: Basic Books, 1975.

Montgomery, G. K. Effects of performance evaluation and anxiety on cardiac response in anticipation of difficult problem solving. *Psychophysiology*, 1977, *14*, 251–257.

Morris, L. W., & Liebert, R. M. Relationship of cognitive and emotional components of test anxiety to physiological arousal and academic performance. *Journal of Consulting and Clinical Psychology*, 1970, *35*, 332–337.

Naliboff, B. D., Rickles, W. H., Cohen, M. J., & Naimark, R. S. Interactions of marijuana and induced stress: Forearm blood flow, heart rate, and skin conductance. *Psychophysiology,* 1976, *13,* 517–522.

Obrist, P. A. The cardiovascular-behavioral interaction—as it appears today. *Psychophysiology,* 1976, *13,* 95–107.

Obrist, P. A., Gaebelein, C. J., Teller, E. S., Langer, A. W., Grignolo, A., Light, K. C., & McCubbin, J. A. The relationship among heart rate, carotid dP/dt, and blood pressure in humans as a function of the type of stress. *Psychophysiology,* 1978, *15,* 102–115.

Obrist, P. A., Howard, J. L., Lawler, J. E., Galosy, R. A., Meyers, K. A., & Gaebelein, C. J. The cardiac-somatic interaction. In P. A. Obrist, A. H. Black, J. Brener, & L. V. DiCara (Eds.), *Cardiovascular psychophysiology: Current issues in response mechanisms, biofeedback, and methodology.* Chicago: Aldine, 1974.

Obrist, P. A., Webb, R. A., & Sutterer, J. R. Heart rate and somatic changes during aversive conditioning and a simple reaction time task. *Psychophysiology,* 1969, *5,* 696–723.

Papsdorf, J. D., Jamieson, J. L., & Ghannam, J. H. *Asymmetric finger temperature response to test anxiety imagery.* Unpublished manuscript, University of Michigan, 1978.

Powell, A. H., Jr., Eisdorfer, C., & Bogdonoff, M. D. Physiologic response patterns observed in a learning task. *Archives of General Psychiatry,* 1964, *10,* 192–195.

Sarason, I. G. Anxiety and self-preoccupation. In I. G. Sarason & C. D. Spielberger (Eds.), *Stress and anxiety* (Vol. 2). Washington, D.C.: Hemisphere, 1975.

Sarason, I. G. The Test Anxiety Scale: Concept and research. In C. D. Spielberger & I. G. Sarason (Eds.), *Stress and anxiety* (Vol. 5). New York: Halsted, 1978.

Schachter, S. The interaction of cognitive and physiological determinants of emotional state. In P. H. Leiderman & D. Shapiro (Eds.), *Psycho-biological approaches to social behavior.* Stanford: Stanford University Press, 1964.

Schell, A. M., & Catania, J. The relationship between cardiac activity and sensory acuity. *Psychophysiology,* 1975, *12,* 147–151.

Schnore, M. M. Individual patterns of physiological activity as a function of task differences and degree of arousal. *Journal of Experimental Psychology,* 1959, *58,* 117–128.

Schwartz, G. E., Davidson, R. J., & Maer, F. Right-hemisphere lateralization for emotion in the human brain: Interactions with cognition. *Science,* 1975, *190,* 286–290.

Smith, D. B., & Wenger, M. A. Changes in autonomic balance during phasic anxiety. *Psychophysiology.* 1965, *1,* 267–271.

Sokolov, E. N. *Perception and the conditioned reflex.* New York: Macmillan, 1963.

Spielberger, C. D., Anton, W. D., & Bedell, J. The nature and treatment of test anxiety. In M. Zuckerman & C. D. Spielberger (Eds.), *Emotions and anxiety: New concepts, methods, and applications.* Hillsdale, N.J.: Lawrence Erlbaum Associates, 1976.

Tecce, J. J. Contingent negative variation (CNV) and psychological processes in man. *Psychological Bulletin,* 1972, *77,* 73–108.

Thayer, R. E. Measurement of activation through self-report. *Psychological Reports,* 1967, *20,* 663–678.

Thayer, R. E. Activation states as assessed by verbal report and four psychophysiological variables. *Psychophysiology,* 1970, *7,* 86–94.

Tucker, D. M., Antes, J. R., Stenslie, C. E., & Barnhardt, T. M. Anxiety and lateral cerebral function. *Journal of Abnormal Psychology,* 1978, *87,* 380–383.

Tursky, B., Schwartz, G. E., & Crider, A. Differential patterns of heart rate and skin resistance during a digit-transformation task. *Journal of Experimental Psychology,* 1970, *83,* 451–457.

Venables, P. H., & Martin, I. (Eds.). *A manual of psychophysiological methods.* New York: Wiley, 1967.

Wilkinson, R. T., El-Beheri, S., & Gieseking, C. C. Performance and arousal as a function of incentive, information load, and task novelty. *Psychophysiology,* 1972, *9,* 589–599.

Williams, R. B., Jr., Bittker, T. E., Buchsbaum, M. S., & Wynne, L. C. Cardiovascular and neurophysiologic correlates of sensory intake and rejection. I. Effects of cognitive tasks. *Psychophysiology*, 1975, *12*, 427–433.

Williams, R., Poon, L., Thompson, L., & Marsh, G. Forearm bloodflow (FBF) response differences occurring during success and failure on a pattern learning task. *Psychophysiology*, 1974, *11*, 234.

Wine, J. Test anxiety and direction of attention. *Psychological Bulletin*, 1971, *76*, 92–104.

Wine, J. D. Anxiety and direction of attention. In H. W. Krohne & L. Laux (Eds.), *Achievement, stress, and anxiety*. Washington, D.C.: Hemisphere, 1978.

Wittmaier, B. C. Test anxiety, mood, and performance. *Journal of Personality and Social Psychology*, 1974, *29*, 664–669.

Wolpe, J. *The practice of behavior therapy* (2nd ed.). New York: Pergamon Press, 1973.

III
CLINICAL AND EDUCATIONAL APPLICATIONS

8

Behavioral Interventions for Alleviating Test Anxiety: A Methodological Overview of Current Therapeutic Practices

George J. Allen
Maurice J. Elias
Susan F. Zlotlow
University of Connecticut

Test anxiety has proven to be a useful target construct for investigating basic behavior change processes as well as a clinical problem deserving attention in its own right. Clinical and laboratory advances have enabled us to cope with and ultimately exploit artifactual influences that we were formerly ignorant of and have extended our knowledge of the methodological trade-offs inherent in therapy outcome research. This chapter surveys the variety of therapeutic strategies used to alleviate test anxiety in terms of methodology and outcome and suggests areas needing further empirical exploration. Our goal is not to criticize individual investigations but rather to draw conclusions about current treatment practices that transcend specific studies, many of which are likely to contain some methodological shortcomings. Following Campbell (1969), we believe that the emergence of consistent trends constitutes strong validity evidence so long as identical specific confoundings are not repeatedly found across the contributing investigations.

AN OVERVIEW OF CURRENT
TREATMENT PRACTICES

Our review encompasses 49 investigations of therapeutic manipulations aimed at alleviating test anxiety in college students. We have arbitrarily excluded: (1) investigations previously reviewed by Allen (1972); (2) single-subject case studies (Bruno & McCullough, 1973; Delprato & DeKraker, 1976; Meyer, 1975; Russell & Sipich, 1973, 1974); (3) studies directed at populations other than college students (Andrews, 1971; Deffenbacher &

Rivera, 1976; Harris & Trujillo, 1975; Little & Jackson, 1974; Mann, 1972; Mann & Rosenthal, 1969); and (4) process studies not directly relevant to outcome (Fisher, 1977; Friedman & Dies, 1974).

Table 8.1 provides descriptive information about the 49 studies, which are presented alphabetically within year of publication. The "Subjects" column describes the number of participants/number of dropouts and any formal criteria used in selection. The "Therapists" column describes therapist characteristics, with *A* or *NA* indicating that possible effects of multiple therapists on outcome were either assessed or not assessed. Specific therapeutic operations are summarized in the "Treatment Groups" column, preceded by two letters designating mode of treatment presentation and format of therapy. *L* indicates that therapy was presented by a live therapist, and *A* indicates use of an automated procedure (e.g., tape recordings, videotapes, study counseling manuals, etc.). *G* or *I* designates that therapy was conducted with groups or individuals, respectively. Under "Time," the number of sessions is followed by the length of time per session (italicized minutes represent the total duration of treatment across all sessions). The final two columns list respective self-report and performance measures used to assess outcome. A question mark indicates that the pertinent information was unavailable in the published report.

The table provides considerable information about the current status of therapeutic endeavors. Willingness to participate in treatment was a universal selection criterion. Therapy in all 49 investigations was conducted with volunteers; more restrictive criteria for inclusion were employed in 22 studies. A high degree of self-reported test anxiety was the most frequently used screening criterion, with the Test-Anxiety Scale (I. Sarason, 1957; 1972), Test Anxiety Behavioral Scale (Suinn, 1969b), and Anxiety Achievement Test (Alpert & Haber, 1960) being used in 8, 5, and 5 studies, respectively. Grade point average was used in only two investigations (Anton, 1976; McReynolds & Church, 1973). Thus, within constraints imposed by the volunteer status of participants, therapy has been directed toward a heterogeneous population of college students.

Attrition rates could be determined in 33 studies (in some cases by analyzing the degrees of freedom reported). Percentage of dropouts ranged from 0% (in 13 studies) to 28%, with attrition averaging 7.5%. Failure to complete treatment tended to be highest in studies that employed self-administered treatments (Allen, 1973; Beneke & Harris, 1972). The former found dropouts to have achieved lower scores on a pretherapy course examination, whereas the latter reported no differences on pretreatment grades. Other than this, very little is known about the personal characteristics of early terminators.

The impact of the therapist has been largely ignored by test anxiety researchers. Single therapists were employed in 15 studies whereas over 30%

of the investigations provided no information about therapists. Graduate students were found to be serving as therapists twice as frequently as Ph.D.-level personnel. Although multiple therapists were employed in 19 of the 49 investigations, possible interactions between therapist attributes and differential outcome were examined statistically in six studies (Aponte & Aponte, 1971; Calef, Calef, Sundstrom, Jarrett, & Davis, 1974; Goldfried, Linehan, & Smith, 1978; Holroyd, 1976; Horne & Matson, 1977; Osterhouse, 1972) and mentioned anecdotally by Smith and Nye (1973). No reliable therapist differences were reported in any of these studies. Although tempting, it is obviously premature to conclude that therapist characteristics do not mediate outcome, given the paucity of studies examining such interactions.

In terms of treatment modality, a decided preference exists for live therapist contact (in 67% of the studies) over automated procedures. In seven studies that contained combinations of live and automated treatments, one (Taylor, 1971) favored live, one (Anton, 1976) favored automated, and the remainder (Allen, 1973; Beneke & Harris, 1972; Cornish & Dilley, 1973; Suinn & Hall, 1970; Suinn & Richardson, 1971) indicated no differences. A marked preference for group treatment (69% of the studies) over individual therapy (10%) also exists. Of five additional studies that combined group and individual formats, two (McReynolds & Church, 1973; Meichenbaum, 1972) that did not confound modality and format indicated no outcome differences as a result of type of client contact. Firm generalizations about the effects of both mode and format of therapy cannot be drawn, because of the small number of relevant investigations and the existence of interactions between these two elements and specific treatment procedures.

Frequency of therapeutic contact ranged between 1 and 23 sessions ($M = 6.6$) in the 41 studies that held contact time constant across treatments. The modal investigation contained five sessions, with the median falling between 5 and 6. Within-session contact time was not mentioned in eight studies and was variable in another nine. Participants met for 45 to 60 minutes in 75% of the remaining studies. In general, investigations reporting more extended contact time tended also to involve fewer sessions. Thus, with few exceptions, treatment interventions were of relatively brief duration.

Table 8.1 also indicates that an explosive increase has occurred in the variety of therapeutic operations used to treat test-anxious students. Traditional desensitization and study counseling programs (e.g., Allen, 1971) continue to be used but have been supplemented by: (1) numerous variations of desensitization (e.g., Denney, 1974; Reed & Meyer, 1974; Russell, Miller, & June, 1975; Zemore, 1975); (2) anxiety induction procedures (Dawley & Wenrich, 1973; Smith & Nye, 1973); (3) modeling and vicarious learning techniques (e.g., Hall & Hinkle, 1972; Horne & Matson, 1977; Jaffe & Carlson, 1972; Wisocki, 1973); and (4) direct expectancy and cognitive

TABLE 8.1

Descriptive Characteristics of Test Anxiety Therapy Outcome Studies

Author	Subjects	Therapists	Treatment Groups	Time	Self-Report[a] Measures	Performance[b] Measures
Suinn (1970)	6/0	Author	L G Massed Systematic Desensitization	2-180'	Interview	
Suinn, Edie, & Spinelli (1970)	13/1	2-NA	L G Massed Systematic Desensitization Accelerated Massed Desensitization	1-260' 1-120'	MARS	DAT
Suinn & Hall (1970)	7/1	?	L G Desensitization A G Massed Systematic Desensitization	11-60' 2-240'	STABS	
Aponte & Aponte (1971)	70/? ≥ 75& on STABS	2-A	L G Desensitization L G Nonsimultaneous Desensitization	5-? 5-?	FSS SRO STABS TAQ	GPA Course Grade
Graff, MacLean, & Loving (1971)	84/3 ≥ 22 on TAS	4-NA	L G Relaxation L G Desensitization L G Reciprocal Inhibition	5-? 11-60' 11-25'	IPAT TAS	
Lomont & Sherman (1971)	27/2 ≥ 30 on AAT-D ≤ 23 on AAT-F	2-NA	L G Desensitization L G Implosion	8-50' 8-90'	AAT	Course Exam Reading Test
Meichenbaum & Smart (1971)	54/0	1	L G Positive Expectancy Manipulation L G Neutral Expectancy Manipulation	1-?	Attitudes Toward Classes	Course Grade
Mitchell (1971)	40/? ≥ 84% on AAT-D	?	L G Desensitization	9-50'	AAT	

Study	N/Dropout	Experience	Treatment	Duration	Measure	Outcome
Suinn & Richardson (1971)	143/?	?	A G Massed Systematic Desensitization	1-150'	MARS STABS	DAT
			L G Anxiety Management Training	2-150'		
Taylor (1971)	32/0 ≥ 75% on TAQ	1	L G Desensitization	8-40'	TAQ	
			A G Study Skills Training	8-20'		
Beneke & Harris (1972)	53/15-A	1 Graduate Student	L G Study Skills Training	11-?	Study Time	GPA
			A I Study Skills Training	11-?		
Hall & Hinkle (1972)	53/? ≥ 87% on STABS	?	L ? Desensitization	10-45'	STABS	
			L ? Massed Systematic Desensitization	2-240'		
			A ? Vicarious Desensitization	10-45'		
			A ? Vicarious Massed Desensitization	2-240'		
Jackson & Van Zoost (1972)	47/?	3-NA	A ? Study Skills Training	5-30'	SSHA	GPA
			A ? Study Skills Training + External Reinforcement	5-30'		
			A ? Study Skills Training + Self Reinforcement	5-30'		
Jaffe & Carlson (1972)	30/?	1 Graduate Student	A I Modeling (4 conditions varying model affect and feedback consequence)	1-60'	TAS	Course Exam WAIS Items
McMillan & Osterhouse (1972)	20/2	?	L G Desensitization of High General Anxiety Ss	3-120'	ITA	Course Exam
			L G Desensitization of Low General Anxiety Ss	3-120'		

(continued)

159

TABLE 8.1 (contd.)

Author	Subjects	Therapists	Treatment Groups	Time	Self-Report[a] Measures	Performance[b] Measures
Meichenbaum (1972)	21/0	1 Graduate Student	L IG Desensitization L IG Cognitive Modification	8-60' 8-60'	AAT AD AACL	GPA Digit Symbol Progressive Matrices
Mitchell & Ng (1972)	30/0	1	L G Desensitization L G Study Skills Training L G Desensitization # Study Skills Training L G Serial Desensitization + Study Skills Training	9-50' 9-50' 9-50' 9-50'	AAT IPAT SSHA STABS	GPA
Osterhouse (1972)	54/6	2-A PhD Level	L G Desensitization L G Study Skills Training	6-60' 6-60'	ITA	Course Exam
Allen (1973)	84/20A	2-NA Graduate Students	L G Relaxation + Study Skills Training A I Relaxation + Study Skills Training L G Study Skills Training A I Study Skills Training	7-60' Variable 7-60' Variable	AAT AD STAI TAS TAS	GPA Course Exam
Cornish & Dilley (1973)	39/0	1 Trained Faculty Member	A G Desensitization A G Implosion L G Study Skills Training	4-60' 4-60' 4-60'	AAT FSP	GPA
Dawley & Wenrich (1973)	36/?	?	L ? Implosion	5-30'	TAQ	

Study	Sample	Group	Treatment	Sessions-Duration	Measures	Outcome
McReynolds & Church (1973)	39/? ≥ 63% on ACT ≤ 2.2 GPA	3-NA Graduate Students MA Level Counselor	L IG Study Skills Training L IG Study Skills Training + Self Contracting L I Personal Counseling	10-?' 10-?' 12-?'	SSHA	GPA
Richardson & Suinn (1973)	52/?	?	L G Desensitization L G Accelerated Massed Desensitization	9-45' 2-240'	MARS	DAT
Scissons & Njaa (1973)	30/2 ≥ 85% on STABS	?	A I Desensitization A G Desensitization	2-180' 2-180'	STABs	
Smith & Nye (1973)	34/3 ≥ 84% on TAS	4-A Graduate Students	L I Desensitization L I Implosion	7-45' 7-45'	STAI TAS	GPA WAIS Items
Wisocki (1973) Calef, Calef, Sundstrom, Jarrett, & Davis (1974)	36/? 60/0 ≥ 12 on TAS	Author 2-A	L ? Covert Reinforcement L G Desensitization L G Desensitization + Tone L G Hierarchy + Tone	5-50' 8-60' 8-60' 8-60'	STABS TAS	Otis-Lennon IQ Stanford-Binet Items
Denney (1974)	48/0 ≥ 85% on TAS	8-NA Graduate Students	L I Desensitization L I Active Coping Desensitization L I Vicarious Desensitization L I Active Vicarious Desensitization L I Relaxation L G Covert Reinforcement	$M = 7.9$ $M = 7.4$ $M = 7.9$ $M = 7.4$ $M = 8.1$	FSS STABS	GPA Course Exam Otis IQ Items
Guidry & Randolph (1974)	36/? High on STABS	1 PhD Level	L G Covert Reinforcement	6-30'	STABS STAI TAQ AAT	
Kostka & Galassi (1974)	27/4	2 Non PhD	L G Desensitization L G Covert Reinforcement	10-60' 10-60'	AAT STABS	Anagrams

(continued)

TABLE 8.1 (contd.)

Author	Subjects	Therapists	Treatment Groups	Time	Self-Report[a] Measures	Performance[b] Measures
Reed & Meyer (1974)	21/3	?	? G Active Autogenic Training	?	TAS	Wonderlic
			? G Passive Autogenic Training	?		
Mitchell, Hall, & Piatkowska (1975)	119/0	1 Senior Author	L G Brief Counseling	3–300'	AAT	Course Grade
			L G Counseling + Study Skills Training	23–55'	SSHA	
			L G C + SST + Relaxation	23–55'		
			L G C + SST + Desensitization	23–55'		
Richards (1975)	90/6	1 Author	A G Study Skills Training	4–60'		Course Grade
			A G SST + Stimulus Control	4–60'		Course Exam
			A G SST + Self-Monitoring	4–60'		
			A G SST + SC + SM	4–60'		
Russell, Miller & June (1975)	40/9	3–NA PhD Level	L G Desensitization	6–60'	SRI STAI TAS	GPA
			L G Cue-Controlled Relaxation	6–60'		
Zemore (1975)	40/? High on FSS test and public speaking	1 Graduate Student	L G Active Coping Desensitization	8–45'	AACL FSS STABS	
			L G Desensitization	8–45'		
Anton (1976)	54/1 ≤ 3.25 on GPA	1 Graduate Student	A G Desensitization	8–60'	STAI TAS	GPA
			L G Study Skills Training	4–60'		
Bedell (1976)	50/?	?	? G High Expectancy Desensitization	7–?'	STAI	WRAT
			? G Neutral Expectancy Desensitization	7–?'	TAS	Wonderlic

Study	N	Therapists	Treatment	Duration	Self-report measures	Performance measures
		?	G High Expectancy Relaxation	7-?		
		?	G Neutral Expectancy Relaxation	7-?		
Chang-Liang & Denney (1976)	81/0 ≥ 67% on TAS	?	L G Desensitization	3-45'	FSS IPAT STAI STABS	Wonderlic
			L G Active Coping Relaxation	3-45'	STABS	
			L G Relaxation			
Daniels (1976)	21/?	?	A G Covert Reinforcement	5-60'		
			A G Positive Imagery	5-60'		
			L G Active Coping Relaxation	5-60'	AAT FSS IPAT	
Deffenbacher & Snyder (1976)	11/? ≥ 85% on AAT	1 Second Author				
Holroyd (1976)	60/7 ≥ 87% on AAT	2-A Graduate Students	L G Desensitization	7-60'	AAT AD STAI	GPA Digit Symbol
			L G Cognitive Restructuring	7-60'		
			L G CR + Desensitization	7-60'		
Malec, Park, & Watkins (1976)	21/?	?	L G Modeling	2-?	AAT STAI	Digit Symbol WAIS Items
Russell, Wise, & Stratoudakis (1976)	23/4	3-NA Authors	L G Desensitization	5-45'	AD SRI STAI TAS	
			L G Cue Controlled Relaxation	5-30'		
Spiegler, Cooley, Marshall, Prince, Puckett, & Skenazy (1976)	47/5 ≥ 7% on TAS	3-NA Graduate Students	L G Desensitization	8-50'	FSS TAS	
			L G Active Coping Desensitization	8-50'		
Denney & Rupert (1977)	98/12 ≥ 85% on TAS	14-NA Graduate Students	L I Active Coping	Variable	AAT FSS STABS	GPA Course Grade Wonderlic
			I Rationale + Active Coping Desensitization	Variable		
			L I ACR + Desensitization	Variable		
			L I Standard Rationale + Active Coping Desensitization	Variable		
			L I SR + Desensitization	Variable		

(continued)

TABLE 8.1 *(contd.)*

Author	Subjects	Therapists	Treatment Groups	Time	Self-Report[a] Measures	Performance[b] Measures
Horne & Matson (1977)	100/0 High on TAS & IPAT	4-A Graduate Students	L G Desensitization L G Implosion L G Modeling L G Study Skills Training	10-60' 10-60' 10-60' 10-60'	IPAT TAS *Pulse*	GPA Observation of Test-Taking Anxiety
Snyder & Deffenbacher (1977)	43/0 ≥ 85% on AAT	?	L G Desensitization L G Active Coping Relaxation	6-60'AAT 6-60'	Anagrams IPAT	
Goldfried, Linehan, & Smith (1978)	42/6	2-A Authors	L I Cognitive Restructuring L I Prolonged Exposure	6-60' 6-60'	STABS STAI TAQ	
Romano & Cabianca (1978)	40/0 ≥ 70% on STABS	?	A ? Desensitization ? ? EMG Biofeedback + Desensitization ? ? EMG Biofeedback + Relaxation	13-? 13-20' 13-20'	STABS TAS	Anagrams

[a]Self-report outcome measures are abbreviated as follows: AACL = Affect Adjective Check List, AAT = Anxiety Achievement Test, AD = Anxiety Differential, FSS = Fear Survey Schedule, IPAT = IPAT Anxiety Scale, MARS = Mathematics Anxiety Rating Scale, SRI = S–R Inventory of Anxiousness, STAI = State–Trait Anxiety Inventory, SSHA = Survey of Study Habits and Attitudes, STABS = Suinn Test Anxiety Behavioral Scale, TAS = Test Anxiety Scale, TAQ = Test Anxiety Questionnaire, ITA = Inventory of Test Anxiety. Physiological measures are presented in italicized form in the Self-Reported Outcome column, where FSP = Finger Sweat Print.

[b]Performance outcome measures are abbreviated as follows: DAT = Differential Aptitude Test, GPA = Grade Point Average, WAIS = Wechsler Adult Intelligence Scale, Wonderlic = Wonderlic Personnel Test, and WRAT = Wide Range Achievement Test.

restructuring manipulations (e.g., Bedell, 1976; Goldfried et al., 1978; Holroyd, 1976; Meichenbaum & Smart, 1971). Two potentially important areas of emerging emphasis involve the growing use of traditional relaxation and desensitization procedures within a self-control framework (e.g., Chang-Liang & Denney, 1976; Denney & Rupert, 1977; Richards, 1975; Snyder & Deffenbacher, 1977) and attempts to pinpoint the precise effects of complex multimodal treatment combinations on specific classes of outcome (Mitchell, Hall, & Piatkowska, 1975; Mitchell & Ng, 1972).

With the growth of innovative techniques, there has been a simultaneous increase in the variety of instruments and procedures used to assess therapeutic outcome. Converging methods of measurement (i.e., self-report and performance) were used in 67% of the studies we sampled. A total of 13 self-report instruments was employed in more than one investigation, with the Suinn Test Anxiety Behavioral Scale the most frequently used (in 16 studies). The Test Anxiety Scale, Achievement Anxiety Test, and State–Trait Anxiety Inventory (Spielberger, Gorsuch, & Lushene, 1970) were also popular measures, appearing in 13, 13, and 11 studies, respectively.

With the exception of grade point average and course examination scores (used in 15 and 7 investigations, respectively), little cross-study consistency was found in the use of performance outcome measures. It appears that growing use is being made of subtests from a variety of intelligence tests. We were very surprised to note, however, that assessment of physiological changes resulting from treatment was conducted in only two studies (Cornish & Dilley, 1973; Horne & Matson, 1977). Given the heated controversies that surround alternative conceptions of the basic change mechanisms underlying procedures such as desensitization and implosion, measurement of physiological processes obviously deserves more attention.

In summary, our survey suggests that test anxiety continues to be exploited as a target for investigating the efficacy of a growing number of short-term treatment innovations. The remainder of the chapter addresses major methodological issues that have relevance for this exciting area of research.

METHODOLOGICAL TRADE-OFFS IN TEST ANXIETY THERAPY STUDIES

Although the goal of any therapy outcome study is to unequivocally demonstrate that a particular treatment does indeed reduce test anxiety (Cook & Campbell, 1976; Paul, 1969), in actuality, this proves to be neither a simple nor straightforward task. By necessity, we are dealing with multifaceted therapeutic "packages" that exert multiple effects on various components that define the construct of test anxiety. In addition, the researcher is forced to make many pragmatic trade-offs while selecting participants, implementing treatments, and assessing results.

From a largely methodological perspective, Cook and Campbell (1976) provide a detailed illustration of how such trade-offs operate in affecting four types of validity. *Statistical conclusion validity* refers to the adequacy of statistical evidence purporting to demonstrate systematic variation between treatment and outcome. Covariation, however, does not imply causality unless rival alternative influences can be ruled out. Attempts to discount the effects of such factors constitute the *internal validity* of an experiment. Insuring that the specific therapeutic operations employed in an experiment represent basic underlying behavior-change processes and that outcome measurements adequately sample the hypothetical construct being investigated in theory-relevant terms constitute *construct validity*. Finally, attempts to demonstrate that whatever causal relationships that are postulated are generalizable across people, settings, and time define the domain of *external validity*.

Specific threats to each type of validity exist, and an attempt to increase one source of validity will necessarily decrease another type. In general, internal and external validity are inversely related, as are construct and statistical conclusion validity. In the first instance, selecting participants for therapy on the basis of various anxiety criteria tends to yield a homogeneous sample that generally proves to be more similarly responsive to a specific intervention. Such selection serves to restrict the range of "error" variance but will also narrow the potential generality of obtained outcomes. Similarly, using multiple control groups increases internal validity but often reduces within-treatment cell sizes, thereby heightening the likelihood of Type II statistical errors. In the second case, any therapeutic intervention is considered to be more powerful if it exerts a consistent influence on multiple, independent measures of the construct (e.g., reduces subjective distress, lowers physiological arousal, improves intellectual performance). Yet, the inclusion of the multiple measures needed to adequately sample construct-relevant change increases the probability of Type I statistical errors.

This state of affairs forces us to give careful consideration to the trade-offs we confront and to choose those strategies that best meet our research priorities. Fortunately, this task is simplified if we distinguish between the logical versus the empirical plausibility of specific threats to validity. It is always possible to generate logically plausible alternative explanations for covariation found in a therapy outcome investigation (e.g., use of a single therapist could account for treatment differences). We need to rule out, however, *only* those threats that possess an empirically demonstrable (cross-investigation) effect that is comparable in magnitude to the relationship one seeks to explain (Campbell, 1969).

SPECIFIC METHODOLOGICAL ISSUES IN THE THERAPEUTIC INVESTIGATIONS

Table 8.2 summarizes the 49 investigations in terms of: (1) the presence of a No-Treatment (NT) or Attention-Placebo (AP) control group; (2) the inclusion of follow-up information; (3) the major outcomes presented for self-report and performance measures; and (4) the adequacy of the study on eight relevant methodological criteria. Construction of Table 8.2 involved making a number of relatively arbitrary decisions that are explained later. An attempt was made to identify the credibility of any attention-placebo procedure as low (*LC*), high (*HC*), or as being unknown (*?*).

Because summarizing outcome proved problematic whenever multiple measures within a single measurement channel yielded inconsistent between-group differences, we sequentially employed serveral guidelines to arrive at an overall summary. Whenever possible, we chose the modal outcome; in the case of ties, we chose the outcome of what appeared to be the more relevant measure (e.g., examination scores over intelligence test items in the Jaffe and Carlson (1972) study). Our final strategy was to use the interpretation provided by the authors unless the validity of their conclusion was jeopardized by threats to statistical conclusion validity. Group designations of outcome correspond to the treatment conditions listed for each study in Table 8.1. Wherever applicable, follow-up outcome data are presented in italics underneath the initial outcome summary.

In rating the methodological characteristics of the studies, we attempted to operationalize our belief that threats to validity ought to be viewed in probabilistic terms as opposed to a simplistic existence/nonexistence dichotomy. This required a careful reading of each investigation to determine the utility of experimental procedures in terms of the intent of the investigation. For example, we assumed that the absence of a placebo control condition would be of lesser consequence in process investigations (e.g., Jaffe & Carlson, 1972; McMillan & Osterhouse, 1972; Scissons & Njaa, 1973) that examined interactions between treatment and subject characteristics or within-technique variations. Our methodological grading system uses D to designate that a particular threat to validity definitely exists in an investigation, P to indicate that it possibly influenced the obtained outcome, $?$ to denote our inability to determine whether the threat was operative, and NA to indicate that the threat is not applicable, given the design and purpose of

TABLE 8.2

Outcome and Methodological Characteristics of Test Anxiety Therapy Outcome Studies

Study	Control Groups	Follow-Up	Self-Report Outcome	Performance Outcome	Inadequate Randomization	Lack of NT Control	Nonequivalent Control	Lack of AP Control	Therapist Specificity	Mono-Method Specificity	Format-Therapy Interaction	Statistical Anomalies
Suinn (1970)	None	None	"Reported Improvement"	?	NA	D	NA	NA	D	D	NA	NA
Suinn, Edie, & Spinelli (1970)	None	None	MSD = AMD[a] (Post > Pre)	MSD = AMD (Post > Pre)	?	D	NA	D	P	C	NA	P
Suinn & Hall (1970)	None	None	D = MSD (Post > Pre)	?	?	D	NA	D	P	D	D	P
Aponte & Aponte (1971)	NT	None	D = NSD = R = NT	D = NSD = R = NT	C	C	NA	P	C	C	C	D
Graff, MacLean, & Loving (1971)	NT, AP-LC	8 Week	D = RI > AP = NT; *D = RI > AP = NT*	?	C	C	NA	C	P	D	D	C
Lomont & Sherman (1971)	NT	None	D = I = NT	D = I = NT	C	C	NA	D	P	C	C	C
Meichenbaum & Smart (1971)	NT, AP-?	None	PEM > NEM = NT	PEM > NEM = NT	C	C	NA	C	?	C	NA	C
Mitchell (1971)	NT	4 Week	D > NT	?	C	C	NA	NA	P	D	NA	C
Suinn & Richardson (1971)	NT	None	MSD = AMT = NT	?	D	C	D	D	P	C	D	D
Taylor (1971)	NT	8 Week	D > SST > NT (*D F-U = Post*)[b]	?	P	C	D	D	D	D	D	C
Beneke & Harris (1972)	NT	3 Semester	GSST = ISST	GSST = ISST > NT; *GSST = ISST > NT*	P	C	P	D	D	C	NA	C
Hall & Hinkle (1972)	NT	None	D = MSD = VSD = VMSD > NT; SSTER = SSTSR > SST = NT; *SSTER = SSTSR > SST = NT*	?	D	P	D	D	P	D	C	C
Jackson & Van Zoost (1972)	NT	4 Month	SSTER = SSTSR = SST = NT	SSTER = SSTSR = SST = NT	C	C	NA	D	?	C	C	P
Jaffe & Carlson (1972)	NT	None	M = NT	M > NT	C	C	NA	NA	D	C	C	C

Study												
McMillan & Osterhouse (1972)	None	None	DHGA = DLGA (Post > Pre)	DLGA > DHGA	C	D	NA	NA	P	C	NA	C
Meichenbaum (1972)	NT	1 Month	CM > D > NT *CM > D > NT*	CM = D > NT	C	C	NA	D	D	C	C	C
Mitchell & Ng (1972)	NT	12 Week	SDSST = DSST = SST = D > NT *SDSST = DSST = SST = D > NT*	SDSST = DSST > SST = D = NT *SDSST = DSST = SST = D = NT*	C	C	NA	NA	D	D	C	C
Osterhouse (1972)	NT	None	D = SST = NT	NT > SST = D	D	C	P	D	C	C	D	D
Allen (1973)	NT *AP-?*	None	RSST = SST = AP > NT	RSST = SST > AP = NT	C	C	NA	C	C	C	C	C
Cornish & Dilley (1973)	NT	None	D > I = SST = NT	D = I = SST = NT	C	C	NA	D	D	C	C	C
Dawley & Wenrich (1973)	NT	1 Month	I = AP > NT *I = AP > NT*	?	C	C	NA	C	P	D	NA	P
McReynolds & Church (1973)	NT	None	SSTSC = SST > NT	SSTSC = SST = NT	P	C	NA	C	P	C	NA	P
Richardson & Suinn (1973)	NT	None	D = AMD > NT	D = AMD = NT	C	C	D	D	P	D	C	C
Scissons & Njaa (1973)	NT	None	ID = GD > NT	?	C	C	NA	NA	P	D	C	C
Smith & Nye (1973)	NT	1 Quarter	D > I = NT *D > I = NT*	?	?	C	NA	D	C	?	C	D
Wisocki (1973)	NT	6 Week	CR > NT *CR > NT*	CR = NT	C	C	NA	C	D	D	C	?
Calef, Calef, Sundstrom Jarrett & Davis (1974)	AP-?	None	DT > D > HT = AP	DT = D = HT = AP	D	C	NA	C	C	C	C	C
Denney (1974)	NT	None	ACD = D = AVD = VD = R > NT *CR = AP > NT*	ACD = D > AVD = VD = R = NT	C	C	NA	NA	C	C	C	C
Guidry & Randolph (1974)	NT *AP-?*	3 Week	CR = AP > NT *CR = AP > NT*	?	C	C	NA	C	D	D	NA	C
Kostka & Galassi (1974)	NT	5 Month	D = CR > NT *D = CR > NT*	CR = NT > D	P	C	D	D	P	C	C	C
Reed & Meyer (1974)	None	None	AAT = PAT (Post > Pre)	AAT = PAT (Post > Pre)	C	D	NA	NA	P	C	?	C
Mitchell, Hall, & Piatkowska (1975)	NT	2 Years	CSSTD = CSSTR = SST > BC	CSSTD > CSSTR > SST = BC = NT *CSSTD > CSSTR > SST = BC = NT*	C	C	NA	D	D	C	C	C
Richards (1975)	NT	None	?	SST = SSTSC = SSTSM = SSTSCSM = NT	C	C	C	D	P	D	C	D

(continued)

TABLE 8.2 (contd.)

Study	Control Groups	Follow-Up	Self-Report Outcome	Performance Outcome	Inadequate Randomization	Lack of NT Control	Nonequivalent Control	Lack of AP Control	Therapist Specificity	Mono-Method Specificity	Format-Therapy Interaction	Statistical Anomalies
Russell, Miller, & June (1975)	NT	None	D = CCR > NT	D = CCR = NT	C	C	NA	D	P	C	C	C
Zemore (1975)	NT	None	ACD = D > NT	?	C	C	NA	D	D	D	C	C
Anton (1976)	NT	1 Semester	D > SST = NT	D = SST = NT _D = SST = NT_	C	C	NA	D	D	C	D	C
Bedell (1976)	NT	None	HED = NED = HER = NER > NT	HED = NED = HER = NER = NT	C	C	NA	D	P	C	?	C
Chang-Liang & Denney (1976)	NT	None	ACR > D = R = NT	ACR > D = R = NT	C	C	NA	D	P	C	C	C
Daniels (1976)	NT	None	PI > CR = NT _(Post > Pre)_	?	C	C	NA	D	P	D	C	C
Deffenbacher & Snyder (1976)	None	None		?	NA	D	NA	D	D	D	NA	C
Holroyd (1976)	NT AP-HC	None 1 Month	CRS > CRSD = D = AP > NT _CRS > CRSD > D = AP = NT_	CRS > CRSD = D = AP > NT	C	C	NA	C	C	C	C	C

170

Study		Follow-up	Posttest results	Follow-up results							
Malec, Park, & Watkins (1976)	NT	None	M > NT	M = NT	C	C	NA	D	P	C	NA	C
Russell, Wise, & Stratoudakis (1976)	NT	None	D = CCR > NT	D = CCR = NT	C	C	NA	D	P	C	C	P
Spiegler, Cooley, Marshall Prince, Puckett & Skenazy (1976)	NT	None	ACD > D = NT	?	C	C	NA	D	P	D	C	C
Denney & Rupert (1977)	NT AP-HC	2 Semester	ACRACD = ACRD > SRACD = SRD > AP = NT	ACRACD = ACRD > SRACD = SRD = AP = NT, ACRACD = ACRD > SRACD = SRD = AP = NT	C	C		NA	C	C	C	C
Horne & Matson (1977)	NT	None	M > D > I > SST = NT	M = D > SST = I > NT	C	C	NA	D	C	C	C	C
Snyder & Deffenbacher (1977)	NT	None	D = ACR > NT	D = ACR = NT	C	C	NA	D	P	C	C	C
Goldfried, Linehan & Smith (1978)	NT	6 Week	CRS > PE > NT, CRS > PE	?	C	C	NA	D	C	D	C	C
Romano & Cabianca (1978)	NT	None	EMGD = EMGR = D > NT	EMGD = EMGR = D = NT	C	C	NA	D	?	C	?	C

[a] Significant between-group differences at $p < .05$ are indicated by >, no significant differences by =. See text for further details.
[b] Indicates that Desensitization group maintained gains from posttest to follow-up.

the study. Any investigation that adequately controlled the potential artifact earned a *C* in the appropriate column. More specific scoring criteria derived from the investigations are embedded in the discussion of the specific threats to validity.

Inadequate Randomization

Random assignment of participants to experimental conditions is the most economical procedure for canceling out potential artifactual biases that might systematically affect outcome (Campbell & Stanley, 1963; Kaplan, 1964). The procedure is assumed to distribute error variance in the form of preexisting individual differences equitably across treatments, thus enabling the investigator to attribute differential outcome to broadly defined treatment variation. Random assignment was specifically mentioned as having been conducted in 74% of the investigations, with three studies not reporting this information (*?*), and two additional ones using only a single group (*NA*). Randomization inadequacies found in the remaining seven investigations took the forms of drawing untreated subjects from "leftover" potential participants (Beneke & Harris, 1972; Taylor, 1971) or from samples of nonparticipants (Hall & Hinkle, 1972; Kostka & Galassi, 1974; Osterhouse, 1972; Richardson & Suinn, 1973; Suinn & Richardson, 1971). The consequences of such a selection bias are discussed in the next section.

Deficiencies in Nontreated Control Groups

The second and third criteria in Table 8.2 deal with two interrelated issues that are fundamental to establishing experimental control. Outcome researchers seek to demonstrate that the efficacy of particular therapeutic operations is reliably greater than historical or maturational influences. A minimal requirement for such a demonstration is the inclusion of a no-treatment control group composed of randomly selected volunteers. Allen (1972) noted the necessity of drawing control subjects from the pool of potential participants, suggesting that nonvolunteers are likely to be less motivated and less anxious. Empirical support exists for both speculations. Initial differences in the test anxiety of volunteers and a nonvolunteer no-treatment control group in the Suinn and Richardson (1971) study made it difficult to draw unambiguous conclusions about treatment effectiveness. More important, Gilbreath (1971) found the academic gains made by untreated students who had volunteered for a study-counseling program to be significantly greater than improvement shown by a group of nonparticipants who had been matched on initial grades and academic aptitude.

Only seven investigations failed to include a no-treatment control condition, whereas 86% of the studies employed this control appropriately. Failure to include untreated subjects was especially critical in five studies that examined variations in standard desensitization procedures, such as massed desensitization (Suinn, 1970; Suinn & Hall, 1970), accelerated massed desensitization (Suinn, Edie, & Spinelli, 1970), autogenic training (Reed & Meyer, 1974), and active coping relaxation (Deffenbacher & Snyder, 1976). Although many of these innovations were reported to produce effects comparable to systematic desensitization, lack of nontreated participants fails to guarantee that improvement did not capitalize on regression effects or the volunteer status of the participants.

Concerns pertaining to use of nonequivalent control groups were not applicable to a vast majority (80%) of the studies. Incorporation of a nonparticipant control group, in addition to volunteer control subjects, provides an excellent check on the interaction between pretest sensitization and contextual reactivity (i.e., subtle demands for manifesting anxiety as a prerequisite for participating in a therapy outcome study). Bernstein (1973) documented how such an interaction operates by finding that assessment in a clinical as opposed to a laboratory context elicits greater phobic avoidance. The sensitization-context interaction provides a compelling explanation for the recurring finding that nontreated nonparticipants who are repeatedly assessed on self-report anxiety measures manifest "spontaneous improvement" (Suinn, 1969a; Tasto & Suinn, 1972), whereas nontreated control participants in therapy outcome studies do not. Cook and Campbell (1976) describe this phenomenon as involving "resentful demoralization" by people who receive less desirable treatment. Three investigations (Meichenbaum & Smart, 1971; Mitchell et al. 1975; Richards, 1975) employed nonequivalent nonparticipant control groups, in addition to participating control subjects, to examine the effects generated by volunteering for participation. Although all three studies found no evidence for volunteerism, the sample is too small to conclude that resentful demoralization can be safely ignored in outcome research on test anxiety.

The trade-off between rigorous selection of potential subjects, which provides a clinically relevant sample but simultaneously reduces the size of the sample, is difficult to resolve. Some investigators sought to circumvent this problem by using a nonequivalent sample of nonvolunteers in place of a participant control group. This strategy, however, posed a possible threat to internal validity in two investigations (Beneke & Harris, 1972; Osterhouse, 1972) and represented a definite threat in five others. In these latter studies (Hall & Hinkle, 1972; Kostka & Galassi, 1974; Richardson & Suinn, 1973; Suinn & Richardson, 1971; Taylor, 1971), control subjects were drawn from various nonvolunteer populations, resulting in a confounding of outcome by probable sensitization-context interactions.

Lack of Placebo Control Procedures

The well-documented finding that exposure to theoretically nonfunctional procedures within a therapeutic context facilitates anxiety reduction (e.g., Allen, 1971; Dawley & Wenrich, 1973; Guidry & Randolph, 1974) highlights the importance of including an attention-placebo condition in test anxiety outcome research. Much has been written on this topic in recent years (Allen, 1977; Kazdin & Wilcoxin, 1976; Lick & Bootzin, 1975), resulting in a dramatic increase in our knowledge of what constitutes an adequate placebo control procedure. Demonstrating that the effects of a theoretically relevant treatment are greater than improvement resulting from the mobilization of positive expectancies and other nonspecific factors requires a placebo condition that provides a nonfunctional (i.e., theoretically irrelevant) set of operations and possesses a high level of empirically assessed credibility (Borkovec & Nau, 1972).

Our survey revealed that failure to include such a control was the single most frequent threat to internal validity. Only eight investigations contained a placebo control condition, and, of these, only two (Denney & Rupert, 1977; Holroyd, 1976) provided evidence that the manipulation was credible. Level of plausibility was unknown in five of the investigations and apparently low in the study by Graff, MacLean, and Loving (1971). In the latter investigation, the authors' description of their subjects' reaction to the placebo procedure suggests the existence of resentful demoralization.

Several investigators have devised innovative strategies that reduce the need for a placebo control. Denney (1974) equated all treatment groups on credibility of rationale, thus providing the option of interpreting his least complex therapeutic package as a placebo manipulation. Mitchell and Ng (1972) and Mitchell et al. (1975) used an analogue of a multiple-baseline design in which the effects of particular interventions (e.g., desensitization and study counseling) were sequentially assessed on outcome measures specifically related to each treatment (e.g., subjective distress, study habits, etc.) Holroyd (1976) included bogus outcome measures to determine whether nontreated participants could be differentiated from treated subjects solely on the basis of expectancy factors. In the latter three studies, it was demonstrated that specific treatments produced theory-relevant outcomes on particular measures but failed to similarly influence tangential outcome measures. Such demonstrations make the incorporation of an attention-placebo group superfluous. These promising alternatives can help balance the trade-off between rigor of subject selection and statistical power by reducing the need for an additional control condition in an experiment.

Therapist Specificity

The therapist is obviously a very important component of any treatment package. Interpretation of differential between-group outcome is open to any alternative that systematically covaries with treatment (e.g., fatigue, enthusiasm, expectations, etc.) when a single therapist is employed. This limitation definitely threatened validity in 13 of the investigations.

Incorporating multiple therapists within an experimental design, however, does not by itself guarantee that systematic artifactual covariation does not exist. A substantial percentage of investigations that employed multiple therapists was possibly threatened by failure to either factorially cross therapists with treatments (e.g., Suinn et al., 1970; Lomont & Sherman, 1971; Russell et al., 1975) or assess possible differences when a factorial crossing is made (e.g., Allen, 1973; Russell, Wise, & Stratoudakis, 1976). Two studies (Denney, 1974; Denney & Rupert, 1977) insured a high degree of generalizability without assessing therapist differences by incorporating enough therapists to conduct individual matching of therapists with clients within treatments.

As we noted earlier, interactions between therapist characteristics and treatment procedures deserve more attention. One procedure that could be easily used on a more widespread basis is to collect perceptions of potentially important therapist characteristics from clients. Allen (1971), for example, found two therapists to reliably differ on a number of attributes (e.g., activity level, involvement, etc.), but these differential collective subject perceptions were not related to variation in outcome.

Mono-Method Specificity

Although often treated as a simple target outcome, test anxiety is a complex hypothetical construct that describes relationships between subjective distress, physiological activation, cognitive disruption, behavioral avoidance, scholastic skills, and intellectual performance. Adequate assessment of treatment effects on this complicated network of relationships necessitates multiple *methods* of measurement. It has been conceptually useful to define three basic measurement domains that encompass self-report inventories, methods of recording physiological responses, and devices to assess overt behavior and performance. Investigations of anxiety assessment and reduction (e.g., Allen, 1971; Lang, 1968; Paul, 1966) have shown that data derived from these three domains are relatively independent. It thus becomes possible to "triangulate" the effects of a therapeutic intervention by means of converging operations.

Each measurement method, as opposed to the variety of instruments found within each method, possesses unique functions in anxiety assessment as well as specific and unique limitations. Anxiety questionnaires provide the most direct assessment of subjective distress, but many are open to deliberate distortion as a result of exposure to simple, extra-therapeutic demands for change (Allen, 1970; Bernstein, 1973). Physiological measures are less transparent in terms of being susceptible to conscious distortion, but often suffer from baseline instability. Performance measures tend to be influenced by other forms of reactivity and tend to be somewhat more "remote" indices of therapeutic change. Examination scores,for example, often improve as a result of subsequent testing, and their use as an outcome index requires that they be normalized (Allen 1973; Jaffe & Carlson, 1972; McMillan & Osterhouse, 1972). Grade point average is affected by numerous extra-therapeutic influences, including "grade inflation," entry into upper-level courses, involvement in independent study courses, and so on (Allen & Desaulniers, 1974).

Sole reliance on a single method of measurement, even if multiple instruments are used within that method, provides less compelling support for the efficacy of a therapeutic intervention than does the use of multiple methods. A therapy that reduces subjective distress and improves academic performance is generally viewed as more effective than a procedure that has impact in only one domain. Such persuasiveness is increased by the fact that the inherent limitations that can bias one method of measurement typically are different than the limitations affecting the other domain. Zemore (1975), for example, convincingly demonstrated that treatment for test anxiety also reduced self-reported and performance indices of speech anxiety, but failure to include a performance measure of test anxiety precluded an unambiguous conclusion that similar generalization resulted from treatment of speech anxiety.

Although only eight investigations employed single outcome measures, mono-method specificity was a definite threat to construct validity in 15 studies (14 of which contained only self-report instruments while one (Richards, 1975) relied exclusively on performance measures). In one additional investigation (Smith & Nye, 1973), comparative academic performance data were lost when nontreated subjects were subsequently provided with therapy. This study exemplifies the dilemma of balancing methodological niceties against the ethical responsibilities confronting the therapy outcome researcher.

Two-thirds of the studies adequately controlled for mono-method specificity. Nonetheless, considerably more attention needs to be directed toward adequately assessing physiological and performance components of the test anxiety construct. As mentioned earlier, only two investigations have included physiological assessment, and only Horne and Matson (1977) have attempted to observe overt behavioral indicators of test anxiety. Such omissions reflect more on the general state of the art of anxiety assessment than they do on the sampled investigations. Presently, we are in need of basic normative data about functioning on many physiological and performance measures (e.g., palmar sweat; intelligence test items) that have been employed in test anxiety outcome research. Clearer and more intricate articulation of the nomological network of relationships defining the test anxiety construct is also necessary.

Format-Treatment Interactions

Considerable effort has been directed toward evaluating the efficiency of various therapeutic interventions once their efficacy has been at least tentatively established. This has usually been accomplished by comparing (1) live versus automated methods of therapy presentation (Allen, 1973; Beneke & Harris, 1972; Hall & Hinkle, 1972), (2) individual versus group treatment (McReynolds & Church, 1973; Scissons & Njaa, 1973), or (3) treatments of varying duration (Graff, MacLean, & Loving, 1971; Suinn et al., 1970). Demonstrating differential efficiency requires that the treatment components be identical across format variations. Failure to factorially cross therapy with format variations makes it impossible to attribute differential outcome to either factor.

It is likely that automated therapies and treatment involving brief duration will be perceived by participants as requiring less therapist involvement, possibly resulting in some resentful demoralization. In our sample, this threat to internal validity was definitely operative in seven investigations and impossible to determine in three others. The existence of a format-treatment confounding forces the investigator to gamble that the outcome will be interpretable. For example, in studies that confounded treatment duration with type of therapy, failure to find differential between-therapy outcomes enables one to conclude that the briefer treatment is more efficient (Graff, MacLean, & Loving, 1971; Lomont & Sherman, 1971; Suinn & Hall, 1970; Suinn & Richardson, 1971). If, however, the briefer treatment is less effective, this could be due to either the technique itself or to its shortened duration (Anton, 1976; Taylor, 1971). Although this confounding was not frequently found in the literature, its existence can pose an unnecessary interpretative dilemma for the researcher.

Statistical Anomalies

We encountered a number of debately questionable practices in the statistical treatment of data in the reviewed studies and took these into account when summarizing outcome. The most serious and definite threat to statistical conclusion validity was the use of post hoc comparison of mean differences after an overall analysis revealed, at best, a marginal level of significance (e.g.,

Aponte & Aponte, 1971; Osterhouse, 1972; Richards, 1975). Although we recognize the utility of this strategy in making sense of complex results, we viewed the practice as obfuscating our task of deriving outcomes from the literature in a consistent manner. Whenever this occurred, we chose the overall nonsignificant outcome as appropriate for inclusion in Table 8.2.

A second frequently noted practice that we designated as a possible threat involved using low-power statistical procedures (e.g., correlated t-tests conducted separately on pre- and posttreatment measures) that tend to capitalize on initial between-group pretreatment differences (Dawley & Wenrich, 1973; Jackson & Van Zoost, 1972; Russell et al., 1976; Suinn et al., 1970; Suinn & Hall, 1970). Determining differential outcome in such investigations requires unnecessary inferential leaps between discrete analyses of data.

We also found that a substantial number of investigations contained analysis of simple change scores, although we did not use this as a criterion for judging validity. Although it is widely known that such scores suffer from serious limitations (Cronbach & Furby, 1970), with few exceptions (e.g., Allen, 1973; Denney, 1974), no effort was made to "residualize" them so as to statistically control for preexisting between-group differences and regression effects. Presentation of change scores in tables of descriptive statistics has the additional undesirable effect of retarding the development of normative information about the measures used in test anxiety research.

We recommend that investigators make greater use of more powerful multivariate statistical procedures. To date, only two investigations (Holroyd, 1976; Malec, Park, & Watkins, 1976) employed multivariate analyses of variance, a technique that substantially reduces the need for making often convoluted logical inferences. Hopefully, clarification of the utility of this statistical tool (e.g., Kaplan & Litrownik, 1977) will make its use in test anxiety outcome research more common.

STRENGTHS AND LIMITATIONS OF CURRENT THERAPEUTIC ENDEAVORS

Our survey indicated that test anxiety is indeed a useful target construct for assessing the efficiency and efficacy of a growing number of therapeutic interventions. The methodological adequacy of the literature also appears to be generally good. Although we recognize the limitations in summarizing the overall status of a substantial body of literature, a majority of the investigations employed adequate randomization procedures, utilized appropriate nontreated control groups, triangulated treatment effects through multiple methods of measurement, contained appropriate statistical analyses, and were free from confounded format-treatment interactions. Two vitally important methodological criteria, however, were not, in general, adequately dealt with—(1) specifying and assessing attributes of the therapist as independent factors in promoting change, and (2) demonstrating the efficacy of theoretically relevant treatments to be greater than improvement produced by placebo manipulations. These two crucial limitations restrict the conclusions that can be drawn about the efficacy of therapeutic attempts to alleviate test anxiety.

Table 8.3 summarizes outcome differences between various therapies and no treatment or placebo manipulations as reported in investigations that contain the relevant comparisons. The fact that most methodological confoundings do not appear to systematically affect the literature suggests that conclusions drawn from such a summary will be reasonably valid. The first comparison clearly indicates that therapy-in-general produces reliably greater improvement than no treatment on self-reported assessments of subjective distress and study skills. Over half of the pertinent studies provided unambiguous support for this contention, whereas in an additional 29% of the investigations, some therapeutic interventions were found to be more efficacious than the absence of treatment. Consideration of performance measures, however, yields a less positive conclusion, as 50% of the investigations failed demonstrate the superiority of therapy.

TABLE 8.3
Percentage of Investigations Indicating Therapeutic
Effectiveness on Self-Report and Performance-Outcome
Measures

| | Measurement Method | |
Comparison	Self-Report	Performance
Treatment vs. No Treatment	(n = 38)	(n = 28)
T > NT	58%	18%
T ≥ NT	29%	29%
T = NT	13%	50%
NT > T	0%	3%
Desensitization vs. No Treatment	(n = 26)	(n = 18)
D > NT	77%	11%
D ≥ NT	4%	11%
D = NT	19%	67%
NT > D	0%	11%
Treatment vs. Placebo	(n = 7)	(n = 4)
T > P	29%	25%
T ≥ P	29%	50%
T =	42%	25%
P > T	0%	0%

Analysis of studies containing variations of systematic desensitization (which comprised a majority of relevant investigations) yielded a more magnified form of this same pattern. Relaxation and desensitization procedures are clearly useful in reducing subjectively experienced anxiety, but, by themselves, have little therapeutic impact on measures of intellectual or academic performance. It also cannot be safely concluded that the "typical" therapeutic intervention is superior to the "average" placebo manipulation, as indicated by the third comparison. Although the small sample of relevant studies severely restricts generality, it appears that placebo manipulations promoted equivalent reductions in subjective distress but were somewhat less effective than therapy in improving performance.

Two important exceptions to the latter two rather gloomy generalizations deserve attention. These involve the use of (1) multimodal therapeutic packages which contain combinations of desensitization and study counseling (Horne & Matson, 1977; Mitchell, et al., 1975; Mitchell & Ng, 1972), and (2) cognitive restructuring and desensitization embedded within a self-control framework (Chang-Liang & Denney, 1976; Denney & Rupert, 1977; Holroyd, 1976). Future effort might be profitably directed toward assessing these innovations by using the sequential time series design employed by Mitchell and his associates. This strategy enables one to pinpoint the effects of specific interventions on construct-relevant outcome measures over time.

If our knowledge of relevant therapeutic parameters is to continue to grow, we must also attend more carefully to four additional concerns. First, *we need to more carefully examine relationships between therapist characteristics and therapy outcome.* Since we have repeatedly emphasized the importance of this issue and suggested procedures by which this can be accomplished, we will not belabor this point.

Second, *we must insure that our therapeutic manipulations are construct-valid comparisons of competing models of basic behavior-change processes.* We currently are confronted with a bewildering array of treatment strategies, many of which represent minute variations of standardized therapeutic interventions (e.g., systematic desensitization). The descriptive labeling of these variations (e.g., autogenic training, cue-controlled relaxation, relaxation-as-self-control, accelerated massed desensitization, anxiety-management training, etc.) implies that each is derived from a clearly unique set of underlying behavioral processes. In fact, this labeling confuses the construct validity of treatment endeavors and promotes the growth of what Allen (1977) calls "clinical gimmickery." Horne and Matson (1977) provide an excellent example of a meaningful parametric investigation in terms of both their selection of treatments and the wide scope of assessment measures they employed. Subsequent efforts of this type will obviously require greater attention to physiological indices of change.

Third, *we must make better use of emerging knowledge about nonspecific placebo influences when constructing and assessing therapeutic interventions.* Allen (1977) has noted that the boundary between "true" therapy and placebo treatments is determined by the developmental state of underlying theory. This boundary is in continual flux—today's placebo is likely to become tomorrow's "real" therapy. From this perspective, the use of direct-expectancy manipulations by Meichenbaum and Smart (1971) can be viewed as a forerunner of more systematically developed cognitive restructuring techniques.

The history of therapy outcome research is characterized by the gradual discovery of artifactual influences, followed by attempts to cope with their effects (McGuire, 1969). Ultimately, coping strategies lead to the exploitation of the artifact as an important independent variable. This cycle is evident in the literature we have reviewed. Emerging information is being used to cope with the artifactual influence of "nonspecific" therapeutic effects by developing more credible placebo procedures (Holroyd, 1976), and an effort is being made (e.g., Denney & Rupert, 1977; Goldfried et al., 1978) to exploit such influences by incorporating them into therapeutic "packages." Because it is clear that just about any therapeutic intervention reduces subjective distress when compared to no treatment, inclusion of placebo manipulations ought to be given priority over untreated control groups when limitations on sample size dictate making a choice between the two control alternatives.

Finally, *more attention must be directed toward the long-term effects of treatment.* Historically, follow-ups examining the maintainance of therapeutic changes have been rare in the test anxiety literature (Allen & Desaulniers, 1974). In our survey, follow-up was reported in 13 and five investigations for self-report and performance data, respectively. Only one study (Mitchell & Ng, 1972), however, contained follow-up across both self-report and performance methods of measurement. Even though treatment effects were generally found to be maintained for periods ranging from one month to two years, we currently lack adequate information about long-term treatment effects. In a disturbingly high proportion of the studies we reviewed, participants simply seemed to disappear after posttreatment assessment was completed.

Adequately assessing therapeutic outcome will undoubtedly become an ever-more-complex task as new knowledge develops about operative artifacts, strategies of methodological control, and the construct of test anxiety. This complexity places added burdens on those of us who use the construct to better understand basic behavioral-change processes. At the same time, however, it presents a stimulating challenge to our creativity and our methodological problem-solving abilities. It is only through accepting this challenge that our research will continue to become an increasingly accurate reflection of the real-world complexity upon which our efforts are founded.

REFERENCES

Allen, G. J.   Effect of three conditions of administration on "trait" and "state" measures of anxiety. *Journal of Consulting and Clinical Psychology,* 1970, *34,* 355–359.

Allen, G. J. The effectiveness of study counseling and desensitization in alleviating test anxiety in college students. *Journal of Abnormal Psychology,* 1971, *77,* 282–289.

Allen, G. J. The behavioral treatment of test anxiety: Recent research and future trends. *Behavior Therapy,* 1972, *3,* 253–262.

Allen, G. J. Treatment of test anxiety by group-administered and self-administered relaxation and study counseling. *Behavior Therapy,* 1973, *4,* 349–360.

Allen, G. J. *Understanding psychotherapy: Comparative perspectives:* Champaign, Ill.: Research Press, 1977.

Allen, G. J., & Desaulniers, G. J. Effectiveness of study counseling and desensitization in alleviating test anxiety: A two-year follow-up. *Journal of Abnormal Psychology,* 1974, *83,* 186–191.

Alpert, R., & Haber, R. N. Anxiety in academic achievement situations. *Journal of Abnormal and Social Psychology,* 1960, *61,* 207–215.

Andrews, W. R. Behavioral and client-centered counseling of high school underachievers. *Journal of Counseling Psychology,* 1971, *18,* 93–96.

Anton, W. D. An evaluation of outcome variables in the systematic desensitization of test anxiety. *Behaviour Research and Therapy,* 1976, *14,* 217–224.

Aponte, J. F., & Aponte, C. E. Group preprogrammed systematic desensitization without the simultaneous presentation of aversive scenes with relaxation training. *Behaviour Research & Therapy,* 1971, *9,* 337–346.

Bedell, J. R. Systematic desensitization, relaxation-training, and suggestion in the treatment of test anxiety. *Behaviour Research & Therapy,* 1976, *14,* 309–311.

Beneke, W. M., & Harris, M. B. Teaching self-control of study behavior. *Behaviour Research & Therapy,* 1972, *10,* 35–41.

Bernstein, D. A. Behavioral fear assessment: Anxiety or artifact? In H. Adams & P. Unikel (Eds.), *Issues and trends in behavior therapy.* Springfield, Ill.: Charles Thomas, 1973.

Borkovec, T. D., & Nau, S. D. Credibility of analogue therapy rationales. *Journal of Behavior Therapy and Experimental Psychiatry,* 1972, *3,* 257–260.

Bruno, R., & McCullough, J. Systematic desensitization of an oral examination phobia. *Journal of Behavior Therapy and Experimental Psychiatry,* 1973, *4,* 187–190.

Calef, R. A., Calef, R. S., Sundstrom, P., Jarrett, J., & Davis, B. Facilitation of group densitization of test anxiety. *Psychological Reports,* 1974, *35,* 1285–1286.

Campbell, D. T. Prospective: Artifact and control. In R. Rosenthal & R. L. Rosnow (Eds.), *Artifact in behavioral research.* New York: Academic Press, 1969.

Campbell, D. T., & Stanley, J. C. *Experimental and quasi-experimental designs for research.* Chicago: Rand-McNally, 1963.

Chang-Liang, R., & Denney, D. R. Applied relaxation as training in self control. *Journal of Counseling Psychology,* 1976, *23,* 183–189.

Cook, T. D., & Campbell, D. T. The design and conduct of quasi-experiments and true experiments in field settings. In M. D. Dunnette (Ed.), *Handbook of industrial and organizational psychology.* Chicago: Rand-McNally, 1976.

Cornish, R. D., & Dilley, J. S. Comparison of three methods of reducing test anxiety: Systematic desensitization, implosive therapy, and study counseling. *Journal of Counseling Psychology*, 1973, *20*, 499–503.

Cronbach, L. J., & Furby, L. How we should measure change—or should we? *Psychological Bulletin*, 1970, *74*, 68–80.

Daniels, L. K. Effects of covert reinforcement in modification of test anxiety. *Psychological Reports*, 1976, *38*, 670.

Dawley, H. H., & Wenrich, W. W. Group implosive therapy in the treatment of test anxiety: A brief report. *Behavior Therapy*, 1973, *4*, 261–263.

Deffenbacher, J. L., & Rivera, N. A. A behavioral self-control treatment of test anxiety in minority populations. *Psychological Reports*, 1976, *39*, 1188–1190.

Deffenbacher, J. L., & Snyder, A. L. Relaxation as self-control in the treatment of test and other anxieties. *Psychological Reports*, 1976, *39*, 379–385.

Delprato, D. J., & DeKraker, T. Metronome conditioned hypnotic-relaxation in the treatment of test anxiety. *Behavior Therapy*, 1976, *7*, 379–381.

Denney, D. R. Active, passive, and vicarious desensitization. *Journal of Counseling Psychology*, 1974, *21*, 369–375.

Denney, D. R., & Rupert, P. A. Densensitization and self-control in the treatment of test anxiety. *Journal of Counseling Psychology*, 1977, *24*, 272–280.

Fisher, E. B. Effects of systematic desensitization by trainees in an "exam fear" clinic. *Journal of Behavior Therapy and Experimental Psychiatry*, 1977, *8*, 329–330.

Friedman, M. L., & Dies, R. R. Reactions of internal and external test anxious students to counseling and behavior therapies. *Journal of Consulting and Clinical Psychology*, 1974, *42*, 921.

Gilbreath, S. Comparison of responsive and nonresponsive underachievers to counseling service aid. *Journal of Counseling Psychology*, 1971, *18*, 81–84.

Goldfried, M. R., Linehan, M. M., & Smith, J. L. Reduction of test anxiety through cognitive restructuring. *Journal of Consulting and Clinical Psychology*, 1978, *46*, 32–39.

Graff, R. W., MacLean, G. D., & Loving, A. Group reactive inhibition and reciprocal inhibition therapies with anxious college students. *Journal of Counseling Psychology*, 1971, *18*, 431–436.

Guidry, L. S., & Randolph, D. L. Covert reinforcement in the treatment of test anxiety. *Journal of Counseling Psychology*, 1974, *21*, 260–264.

Hall, R. A., & Hinkle, J. E. Vicarious desensitization of test anxiety. *Behaviour Research & Therapy*, 1972, *10*, 407–410.

Harris, M. B., & Trujillo, A. E. Improving study habits of high school students through self-management versus group discussion. *Journal of Counseling Psychology*, 1975, *22*, 513–517.

Holroyd, K. A. Cognition and desensitization in the group treatment of test anxiety. *Journal of Consulting and Clinical Psychology*, 1976, *44*, 991–1001.

Horne, A. M., & Matson, J. L. A comparison of modeling, desensitization, flooding, study skills and control groups for reducing test anxiety. *Behavior Therapy*, 1977, *8*, 1–8.

Jackson, B., & Van Zoost, B. Changing study habits through reinforcement contingencies. *Journal of Counseling Psychology*, 1972, *19*, 192–195.

Jaffe, P. G., & Carlson, P. M. Modelling therapy for test anxiety: The role of model affect and consequences. *Behaviour Research & Therapy*, 1972, *10*, 329–339.

Kaplan, A. *The conduct of inquiry: Methodology for behavioral science.* San Francisco: Chandler, 1964.

Kaplan, R. M., & Litrownik, A. J. Some statistical methods for the assessment of multiple outcome criteria in behavioral research. *Behavior Therapy*, 1977, *8*, 383–392.

Kazdin, A. E., & Wilcoxin, L. A. Systematic desensitization and nonspecific treatment effects: A methodological evaluation. *Psychological Bulletin*, 1976, *83*, 729–758.

Kostka, M. P., & Galassi, J. P. Group systematic desensitization versus covert positive reinforcement in the reduction of test anxiety. *Journal of Counseling Psychology,* 1974, *21,* 464–468.

Lang, P. J. Fear reduction and fear behavior: Some problems in treating a construct. In J. M. Schlien (Ed.), *Research in psychotherapy* (Vol. 3). Washington, D.C.: American Psychological Association, 1968.

Lick, J., & Bootzin, R. Expectancy factors in the treatment of fear: Methodological and theoretical issues. *Psychological Bulletin,* 1975, *82,* 917–931.

Little, S., & Jackson, B. The treatment of test anxiety through attentional and relaxation training. *Psychotherapy: Theory, Research, and Practice,* 1974, *11,* 175–178.

Lomont, J. F., & Sherman, L. J. Group systematic desensitization and group insight therapies for test anxiety. *Behavior Therapy,* 1971, *2,* 511–518.

Malec, J., Park, T., & Watkins, J. T. Modeling with role playing as a treatment for test anxiety. *Journal of Consulting and Clinical Psychology,* 1976, *44,* 679.

Mann, J. Vicarious desensitization of test anxiety through observation of videotaped treatment. *Journal of Counseling Psychology,* 1972, *19,* 1–7.

Mann, J., & Rosenthal, T. L. Vicarious and direct counterconditioning of test anxiety through individual and group desensitization. *Behaviour Research & Therapy,* 1969, *7,* 359–367.

McGuire, W. J. Suspiciousness of experimenter's intent. In R. Rosenthal & R. L. Rosnow (Eds.), *Artifact in behavioral research.* New York: Academic Press, 1969.

McMillan, J. R., & Osterhouse, R. A. Specific and generalized anxiety as determinants of outcome with desensitization of test anxiety. *Journal of Counseling Psychology,* 1972, *19,* 518–521.

McReynolds, W. T., & Church, A. Self-control, study skills development, and counseling approaches to the improvement of study behavior. *Behaviour Research & Therapy,* 1973, *11,* 233–235.

Meichenbaum, D. H. Cognitive modification of test anxious college students. *Journal of Consulting and Clinical Psychology,* 1972, *39,* 370–380.

Meichenbaum, D. H., & Smart, I. Use of direct expectancy to modify academic performance and attitudes of college students. *Journal of Counseling Psychology,* 1971, *18,* 531–535.

Meyer, R. G. A behavioral treatment of sleepwalking associated with test anxiety. *Journal of Behavior Therapy and Experimental Psychiatry,* 1975, *6,* 167–168.

Mitchell, K. R. Effects of neuroticism on intra-treatment responsivity to group desensitization of test anxiety. *Behaviour Research & Therapy,* 1971, *9,* 371–374.

Mitchell, K. R., Hall, R. F., & Piatkowska, O. E. A group program for the treatment of failing college students. *Behavior Therapy,* 1975, *6,* 324–336.

Mitchell, K. R., & Ng, K. T. Effects of group counseling and behavior therapy on the academic achievement of test anxious students. *Journal of Counseling Psychology,* 1972, *19,* 491–497.

Osterhouse, R. A. Densitization and study skills training as treatment for two types of test anxious students. *Journal of Counseling Psychology,* 1972, *19,* 301–307.

Paul, G. L. *Insight versus desensitization in psychotherapy.* Stanford: Stanford University Press, 1966.

Paul, G., L. Behavior modification research: Design and tactics. In C. M. Franks (Ed.), *Behavior therapy: Appraisal and status.* New York: McGraw-Hill, 1969.

Reed, R., & Meyer, R. G. Reduction of test anxiety via autogenic therapy. *Psychological Reports,* 1974, *35,* 649–650.

Richards, C. S. Behavior modification of studying through study skills advice and self-control procedures. *Journal of Counseling Psychology,* 1975, *22,* 431–436.

Richardson, F. C., & Suinn, R. M. A comparison of traditional systematic desensitization, accelerated massed desensitization, and anxiety management training in the treatment of mathematics anxiety. *Behavior Therapy,* 1973, *4,* 212–218.

Romano, J. L., & Cabianca, W. A. EMG biofeedback training versus systematic desensitization for test anxiety reduction. *Journal of Counseling Psychology,* 1978, *25,* 8–13.

Russell, R. K., Miller, D. E., & June, L. N. A comparison between group systematic desensitization and cue-controlled relaxation in the treatment of test anxiety. *Behavior Therapy,* 1975, *6,* 172–177.

Russell, R. K., & Sipich, J. F. Cue-controlled relaxation in the treatment of test anxiety. *Journal of Behavior Therapy and Experimental Psychiatry,* 1973, *4,* 47–49.

Russell, R. K., & Sipich, J. F. Treatment of test anxiety by cue-controlled relaxation. *Behavior Therapy,* 1974, *5,* 673–676.

Russell, R. K., Wise, F., & Stratoudakis, J. P. Treatment of test anxiety by cue-controlled relaxation and systematic desensitization. *Journal of Counseling Psychology,* 1976, *23,* 563–566.

Sarason, I. G. Test anxiety, general anxiety, and intellectual performance. *Journal of Consulting Psychology,* 1957, *21,* 485–490.

Sarason, I. G. Experimental approaches to test anxiety: Attention and the uses of information. In C. D. Spielberger (Ed.), *Anxiety: Current trends in theory and research.* (Vol II). New York: Academic Press, 1972.

Scissons, E. H., & Njaa, L. Systematic desensitization of test anxiety: A comparison of group and individual treatment. *Journal of Consulting and Clinical Psychology,* 1973, *41,* 470.

Smith, R. E., & Nye, S. L. A comparison of implosive therapy and systematic desensitization in the treatment of test anxiety. *Journal of Consulting and Clinical Psychology,* 1973, *41,* 37–42.

Snyder, A. L., & Deffenbacher, J. L. Comparison of relaxation as self-control and desensitization in the treatment of test anxiety. *Journal of Consulting and Clinical Psychology,* 1977, *45,* 1202–1203.

Spiegler, M. D., Cooley, E. J., Marshall, G. J., Prince, H. T., Puckett, S. P., & Skenazy, J. A. A self-control versus a counterconditioning paradigm for systematic desensitization: An experimental comparison. *Journal of Counseling Psychology,* 1976, *23,* 83–86.

Spielberger, C. D., Gorsuch, R. L., & Lushene, R. E. *Manual for the state–trait anxiety inventory.* Palo Alto, Calif.: Consulting Psychologists Press, 1970.

Suinn, R. M. Changes in nontreated subjects over time: Data on a fear survey schedule and the test anxiety scale. *Behaviour Research & Therapy,* 1969, *7,* 205–206. (a).

Suinn, R. M. The STABS, a measure of test anxiety for behavior therapy: Normative data. *Behaviour Research & Therapy,* 1969, *7,* 335–339. (b).

Suinn, R. M. Short-term desensitization therapy. *Behaviour Research & Therapy,* 1970, *8,* 383–384.

Suinn, R. M., Edie, C. A., & Spinelli, P. R. Accelerated massed desensitization: Innovation in short term treatment. *Behavior Therapy,* 1970, *1,* 303–311.

Suinn, R. M., & Hall, R. Marathon desensitization groups: An innovative technique. *Behaviour Research & Therapy,* 1970, *8,* 97–98.

Suinn, R. M., & Richardson, F. Anxiety management training: A nonspecific behavior therapy program for anxiety control. *Behavior Therapy,* 1971, *2,* 498–510.

Tasto, D. L., & Suinn, R. M. Fear Survey Schedule: Changes on total and factor scores due to nontreatment effects. *Behavior Therapy,* 1972, *3,* 275–278.

Taylor, D. W. A comparison of group desensitization with two control procedures in the treatment of test anxiety. *Behaviour Research & Therapy,* 1971, *9,* 281–284.

Wisocki, P. A. A covert reinforcement program for the treatment of test anxiety: Brief report. *Behavior Therapy,* 1973, *4,* 264–266.

Zemore, R. Systematic desensitization as a method of teaching a general anxiety skill. *Journal of Consulting and Clinical Psychology,* 1975, *43,* 157–161.

9

Toward a Conceptual Model for the Treatment of Test Anxiety: Implications for Research and Treatment

Donald Meichenbaum
Lynda Butler

University of Waterloo
Waterloo, Ontario, Canada

PROLOGUE

An often-cited finding in the literature is that *uncertainty* causes anxiety. We propose that *redundancy* can also engender anxiety. As we received the chapter outlines from each of the contributors to this volume, we began to wonder what was left for us to discuss concerning test anxiety. Have so many ever written so much about one topic? It was enough to make one anxious!

Our task was to review the literature on the cognitive-behavioral treatment of test anxiety, but this literature has already been reviewed elsewhere in some detail (Goldfried, 1977; Meichenbaum, 1977; Spielberger, Anton, & Bedell, 1976) as well as by some of the contributors to this volume (Deffenbacher; Denney). Moreover, Meichenbaum and Genest (1977) have recently described a procedure for the treatment of test-anxious clients by means of cognitive-behavior modification.

The question remained: How could we reduce our anxiety about finding something to say that had not already been said? Indeed, could we come to view this anxiety as facilitative instead of debilitative? What was the state of our worry and emotionality? "Now, no self-preoccupying thoughts. Focus attention. View this as a problem to be solved, a challenge, not as an occasion for irrational self-statements and catastrophizing images."

Our solution was to try to integrate the test anxiety literature by proposing a conceptual model that has implications for the treatment of this problem. How therapeutically or heuristically valuable this model will prove to be for test-anxious clients is a question for future research to examine, but we can attest to its usefulness in the reduction of anxiety in two authors.

OVERVIEW OF THE CHAPTER

Having shared some of our initial anxiety, we should now like to share some of our more task-oriented thoughts about the problem of test anxiety. Our impression, based on a review of the literature and on our work with test-anxious clients, is that something *more* is going on in test anxiety than has been studied to date. We think test anxiety is more than physiological arousal, more than negative self-preoccupation, more than poor study habits, and more than a deficit in stress-related coping skills. In fact, we think it is more than a *combination* of these factors. The model that we present in this chapter is our first attempt to describe these and other elements that we think central to the problem of test anxiety and to consider the complex ways in which they may interact.

Following the tradition of George Kelley (1955), we employ an analogy of the scientist's behavior in order to convey the various elements of our model and their interrelationships. After this brief introduction, we describe each of the model's components in some detail, discussing relevant findings in the test anxiety literature and presenting suggestions for future research. The final section of the chapter discusses implications of the model for the treatment of test anxiety.

THE SCIENTIST: AN ANALOGY

A consideration of how we, as scientists, go about the task of developing theories, collecting data, and so on, may prove useful in understanding what goes on in test anxiety. Indeed, as we learn more about how scientists function (consider, for example, the work of Brush, 1974; Hebb, 1975; Mahoney, 1976; and Polanyi; 1958), the better the fit between scientists and our clients. As each of these authors underlines, for example, the role of passion is equally evident in both populations.

Most simplistically, we can consider that the scientist holds a set of explicit or implicit beliefs, a type of meaning system. These beliefs (or what we will describe as *cognitive structures*) about the phenomena under investigation give rise to conscious thought (or what we shall call *internal dialogue*) in the scientist. The scientist's internal dialogue represents the hypotheses and hunches that guide and influence *behavioral acts,* (i.e., what phenomena will be attended to, the appraisal and evaluation of these phenomena, and most important, what kind of experiments will be undertaken). The scientist's observations and experiments yield data (or *behavioral outcomes*) that may be viewed as being either consistent or anomalous with the scientist's cognitive structures; this will lead to the acceptance or rejection of the data. What the scientist says to himself or herself about the behavioral outcomes of experiments will determine whether he or she considers the results as *evidence*, and this will in turn alter or confirm the initial beliefs. The situation becomes more complicated when we recognize that the scientist, like many of our clients, has a host of defensive rationalizations and cognitive techniques to discount, obscure, "fudge", or even occasionally simply accept the importance of data derived from behavioral outcomes. As we shall see, the issue of what constitutes evidence is not only critical for the scientist, but also has important implications in the treatment of clients whose central concern is anxiety about evaluation in test situations.

What we have described, in effect, is an *evidential* model of human behavior. The model includes the concepts of cognitive structures, internal dialogue, behavioral acts, and behavioral outcomes. Let us now briefly consider each of these components of the model and indicate how they apply to the problem of test anxiety. We begin with a consideration of internal dialogue because this concept has received the most attention in the test anxiety literature. Then, we discuss behavioral acts and behavioral outcomes and end with the difficult but, we believe, important construct of cognitive structures. Even though these components are described separately, it is important to appreciate that, according to the model, they are considered to be highly interdependent as they interweave in contributing to the problem of test anxiety and its treatment.

INTERNAL DIALOGUE

An individual's internal dialogue refers to the conscious thoughts (self-statements and images) which he or she can report to someone else (see Meichenbaum, 1977, for a fuller discussion of the nature of the internal dialogue). An examination of the test anxiety literature indicates that most of the research has focused on the role of internal dialogue in relation to test performance. A repeated observation is that highly anxious individuals react to the stress of test situations with personalized responses of a negative character, which direct attention away from the task at hand. For example, Deffenbacher (1978) found that for the highly anxious individual only, evaluative stress elicited interfering anxiety in the form of attention to worrisome thoughts and ruminations, physiological arousal and upset, and other elements of task irrelevancies. A low-stress condition did not elicit a similar internal dialogue in these individuals. Self-preoccupation, consisting of self-awareness, self-doubt, and self-depreciation, was found to characterize high-anxious subjects in studies by Heckhausen (in press); Holroyd, Westbrook, Wolf, and Badhorn (1978); Houston (1978); and Sarason and Stoops (1978).

In a recent study, Hollandsworth, Glazeski, Kirkland, Jones, and van Norman (1978) employed an innovative method of assessing aspects of the test-anxious individual's internal dialogue. Subjects (all female) were videotaped while individually taking a test. Immediately after testing, they reviewed their tape with an experimenter and reconstructed what they were thinking and feeling as they worked on the test. In addition to assessing the subjects' internal dialogues by means of this videotape reconstruction procedure, Hollandsworth et al. monitored the subjects' physiological reactions during testing. As was expected, they found that high-test-anxious subjects engaged in more task-irrelevant thinking and negative rumination than low-anxious subjects. Interestingly, the low-anxious subjects in this study showed *more* physiological arousal than the high-anxious subjects, but they described their anxiety on the Alpert-Haber (1960) scale as facilitative rather than debilitative. Thus, it did not appear to be the level of arousal per se that had a critical debilitating impact on test performance but what the subjects said to themselves about the arousal they experienced. This observation is consistent with the findings of Meichenbaum (1972) and Wine (1970).

In a therapist manual for treating test anxiety, Richardson (1973) has suggested the following categorization of the thinking processes of high-test-anxious individuals:

1. Worrying about one's performance, including how well others are doing as compared with oneself.
2. Ruminating too long and fruitlessly over alternative answers or responses.
3. Being preoccupied with bodily reactions associated with anxiety.
4. Ruminating about possible consequences of doing poorly on the test: disapproval, punishment, loss of status or esteem, damage to academic record or job changes.
5. Thoughts or feelings of inadequacy, including active self-criticism or self-condemnation, calling oneself "stupid," considering onself worthless.

In summary, the maladaptive quality of the high-anxious individual's thinking is evident in the following aspects of the internal dialogue: (1) it is self-oriented rather than task-oriented, which serves to deflect attention from the task at hand; (2) its basic orientation is negative rather than positive, which serves to deflate motivation; and (3) it has an automatic, stereotyped, "run-on" character, which has the effect of escalating rather than controlling anxiety.

Although we have a descriptive account of the internal dialogue of test-anxious individuals, in fact this descriptive account is quite general in nature. Exactly how test-anxious individuals differ in their internal dialogue from low-anxious individuals is something we actually know very little about this point. This is largely because we know very little about the internal dialogue of the individual who copes adequately with examination stress. Is, for example, the critical difference the *lack* of negative ideation in low-test-anxious individuals, or do these low-anxious individuals interrupt negative ideation and employ coping skills and adaptive defenses such as attention-focusing, compartmentalization, positive labeling of arousal, humor, and so on? What are the situational cues that will lead a low-test-anxious individual to produce negative self-referent ideation? The answer to questions such as these will help explicate the role of internal dialogue as a contributor to test anxiety.

We have argued elsewhere (Meichenbaum, 1977; Meichenbaum & Butler, 1978) for the development of a *cognitive ethology* that will help us map the cognitive domain (thought content, frequency, and most important, patterning) of high- and low-test-anxious individuals, as well as other clients, in much the same way that the ethologists describe sequences of overt behaviors, looking for explanatory constructs such as fixed-action patterns, releasing stimuli, etc. Cognitive ethology requires the development of an armamentarium of techniques (interviews, questionnaires, think-aloud protocols, videotape reconstruction, thought sampling, etc.) to assess more adequately the subject's cognitive processes or what we are calling internal dialogue. We could use this assessment methodology, for example, to explicate the effect of cognitive factors on performance across tasks and populations because a number of studies suggest a common patterning of self-referent negative ideation situations. These studies include such settings as taking an examination (Hollandsworth et al., 1978), responding to social challenges (Smye, 1977), tolerating pain (Genest, Turk, & Meichenbaum, 1977), performing in athletic competition (Mahoney & Avener, 1977; O'Hara, 1977), and producing creative cartoon captions and creative responses on tests of divergent thinking (Henshaw, 1978). Meichenbaum, Henshaw, and Himel (in press) have even gone so far as to speculate that a common pattern of thinking processes (which they characterize as a failure to adopt a problem-solving set) contributes to inadequate performance on a variety of tasks. (See Cacioppo and Petty, 1978, and Meichenbaum and Butler, 1978, for a discussion of the advantages and pitfalls of these cognitive assessment procedures.)

Whether commonalities in thought processes can be identified across stressful situations in a provocative hypothesis worth testing. Confining ourselves in the meantime to the problem of test anxiety, we would argue for the importance of using such cognitive assessment procedures as we have available to attempt to identify *patterns* of thought in individuals confronted with academic evaluative situations. We are proposing that identification of individual thought patterns may give us some clue to the broader "meaning" of test anxiety for the individual and help us understand why some individuals experience this problem and others in similarly stressful situations do not. It is our hunch that the negative self-referent internal dialogue of the test-anxious individual may reflect more general, embedded, and, in some cases, quite rigid structures of thought about oneself and the environment with which one is confronted. We return to this issue later in our discussion of cognitive structures.

BEHAVIORAL ACTS

Whereas internal dialogue involves the content, frequency, and patterning of an individual's thought (self-statements and images) in a given situation, the concept of behavioral acts focuses on directly observable behaviors. Such behavioral acts have received relatively little attention in the test anxiety literature, although we think this is an area worthy of further investigation.

One class of behavioral acts which has been examined to some extent is study habits. Desiderato and Koskinen (1969) showed that high test anxiety was related to poor study habits, and these in turn were related to a lower academic achievement level. Allen (1971) found that a combination of desensitization and study counseling was more effective in reducing physiological activation due to examination stress, and in improving academic performance (GPA and two measures of examination performance) than either type of treatment used by itself. Although poor study habits appear to play a role in the inadequate performance of at least some test-anxious students, more direct assessment in a natural setting of study behaviors of high- and low-test-anxious subjects (amount and efficient use of study time, coverage of material, and so on) would be valuable in assessing the relationship between study skills and test anxiety.

A second class of behavioral acts that merits further attention is that of interpersonal behavior in preparation for stressful evaluative situations. An interesting prototype for the kind of naturalistic research which might be undertaken is the work of Mechanic (1962), who studied the way in which graduate students preparing for comprehensive examinations negotiated their relationships with faculty and fellow students. Mechanic found that students who were effective in controlling their anxiety about the upcoming examinations sought out contacts with faculty members in order to get information about the examinations and how to prepare for them and to receive support and reassurance. In their contacts with fellow students who were also anxiously preparing for the examinations, they sought information exchange and reassurance but avoided social comparison situations (with highly competitive students or "anxiety carriers," for example) that might undermine their self-confidence and ability to cope. Upon reading Mechanic's provocative study, we were immediately led to wonder whether high- and low-test-anxious individuals also differ in preexamination interpersonal behavior. It seems unlikely that an intense preoccupation with evaluation would be confined only to behavior in actual test-taking situations.

A third class of behavioral acts that we find potentially interesting is that of actual test-taking behavior. An illustrative study on test-taking skills was conducted by Bruch (1978), who examined in a 2 × 2 design the role of various model characteristics (model verbalization of problem-solving rules vs. coping self-statements, and presence or absence of model reinforcement) in reducing evaluation anxiety in a laboratory anagram task. The subjects were asked to fill out a self-report protocol about the cognitive tactics they were employing at three different points during post-test performance. The results indicated that cognitive modeling of problem-solving rules was the only variable that consistently influenced performance and imitative responding. These results were moderated by level of task difficulty, client characteristics, and model reinforcement. Bruch's (1978) general findings are consistent with those of Sarason, Pederson, and Nyman (1968), who permitted college students to observe a model perform on a serial learning task prior to their own performance on a similar task. They found that the performance of high-test-anxious subjects increased more as a function of opportunity to observe a model than did that of low-test-anxious subjects. The test-taking situations with which university students, in particular, are confronted require complex and sophisticated test-taking skills (multiple-choice strategies, selection of essay questions, organization of material, and so on). Whether high- and low-test-anxious subjects differ in the possession *or* in the employment of such skills in an actual examination situation is an important question for future research.

Although we have discussed separately the potential importance of three classes of behavioral acts (study behavior, test-taking behavior, and interpersonal behavior), we believe that such behaviors are intimately interconnected and may interact in a variety of ways to contribute to test anxiety. At the same time, we would also like to stress the interaction of test-related behaviors and the internal dialogue. An illustration of the necessity for considering the interrelationship between the test-anxious individual's internal dialogue and behavior is to be found in Goldfried's (1977) review of the evidence for a cognitive (coping) component in traditional approaches (relaxation training, systematic desensitization) to the treatment of test anxiety. (Relaxation is, of course, one of a class of behavioral acts, i. e., coping behaviors, which are of considerable importance in controlling anxiety in stressful situations). Goldfried (1977) argued that the effective ingredient in traditional behavioral approaches to anxiety management is the subject's acquisition of a coping skill (for example, relaxation) which provides a *sense of control* over anxiety that was previously perceived as debilitating.

Studies that have added a coping component to either standard relaxation training (for example, Goldfried & Trier, 1974; Chang-Liang & Denney, 1976) or systematic desensitization (Meichenbaum, 1972; Denney & Rupert,

1977 have consistently found "coping plus behavioral" treatments superior to standard behavioral approaches in the modification of a variety of anxiety-related problems, including test anxiety. Moreover, treatments such as rational restructuring, which directly attack the individual's belief systems and internal dialogue *without* providing relaxation skills, are as effective (Goldfried, Linehan, & Smith, 1978) or more effective (Holroyd, 1976) than single or combined cognitive-behavioral approaches. It appears to be the case, then, that the employment of relaxation skills to control excessive anxiety is not effective because of the reduction of physiological arousal per se but because the test-anxious individual's internal dialogue about that arousal has in some respects changed from one of panic to one of coping.

We need, then, to examine the ways in which a test-anxious individual's internal dialogue about his anxiety affects his interpersonal (information- and support-seeking) and school-related (study or test-taking) behaviors, or how lack of skills in these areas may magnify the threat of evaluation and engender "catastrophizing" ideation. An examination (i.e., Schwartz & Gottman, 1976) of whether test-anxious individuals lack the knowledge of, or simply do not employ, interpersonal and task skills that might assist them in evaluative situations is a needed first step in this direction.

BEHAVIORAL OUTCOMES

Closely akin to the concept of behavioral acts is the notion of behavioral consequences. Under the concept of behavioral outcomes are subsumed a wide range of events to which the individual has some cognitive or behavioral reaction. These may include tangible results, such as the grade or other feedback one receives on an examination, as well as either positive or negative social reinforcement (praise, respect, criticism, derision, etc.). Behavioral outcomes may also refer to internal events, such as physiological reactions, mood states, and so on.

The evidential nature of our model of human behavior is most apparent when we examine how test-anxious individuals react to behavioral outcomes. The reader will recall Hollandsworth et al.'s (1978) high-test-anxious subjects, who defined their arousal as debilitative rather than facilitative. Goldfried (1977), Meichenbaum (1972), and Wine (1970) have demonstrated that cognitive-behavioral treatment can help test-anxious subjects come to view their anxiety more positively as a cue to cope. We know something about the interaction of internal dialogue and physiological arousal; however, we know considerably less about the test-anxious individual's reaction to other behavioral outcomes. What, for example, constitutes praise or criticism for this individual in comparison with his or her low-anxious counterpart? Does the test-anxious person even "hear" praise in contrast to critical feedback? We are not sure. How do high- versus low-test-anxious individuals differ in their criteria for success or failure or in their definition of "adequate" performance? What are their causal attributions when success or failure occurs? Heckhausen (in press) has called for a closer examination of the complex interaction of factors such as these in relation to performance outcome.

In summary, it is our belief that the test-anxious client, like our scientist confronting his or her experimental data, plays a central role in defining what constitutes a behavioral outcome and how he or she evaluates this. Individual differences in interpretation of behavioral outcomes can, in turn, have an important motivating impact on concurrent and future test performance. By asking the following questions, we can begin to tap how behavioral outcomes are individually defined and how clients may best be treated: (1) What are the data that the client uses to indicate that he or she is test-anxious? (2) What alterations in these data would be viewed as being anomalous with his or her self-definition as a test-anxious person? The answer to such questions will suggest the conditions under which the client may begin to consider and weigh outcomes in a more adaptive fashion. Changes in what he or she views as evidence can in turn contribute to changes in underlying belief systems or cognitive structures, and to improvements in test performance. The treatment implications of this process of evidential change are discussed in more detail later.

COGNITIVE STRUCTURES

When we began our treatment research on test anxiety (Meichenbaum, 1972), the focus of attention was the internal dialogue of the test-anxious individual. The treatment regimen attempted to alter the way in which this individual appraised the test situation and the nature of his or her self-statements and images in evaluative situations. The test-anxious clients were trained to develop a variety of cognitive and behavioral strategies in order to shift the focus of their attention from that of excessive preoccupation with their personal deficiencies to more adaptive task-relevant cognitions. The initial results of this treatment approach have proven quite encouraging (for example, Holroyd, 1976; Meichenbaum, 1972; and other studies reviewed by Denney in this volume).

Several clinical observations, however, led us to question the adequacy of a cognitive-behavioral treatment approach that limited its focus to the test-anxious client's internal dialogue. For example, in *some* instances test-anxious clients following cognitive-behavioral treatment reported that while taking an examination they would employ the host of behavioral and cognitive coping responses in which they had been trained but that they would often become anxious anyway. Some of the clients indicated that there was an accompanying set of thoughts which took the following form: "I must *really* be anxious if I have to use all these techniques." What these clients said to themselves about using coping responses—which reflects the (negative) *meaning* they imposed on the use of these procedures—influenced their efficacy. Treatment outcome was apparently influenced not only by the possession of specific coping skills, but also by how they "fit" into the individual's meaning system.

A second observation that led us to question the relationship between internal dialogue and performance was the rather frequent experience of encountering students who constantly bemoaned their chances of doing well on an examination, who following the examination similarly decried their performance—but who invariably did well in spite of (or because of?) their protestations. Whether such personal styles serve a defensive or attention-getting function, we do not know. The point to be made, however, is that an anxious, self-deprecating dialogue does not seem necessarily to result in debilitated performance, perhaps because evaluation has a different *meaning* for these individuals than for the highly test-anxious person.

Finger and Galassi (1977) have called for a more careful examination of the relationship between anxiety and performance. We agree. We need to know *why* (as well as *how*) high- and low-test-anxious subjects differ in their internal dialogue, behavioral acts, and interpretation of behavioral outcomes. We need to know *why* test-anxious individuals who have an extensive natural repertoire of coping skills (and our clinical experience convinces us that many do) do not employ them in this, and perhaps other, evaluative situations. We need to know *why* treatments that effect changes in the internal dialogue (via rational restructuring or coping self-statements) and in behavior (by training in relaxation or study skills) work for some individuals and not for others. We are curious about *why* some individuals who appear very anxious about evaluation actually perform well in test situations.

It was our concern to understand some of these individual differences and their treatment implications that led us to introduce the construct of cognitive structures into the present model. Although the construct is a difficult one and has in fact been characterized (Meichenbaum, 1977) as the cognitive psychologist's Rorschach card or "Linus-blanket" (one can see anything one wants in it, and it gives one a sense of security), it has nevertheless captured the attention of a large number of eminent psychologists over the years.

The term *cognitive structures* was first made familiar by Tolman (1932) and Lewin (1935). Since then, under the banner of cognitive structures have fallen such concepts as Bandura's (1978) "self-system"; Bartlett's (1932) "schema"; Hilgard's (1976) "control systems"; Miller, Galanter, and Pribram's (1960) "images and plans"; Morris's (1975) "structures of meaning"; Parkes's (1971) and Frank's (1961) "assumptive worlds"; Klinger's (1977) "current concerns";

Piaget's (1954) "schemata"; Sarbin's "roles" (Sarbin & Coe, 1972); and Schank and Abelson's (1978) "scripts." As varied as the terminology is, however, Averill (inpress) has pointed out that the basic idea behind cognitive structures is the same:

Events are only meaningful to the extent that they can be assimilated into some existing cognitive model or structure; and if they cannot be assimilated, then the relevant cognitive structures must be altered to accommodate the environmental input [p. 24].

In the context of the present model, we were interested in a conceptualization of cognitive structures that seemed to account for the motivation, direction, and organization of behavior. We wanted to use such a construct in order to understand why individuals differ in their responses to the same environmental stimuli (in the case of test anxiety, to evaluative situations). We have also been struck repeatedly in our research and clinical experience with test-anxious individuals by the automatic, stereotyped quality of their thinking in a situation in which even the test-anxious individual was aware that it was highly inappropriate to the task demands, and by the persistence of this behavior even when alternative (and more adaptive) ways of dealing with the situation were available to the individual. Our second concern, therefore, was a conceptualization of cognitive structures that could account for the stereotypy and persistence of maladaptive behavior in certain situations.

The conception of cognitive structures that we have chosen to focus upon is what we call the individual's *meaning system* (a concept somewhat akin to Klinger's, 1977, "current concerns"). As we have suggested earlier, we believe that the test situation may hold a somewhat different meaning for each individual. We see this meaning as part of a broader network of concerns or goals (i.e., the individual's meaning system) that determines what are important issues in an individual's life and the position he or she takes in relation to them. These concerns may vary in intensity (how important or central they are) and in valence (positive or negative). An individual will normally have a multiplicity of concerns, some of which support and others which compete with one another, in situations the individual encounters. In any given situation with which the individual is confronted (for example, a test), the overall meaning which he or she attaches to the situation will determine whether he or she will participate, what aspects of the situation he or she will attend and respond to, how intense the involvement will be, and the general positive or negative orientation of behavior in that situation.

In short, we see the individual's meaning system as a kind of "executive processor" which holds the "blueprints" for both thinking and behavior. The meaning system functions to set behavior in motion, to guide the choice and direction of particular sequences of thought and behavior, and to determine their continuation, interruption, or change of direction. In this sense, meaning systems control the "scripts" from which internal dialogues and behavioral acts borrow. (Here we use "scripts," or stereotyped thought and behavior, in the spirit of Abelson, 1978; Gagnon and Simon, 1973; Langer, 1978; Schank and Abelson, 1978; and Tompkins, (1978). The concept of meaning system also helped us make sense of the highly automatic, predictable, stereotyped quality of many individuals', and particularly test-anxious individuals', behavior in evaluative situations. We first discuss the implications of the concept of meaning system for test anxiety and then deal with the scripted or stereotyped behavior to which the meaning system gives rise.

In terms of meaning systems, we can envisage a variety of possible concerns or meanings that might influence the behavior of individuals confronted with evaluative situations. Consider the following examples: (1) concern over loss of control, fear of being overwhelmed by anxiety; (2) concern to gain the esteem of authority figures and/or peers; (3) concern by a student that high academic achievement might jeopardize social relationships with members of the opposite sex; (4) concern for job sucess or entry into graduate school; or (5) concern by a male that academic failure would result in being subject to the military draft. Note that some of these concerns are specific and some general, some are negative and some positive in valence, but in each case they represent the meaning which academic evaluative situations holds for the *individual*. Our concern is that the treatment techniques thus far employed (and especially behavioral interventions such as desensitization) have failed to deal with the broader personal meaning(s) of evaluation.

It is important to note that competing concerns or meanings might produce alternating or ambivalent behavior in test situations. The reader will recall our earlier example of the individual who showed every evidence of severe anxiety about evaluation but who performed well nonetheless. It is possible that, whatever this individual's negative feelings about evaluation (for example, loss of his professor's esteem, fear of being overwhelmed), more adaptive competing concerns (future goals, for example) were more salient for him in the actual test situation.

One of the important implications that follows from this argument is that we should not impose a "uniformity myth" (Kieslar, 1966) on test-anxious subjects. Different meaning systems may underlie many of the same behaviors. What we have assessed in these individuals as hypervigilance to evaluation cues—self-deprecating, ruminative internal dialogue, or inefficient study habits—may represent final common pathways for a variety of different concerns. One must be concerned with the entire constellation of important concerns the individual brings to bear on the test situation and with where negative concerns (for example, loss of control) fit in with other more adaptive goals that may be present (such as academic and job success). From the viewpoint of therapy, with some test-anxious clients the objective could be to influence the valence and priority of the respective meanings they attach to evaluative situations. The present analysis also implies that just as high-test-anxious individuals should be viewed as a heterogeneous population, low-test-anxious individuals should be viewed as heterogeneous as well. It is our hunch that at least some low-test-anxious individuals experience considerable negative affect and ideation in evaluative situations but perform adequately, nonetheless, because the overall valence of competing concerns leads to the use of cognitive and behavioral coping techniques. Other low-anxious individuals may quite simply have few negative concerns related to evaluation and thus little anxiety in test situations.

We suggest, moreover, that the nature and number of an individual's concerns should be predictive of the magnitude of anxiety in test situations and its amenability to treatment intervention. The prognosis for an individual with a large number of intensely negative concerns would be less favorable than that for a person who has either a relatively specific concern or intense positive concerns that override the negative meaning he or she attaches to test situations. In addition, the nature of the individual's concerns should be predictive of the generality of evaluation anxiety across situations and the particular kind of situations in which it would most likely occur. This suggestion is consistent with the conclusion (Bem & Allen, 1974; Ekehammer, Schalling, & Magnusson, 1973; Magnusson & Ekehammer, 1975) that situational variables are important insofar as the person perceives them to be and that cross-situational consistency of behavior depends upon the individual's perception of similarity in situations. What we are proposing, in effect, is that the individual's meaning system influences such perceptions and defines what is similar across situations; this, in turn, will influence the range of situations in which the individual manifests evaluation anxiety.

An interesting way to assess the meaning system's impact upon behavior would be to employ a methodology similar to that proposed by Pervin (1976). After asking subjects to list current life situations and give free descriptions and ratings of them, Pervin grouped situations, by means of cluster analysis, toward which individuals showed similar patterns of feelings and behavior. Using this methodology, we might be able to descriminate among high-test-anxious individuals who have quite different meaning systems contributing to their evaluation anxiety. It might be that the same kind of internal dialogue would characterize each subgroup of high-anxious individuals in evaluative situations but that they would differ in other ways (for example, frequency of anxiety experiences, situational threshold for anxious behavior, situational specificity, etc.)

Thus far, we have discussed the ways in which the meaning system that individuals bring to bear on test situations may influence their cognitive and overt behavior in such situations. Let us now consider the stereotypic aspects of that behavior. *Behavioral stereotypy,* we suggest, may be a function of stored personal predictions about what typically happens in situations involving the individual (what thoughts and feelings one will have, what behaviors one will engage in, how others will react, what the outcome will be, etc.). These stored predictions are most likely the result of repeated personal experience with similar situations in the past. In any given situation, these stored predictions may give rise to specific thought and behavioral sequences (what Abelson, 1978, calls "behavioral scripts") that have a quality of automaticity, if not rigidity and stereotypy. These personal predictions are activated (i.e., transformed into behavior) by a combination of environmental and internal cues, cues to which the individual is highly sensitized because of the meaning or meanings that the situation holds for him or her. In this sense, the individual's meaning system determines what specific stereotyped thinking and behavioral sequences are called into play in any given situation and whether these will be interrupted or replaced with other sequences of thought and behavior.

Let us consider some examples of behavioral stereotypy in test situations. We are all familiar with the ruminative, self-deprecating cognitive scripts (internal dialogue) of the highly test-anxious individual in examination situations, although we know less about his or her behavioral scripts (for example, test-taking strategies or rituals) in such situations. We also think it possible that highly practiced behavioral and cognitive scripts may be called into play in other test-relevant situations (studying, interpersonal behavior, etc.). Here we are vividly reminded of Mechanic's (1962) highly anxious graduate students who repeatedly sought out others in the same situation for anxiety-raising ruminations and speculations about the upcoming examinations.

Nor do we need to see scripted behaviors as necessarily performance-debilitating. The following example of a mixed script (one which may reflect competing concerns) comes from our clinical work with test-anxious students. One highly test-anxious individual reported that before going to each exam she planned exactly where she would sit (the same place each time); she timed her arrival (the same time) so as not to interact with other students who might discuss the course material, and she focused her attention on concrete aspects of the situation so as not to dwell on her worries about the upcoming examination. This stereotyped behavior was activated by a deep concern about not "losing control" and reflected the client's attempt to cope. At the same time, her behavior reflected her personal prediction that she would be highly anxious in the test situation; her anxiety was presumably motivated by some combination of negative meanings that the situation held for her.

Although behavioral stereotypy is most evident in highly test-anxious individuals, it may be characteristic to some extent of low-test-anxious individuals as well. We need to assess personal predictions and the stream of behavior in both kinds of individuals more carefully in order to determine where differences between these groups lie. Is it for example, the general *content* of their scripts (positive or negative, success or failure, coping vs. panic) which differs? Or is it the degree of *rigidity* or automaticity which is the essential difference in the behavior of high- and low-test-anxious individuals? Do low-test-anxious individuals, for example, monitor, interrupt, and change their predictions and behavior more flexibly in response to situational demands and environmental feedback than high-test-anxious individuals (where the meaning(s) of the situation so constrains their attention and predictions that stereotyped maladaptive thinking and behavior "runs on" to the detriment of their test performance)? The exploration with test-anxious clients of their personal predictions and the impact these have on behavior may prove a useful addition to our treatment armamentarium and has in fact been used effectively, if informally, in cognitive-behavioral group treatment approaches (Meichenbaum & Genest, 1977).

Let us now consider some general treatment implications of the proposed model.

IMPLICATIONS FOR TREATMENT

The outcome data for the treatment of test anxiety has produced somewhat mixed results. Finger (1975) reported that performance improvements were obtained in only 16 of 54 (29.6%) treatment studies of test anxiety. Denney in this volume has indicated that performance improvement varied from 33% when relaxation techniques were used to treat test-anxious subjects to 71% when cognitive-behavioral coping training procedures were employed. Although one can be encouraged by the increased improvement evident in more cognitively oriented coping-skills training programs (which is consistent with our suggestion of substantial cognitive mediation of test-anxious behavior), there still remains room for a good deal of improvement.

One set of implications that derives from the present conceptual model is the need to perform a careful analysis of the client's test anxiety. As indicated previously, individuals may be test-anxious for different reasons, and the therapist needs to determine the mediating role of the individual's meaning system on factors such as his or her internal dialogue, behavioral acts, and interpretation of behavioral outcomes. For example, while editing this chapter, the senior author was approached by a chairperson of a mathematics department who was distressed over the math anxiety experienced by students at her university. She was concerned, in particular, about minority students restricting their career options, because a number of these mathematics courses were prerequisites for certain professional programs. Assuming that the chairperson had correctly diagnosed the problem, one can begin to wonder how to analyze and intervene with this supposedly math-anxious population. What would be the nature of the meaning systems that such students brought to bear on exam situations influencing major career choices? What might be the stereotyped thinking and behavior that they had built up over years of experience in such situations? What would be the impact of these factors on their employment of cognitive and behavioral coping skills? What would be the most effective level of treatment intervention?

A second set of implications of the present model is that a treatment approach will be most effective if it influences in some way the entire chain of events (viz., meaning system, internal dialogue, behavioral acts, and interpretation of behavioral outcomes) rather than focusing on only one aspect of the process. In contrast, a consideration of the various treatment procedures described in the literature indicates that the focus of the various forms of intervention is usually limited to only one component process. For example, cognitive restructuring and rational restructuring focus primarily on altering cognitive structures (i.e., altering beliefs, basis for self-appraisals, etc.), whereas coping-skills training, attentional training, and thought stopping focus primarily on the role of the high-test-anxious subject's internal dialogue (i.e., self-referent and task-irrelevant ideation). Various relaxation training procedures and study skills programs attempt to alter the high-test-anxious subject's behavioral acts, whereas in vivo rehearsal and reinforcement programs primarily focus on influencing behavioral outcomes.

The recent treatment study by Finger and Galassi (1977), who compared attentional training versus relaxation training in the reduction of test anxiety illustrates the difficulties associated with the "compartmentalization" view of test anxiety which is prevalent in the field. The objective of the study was to test the Liebert and Morris (1967) view of test anxiety as involving two components: cognitive worry and emotionality. Finger and Galassi's notion was that the two treatments would differentially influence these components of test anxiety (attentional training affecting worry, and relaxation training affecting emotionality). They found no evidence for such a differential treatment effect. Both component treatments reduced test anxiety on self-report measures but not on performance measures. Given the present conceptual model of test anxiety, one can question whether one should expect various treatments to have such differential effects. It is likely that attentional training may convey a sense of control to test-anxious subjects that would result in alterations in emotional reactions, and so forth. Similarly, relaxation training may result in a decrease in the likelihood of anxiety-focused, task-irrelevant ideation. Indeed, Finger and Galassi found, contrary to prediction but consistent with the present model, that significant reduction in worry and emotionality occurred regardless of whether that treatment included a specific focus on the cognitive component of test anxiety.

A treatment approach, according to the present model, may be particularly effective in several ways. It may influence several important components of the process (for example, training in study habits or coping skills), which have an impact on the valence or intensity of concerns and on the behavior they control. For example, improvement in grades is most often found in treatment studies that have combined desensitization *and* some form of study counseling (Allen, 1971; Katahn, Strenger, & Cherry, 1966; McManus, 1971; Mitchell & Ng, 1972), perhaps because the possession of such skills changes the individual's feelings about exam situations. Alternatively, it may be most effective to intervene directly upon central cognitive mediating mechanisms (for example, meaning structures, self-appraisals, or personal predictions), thus setting in motion a chain of events which permits the individual to employ skills which are already in his or her possession.

Some support for the central mediating role of cognitive processes comes from a number of studies which focus upon cognitive restructuring (see, for example, our earlier discussion of Goldfried, 1977). Another example comes from a recent study by Glogower, Fremouw, and McCraskey (in press) who conducted a component analysis of cognitive restructuring therapy for the treatment of communication-anxious subjects. One treatment group focused on insight into negative self-statements, whereas the comparison group focused on knowledge and rehearsal of coping self-statements. Relative to both an extinction (discussion) group and an insight group, the coping self-statement group improved the most. But pertinent to the present point, the treatment group that *combined* both insight into negative self-statements (i.e., a focus on cognitive structures) and coping self-statements (i.e., a focus on internal dialogue) demonstrated the most improvement.

Further evidence that complex alterations in cognitive processes contribute to change in test anxiety has been offered by Houston and his colleagues. Houston (1978) found that, prior to treatment, high-anxious subjects tended to lack organized ways of coping with stress and instead ruminated about themselves and the situation in which they found themselves. Hutchings, Denney, Basgall, and Houston (1978) demonstrated that anxiety management training, a cognitively based treatment developed by Suinn and Richardson (1971), significantly reduced test-anxious subjects' preoccupation with either themselves or the situation and increased their use of cognitive strategies for coping with stress. These changes in basic cognitive processes were accompanied by changes on laboratory performance measures but not physiological changes.

The treatment research on cognitive restructuring and coping-skills training cited previously indicates that directly influencing the evaluation-anxious subject's cognitive structures and internal dialogue provides a useful mode of intervention. What is missing from these studies, and what might mitigate the efficacy of treatment, is assessment of and intervention directed at the client's broader meaning system about academic evaluation and the impact of this on his stereotyped cognitive and overt behaviors.

In *summary,* the present model proposes that test anxiety can be best conceptualized as consisting of several interacting components that operate on one another to produce a kind of self-perpetuating cycle, elements of which may be operating at a very automatic stereotyped level. A pattern emerges whereby the individual's meaning system leads him or her to view physical symptoms as anxiety, which leads to self-referent ideation, which influences arousal and leads to avoidant behavior, which only serves to further increase anxiety, and so forth. The individual is caught in a type of vicious cycle, a self-perpetuating trap in which the meaning system, internal dialogue, behavioral acts, and interpretation of consequences feed upon each other. In this framework, test anxiety should not merely be equated with poor study skills, or task-irrelevant internal dialogue, or irrational beliefs, or unrealistic expectations. Instead, test anxiety is a construct that summarizes this entire chain of events.

Such a view is consistent with the recent reciprocal determinism system offered by Bandura (1978). Bandura indicates that psychological functioning involves continuous reciprocal interaction between behavioral, cognitive, and environmental influences. The individual's "self-system," comprising cognitive structures and subfunctions for perceiving, evaluating, and regulating behavior, is viewed by Bandura as central. When we come to appreciate the complexity of the nature of the negative motivation or skills deficit in test anxiety, we will begin to develop more multifaceted treatment approaches that interrupt the vicious cycle and replace it with more adaptive behaviors. One must help the client deautomatize the vicious cycle; one must be concerned with the role of the client's meaning system surrounding the evaluative situation as well as with the nature of the client's coping behaviors and cognitive strategies.

A cognitive-behavioral treatment approach that is designed to do this is stress-inoculation training. Space does not permit a detailed description of this treatment program, but the main elements are listed. (See Jaremko, 1978; Meichenbaum, 1977; Meichenbaum and Genest, 1977, for a fuller discussion). The stress-inoculation program has three components: (1) an educational component, which provides clients with an understanding of their stress response and of stress in general; (2) a rehearsal component, which consists of the use of physical coping skills (for example, relaxation), cognitive restructuring, and cognitive strategies (i.e., programming of specific self-statements that individuals can follow in coping with stress); and (3) an application phase, during which the client can practice the acquired cognitive and behavioral skills with either a real or imagined stressor. This multifaceted treatment approach is designed to influence each of the components of the conceptual model that has been described. Although the initial results with this approach are encouraging (for example, Jaremko, 1978), more research is needed to assess its therapeutic benefits.

The present conceptual model has attempted to frame questions, the answers to which we feel will lead to a more comprehensive understanding and treatment of test anxiety. These questions include:

1. What is the nature (competence) of the test-anxious individual's behavioral acts (for example, study habits, test-taking behavior, interpersonal style) surrounding the evaluative episode?
2. What is the nature of the high-test-anxious individual's internal dialogue (self-statements and images), and how does this relate to the behavioral acts?
3. What is the nature of the cognitive structures or meaning system that give rise to the particular cognitive and overt behaviors?
4. Exactly how do high- versus low-test-anxious individuals differ on each of these questions?

When we can begin to answer these questions, we will be able to tailor our mode of treatment interventions to the characteristics of the specific test-anxious client. We feel the field should shift emphasis from comparative outcome studies (a kind of batting average tally) to a consideration of *why* treatments work when they do and, more important, *why* they fail.

ACKNOWLEDGMENT

The authors are indebted to Myles Genest for his thoughtful comments.

REFERENCES

Abelson, R. *Scripts.* Paper presented at the meeting of the Midwestern Psychological Association, Chicago, April 1978.

Allen, G. Effectiveness of study counseling and desensitization in alleviating test anxiety in college students. *Journal of Abnormal Psychology,* 1971, *77,* 282–289.

Alpert, R., & Haber, R. Anxiety in academic achievement situations. *Journal of Abnormal Social Psychology,* 1960, *61,* 207–215.

Averill, J. A selective review of cognitive and behavioral factors involved in the regulation of stress. In R. Depue (Ed.), *The psychobiology of depressive disorders: Implications for the effects of stress.* New York: Academic Press, in press.

Bandura, A. The self-system in reciprocal determinism. *American Psychologist,* 1978, *33,* 344–358.

Bartlett, F. *Remembering.* Cambridge, England: Cambridge University Press, 1932.

Bem, D., & Allen, A. On predicting some of the people some of the time: The search for cross-situational consistencies in behavior. *Psychological Review*, 1974, *81*, 506–520.

Bruch, M. Type of cognitive modeling, imitation of modeled tactics, and modification of test anxiety. *Cognitive Therapy and Research*, 1978, *2*, 147–164.

Brush, S. Should the history of science be rated X? *Science*, 1974, *183*, 1164–1172.

Cacioppo, J., & Petty, R. *Inductive techniques for the assessment of cognitive response.* Unpublished manuscript, University of Notre Dame, 1978.

Chang-Liang, R., & Denney, D. Applied relaxation as training in self-control. *Journal of Counseling Psychology*, 1976, *23*, 183–189.

Deffenbacher, J. Worry, emotionality and task generated interference in test anxiety: An empirical test of attentional theory. *Journal of Educational Psychology*, 1978, *70*, 248–254.

Denney, D., & Rupert, P. Desensitization and self-control in the treatment of test anxiety. *Journal of Counseling Psychology*, 1977, *45*, 272–280.

Desiderato, O., & Koskinen, P. Anxiety, study habits and academic achievement. *Journal of Consulting Psychology*, 1969, *16*, 162–165.

Ekehammer, B., Schalling, D., & Magnusson, D. Dimensions of stressful situations: A comparison between a response analytical and a stimulus analytical approach. *Multivariate Behavior and Research*, 1973, *10*, 155–164.

Finger, R. *The effects of modifying cognitive versus emotionality responses in the treatment of test anxiety.* Doctoral dissertation, University of North Carolina at Chapel Hill, 1975.

Finger, R., & Galassi, J. Effects of modifying cognitive versus emotionality responses in the treatment of test anxiety. *Journal of Consulting and Clinical Psychology*, 1977, *45*, 280–287.

Frank, J. *Persuasion and healing.* Baltimore: John Hopkins Press, 1961.

Gagnon, J., & Simon, W. *Sexual conduct. The social avarices of human sexuality.* Chicago, Ill.: Aldine, 1973.

Genest, M., Turk, D., & Meichenbaum, D. *A cognitive behavioral approach to the management of pain.* Paper presented at the meeting of the Association for the Advancement of Behavior Therapy, Atlanta, December 1977.

Glogower, F., Fremouw, W. & McCraskey, J. A component analysis of cognitive restructuring. *Cognitive Therapy and Research*, in press.

Goldfried, M. The use of relaxation and cognitive relabeling as coping skills. In R. Stuart (Ed.), *Behavioral self-management.* New York: Brunner/ Mazel, 1977.

Goldfried, M., Linehan, M., & Smith, J. Reduction of test anxiety through cognitive restructuring. *Journal of Consulting and Clinical Psychology*, 1978, *46*, 32–39.

Goldfried, M., & Trier, C. Effectiveness of relaxation as an active coping skill. *Journal of Abnormal Psychology*, 1974, *83*, 348–355.

Hebb, D. Science and the world of imagination. *Canadian Psychological Review*, 1975, *16*, 4–12.

Heckhausen, H. Task-irrelevant cognitions during an exam: Incidence and effects. In H. Krohne & L. Laux (Eds.), *Achievement, stress and anxiety.* Washington, D.C.: Hemisphere, in press.

Henshaw, D. *A cognitive analysis of creative problem-solving.* Unpublished doctoral dissertation, University of Waterloo, 1978.

Hilgard, E. Neodissociation theory of multiple cognitive control systems. In G. Schwartz and D. Shapiro (Eds.), *Consciousness and self-regulation* (Vol. 1). New York: Plenum Press, 1976.

Hollandsworth, J., Glazeski, R., Kirkland, K., Jones, G., & Van Norman, L. *An analysis of the nature and effects of test anxiety: Cognitive, behavioral and physiological components.* Unpublished manuscript, University of Southern Mississippi, 1978.

Holroyd, K. Cognition and desensitization in the group treatment of test anxiety. *Journal of Consulting and Clinical Psychology*, 1976, *44*, 991–1001.

Holroyd, K., Westbrook, T., Wolf, M., & Badhorn, E. *Performance, cognition and physiological responding in test anxiety.* Unpublished manuscript, Ohio University, 1978.

Houston, K. Trait anxiety and cognitive coping behavior. In H. Krohne and L. Laux (Eds.), *Achievement, stress and anxiety*. Washington, D.C.: Hemisphere, 1978.

Hutchings, D., Denney, D., Basgall, J., & Houston, B. *Anxiety management and applied relaxation in reducing chronic anxiety*. Unpublished manuscript, University of Kansas, 1978.

Jaremko, M. *A component analysis of stress inoculation: Review and prospects*. Unpublished manuscript, University of Richmond, 1978.

Katahn, M., Strenger, S., & Cherry, N. Group counseling and behavior therapy with text anxious college students. *Journal of Counseling Psychology*, 1966, *30*, 544–549.

Kelley, G. *The psychology of personal constructs* (2 vols.) New York: Norton & Company, 1955.

Kieslar, D. Some myths of psychotherapy research and the search for a paradigm. *Psychological Bulletin*, 1966, *65*, 110–136.

Klinger, E. *Meaning and void: Inner experience and the incentives in people's lives*. Minneapolis: University of Minnesota Press, 1977.

Langer, E. Rethinking the role of thought in social interaction. In J. Harvey, W. Ickes, & R. Kidd (Eds.), *New directions in attribution research* (Vol. 2). Hillsdale, N.J.: Lawrence Erlbaum, Associates, 1978.

Lewin, K. *A dynamic theory of personality*, New York: McGraw-Hill, 1935.

Liebert, R. & Morris, L. Cognitive and emotional components of test anxiety: A distinction and some initial data. *Psychological Reports*, 1967, *20*, 975–978.

Magnusson, D., & Ekehammer, B. Anxiety profiles based on situational response factors. *Multivariate Behavior and Research*, 1975, *10*, 27–43.

Mahoney, M. *Scientist as subject: The psychological imperative*. Cambridge, Mass.: Ballinger Publishing Company, 1976.

Mahoney, M., & Avener, M. Psychology of the elite athlete: An explanatory study. *Cognitive Therapy and Research*, 1977, *1*, 135–142.

McManus, M. Group desensitization of test anxiety. *Behaviour Research & Therapy*, 1971, *9*, 51–56.

Mechanic, D. *Students under stress: A study of the social psychology of adaptation*. New York: Free Press of Glencoe, 1962.

Meichenbaum, D. Cognitive modification of test anxious college students. *Journal of Consulting and Clinical Psychology*, 1972, *39*, 370–380.

Meichenbaum, D. *Cognitive-behavior modification: An integrative approach*. New York: Plenum Press, 1977.

Meichenbaum, D., & Butler, L. *Cognitive ethology: Assessing the streams of cognition and emotion*. Paper presented at the Erindale Conference on the Assessment of Emotion, Erindale College, University of Toronto, 1978.

Meichenbaum, D., & Genest, M. Treatment of anxiety. In G. Harris (Ed.), *The group treatment of human problems: A social learning approach*. New York: Grune & Stratton, 1977.

Meichenbaum, D., Henshaw, D., & Himel, N. Coping with stress as a problem-solving process. In W. Krohne & L. Laux (Eds.), *Achievement stress and anxiety*. Washington, D.C., Hemisphere, in press.

Miller, G., Galanter, E., & Pribram, K. *Plans and the structure of behavior*. New York: Holt, 1960.

Mitchell, K., & Ng, K. Effects of group counseling and behavior therapy on the academic achievement of test anxious students. *Journal of Counseling Psychology*, 1972, *19*, 491–497.

Morris, P. *Loss and change*. Garden City, New York: Anchor Press/Doubleday, 1975.

O'Hara, T. *A demonstration of the relationship between cognitive experience and performance debilitation in high evaluation conditions*. Paper presented at the Ninth Canadian Psychomotor learning and sport symposium, Banff, October 1977.

Parkes, C. Psychosocial transitions: A field for study. *Social Science and Medicine*, 1971, *5*, 101–115.

Pervin, C. A free response description approach to the analysis of person-situation interaction. *Journal of Personality and Social Psychology,* 1976, *49,* 237–247.

Piaget, J. *Construction of reality in the child* (Trans. M. Cook). New York: Basic Books, 1954.

Polanyi, M.   *Personal knowledge: Towards a post-critical philosophy.* Chicago: University of Chicago Press, 1958.

Richardson, F. *Coping with test anxiety: A guide.* Unpublished manual, University of Texas at Austin, 1973.

Sarason, I., Pederson, A., & Nyman, B. Test anxiety and the observation of models. *Journal of Personality,* 1968, *36,* 493–511.

Sarason, I., & Stoops, R. Test anxiety and the passage of time. *Journal of Consulting and Clinical Psychology,* 1978, *46,* 102–109.

Sarbin, T., & Coe, W. *Hypnosis: A social psychological analysis of influence communication.* New York: Holt, Rinehart & Winston, 1972.

Schank, R., & Abelson, R. *Scripts, plans, goals, and understanding.* Hillsdale, N.J.: Lawrence Erlbaum Associates, 1978.

Schwartz, R., & Gottman, J. Toward a task analysis of assertive behavior. *Journal of Consulting and Clinical Psychology,* 1976, *44,* 910–920.

Smye, M. *Verbal, cognitive and behavioral correlates of social anxiety.* Unpublished doctoral dissertation, Ontario Institute for Studies in Education, University of Toronto, 1977.

Spielberger, C., Anton, W., & Bedell, J. The nature and treatment of test anxiety. In M. Zuckerman & L. Spielberger (Eds.), *Emotion and anxiety: New concepts, methods and applications.* Hillsdale, N.J.: Lawrence Erlbaum Associates, 1976.

Suinn, R., & Richardson, F. Anxiety management training: A non-specific behavior therapy program for anxiety control. *Behavior Therapy,* 1971, *4,* 498–571.

Tolman, E. *Purposive behavior in animals and men.* New York: Century, 1932.

Tompkins, S. Script theory: Differential magnification of affects. *Nebraska Symposium on Motivation.* Lincoln: University of Nebraska Press, 1978.

Wine, J. *Investigations of attentional interpretation of test anxiety.* Unpublished doctoral dissertation, University of Waterloo, Ontario, Canada 1970.

10 Self-Control Approaches to the Treatment of Test Anxiety

Douglas R. Denney
University of Kansas

Behavioral approaches to the treatment of anxiety have been developing at a steadily accelerating pace for two decades, since the publication of Wolpe's (1958) seminal work, *Psychotherapy by Reciprocal Inhibition.* Throughout this development, test anxiety has been a common target of therapy—to the extent that a review of the treatment literature bearing on test anxiety would effectively summarize the overall evolution of behavioral approaches to anxiety reduction. The present chapter focuses upon one particularly important branch of this evolutionary course, pertaining to self-control procedures for the management of anxiety. These procedures share a common feature: All of them emphasize the attainment of coping skills that the client can effectively apply toward the management and reduction of anxiety when it arises in real life situations.

The current emphasis upon self-control approaches to the treatment of anxiety can be traced to two crucial papers by Joseph Cautela (1969) and Marvin Goldfried (1971). The ultimate effect of these papers was to lay aside mechanistic accounts of systematic desensitization involving principles of counterconditioning and extinction and to prepare a way for cognitive-mediational interpretations of this procedure.

Cautela (1969) was concerned about the lack of generalization in the treatment effects stemming from systematic desensitization and the failure of behavior therapists to teach skills that would assist clients to avoid developing future fears. His was the first paper to offer a view of relaxation training as a self-control procedure. He suggested that clients should learn to use relaxation on their own at night in order to desensitize themselves to troublesome events arising during the day.

Cautela sought to preserve systematic desensitization in tact as a self-control procedure. However, Goldfried went considerably further in offering a reinterpretation of systematic desensitization as training in self-control. To Goldfried (1971):

> [it seemed] appropriate to construe systematic desensitization as more of an active process, directed toward learning of a general anxiety-reducing skill, rather than the passive desensitization to specific aversive stimuli.... During the process of systematic desensitization, the client is taught to become sensitive to his proprioceptive cues for tension and to react to these cues with his newly acquired skill in muscular relaxation.... According to this view, then, what the client learns is a means of actively coping with anxiety, rather than an immediate replacement for it [pp. 228–229].

Goldfried (1971) proceeded to recommend a number of modifications in systematic desensitization to further exploit its potential as a method for training self-control. The modifications can be divided into two types, those involving the treatment rationale advanced to the client and those involving the procedure of desensitization itself. With regard to the rationale, clients were to be told they would be learning a relaxation skill that they could actively use in order to cope with anxiety engendered in any setting. The purposes of the treatment sessions were thus to train clients in methods of relaxation, to assist them to recognize tension cues as signals to initiate relaxation, and to allow them to practice relaxing away anxiety arising from a set of imaginary scenes presented by the therapist. Having demonstrated to themselves that they could relax away anxiety within the relative safety of the consultation setting, clients were to actively apply their emergent relaxation skills outside of treatment to reduce anxiety occurring in any life setting.

As for procedural modifications, Goldfried recommended that greater attention be paid to relaxation training—not only to assist clients to achieve voluntary control over their relaxation response, but also to permit them to learn to discriminate proprioceptive cues of tension and relaxation. Hierarchies need not be constructed around a common theme but could instead include scenes of several diverse events, all of which elicited anxiety in the client. Unlike Wolpe's procedure, clients were not to be allowed to terminate a scene whenever they signaled a disruption in their state of relaxation. Instead they were to continue to imagine the scene while attempting to relax away the accompanying feelings of anxiety. Clients were instructed to signal a second time when they had succeeded in regaining a state of deep relaxation, and only then were they allowed to terminate the scene. Finally, Goldfried recommended that clients be instructed to use relaxation to inhibit anxiety in real-life settings and that time be set aside within the treatment sessions so that clients could discuss their successes and failures with this continuing assignment.

A Continuum of Self-Control Procedures

A variety of self-control procedures is described in the treatment literature, and a variety of labels have been used to refer to these procedures. As is common in such instances, the correspondence between labels and procedures is less than perfect. An important objective of the present chapter is to bring some semblance of order to the topic of self-control procedures by offering a taxonomy of such procedures. To begin this task, it is useful to distinguish between applied relaxation techniques, self-control training techniques, and cognitive coping techniques. These terms are used as generic labels to refer to ranges along a continuum of self-control procedures, as illustrated in Figure 10.1.

Applied relaxation techniques constitute the simplest examples of self-control procedures for the reduction of anxiety. The procedures that are classified as applied relaxation techniques share three common features. First, these procedures are introduced with a self-control rationale similar to the one advocated by Goldfried (1971). Clients are typically informed that the purpose of treatment is to teach them effective means for actively coping with anxiety. They are led to construe the relaxation training they receive as a method for helping them to bring the response of relaxation under voluntary control. They are told that, with practice, they will become increasingly proficient at voluntarily inducing relaxation and that with this greater proficiency will come the ability to apply relaxation to reduce feelings of anxiety in stressful situations encountered outside of treatment.

The second feature common to applied relaxation techniques is training in the induction of relaxation. Progressive muscle-relaxation exercises (Rimm & Masters, 1974), adapted from Jacobson's (1938) work, remain the most common method for inducing relaxation. However, some investigators (e.g. Deffenbacher & Snyder, 1976) have been particularly inventive in supplementing progressive muscle relaxation with a variety of other exercises especially suited to the goals of applied relaxation. Some of these supplementary exercises are included for deepening relaxation and shortening the time necessary for its induction. Breathing exercises (e.g., Deffenbacher & Snyder, 1976; Meichenbaum, 1972), special muscle exercises (Deffenbacher & Snyder, 1976), imagery exercises (Samuels & Samuels, 1975; Singer, 1974), autogenic exercises (Reed & Meyer 1974; Schultz & Luthe, 1959; Snider & Oetting, 1966), and biofeedback-assisted relaxation (Romano & Cabianca, 1978; Wickramasekera, 1972) are all potentially useful for these purposes. Other supplementary exercises, such as differential relaxation (Davison, 1965) and cue-controlled relaxation (Cautela, 1966; Russell & Sipich, 1973), are used because they provide clients with induction methods that can be readily employed within stressful settings. When a variety of relaxation exercises are introduced in applied relaxation techniques, an attempt is usually made to fashion an individualized

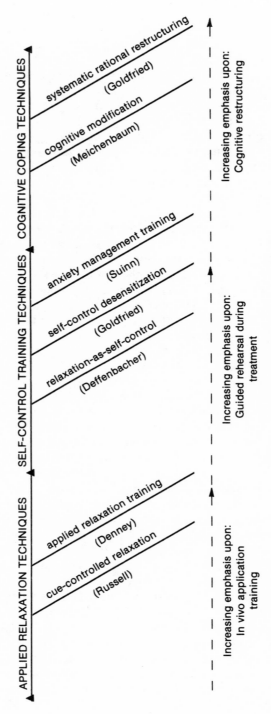

FIG. 10.1. A continuum of self-control procedures.

APPLIED RELAXATION TECHNIQUES   SELF-CONTROL TRAINING TECHNIQUES   COGNITIVE COPING TECHNIQUES

systematic rational restructuring (Goldfried)

cognitive modification (Meichenbaum)

anxiety management training (Suinn)

self-control desensitization (Goldfried)

relaxation-as-self-control (Deffenbacher)

applied relaxation training (Denney)

cue-controlled relaxation (Russell)

Increasing emphasis upon: Cognitive restructuring

Increasing emphasis upon: Guided rehearsal during treatment

Increasing emphasis upon: In vivo application training

relaxation program according to the particular needs of the client (Deffenbacher & Snyder, 1976; Marston & Feldman, 1972; Meichenbaum, 1973).

The third feature of applied relaxation techniques involves training in the application of relaxation within stressful settings encountered outside of treatment. Relatively little attention has been paid to application training in self-control procedures. Typically, clients are merely instructed to begin applying relaxation outside of treatment, and time is set aside to allow them to discuss their successes and failures in these attempts. However, four additional recommendations might be considered. First, application training should be initiated in the later treatment sessions after clients have attained considerable proficiency at inducing relaxation. Prior to this time, homework assignments should require clients to practice their relaxation exercises only in quiescent, nonstressful settings. Second, whenever possible, clients should be instructed to attempt their initial applications of relaxation within settings that are only moderately stressful. Third, clients should be introduced to the notion of preparatory relaxation; that is, the importance of placing themselves in a state of relaxation just before the actual confrontation with a stressful situation. Finally, clients should be prepared for limited success in their early attempts at applying relaxation. They should be informed that they may indeed feel anxious in the stressful setting but that they should be able to keep their anxiety under better control and thus prevent it from interfering with their performance. Without this latter preparation, the anxiety that clients may feel upon encountering a stressful situation may have the effect of undoing their prior training and retraumatizing them to the stressful event.

Self-control training techniques are found in the middle of the continuum in Figure 10.1. The procedures in this category include the same three features found in applied relaxation techniques. However, in addition, all of the self-control training techniques include a fourth feature, guided rehearsal, which is introduced after relaxation induction training. During guided rehearsal, clients are confronted with some type of stressful stimulus presented within the consultation setting. Usually, the stressful stimuli are evoked by having the client imagine certain scenes, although role playing and other simulations have been used to evoke stress during guided rehearsal. When clients begin to experience tension as a result of the stressful stimulus, they are instructed to indicate this fact to the therapist and to concentrate on the experience of tension, noting the locations in their body where they typically feel tension and anxiety. They are then instructed to use their coping skills to reduce the feelings of tension and anxiety, continuing until they have eliminated these feelings and have regained a state of complete relaxation. Accordingly, guided rehearsal has two major objectives. The first is tension cue discrimination training. Clients are helped to discriminate cues of tension and anxiety, to detect these cues early in their development, and to use these cues as signals to begin actively applying their coping skills. The second objective is simply one of allowing clients an opportunity to practice the application of their coping skills in the actual reduction of anxiety. Practicing this sequence during treatment sessions may enhance its successful deployment in real-life settings during application training.

Cognitive coping techniques are arrayed along the right-hand portion of the continuum of self-control procedures. These techniques typically encompass all four features of the self-control training techniques as well as one additional feature termed cognitive restructuring. Three basic objectives are pursued in connection with cognitive restructuring. The first is to persuade clients that the beliefs that they entertain while confronting certain situations affect the emotional reactions they have in these situations. As they come to accept this basic premise underlying cognitive restructuring, clients are next encouraged to identify the particular negative self-statements that they make when confronting a stressful situation. Finally, clients are helped to formulate more positive and rational self-statements with which to replace the negative self-statements and thereby attenuate their anxiety in the stressful situations. The first objective of cognitive restructuring is usually appended to the self-control rationale, whereas the latter two objectives are incorporated within guided rehearsal. In general, cognitive coping techniques attempt to provide clients with an additional repertoire of coping skills beyond those of relaxation.

Applied relaxation techniques, self-control training techniques, and cognitive coping techniques are arranged along a continuum in order to represent their relative procedural complexity. As one traces from left to right along the portion of the continuum devoted to applied relaxation techniques, one encounters procedures that not only are procedurally more complex, but also place relatively greater emphasis upon the application of relaxation in real-life settings. Similarly, as one traces from left to right along the self-control training techniques, one finds procedures that place relatively greater emphasis upon the guided rehearsal component that differentiates these procedures from applied relaxation techniques. Finally, as one traces from left to right along the cognitive coping techniques, the specific procedures place relatively greater emphasis upon cognitive restructuring rather than relaxation as the type of coping skill imparted through treatment. This continuum of self-control procedures provides an organizational format with which to review the self-control approaches to the treatment of test anxiety.

APPLIED RELAXATION TECHNIQUES

In an effort to determine the effective components operating within systematic desensitization, a number of investigators designed studies that included a relaxation-only group wherein subjects received only training in progressive relaxation. Some of these studies indicated that relaxation training alone was completely ineffective in reducing specific fears (Aponte & Aponte, 1971; Cooke, 1968; Davison, 1968; Johnson & Sechrest, 1968; Lang, Lazovik, & Reynolds, 1965; Rachman, 1965, 1968; Rimm & Medeiros, 1970). However, in other instances, relaxation training alone effected significant reductions in subjects' fears relative to untreated controls (Bedell, 1976; Denney, 1974; Folkins, Lawson, Opton, & Lazarus, 1968; Freeling & Shemberg, 1970; Laxer, Quarter, Kooman, & Walker, 1969; Laxer & Walker, 1970; Snider & Oetting, 1966; Spiegler, Liebert, McMains, & Fernandez, 1969; Trexler & Karst, 1972). Occasionally, the reductions brought about through relaxation training alone were as great as those of systematic desensitization (e.g. Bedell, 1976; Denney, 1974).

A possible explanation for the discrepancy in these results may lie in the manner in which subjects construed the relaxation training they received. In some instances, subjects may have been encouraged to view their relaxation training from a self-control perspective and may have concluded that they should apply these relaxation skills in real-life encounters with fearful objects and events. This type of self-control perspective could substantially enhance the effectiveness of relaxation training.

Studies by Zeisset (1968) and by Goldfried and Trier (1974) illustrated the fact that relaxation training could be an effective procedure for reducing specific fears when such training was combined with a self-control rationale and explicit instructions concerning the application of relaxation in real-life settings. Zeisset found that such an applied relaxation procedure was as effective as systematic desensitization in reducing interview anxiety among psychiatric inpatients. Goldfried and Trier (1974) evaluated the contribution of self-control rationales and application training in a more direct fashion by comparing two groups of speech-anxious subjects. Although both groups received detailed training in relaxation, the applied relaxation group also received an active, self-control rationale and instructions concerning the application of relaxation. Subjects in the relaxation-only group received a passive, automatic rationale emphasizing counterconditioning and no instructions concerning the application of relaxation. The applied relaxation procedure resulted in more consistently significant changes from the pretest to the posttest on both behavioral and self-report measures of speech anxiety than did the relaxation-only procedure.

Thus, the early component analytic research concerning systematic desensitization served as a background for the development of applied relaxation techniques. The two principal applied relaxation techniques that have been used in the treatment of test anxiety are cue-controlled relaxation training and applied relaxation training. The location of these procedures along the continuum in Figure 10.1 is determined by the extent to which each procedure emphasizes the application of relaxation in actual testing situations. Table 10.1 summarizes the controlled outcome studies pertaining to each of these procedures.

TABLE 10.1
Applied Relaxation Techniques

| Study | Conditions | No. of Treatment Sessions | Weeks of Follow-Up | Self-Report Measures | | | | | Performance Measures | | General Anxiety or Nontargeted Fears |
				Debilitating Test Anxiety (Trait)	Facilitating Test Anxiety (Trait)	Emotionality (State)	Worry (State)	Test Anxiety (State)	Abilities Test	Academic Measure	
Russell, Miller, & June (1975)	1. cue-controlled relaxation 2. systematic desensitization training 3. no-treatment control	6	0	SRIA-E: 1 = 2 < 3 TAS: 1 = 2 < 3						GPA: NS	SRIA-S: NS STAI-T: NS
Russell, Wise, & Stratoudakis (1976)	1. cue-controlled relaxation 2. systematic desensitization 3. no-treatment control	5	0	SRIA-E: 1 = 2 < 3 TAS: 1 = 2 < 3				AD: 1 = 2 < 3	WAIS-S: NS		STAI-T: 1 = 2 < 3

Marchetti, McGlynn, & Patterson (1977)	1. cue-controlled relaxation 2. placebo (neutral) imagery 3. no-treatment control	6 (2/wk)	0	SRIA-E: 2 < 1 = 3 TAS: NS	PM-HR: NS PM-SC: NS	GPE: NS(?)	SRIA-S: NS
Chang-Liang & Denney (1976)	1. applied relaxation training 2. systematic desensitization 3. relaxation-only 4. no-treatment control	3	0	STABS: NS	STAI-S: 1 < 4	WPT: 1 > 2 = 3 = 4	STAI-T: 1 < 3 = 4 IPAT: 1 < 3 = 4 FSS: NS

[a]AD—Anxiety Differential; FSS—Fear Survey Schedule; GPA—Grade Point Average; GPE—General Psychology Exam; IPAT—Anxiety Scale; PM-HR—Physiological measure (heart rate); PM-SC—Physiological measure (skin conductance); SRIA-E—SR Inventory of Anxiousness (Exam); SRIA-S—SR Inventory of Anxiousness (Speech); STABS—Suinn Test Anxiety Behavior Scale; STAI-S—State-Trait Anxiety Inventory (State); STAI-T—State-Trait Anxiety Inventory (Trait); TAS—Test Anxiety Scale; WAIS—WAIS subtests; WPT—Wonderlic Personnel Test.

217

Cue-controlled relaxation was first suggested by Cautela (1966) as a means of establishing a verbal cue that was capable of eliciting relaxation responses in previously anxious clients. The procedure consisted of two phases. Clients were first trained in progressive relaxation. After they attained a deeply relaxed state, they were instructed to concentrate on their breathing and to subvocalize a verbal cue such as the word "calm" or "relax" with each exhalation. This second phase served to pair the verbal cue with the client's relaxation. Since clients were supposed to self-produce this cue when they felt themselves becoming anxious outside the consultation setting, the procedure qualifies as an applied relaxation technique. Nevertheless, relatively little emphasis was placed upon application training.

Russell and his colleagues (Russell, Miller, & June, 1974; Russell & Sipich, 1973, 1974) have reported several case studies in which cue-controlled relaxation training has been successfully used to treat individuals and groups suffering from test anxiety. Russell, Miller, and June (1975) compared group-administered cue-controlled relaxation training with systematic desensitization and an untreated control condition. Subjects in the cue-controlled relaxation training condition received six 1-hour treatment sessions during which they were instructed in progressive relaxation and were then told to focus on their breathing and to subvocalize the word "calm" with each of 40 exhalations. Subjects were instructed to practice this same procedure each day between treatment sessions and to try self-producing the relaxation cue to counter anxiety during testing situations at school. Subjects in the systematic desensitization condition received the same number of treatment sessions during which they were trained in progressive relaxation and worked through a standard 12-item test anxiety hierarchy. Cue-controlled relaxation training and systematic desensitization were equally effective in reducing self-reports of debilitating test anxiety compared to the untreated control condition. However, neither procedure effected changes in a performance measure (grade point average) or in self-reported generalization measures.

Cue-controlled relaxation training and systematic desensitization were again compared in a study by Russell, Wise, and Stratoudakis (1976). The principal difference between this study and the preceding one lay in the measures used to assess outcome. The present study employed both trait and state measures of test anxiety as well as an abilities test to serve as the performance measure of test anxiety. Once again, cue-controlled relaxation training and systematic desensitization were equally effective in reducing self-reports of test anxiety on both state and trait measures, but there were no significant effects for either condition on the performance measure.

The somewhat limited success of cue-controlled relaxation training is open to even further question when one considers a carefully designed study by Marchetti, McGlynn, and Patterson (1977). Cue-controlled relaxation training, conducted in the manner described by Russell and Sipich (1973,

1974) was compared with a placebo and an untreated control condition. Subjects in the placebo condition received training in muscle relaxation and were then instructed to imagine irrelevant neutral scenes while relaxing. Unlike the cue-controlled relaxation training condition, subjects in the placebo condition were provided no instructions regarding the application of relaxation. Self-report measures of test anxiety and speech anxiety as well as physiological measures (heart rate and skin conductance) collected during performance on an actual course examination in general psychology failed to show any significant effects for cue-controlled relaxation beyond those of the placebo condition.

Cue-controlled relaxation training would seem to be a valuable procedure for establishing a relaxation response that might readily be evoked in fear-provoking settings. As such, it might be included among the relaxation induction methods used in other applied relaxation techniques. However, most investigators of cue-controlled relaxation training have placed insufficient emphasis upon the other features common to applied relaxation techniques, the self-control rationale and, more important, application training. This failure perhaps accounts for the relatively poor results of cue-controlled relaxation training as a treatment of test anxiety.

Relative to cue-controlled relaxation training, applied relaxation training places far greater emphasis upon a self-control rationale and upon application training. Rosa Chang-Liang and I (Chang-Liang & Denney, 1976) conducted a study that illustrates the effectiveness of applied relaxation training in the treatment of test anxiety . Applied relaxation training was compared with systematic desensitization, relaxation alone, and an untreated control condition. Subjects in all three treatment groups received the same training in progressive relaxation. Subjects in the applied relaxation training group also received an active, self-control rationale by way of introduction to their treatment procedure and explicit instructions concerning the application of relaxation skills on testing situations. Subjects in the systematic desensitization and relaxation-only conditions were given a passive, counterconditioning rationale emphasizing the "automatic" reciprocal inhibition of anxiety by relaxation and were not told to apply relaxation outside of therapy. In addition, subjects in the systematic desensitization condition received training in desensitization using a standard 15-item test anxiety hierarchy. All treatment conditions were conducted during three weekly treatment sesssions.

In order to assess the effects of these treatments on test anxiety, we included self-report trait and state measures of test anxiety and an abilities test to serve as a performance measure. Furthermore, we reasoned that one advantage of applied relaxation training over systematic desensitization might be in terms of generalization to other types of anxiety. Accordingly, we included three measures of general anxiety along with our test anxiety measures.

The results of this study indicated some noteworthy advantages of applied relaxation training. Although all three treatment conditions were equally effective in reducing the trait measure of test anxiety, applied relaxation training also resulted in significant decreases in the state measure of test anxiety, significant improvement on the performance measure, and significant declines on two of the three general anxiety measures. The systematic desensitization condition did not differ from relaxation alone or untreated controls on any of these latter outcome measures. Thus, subjects who were instructed to apply relaxation in order to cope with the tension arising during tests were able to improve their test performance as well as to reduce their feelings of test anxiety. Furthermore, applied relaxation training appeared to impart a general coping skill that subjects could successfully employ to reduce their anxiety in a variety of other situations.

The applied relaxation training procedure could be strengthened in many ways. Although we were careful to use the same type of progressive relaxation training in all three treatment conditions, there are many additional relaxation induction techniques that could have been introduced during applied relaxation training (see page 211), including the cue-controlled relaxation method discussed earlier. Having sampled a variety of relaxation induction methods, subjects could have then formulated an individualized program of relaxation uniquely suited to their needs. Application training might also have been augmented by adopting some of the suggestions offered on page 213. Finally, the number of treatment sessions could certainly have been expanded beyond the three which we used in our study. Thus, the study that Chang-Liang and I completed should be considered as only a conservative index of the potential effectiveness of applied relaxation training.

SELF-CONTROL TRAINING TECHNIQUES

Table 10.2 presents the controlled outcome studies pertaining to the second major category of self-control procedures. Self-control training techniques differ from the applied relaxation techniques of the preceding section in that they include guided rehearsal during at least some of the treatment sessions. During guided rehearsal, clients are encouraged to examine their experience of anxiety and to practice reducing these feelings through relaxation. In general, as one proceeds from left to right along the portion of the continuum in Fig. 10.1 devoted to self-control training techniques, the procedures place increasingly heavier emphasis upon guided rehearsal.

Guided rehearsal is given least attention in a procedure devised by Jerry Deffenbacher (1976), known as "relaxation-as-self-control." In this procedure, clients are provided with an elaborately designed program of relaxation training which includes progressive muscle relaxation, breathing exercises, relaxing imagery, differential relaxation, and cue-controlled relaxation. Ultimately, clients assemble an individualized relaxation induction from these elements in much the same way that I have advocated for applied relaxation training. Clients are then instructed to begin applying relaxation to reduce anxiety that arises outside of treatment, and time is allotted during the sessions for clients to discuss these attempts. Guided rehearsal is typically introduced during the last two or three sessions. In the case of test anxiety, clients are presented with sample tests and are encouraged to discriminate tension cues elicited by the tests and then to use their relaxation skills to dissipate their anxiety.

Using this relaxation-as-self-control procedure, Deffenbacher (1976) successfully treated four highly test-anxious clients whose lives were quite impaired by test anxiety. The procedure led to substantial decreases in self-reported debilitating test anxiety and substantial increases in both facilitating test anxiety and test performance. These results were confirmed in a somewhat better study by Deffenbacher & Snyder (1976). Eleven test-anxious subjects were treated with the relaxation-as-self-control procedure following a 4-week baseline period. Subjects showed significant declines in debilitating test anxiety and significant increases in facilitating test anxiety following five sessions of relaxation-as-self-control training, whereas no such changes occurred during the baseline peirod. In addition, Deffenbacher and Snyder found significant reductions in subjects' levels of general anxiety resulting from the relaxation-as-self-control procedure.

In the first independently controlled outcome study of the relaxation-as-self-control procedure, Snyder and Deffenbacher (1977) compared this procedure with a modified version of systematic desensitization and an untreated control condition. The modified desensitization procedure incorporated elements of both Wolpe's (1958) and Goldfried's (1971) approach. For example, the desensitization procedure included both passive counterconditioning and active, self-control rationales. Furthermore, scenes were terminated whenever subjects signaled anxiety; however, following the termination of a scene, subjects were given an opportunity to (1) discriminate tension cues, and (2) relax away these cues by rehearsing their relaxation skills. Finally, the modified version of desensitization included application training.

Snyder and Deffenbacher found both the relaxation-as-self-control procedure and the modified desensitization procedure to be equally effective at reducing self-reports of debilitating test anxiety, worry, and state anxiety before a test. Although subjects in both treatment groups rated themselves to be more able to perform on an abilities test than did untreated control subjects, there were no differences in the actual scores achieved on the abilities test. Both treatment groups showed significant reductions on one of two

TABLE 10.2
Self-Control Training Technique

Study	Conditions	No. of Treatment Sessions	Weeks of Follow-Up	Self-Report Measures					Performance Measures		General Anxiety or Nontargeted Fears
				Debilitating Test Anxiety (Trait)	Facilitating Test Anxiety (Trait)	Emotionality (State)	Worry (State)	Test Anxiety (State)	Abilities Test	Academic Measure	
Snyder & Deffenbacher (1977)	1. relaxation-as self-control 2. modified desensitization 3. no-treatment control	6	0	AAT: 1 = 2 < 2 > 3	AAT: NS	LM: 1 = 2 < 3	LM: 1 = 2 < 3	LM: NS	ANAG:	NS	IPAT: FSS: 1 = 2 < 3
Deffenbacher, Mathis, & Michaels (1978)	1. self-control desensitization 2. relaxation-as self-control 3. no-treatment control	7	6	AAT: 1 = 2 < 3	AAT: 1 = 2 > 3	LM: 1 = 2 < 3 OITA: 1 = 2 < 3	LM: 1 = 2 < 3 OITA: 1 = 2 < 3	OITA: 1 = 2 < 3	WPT: NS DS: NS	GPG: 1 = 2 > 3	STAI-T: 1 = 2 < 3 FSS: 1 = 2 < 3
Spiegler et al., (1976)	1. self-control desensitization 2. systematic desensitization 3. no-treatment control	8	4	TAS: 1 = 2 < 3							FSS: NS
Zemore (1975)	1. self-control desensitization 2. systematic desensitization 3. no-treatment control	8	0	STABS: 1 = 2 < 3							PRCS: 1 = 2 < 3

Study	Treatment	n						
Deffenbacher & Parks (1979)	1. self-control desensitization	8	TAS: 1 = 2 < 3	OITA: NS	OITA: 1 = 2 < 3	OITA: 1 = 2 < 3	WPT: NS DS: NS	IPAT: 1 < 3 FSS: 1 = 2 < 3
	2. systematic desensitization	8						
	3. no-treatment control	8						
Denney & Rupert (1977)	1. self-control desensitization	7+	STABS: 1,2,3,4 < 5 < 6 ATT 1 > 2,3,4,5,6 ATT: 1,2,3,4 < 5 = 6				WPT: 1 > 2,3,4, 5,6 DS: NS	GPA: 1 = 2 =3 > 4 = NS 5 = 6 GPG: NS FSS: NS
	2. self-control rationale + standard procedure	0						
	3. counterconditioning rationale + self-control procedure							
	4. systematic desensitization							
	5. placebo (scene only)							
	6. no-treatment control							
Richardson & Suinn (1974)	1. anxiety management training	1 (3 hrs)	STABS: 2 < 1 = 3 < 4					FSS: NS
	2. systematic desensitization	6						
	3. accelerated massed desensitization	1 (3 hrs)						
	4. no-treatment control	0						
Deffenbacher & Shelton (1978)	1. anxiety management training	5	TAS: 1 = 2 STABS: 1 = 2					STAI-T: 1 < 2 FSS: 1 = 2
	2. systematic desensitization	6						

[a]Results reported for posttest only. AAT—Alpert Haber Achievement Anxiety Test; ANAG—Anagrams; DS—Digit Span; FSS—Fear Survey Schedule; GPA—Grade Point Average; GPG—General Psychology Grade; IPAT—IPAT Anxiety Scale; LM—Liebert & Morris Test Anxiety Scale; OITA—Osterhouse Inventory of Test Anxiety; PRCS—Personal Report of Confidence as a Speaker; STABS—Suinn Test Anxiety Behavior Scale; STAI-T—State-Trait Anxiety Inventory (Trait); TAS—Test Anxiety Scale.

general anxiety measures included to assess the generalization of treatment effects. In only one instance did the two treatment groups differ. Subjects receiving modified desensitization scored significantly higher in self-reported facilitating test anxiety than control subjects, whereas subjects in the relaxation-as-self-control condition did not.

The essential comparability between the effectiveness of relaxation-as-self-control and modified desensitization was replicated in a study by Deffenbacher and Payne (1977) dealing with speech anxiety rather than test anxiety. Unfortunately, both of these controlled outcome studies lacked a placebo condition to control for nonspecific treatment effects. Furthermore, the modified version of desensitization employed in each study was neither a pure representation of Wolpe's systematic desensitization procedure nor of Goldfried's self-control desensitization procedure. Thus it is difficult to decide whether or not the essential comparability in the effectiveness of relaxation-as-self-control and modified desensitization is the result of the self-control features common to both of these procedures.

Self-control desensitization encompasses all the rationale and procedural modifications in systematic desensitization that were first recommended by Goldfried (1971). Clients receive an active self-control rationale emphasizing that the purpose of treatment is to teach them a relaxation skill for voluntarily coping with anxiety. The actual procedure of desensitization is conducted as a guided rehearsal in tension cue discrimination and practice at using relaxation to reduce tension. Clients are instructed to signal if they experience any feelings of anxiety while imagining a particular scene. If clients do signal, they are instructed to continue imagining the scene, to focus their attention on the experience of anxiety, and then to reduce this anxiety by voluntarily relaxing it away. When clients signal a second time to indicate that they have eliminated their feelings of anxiety and regained a state of deep relaxation, the scene is terminated. During later treatment sessions, clients are instructed to apply their relaxation skills in any real-life settings which elicit anxiety, and the successes and failures that clients have in these attempts are discussed during each subsequent session.

The effectiveness of self-control desensitization is documented in seven studies (Deffenbacher, Mathis, & Michaels, 1978; Deffenbacher & Parks, 1979; Denney & Rupert, 1977; Goldfried & Goldfried, 1977; Jacks, 1972; Spiegler, Cooley, Marshall, Prince, Puckett, & Skenazy, 1976; Zemore, 1975). Five of these studies are concerned with test anxiety, the exceptions being studies by Goldfried and Goldfried (1977), which focused upon speech anxiety, and Jacks (1972), which dealt with acrophobia.

Deffenbacher, Mathis, and Michaels (1978) compared self-control desensitization with the relaxation-as-self-control procedure discussed previously. The latter procedure included the more elaborate training in relaxation induction described earlier, and the guided rehearsal portion of the procedure permitted subjects to become aware of and to relax away feelings of anxiety while taking simulated abilities tests. Subjects in the self-control desensitization condition received relatively less training on relaxation and more guided rehearsal. This rehearsal was structured around imagined scenes from a test anxiety hierarchy rather than simulated tests. Beyond these distinctions, the two procedures were highly similar, and as one might expect, the procedures did not differ on any of the outcome measures. Compared to untreated controls, subjects in both conditions reported significantly less debilitating test anxiety, less worry, and emotionality before an abilities test, more facilitating test anxiety, and more generalization to nontargeted fears. Although no differences occurred on the abilities test, subjects in both treatment conditions achieved higher grade point averages at the end of the semester than did the controls.

All four of the remaining test anxiety studies involve comparisons between self-control desensitization and traditional systematic desensitization. Spiegler et al (1976) and Zemore (1975) employed only self-report measures of debilitating test anxiety. On such measures, self-control desensitization and systematic desensitization were found to be equally effective, and both procedures produced significantly greater changes than an untreated control condition. Deffenbacher and Parks (1979) used a much wider variety of test anxiety measures, encompassing debilitating test anxiety, worry and emotionality, and performance on two abilities tests. Self-control desensitization and systematic desensitization were equally effective at reducing the self-report measures of test anxiety, relative to an untreated control condition. Both procedures also resulted in generalization of treatment effects to nontargeted fears. However, neither procedure was found to have a significant impact upon subjects' scores on the abilities tests.

The study that I conducted along with Patricia Rupert represents perhaps the most extensive comparison between self-control desensitization and systematic desensitization. To begin with, we distinguished between the rationale modifications and the procedural modifications which Goldfried (1971) had recommended for systematic desensitization. Four treatment procedures were devised by combining either an active, self-control or a passive, counterconditioning rationale with either a self-control or a standard procedure. The combination of the active, self-control rationale and the self-control procedure resulted in Goldfried's self-control desensitization, and of course, the combination of the passive, counterconditioning rationale and the standard procedure resulted in Wolpe's systematic desensitization. In addition to this two-by-two factorial design, we appended two additional groups: a placebo group in which subjects merely visualized scenes from a test anxiety hierarchy, and an untreated control group.

Like Deffenbacher and Parks (1979), we included a wider variety of test anxiety measures in the hope of finding some superiority for the self-control form of desensitization. Our results replicated all the preceding test anxiety studies by showing that self-control desensitization and systematic desensitization were equally effective on self-report measures of debilitating test anxiety. In fact, all four treatment groups had significantly lower debilitating test anxiety scores than the placebo and the no-treatment control groups. However, Rupert and I found that self-control desensitization, combining both the rationale and procedural recommendations made by Goldfried, was significantly more effective than systematic desensitization at increasing scores on facilitating test anxiety and improving performance on an abilities test. It seemed as though the rationale and procedural modifications recommended by Goldfried interacted in a synergistic fashion to produce a technique which was substantially more effective than systematic desensitization.

The last technique to be considered in this section is anxiety management training, developed by Richard Suinn. Although Suinn initially discussed anxiety management training in conditioning terms (e.g. Suinn, 1975), the procedure clearly belongs in the category of self-control training techniques because it involves the elements of self-control rationales, relaxation training, guided rehearsal, and application training that are common to this category. Clients are presented with self-control rationales emphasizing the acquisition of coping skills that can be used voluntarily to reduce or eliminate anxiety whenever tension cues are recognized. Clients are trained in relaxation exercises and instructed to practice these exercises as homework assignments between sessions. There seems to be somewhat greater variety in the relaxation exercises introduced in anxiety management training compared with self-control desensitization. As in the case of the relaxation-as-self-control procedure, clients are often encouraged to continue practicing those exercises that seem to be most conducive to relaxation. In the later sessions, clients are instructed to apply relaxation in anxiety-provoking settings outside of treatment, and discussion of successes and failures in these attempts is encouraged (Suinn, 1975, 1976, 1977).

Anxiety management training places the greatest emphasis upon the guided rehearsal component and, for this reason, is located the furthest to the right among the self-control training techniques on the continuum in Fig. 10.1. It is within the guided rehearsal component that most of the differences between anxiety management training and other self-control training techniques occur. In contrast to self-control desensitization, hierarchial arrangements of fear-provoking scenes are not used in anxiety management training, and there is a much greater emphasis upon purposefully inducing feelings of anxiety and tension by whatever means are most effective. Since Suinn contends that the stimuli used to elicit anxiety in guided rehearsal need bear no relation to the fearful stimuli in the clients' lives, a wider variety of potentially fearful stimuli have been considered for use in the guided rehearsal component of anxiety management training. Clients have been asked to recall anxiety-provoking memories from their past, to focus attention on physiological arousal, or to contemplate receiving a painful electric shock. Their anxiety has been facilitated further by means of frightening passages from Edgar Allen Poe or by electronic "mood" music. Although anxiety-evoking images are most commonly employed and most of these alternative means have been abandoned as the procedure evolved, the emphasis upon the purposeful induction of anxiety during guided rehearsal is evident from the many methods that have been tried.

As in all of the self-control training techniques, the guided rehearsal component of anxiety management training is designed to provide clients the opportunity first to detect and identify physical cues indicative of anxiety (i.e. tension cue discrimination) and then to rehearse their relaxation skills to bring about a reduction in this anxiety. As anxiety management training is currently practiced, clients are first instructed to divert their attention away from the anxiety-provoking images when they begin relaxing away their anxiety. In later stages of guided rehearsal, clients are encouraged to continue attending to the anxiety-evoking images (i.e. to "stay in" the arousing scene) while practicing relaxation.

Anxiety management training was developed for treating individuals who suffered from generalized forms of anxiety not clearly associated with particular stimulus settings. Accordingly, most of the outcome research involving anxiety management training has employed subjects who suffer from chronic anxiety (Basgall, Denney, Hutchings, & Houston, 1978; Edie, 1972; Hutchings, Denney, Basgall, & Houston, 1978; Shoemaker, 1976) and anxiety-related disorders such as hypertension (Bloom & Cantrell, 1977; Suinn & Bloom, 1977). However, in a few early studies of anxiety management training, mathematics anxiety and test anxiety were targeted for treatment. Suinn and Richardson (1971) showed that anxiety management training and systematic desensitization were equally effective at reducing self-reports of mathematics anxiety and increasing scores on a mathematics performance test. The effects of both treatment procedures generalized to a self-report measure of test anxiety as well. The data from the anxiety management training condition in Suinn and Richardson's (1971) first study were later compared with the data from two other treatment conditions, systematic desensitization and a variant of desensitization known as accelerated massed desensitization (Richardson & Suinn, 1973). Anxiety management training again appeared to be as effective as the two desensitization procedures for reducing self-reported mathematics anxiety and improving mathematics performance. All three procedures were more effective than an untreated control condition.

Richardson and Suinn (1974) compared anxiety management training, systematic desensitization, and accelerated massed desensitization in the treatment of test anxiety. Unfortunately, only a single, self-report measure was used to evaluate subjects' test anxiety in this study. On this one measure, all three treatment procedures resulted in significant reductions of test anxiety relative to an untreated control condition. However, the scores for the anxiety management training subjects remained significantly higher than those of the systematic desensitization subjects at the time of the posttest.

A more elaborate comparison of anxiety management training and systematic desensitization in the treatment of test anxiety was conducted by Deffenbacher and Shelton (1978). Following five treatment sessions, subjects in both treatment conditions showed a significant reduction in their levels of test anxiety, as indicated by two self-report measures. Subjects who received anxiety management training maintained this improvement over the course of a 6-week follow-up period, whereas subjects in the systematic desensitization condition tended to revert toward their pretest levels of test anxiety. In addition, anxiety management training was found to be more effective than systematic sensitization in terms of generalization to a measure of chronic anxiety.

Like the other self-control training techniques reviewed in this section, anxiety management training would seem to be a promising procedure for the treatment of test anxiety. Unfortunately, the outcome studies investigating the effects of anxiety management training upon test anxiety are limited in their designs. Only self-report measures of test anxiety have been used to assess outcome, and placebo groups to control for nonspecific treatment effects are completely absent. Anxiety management training represents a procedure lying squarely within the realm of self-control treatments. Its effectiveness in alleviating test anxiety deserves more careful investigation.

COGNITIVE COPING TECHNIQUES

The introduction of cognitive-mediational theories has led to two important developments in the field of behavior therapy. On the one hand, the adoption of a cognitive-mediational perspective permitted a valuable reinterpretation of existing behavior therapy procedures. Nowhere is this dividend better illustrated than in Goldfried's (1971) paper concerning the self-control features of desensitization. Of perhaps greater significance, however, is the expansion of behavior therapy procedures that has followed the assimilation of cognitive-mediational theories. The cognitive coping techniques discussed in the present section are all representative examples of this latter development.

Any discussion of cognitive coping techniques must begin with a consideration of the work of Albert Ellis (1962). It has long been recognized that the way in which individuals construe situations that they confront has a substantial effect upon the emotional reactions that follow. Empirical support for this fact is available from a number of studies (Goldfried & Sobocinski, 1975; May & Johnson, 1973; Rimm & Litvak, 1969; Russell & Brandsma, 1974; Velten, 1968). However, Ellis' (1962) contribution lay in helping us to appreciate the therapeutic significance of this fact, as summarized in the following statement:

> If...people essentially become emotionally disturbed because they unthinkingly accept certain illogical premises or irrational ideas, then there is a good reason to believe that they can somehow be persuaded or taught to think more logically and rationally and thereby undermine their own disturbance [p. 161].

In rational emotive therapy, the method Ellis employs for altering the irrational beliefs of his clients consists of a fairly direct verbal assault upon their thinking. As Brehm (1966) has indicated through his concept of reactance, such an assault could easily provoke clients into a more tenacious position if they feel they are being coerced into changing their beliefs. Outcome research with respect to the effectiveness of rational emotive therapy is sparse and methodologically poor, and a review of this research—like the treatment procedure itself—lies outside the scope of this chapter (see review by Mahoney, 1974).

The assimilation of Ellis' work within the field of behavior therapy has led to three results. First, rational emotive therapy has been systematized into a more clearly operationally defined procedure (Goldfried, Decenteceo, & Weinberg, 1974). Second, research dealing with the impact of cognitive interventions in the context of therapy has been conducted with much greater methodological sophistication. Finally, cognitive interventions themselves have become somewhat more focused, deemphasizing the alteration of pervasive "irrational beliefs" in favor of a more concentrated assault upon specific negative and counterproductive self-statements which clients emit in certain contexts.

The procedures in the present section all share a cognitive restructuring component that distinguishes them from self-control training techniques. As we trace from left to right along the continuum in Fig. 10.1, we encounter cognitive coping techniques that place increasing emphasis upon cognitive restructuring rather than relaxation as a means of reducing anxiety. The use of cognitive restructuring as a coping skill in the treatment of text anxiety is largely predicated upon the attentional theory of test anxiety, which Jeri Wine has discussed in Chapter 16. In brief, this theory proposes that highly test-anxious individuals divide their attention between task-relevant and task-irrelevant thoughts while working on tests. The task-irrelevant thoughts are usually self-evaluative and self-deprecatory in nature. Their effect is to draw the person's attention away from the task at hand and thus detract from test performance. Within the context of test anxiety, cognitive restructuring is aimed at helping clients to identify the task-irrelevant thoughts they entertain during tests, to eclipse such thoughts, and to substitute positive self-statements which redirect their attention to the test.

Table 10.3 summarizes the controlled outcome studies involving cognitive coping techniques. The first such technique to be considered here was devised by Donald Meichenbaum (1972) and is known as cognitive modification. As applied to test anxiety, this procedure begins with a self-control rationale that includes an emphasis upon the role of negative self-statements in distracting individuals during their performance on tests. During an "insight" phase, clients discuss various irrational thoughts that they have during tests and the internal and external cues that lead to such thoughts. Clients are then taught relaxation. During guided rehearsal, clients are asked to imagine themselves taking tests and to cope with feelings of anxiety by using relaxation and self-generated instructions to focus their attention upon the task.

Meichenbaum (1972) compared cognitive modification with a modified type of desensitization in the treatment of test anxiety. The latter treatment differed from systematic desensitization in that subjects were instructed to apply the skills they acquired during actual tests. The same application training was, of course, also included in the cognitive modification procedure. Both cognitive modification and desensitization were equally effective in reducing self-reports of debilitating test anxiety, relative to an untreated control group. However, subjects in the cognitive modification condition also scored higher on a measure of facilitating test anxiety, achieved higher grade point averages, and reported feeling less fear before completing an abilities test than subjects in the desensitization condition. Moreover, the superiority of cognitive modification over desensitization was even more evident after a one-month follow-up.

Subsequent to Meichenbaum's (1972) study, several additional comparative outcome studies were conducted to assess the relative efficacy of cognitive modification and either a systematic or self-control form of desensitization (Holroyd, 1976; Lavigne, 1974; Scrivner, 1974; Thompson, 1976). Although isolated differences between cognitive modification and desensitization were occasionally reported for debilitating test anxiety (Lavigne, 1974), facilitating test anxiety (Scrivner, 1974), or abilities test performance (Holroyd, 1976), the general impression obtained from these later studies is that cognitive modification and desensitization, particularly the self-control form of desensitization, are about equally effective in the treatment of test anxiety. A similar conclusion may be drawn from comparative outcome studies dealing with speech anxiety (Meichenbaum, Gilmore, & Fedoravicious, 1971; Norman, 1975).

In addition to the comparative outcome studies, component analytic studies of cognitive modification have been conducted by Wine (1971a),

Holroyd (1976), and Hahnloser (1974). In Wine's (1971a) study, test-anxious subjects were assigned to three conditions: cognitive modification, which combined both relaxation and attentional training (i.e., cognitive restructuring); attentional training alone; and placebo, which required subjects merely to focus on their thoughts and feelings while taking simulated tests. Wine's cognitive modification procedure differed from Meichenbaum's in two notable respects. First, Wine used simulated tests rather than imaginal scenes and coping imagery during guided rehearsal. Second, she included models of test-anxious persons making derogatory and unproductive self-statements and also redirecting their attention to tests through more positive, task-relevant self-statements.

Wine's results indicated that attentional training was responsible for changes in test anxiety. Subjects in both the cognitive modification and the attentional training conditions reported significant decreases in debilitating test anxiety and raised their scores on two performance tests, relative to the placebo condition. The only difference between the two treatments occurred on a measure of facilitating test anxiety, and here subjects in the attentional training condition showed more improvement than those in the cognitive modification condition.

Holroyd (1976) compared cognitive modification, attentional training alone, systematic desensitization, a placebo condition involving meditation upon irrelevant scenes, and an untreated control condition. The four treatment conditions, including the placebo, were equally effective in reducing self-reports of debilitating test anxiety. However, as in the case of Wine's study, Holroyd found evidence that cognitive restructuring was more important than relaxation training in the cognitive modification procedure. Subjects in both the cognitive modification condition and the attentional training condition improved their scores on a performance test, relative to subjects in the three remaining conditions. Furthermore, subjects who received attentional training alone reported lower levels of test anxiety before attempting the performance test and also achieved higher grade point averages than all other groups.

Finally, Hahnloser (1974) compared cognitive modification, attentional training alone, relaxation training alone, and an untreated control condition. In contrast to the results obtained by Wine and Holroyd, the cognitive modification procedure was found to be significantly more effective than either of its component procedures in terms of reducing debilitating test anxiety and increasing facilitating test anxiety. Furthermore, no significant differences were found on performance measures of test anxiety—another result which varies from Wine's and Holroyd's findings. Therefore, while two of the component analytic studies suggest that attentional training or cognitive restructuring is the more essential coping skill in cognitive modification, the third study indicates that a synergistic combination of

TABLE 10.3
Cognitive Coping Technique

				Self-Report Measures					Performance Measures		
Study	Conditions	No. of Treatment Sessions	Weeks of Follow-Up	Debilitating Test Anxiety (Trait)	Facilitating Test Anxiety (Trait)	Emotionality (State)	Worry (State)	Test Anxiety (State)	Abilities Test	Academic Measure	General Anxiety or Nontargeted Fears
Meichenbaum (1972)	1. cognitive modification 2. modified desensitization 3. no-treatment control	8	4	AAT: 1 = 2 < 3	AAT: 1 = 2 > 3			AACL: 1 < 2 = 3 AD: 1 < 2 < 3	DS: 1 = 2 > 3 RM: NS	GPA: 1 > 2 > 3	
Holroyd (1976)	1. cognitive modification 2. attentional training 3. systematic desensitization 4. placebo (meditation) 5. no-treatment control	7	4	AAT: 1,2,3,4 < 5	AAT: NS			STAI-S: 2 < 1 = 3 = 4 < 5 AD: 2 < 1 = 3 = 4 < 5	DS: 1 = 2 > 3,4,5	GPA: 2 > 1 = 3 = 4 > 5	
Lavigne (1974)	1. cognitive modification 2. systematic desensitization 3. no-treatment control	8	0	AAT: 1 = 2 < 3 TTAQ: 1 < 2 < 3	AAT: NS TTAQ: NS				WPT: 1 = 2 > 3	GPA: NS	
Scrivner (1974)	1. cognitive modification 2. modified desensitization	8	0	AAT: 1 = 2	AAT: 1 > 2	OITA: 1 = 2	OITA: 1 = 2	OITA: 1 = 2	WPT: 1 = 2		

Study	Treatments										
Wine (1971a)	1. cognitive modification 2. attentional training 3. placebo (self-focussing)	6	0	AAT: 2<3 TAQ: 1=2<3	AAT: 2>1=3	LM: NS	LM: NS		WPT: 1=2>3 DS: 1=2>3		STAI-T: NS
Hahnloser (1974)	1. cognitive modification 2. attentional training 3. relaxation training 4. no-treatment control	4	0	AAT: 1<2=3<4	AAT: 1>2=3=4 NS	LM: 1=2 NS	LM: 1=2= 3<4		WPT: NS DS: NS	GPE: NS	
Goldfried, Linehan, & Smith (1978)	1. systematic rational restructuring 2. placebo (scene only) 3. no-treatment control	6	6	AAT: 1<2<3 TAQ: NS STABS: 1<2<3 SRIA-E: 1<2<3	AAT: NS	EQ: NS	EQ: 1<3	STAI-S: NS AD: NS	WPT: NS DS: NS	1<3	STAI-T: NS SRIA-S:
Osarchuk (1974)	1. systematic rational restructuring 2. self-control desensitization 3. combined treatment 4. placebo (scene only)	6	8	AAT: 1=2=3<4	AAT: NS	LM: 1=2= 3<4	LM: 1=2=3<4		WPT: 1=2=3>4		FNE: 1<2=3 SADS: 1<2=3

[a]Results reported for posttest only. AAT—Alpert Haber Achievement Test; AACL—Affect Adjective Checklist; AD—Anxiety Differential; DS—Digit Span; EQ—Experience Questionnaire; FNE—Fear of Negative Evaluation; GPA—Grade Point Average; GPE—General Psychology Exam; LM—Liebert & Morris Test Anxiety Scale; OITA—Osterhouse Inventory of Test Anxiety; RM—Raven Matrices; SADS—Social Avoidance and Distress Scale; SRIA-E—SR Inventory of Anxiousness (Exam); SRIA-S—SR Inventory of Anxiousness (Speech); STABS—Suinn Test Anxiety Behavior Scale; STAI-S—State–Trait Anxiety Inventory (State); STAI-T—State–Trait Anxiety Inventory (Trait); TAQ—Test Anxiety Questionnaire; TTAQ—Target Test Anxiety Questionnaire; WPT—Wonderlic Personnel Test.

cognitive restructuring and relaxation training may be responsible for the success of Meichenbaum's procedure.

Whereas cognitive modification embraces both relaxation and cognitive restructuring as coping skills in the reduction of anxiety, Marvin Goldfried's procedure, known as systematic rational restructuring, employs only cognitive restructuring and thus is located further to the right along the continuum of self-control procedures (Goldfried, 1977; Goldfried & Davison, 1976; Goldfried et al., 1974). Systematic rational restructuring incorporates many of the tenets of rational emotive therapy and, in fact might be viewed as a more systematized rendition of Ellis' therapeutic approach. However, Goldfried has embedded Ellis' approach within a self-control framework. Systematic rational restructuring includes a self-control rationale, guided rehearsal, and application training along with cognitive restructuring. Clients are first introduced to the premise that their beliefs substantially determine the emotions they experience within certain settings and are helped to identify the particular irrational and counterproductive self-statements they make when confronting a stressful situation. Guided rehearsal permits clients an opportunity to discriminate anxiety cues, to identify the negative self-statements they may be making, and to reduce their anxiety by self-verbalizing positive coping statements.

The effectiveness of systematic rational restructuring has been examined in terms of the treatment of speech anxiety (Casas, 1975), interpersonal anxiety (Goldfried, 1977; Kanter & Goldfried, 1976), and unassertiveness (Glass, Gottman, & Shmurak, 1976; Thorpe, 1975) as well as test anxiety.

Goldfried, Linehan, and Smith (1978) examined the effectiveness of systematic rational restructuring in the reduction of test anxiety. Test-anxious undergraduates from two separate universities were randomly assigned to systematic rational restructuring, prolonged exposure, and no-treatment control conditions. The subjects in the systematic rational restructuring condition began by observing a model illustrating the use of coping self-statements spoken aloud in order to reduce anxiety and to refocus attention on a simulated test. Subjects were then asked to imagine a scene from a test anxiety hierarchy, to identify any irrational self-statements that arose during the scene, and to reduce their anxiety by substituting more positive and rational self-statements. Fifteen scenes were used in the rational restructuring condition, and each scene was presented for four 1-minute exposures. Subjects in the prolonged exposure condition visualized the same scenes but were instructed merely to focus upon their emotional reactions to the scenes.

The results of this study generally indicate greater effectiveness for systematic rational restructuring as opposed to the prolonged exposure and untreated control conditions. Subjects in the former group reported greater reductions on various self-report measures of debilitating test anxiety and on generalization measures involving other types of fear. These differences were maintained over a 6-week follow-up period. However, it should be noted that there were no differences between the three conditions in terms of facilitating test anxiety or (presumably) in terms of the performance measures of test anxiety.

The only additional study involving systematic rational restructuring in the treatment of test anxiety was a comparative outcome study conducted by Osarchuk (1974). In this study, systematic rational restructuring was compared with self-control desensitization, a condition combining both procedures, and a placebo condition involving prolonged scene exposures only. The results revealed no differences between the three active treatment conditions, whereas all three treatments were significantly more effective than the placebo condition on both self-report and performance measures of test anxiety. A similar result was obtained by Casas (1975) in a study comparing systematic rational restructuring and self-control desensitization in the treatment of speech anxiety.

CONCLUSION

The behavior therapy literature pertaining to the treatment of test anxiety has been reviewed by Allen (1972) and Wine (1973) (see Chapter 8 by Allen, Elias, and Zlotlow). With well over 50 controlled outcome studies appearing in the literature, systematic desensitization still remains the most common procedure for treating test anxiety. Although reductions in self-reports of debilitating test anxiety are typically observed in these studies, concomitant improvements in abilities test performance and academic measures have been observed with far less consistency. As pointed out in Chapter 8, 50% of all recent behavior therapy studies and 67% of those studies involving systematic desensitization have failed to find differences between treated and untreated control conditions on performance measures of test anxiety.

One might ask whether the self-control procedures reviewed in the present chapter are any more successful in promoting changes on such performance measures. An overall tally of the self-control procedures summarized in Tables 10.1, 10.2, and 10.3 reveals that 54% of the 15 studies that included performance measures in assessing outcome reported significant differences between treated and untreated control conditions on at least one such measure, a success rate which compares closely with the figures reported in Chapter 8. However, somewhat greater optimism is afforded if one examines the results for the studies within each of the three categories of self-control procedures. Only 33% (1 of 3) of the studies in the category of applied relaxation techniques and 50% (4 of 8) of the studies in the category of self-control training techniques revealed improvements on performance measures, whereas 71% (5 of 7) of the studies in the category of cognitive coping techniques demonstrated improvements in these types of measures. In other words, as one moves from left to right along the continuum of self-control procedures illustrated in Figure 10.1, the success rate on performance measures of test anxiety increases markedly.

When differences on performance measures between treated and untreated control conditions are reviewed across a number of separate studies, cognitive coping techniques, which incorporate some form of cognitive restructuring, are observed to have a higher rate of success than self-control training or applied relaxation techniques. This observation is relevant to another issue concerning self-control procedures—namely, the relative effectiveness of cognitive restructuring as opposed to relaxation as a coping strategy for reducing test anxiety. In addition to the preceding observation regarding success rates on performance measures, two types of studies have been conducted which bear on this issue. The first involves an analysis of the effective components of the cognitive modification procedure. Since cognitive modification combines both relaxation and cognitive restructuring as coping strategies, several investigators (Hahnloser, 1974; Holroyd, 1976; Wine, 1971a) have been interested in conducting component analytic studies to determine which of the two strategies was more conducive to changes in test anxiety. The other type of study involves a more global comparison between one of the cognitive coping techniques and self-control desensitization. Because cognitive coping techniques incorporate cognitive restructuring, either alone or in combination with relaxation, and self-control desensitization employs only relaxation, these comparative outcome studies (Meichenbaum, 1972; Osarchuk, 1974; Scrivner, 1974; Thompson, 1976) also bear on the question of the relative effectiveness of cognitive restructuring and relaxation training.

Both the component analytic studies and the comparative outcome studies were reviewed in the preceding section dealing with cognitive coping techniques. Two of the component analytic studies (Wine, 1971a; Holroyd, 1976) indicated that cognitive restructuring (i.e., attentional training) was the effective coping strategy operating in cognitive modification, whereas the remaining study (Hahnloser, 1974) indicated that both cognitive restructuring and relaxation had to be available in combination for cognitive modification to be effective. The results for the comparative outcome studies are also fairly indecisive. Meichenbaum (1972) found several important advantages of cognitive modification over modified desensitization. Scrivner (1974) found only one relatively minor advantage involving facilitating test anxiety. The remaining studies showed no differences between cognitive modification (Thompson, 1976) or systematic rational restructuring (Osarchuk, 1974) and self-control desensitization.

The component analytic and comparative outcome studies conducted thus far offer no firm conclusion regarding the relative effectiveness of cognitive restructuring and relaxation as coping strategies to be employed in self-control procedures. One of the problems accounting for the lack of consensus among these studies may be the insensitivity of available outcome measures of test anxiety. These measures may simply lack the power to discriminate the relative effectiveness of one component of cognitive modification from another or to discriminate the relative effectiveness of a cognitive coping technique and a self-control training technique. Self-report measures offer relatively more direct assessments of test anxiety than performance measures and thus may possess more sensitivity to differential treatment effects. Nevertheless, they are also more subject to distortion due to differences in demand and expectation.

Another problem affecting comparisons between cognitive restructuring and relaxation as coping strategies lies in the greater complexity of cognitive restructuring. Several studies have shown that subjects who are exposed to stressful situations have difficulty employing complex mental operations in order to cope with the stress (Gaudry & Spielberger, 1971; Lazarus, 1966). By the same token, self-control procedures that incorporate fairly complex coping strategies may exceed the capacity of some test-anxious individuals when they are confronting important tests and thus may seem to be less effective than simpler procedures relying exclusively upon relaxation. In this instance, the lack of effectiveness of cognitive restructuring is an artifact of its greater complexity and perhaps also a function of individual differences in anxiety levels.

Another factor governing the relative effectiveness of relaxation and cognitive restructuring as coping strategies in self-control procedures may be the nature of the anxiety being treated. Goldfried (1977) reviewed a number of self-control treatment studies and concluded that relaxation was as effective as cognitive restructuring for dealing with relatively circumscribed fears, such as speech anxiety and test anxiety. However, cognitive restructuring appeared to be somewhat more effective when dealing with more pervasive forms of anxiety—especially those involving a heavy social-evaluative component.

A somewhat similar argument might be made in the case of test anxiety itself. The relative efficacy of cognitive restructuring and relaxation may depend upon the nature of clients' test anxiety. Liebert and Morris (1967) have distinguished between worry and emotionality as features of test anxiety. In brief, worry refers to the cognitive concern that persons have about the adequacy of their test performance, whereas emotionality refers to the autonomic arousal elicited by tests (see Chapter 6 by Jerry Deffenbacher for a further discussion of this distinction). It would seem reasonable to suppose that relaxation is a more effective skill for coping with emotionality, whereas cognitive restructuring might be more effective for altering ruminative and task-irrelevant worries.

In future research bearing on cognitive restructuring and relaxation as coping strategies, it will be important to assess the "domains of effectiveness" (Sherman, Mulac, & McCann, 1974) of these strategies in conjunction with the distinction between worry and emotionality. A study recently published by Finger and Galassi (1977) offers an excellent model for such research. The treatment procedure used by Finger and Galassi was covert positive reinforcement. Since this procedure encompasses almost none of the features characteristic of self-control procedures, their study does not technically qualify for inclusion in this chapter. However, because these investigators distinguished between worry and emotionality and found evidence that the apparent effectiveness of relaxation and attentional training depended upon the type of outcome measure employed, it is instructive to review this study.

Finger and Galassi covertly reinforced various types of self-instructions while subjects imagined scenes having to do with preparing for and taking examinations. Subjects in one condition were reinforced for attentional self-instructions, whereas those in another condition were reinforced for relaxational self-instructions, and those in a third condition were reinforced for both types of self-instructions. All three conditions were compared with an untreated control group, using both self-report measures of worry and emotionality and performance measures. Although no differences occurred on the performance measures, some very interesting results were obtained on the self-report measures. Subjects in all three treatment conditions scored significantly lower than controls on a global measure of debilitating test anxiety. However, subjects in the relaxation condition and the combined condition reported significantly less emotionality than subjects in the attentional training condition, whereas subjects in the attentional training condition and the combined condition reported significantly less worry than subjects in the relaxation condition. Thus, the apparent effectiveness of relaxation and attentional training depended upon the type of test anxiety measure being applied to assess treatment outcome.

In her review of the literature, Wine (1971b) concluded that studies concerned with the treatment of test anxiety "have evolved from interest in specific treatment techniques rather than from an analysis of the nature and effects of test anxiety [p. 101]." In a similar but more specific vein, it may only be fruitful to compare cognitive restructuring and relaxation as coping strategies in self-control procedures by considering each strategy's domain of effectiveness in conjunction with a multifaceted construct of test anxiety. A distinct advantage of the self-control procedures reviewed in the present chapter is that they possess the flexibility to accommodate our current and emergent understanding regarding the nature of this problem.

REFERENCES

Allen, G. J. The behavioral treatment of test anxiety: Recent research and future trends. *Behavior Therapy,* 1972, *3,* 253–262.

Aponte, J. F., & Aponte, C. E. Group preprogrammed systematic desensitization without the simultaneous presentation of aversive scenes with relaxation training. *Behaviour Research & Therapy,* 1971, *9,* 337–346.

Basgall, J., Denney, D. R., Hutchings, D., & Houston, B. K. *Anxiety management training and meditation in the reduction of chronic anxiety.* Unpublished manuscript, University of Kansas, Lawrence, Kans., 1978.

Bedell, J. R. Systematic desensitization, relaxation-training, and suggestion in the treatment of test anxiety. *Behaviour Research & Therapy,* 1976, *14,* 309–311.

Bloom, L., & Cantrell, D. *Anxiety management training for essential hypertension in pregnancy.* Unpublished manuscript, Colorado State University, Fort Collins, Colo., 1977.

Brehm, J. W. *A theory of psychological reactance.* New York: Academic Press, 1966.

Casas, J. M. *A comparison of two mediational self-control techniques for the treatment of speech anxiety.* Unpublished doctoral dissertation, Stanford University, Palo Alto, Calif., 1975.

Cautela, J. R. A behavior therapy treatment of pervasive anxiety. *Behaviour Research and Therapy,* 1966, *4,* 99–109.

Cautela, J. R. Behavior therapy and self control: Techniques and implications. In C. M. Franks (Ed.), *Behavior therapy: Appraisal and status.* New York: McGraw-Hill, 1969.

Chang-Liang, R., & Denney, D. R. Applied relaxation as training in self-control. *Journal of Counseling Psychology,* 1976, *23,* 183–189.

Cooke, G. Evaluation of the efficacy of the components of reciprocal inhibition psychotherapy. *Journal of Abnormal Psychology,* 1968, *73,* 464–467.

Davison, G. C. Relative contributions of differential relaxation and graded exposure to in vivo desensitization of a neurotic fear. *Proceedings of the 73rd Annual Convention of the American Psychological Association,* 1965, *1,* 209–210.

Davison, G. C. Systematic desensitization as a counterconditioning process. *Journal of Abnormal Psychology,* 1968, *73,* 91–99.

Deffenbacher, J. L. Relaxation in vivo in the treatment of test anxiety. *Journal of Behavior Therapy and Experimental Psychiatry,* 1976, *1,* 289–292.

Deffenbacher, J. L., Mathis, H., & Michaels, A. C. *Self-control procedures in the reduction of targeted and nontargeted anxieties.* Unpublished manuscript, Colorado State University, Fort Collins, Colo., 1978.

Deffenbacher, J. L., & Parks, D. H. A comparison of traditional and self-control systematic desensitization. *Journal of Counseling Psychology,* 1979, *26,* 93–97.

Deffenbacher, J. L., & Payne, D. M. J. Two procedures for relaxation as self-control in the treatment of communication apprehension. *Journal of Counseling Psychology,* 1977, *24,* 255–258

Deffenbacher, J. L., & Shelton, J. L. Comparison of anxiety management training and desensitization in reducing test and other anxieties. *Journal of Counseling Psychology,* 1978, *25,* 277–282.

Deffenbacher, J. L., & Snyder, A. L. Relaxation as self control in the treatment of test and other anxieties. *Psychological Reports,* 1976,*39,* 379–385.

Denney, D. R. Active, passive, and vicarious desensitization. *Journal of Counseling Psychology,* 1974, *21,* 369–375.

Denney, D. R., & Rupert, P. A. Desensitization and self-control in the treatment of test anxiety. *Journal of Counseling Psychology,* 1977, *45,* 272–280.

Edie, C. *Uses of anxiety management training in treating trait anxiety.* Unpublished doctoral dissertation, Colorado State University, Fort Collins, Colo., 1972.

Ellis, A. *Reason and emotion in psychotherapy.* New York: Lyle Stuart, 1962.

Finger, R., & Galassi, J. P. Effects of modifying cognitive versus emotionality responses in the treatment of test anxiety. *Journal of Consulting and Clinical Psychology,* 1977, *45,* 280–287.

Folkins, C., Lawson, K., Opton, E., & Lazarus, R. Desensitization and the experimental reduction of threat. *Journal of Abnormal Psychology,* 1968, *73,* 100–113.

Freeling, N. W., & Shemberg, K. M. The alleviation of test anxiety by systematic desensitization. *Behaviour Research & Therapy,* 1970, *8,* 293–299.

Gaudry, E., & Spielberger, C. D. *Anxiety and Educational Achievement.* New York: Wiley, 1971.

Glass, C. R., Gottman, J. M., & Shmurak, S. H. Response acquistion and cognitive self-statement modification approaches to dating skills training. *Journal of Counseling Psychology,* 1976, *23,* 520–526.

Goldfried, M. R. Systematic desensitization as training in self-control. *Journal of Consulting and Clinical Psychology,* 1971, *37,* 228–234.

Goldfried, M. R. The use of relaxation and cognitive relabeling as coping skills. In R. B. Stuart (Ed.), *Behavioral self management: Strategies, techniques, and outcomes.* New York: Brunner/Mazel, 1977.

Goldfried, M. R. & Davison, G. C. *Clinical behavior therapy.* New York: Holt, Rinehart & Winston, 1976.

Goldfried, M. R., Decenteceo, E. T., & Weinberg, L. Systematic rational restructuring as a self-control technique. *Behavior Therapy,* 1974, *5,* 247–254.

Goldfried, M. R., & Goldfried, A. P. Importance of hierarchy content in self-control of anxiety. *Journal of Consulting and Clinical Psychology,* 1977, *45,* 124–134.

Goldfried, M. R., Linehan, M. M., & Smith, J. L. Reduction of test anxiety through cognitive restructuring. *Journal of Consulting and Clinical Psychology,* 1978, *46,* 32–39.

Goldfried, M. R., & Sobocinski, D. The effect of irrational beliefs on emotional arousal. *Journal of Consulting and Clinical Psychology,* 1975, *43,* 504–510.

Goldfried, M. R., & Trier, C. S. Effectiveness of relaxation as an active coping skill. *Journal of Abnormal Psychology,* 1974, *83,* 348–355.

Hahnloser, R. M. *A comparison of cognitive restructuring and progressive relaxation in test anxiety reduction.* Unpublished doctoral dissertation, University of Oregon, Eugene, Oreg. 1974.

Holroyd, K. A. Cognition and desensitization in the group treatment of test anxiety. *Journal of Consulting and Clinical Psychology,* 1976, *44,* 991–1001.

Hutchings, D., Denney, D. R., Basgall, J., & Houston, B. K. *A comparison of anxiety management training and applied relaxation in the treatment of chronic anxiety.* Unpublished manuscript, University of Kansas, Lawrence, Kans., 1978.

Jacks, R. N. *Systematic desensitization versus a self-control technique for the reduction of acrophobia.* Unpublished doctoral dissertation, Stanford University, Palo Alto, Calif., 1972.

Jacobson, E. *Progressive relaxation.* Chicago: University of Chicago Press, 1938.

Johnson, S. M., & Sechrest, L. Comparison of desensitization and progressive relaxation in treating test anxiety. *Journal of Consulting and Clinical Psychology,* 1968, *32,* 280–286.

Kanter, N. J., & Goldfried, M. R. *Relative effectiveness of rational restructuring and self-control desensitization for the reduction of interpersonal anxiety.* Unpublished manuscript, State University of New York at Stony Brook, N.Y., 1976.

Lang, P., Lazovik, A., & Reynolds, D. Desensitization, suggestibility, and pseudotherapy. *Journal of Abnormal Psychology,* 1965, *70,* 395–402.

Lavigne, J. V. *The relative efficacy of cognitive-behavior rehearsal and systematic desensitization on the treatment of test anxiety.* Unpublished doctoral dissertation, University of Texas, Austin, Tex., 1974.

Laxer, R. M., Quarter, J., Kooman, A., & Walker, K. Systematic desensitization and relaxation of high-test-anxious secondary school students. *Journal of Counseling Psychology,* 1969, *16,* 446–451.

Laxer, R. M., & Walker, K. Counterconditioning versus relaxation in the desensitization of test anxiety. *Journal of Counseling Psychology,* 1970, *17,* 431–436.

Lazarus, R. S. *Psychological stress and the coping process,* New York: McGraw-Hill, 1966.

Liebert, R. M., & Morris, L. W. Cognitive and emotional components of test anxiety: A distinction and some initial data. *Psychological Reports,* 1967, *20,* 975–978.

Mahoney, M. J. *Cognitive and behavior modification.* Cambridge, Mass.: Ballinger, 1974.

Marchetti, A., McGlynn, F. D., & Patterson, A. S. Effects of cue-controlled relaxation, a placebo treatment, and no treatment on changes in self-reported and psychophysiological indices of test anxiety among college students. *Behavior Modification,* 1977, *1,* 47–72.

Marston, A. R., & Feldman, S. F. Toward the use of self-control in behavior modification. *Journal of Consulting and Clinical Psychology,* 1972, *39,* 429–433.

May, J. R., & Johnson, J. H. Physiological activity to internally elicited arousal and inhibitory thoughts. *Journal of Abnormal Psychology,* 1973, *82,* 239–245.

Meichenbaum, D. H. Cognitive modification of test anxious college students. *Journal of Consulting and Clinical Psychology,* 1972, *39,* 370–380.

Meichenbaum, D. H. Cognitive factors in behavior modification: Modifying what clients say to themselves. In R. D. Rubin, J. P. Brady, & J. D. Henderson (Eds.), *Advances in behavior therapy* (Vol.4). New York: Academic Press, 1973.

Meichenbaum, D. H., Gilmore, J. B., & Fedoravicious, A. Group insight versus group desensitization in treating speech anxiety. *Journal of Consulting and Clinical Psychology,* 1971 *36,* 410–421.

Moore, N. Behavior therapy in bronchial asthma: A controlled study. *Journal of Psychosomatic Research,* 1965, *9,* 257–274.

Norman, W. H. *The efficacy of self-instructional training in the treatment of speech anxiety.* Unpublished doctoral dissertation, Pennsylvania State University, University Park, Pa., 1975.

Osarchuk, M. M. *A comparison of a cognitive, a behavior therapy, and a cognitive-and-behavior therapy treatment of test anxious college students.* Unpublished doctoral dissertation, Adelphi University, N.Y., 1974.

Rachman, S. Studies in desensitization: I. The separate effects of relaxation and desensitization. *Behaviour Research & Therapy,* 1965, *3,* 245–252.

Rachman, S. The role of muscle relaxation in desensitization therapy. *Behaviour Research & Therapy,* 1968, *6,* 159–166.

Reed, R., & Meyer, R. G. Reduction of test anxiety via autogenic training. *Psychological Reports,* 1974, *35,* 649–650.

Richardson, F. C., & Suinn, R. A. A comparison of traditional systematic desensitization, accelerated desensitization, and anxiety management training in the treatment of mathematics anxiety. *Behavior Therapy,* 1973, *4,* 212.

Richardson, F. C., & Suinn, R. Effects of two short-term desensitization methods in the treatment of test anxiety. *Journal of Counseling Psychology,* 1974, *21,* 457–458.

Rimm, D. C., & Litvak, S. B. Self-verbalization and emotional arousal. *Journal of Abnormal Psychology,* 1969, *74,* 181–187.

Rimm, D. C., & Masters, J. C. *Behavior therapy: Techniques and empirical findings.* New York: Academic Press, 1974.

Rimm, D., & Medeiros, D. The role of muscle relaxation in participant modeling. *Behaviour Research & Therapy,* 1970, *8,* 127–132.

Romano, J. L., & Cabianca, W. A. EMG biofeedback training versus systematic desensitization for test anxiety reduction. *Journal of Counseling Psychology,* 1978, *25,* 8–13.

Russell, P. L. & Brandsma, J. M. A theoretical and empirical integration of the rational-emotive and classical conditioning theories. *Journal of Consulting and Clinical Psychology,* 1974, *42,* 389–397.

Russell, R. K., Miller, D. E., & June, L. N. Group cue-controlled relaxation in the treatment of test anxiety. *Behavior Therapy,* 1974, *5,* 572–573.

Russell, R. K., Miller, D. E., & June, L. N. A comparison between group systematic desensitization and cue-controlled relaxation in the treatment of test anxiety. *Behavior Therapy,* 1975, *6,* 172–177.

Russell, R. K., & Sipich, J. F. Cue-controlled relaxation in the treatment of test anxiety. *Journal of Behavior Therapy and Experimental Psychiatry,* 1973, *4,* 47–49.

Russell, R. K., & Sipich, J. F. Treatment of test anxiety by cue-controlled relaxation. *Behavior Therapy,* 1974, *5,* 673–676.

Russell, R. K., Wise, F., & Stratoudakis, J. P. Treatment of test anxiety by cue-controlled relaxation and systematic desensitization. *Journal of Counseling Psychology,* 1976, *23,* 563–566.

Samuels, M., & Samuels, N. *Seeing with the mind's eye: The history, techniques and uses of visualization.* New York: Random House, 1975.

Schultz, J. H., & Luthe, W. *Autogenic training: A physiologic approach in psychotherapy.* New York: Grune & Stratton, 1959.

Scrivner, R. W. *Systematic desensitization and cognitive modification with high emotionality and high worry subjects.* Unpublished doctoral dissertation, University of Texas, Austin, Tex., 1974.

Sherman, A. R., Mulac, A., & McCann, M. J. Synergistic effect of self-relaxation and rehearsal feedback in the treatment of subjective and behavioral dimensions of speech anxiety. *Journal of Consulting and Clinical Psychology,* 1974, *42,* 819–827.

Shoemaker, J. E. *Treatments for anxiety neurosis.* Unpublished doctoral dissertation, Colorado State University, Fort Collins, Colo., 1976.

Singer, J. *Imagery and daydream methods in psychotherapy and behavior modification.* New York: Academic Press, 1974.

Snider, J. G., & Oetting, E. R. Autogenic training and the treatment of examination anxiety in students. *Journal of Clinical Psychology,* 1966, *22,* 111–114.

Snyder, A. L., & Deffenbacher, J. L. Comparison of relaxation as self-control and systematic desensitization in the treatment of test anxiety. *Journal of Consulting and Clinical Psychology,* 1977, *45,* 1202–1203.

Spiegler, M. D., Cooley, E. J., Marshall, G. J., Prince, H. T., Puckett, S. P., & Skenazy, J. A. A self-control versus a counterconditioning paradigm for systematic desensitization: An experimental comparison. *Journal of Counseling Psychology,* 1976, *23,* 83–86.

Spiegler, M. D., Liebert, R. M., McMains, M. J., & Fernandez, L. E. Experimental development of a modeling treatment to extinquish persistent avoidant behavior. In R. D. Rubin & C. M. Franks (Eds.), *Advances in behavior therapy, 1968.* New York: Academic Press, 1969.

Suinn, R. M. Anxiety management training for general anxiety. In R. M. Suinn & R. Weigel (Eds.), *The innovative psychological therapies.* New York: Harper & Row, 1975.

Suinn, R. M. Anxiety management training to control general anxiety. In J. Krumboltz & C. Thorensen (Eds.), *Counseling methods.* New York: Holt, Rinehart & Winston, 1976.

Suinn, R. M. *Manual for anxiety management training (AMT).* Unpublished manuscript, Colorado State University, Fort Collins, Colo., 1977.

Suinn, R. M., & Bloom L. *Stress management training for Type A persons.* Unpublished manuscript, Colorado State University, Fort Collins, Colo., 1977.

Suinn, R. M., & Richardson, F. Anxiety management training: A non-specific behavior therapy program for anxiety control. *Behavior Therapy,* 1971, *4,* 498.

Thompson, J. W. *A comparison of four behavior therapies in the treatment of test anxiety in college students.* Unpublished doctoral dissertation, University of Arkansas, Fayetteville, Ark., 1976.

Thorpe, G. L. Desensitization, behavior rehearsal, self-instructional training and placebo effects on assertive-refusal behavior. *European Journal of Behavioural Analysis and Modification,* 1975, *1,* 30–44.

Trexler, L., & Karst, T. Rational-emotive therapy, placebo, and no treatment effects on public-speaking anxiety. *Journal of Abnormal Psychology,* 1972, *79,* 60–67.

Velten, E. A laboratory task for induction of mood states. *Behaviour Research & Therapy,* 1968, *6,* 473–482.

Wickramasekera, I. Instructions and EMG feedback in systematic desensitization: A case report. *Behavior Therapy,* 1972, *3,* 460–465.

Wine, J. *An attentional approach to the treatment of test anxiety.* Unpublished manuscript, Counseling Services Report, University of Waterloo, Ontario, Canada, 1971. (a)

Wine, J. Test anxiety and the direction of attention. *Psychological Bulletin,* 1971, *76,* 92–104. (b)

Wine, J. *Cognitive-attentional approaches to test anxiety modification.* Paper presented at the meeting of the American Psychological Association, Montreal, Canada, August, 1973.

Wolpe, J. *Psychotherapy by reciprocal inhibition.* Stanford: Stanford University Press, 1958.

Zeisset, R. M. Desensitization and relaxation in the modification of psychiatric patients' interview behavior. *Journal of Abnormal Psychology,* 1968, *73,* 18–24.

Zemore, R. Systematic desensitization as a method of teaching a general anxiety-reducing skill. *Journal of Consulting and Clinical Psychology,* 1975, *43,* 157–161.

11

Modeling Approaches to Test Anxiety and Related Performance Problems

Ted L. Rosenthal
University of Tennessee Center for the Health Sciences and MidSouth Hospital, Memphis

Fears are largely maintained by stressful anticipations about what one will face before entering the threatening situation. Anxious reveries are practiced at the expense of constructive planning. Thus, both "cognitive" and "affective" elements are involved and often defy distinction. Efforts to treat skill aspects versus emotional features separately challenge any dichotomy for examination (Finger & Galassi, 1977) or social (Trower, Yardley, Bryant, & Shaw, 1978) anxieties. Typically, when one emphasis surpasses the other, its superiority is slight. Its advantages may stem from including more comprehensive techniques rather than from any natural cleavage between affect and cognition (Curran & Gilbert, 1975; Wright, 1976). Hence, it seems premature to segregate the roles of arousal and thought in creating avoidance problems (Levine, Rotkin, Jankovic, & Pitchford, 1977; Rachman, 1977; Rosenthal & Bandura, 1978). The strands intermingle.

If the people anticipate inability to master some situation, they question their skills and magnify dangers. They worry about how to cope, how to fend off failure and embarrassment, and how to manage the consequences of expected poor performance. These ruminations further pave the way to disappointment. Attention is diverted from preparing and rehearsing effective solutions. One fails to analyze the key features of effective conduct and to organize them into workable plans that can steer future action. Instead, time is spent in seeking to ward off blunders, in dealing with distress triggered by imagined hazards, and in devising costly detours that might allow one to avoid the feared events. With such backgrounds to action, there is little wonder that actual performance suffers. People misread test questions, forget easy answers, lose their train of thought and garble sentences when speaking in public, or allow their legitimate rights to be usurped by more forceful companions. Those failures validate people's prior doubts about mastering tests, talking to groups, or asserting their rights with partners. The pattern of fearful anticipations hampering competent behavior continues or worsens. Fortunately, recent advances in treatment offer hope to those in need.

FEAR-REMOVAL MEDIA

Guidance information can be conveyed by a host of communication formats. Sometimes, alternative modes of presenting content prove comparable and choice is elective. But often, the form in which information is cast will determine the impact of guidance. Teaching by demonstration is widely used because it is versatile as well as effective. Exemplary modeling works very well to convey a broad range of knowledge. It is usually among the best, and rarely the worst, of competing methods to introduce abstract principles (Rosenthal & Zimmerman, 1978; Woodson, 1974) and social perceptions. Thus, audio- and videotaped episodes depicting human problems were equally able to elicit compassion from judges, but reading the same content created less sympathy (Baum, 1974). Likewise, student counselors learned best from taped demonstrations of how to adopt an empathic style of interaction; reading about empathy helped less; and giving or withholding didactic instructions had no effect (Dalton, Sunblad, & Hylbert, 1973; Eskedal, 1975; Perry, 1975). Modeling can enhance other guidance thrusts, e.g., structured modular programs, to foster diverse skills such as how to study (Kunce, Bruch, & Thelen, 1974) or to obtain vocational information (Fisher, Reardon, & Burck, 1976). Demonstrations are efficient as well as effective. Among trainees learning to express interpersonal warmth, 90 minutes of exemplary modeling led to as much progress as did 10 hours of other guidance (Dalton & Sunblad, 1976). Such results foreshadow the treatment value of modeling techniques for the problems of present concern and for other clinical fears (see Bandura, 1977a; Rosenthal & Bandura, 1978).

Current treatment strategies are robust in that a basic method can be applied to many specific types of fear and avoidance problems. Therapists may adopt the same strategy to teach calm, effective conduct during tests, speeches, or social exchanges even though the details of content will differ. Most methods develop competence by encouraging clients to face problem situations in gradual steps, mounting from easy to hardest tasks. Also, the benefits created by nearly all techniques involve support and therapeutic social influence exerted by a trusted counselor (Rosenthal, 1976, 1979; Rosenthal, Hung, & Kelley, 1977). A major difference concerns the mode of coping practice. Do clients perform: (1) symbolically, e.g., by imagining themselves approaching feared events; or (2) more literally, by enacting some approximation of the naturalistic task, e.g., taking sample examinations?

Surrogate Approach Scenarios

Learning is regulated by cognitive processes which interpret cues and organize meanings. Hence, much treatment information can be derived from symbolic approach episodes (Bandura, 1977a, b; Mahoney, 1974; Rosenthal & Zimmerman, 1978). As the earliest example of behavioral techniques for overcoming fear, *systematic desensitization* is the forebear of present symbolic performance methods. It is often used as a comparison standard to test the worth of other treatments. In traditional format, a hierarchy of problem-related scenes is constructed and clients are taught muscular relaxation. While relaxed, they visualize scenes starting with easy ones (e.g., taking an easy test from a kindly instructor) and progressing to items of peak difficulty (e.g., taking a final exam that affects graduation from a stern teacher). Desensitization requires minimal apparatus but still works well. It reduces test and social fear problems with success rates comparable to some more elaborate methods (e.g., Finger & Galassi, 1977; Trower et al., 1978). Thus, test-anxious college students gained as much from an automated form of desensitization as did other test-fearful peers, who were instead taught to control their arousal via biofeedback of muscle activity from complex instruments (Romano & Cabianca, 1978). Relaxation training is not essential for desensitization to work, nor must scenes adhere to rigid rules. For example, changing test-taking scenes into pleasant versions (e.g., imagining success on exams) aided clients (Guidry & Randolph, 1974). Such *positive imagery* methods work roughly as well but may require less time. One study found that a positive imagery technique required two fewer therapy sessions to achieve results as good as or better than desensitization (Kostka & Galassi, 1974). If they are plausible to clients, various modifications of the desensitization strategy can reduce such performance fears as public-speaking anxiety (Kirsch & Henry, 1977). In common, these tactics bring people into progressively harder mental contacts with threats they normally avoid. Because observing events conveys much information, what would happen if some clients witnessed the desensitization of others?

Vicarious Desensitization. A first trial used test-anxious junior high school students. Some were desensitized individually while observed by a peer. Others received group desensitization while observed by a group of peers. In a final version, a group of clients observed desensitization given to a peer model. Collectively, all formats surpassed untreated controls on fear ratings and worksample exams. But direct desensitization was no better than observation. The vicarious and direct treatments were equal, as were the individual and group formats (Mann & Rosenthal, 1969). Next, treatment was filmed and shown to groups of test-anxious adolescents. Some watched and emulated all steps of desensitization, e.g., relaxation exercises. Others observed without overt practice. Relaxation was omitted for a last group; they only observed the test-taking scene presentations. Yet all modeling formats made ample but equivalent progress (Mann, 1972). Similar results were found with college students. Vicarious clients did at least as well as those given two forms of desensitization for test anxiety (Denney, 1974). Likewise, one study compared traditional desensitization, desensitization plus images of effective coping, and desensitization plus statements for clients' self-guidance as means to treat speaking fears. Each form of therapy was administered directly to some clients and was videotaped and observed by others. The alternative treatments proved about equally beneficial, but overt was no better than vicarious guidance (Weissberg, 1977). Whatever the essential components of desensitization, they seem as readily conveyed vicariously as directly—with the added advantage that treatment recordings can be reused for future clients. These data illustrate the capacity of observational guidance as a therapy medium. Nor are its virtues confined to use with desensitization-like formats.

Symbolic Modeling. Observing live or recorded guidance episodes portrayed by others is called symbolic modeling. Exemplary demonstrations are an ancient teaching strategy. They illustrate the meaning of events in concrete, sequentially organized terms. They can teach new behavior or how to recombine familiar acts into novel patterns and solutions. They can disinhibit responses available to observers by depicting approach to feared cues without adverse consequences, thus raising clients' optimism and willingness to attempt deeds usually suppressed. They socially facilitate approach by influencing people to follow the modeled precedents as guides. And they can alter the cognitive standards and aspirations which people use to regulate conduct. Thus, observing models approach and master situations which clients fear has brought consistent benefits across a broad span of clinical handicaps (Rosenthal & Bandura, 1978).

Indeed, watching live or filmed approach demonstrations has reliably equaled or surpassed desensitization for such diverse problems as animal phobias (Bandura, Blanchard, & Ritter, 1969; Denney & Sullivan, 1976), dating inhibitions (Curran, 1975; Curran & Gilbert, 1975), and frigidity in women (Caird & Wincze, 1974; Wincze & Caird, 1976). In the foregoing studies, symbolic modeling exceeded desensitization on some dependent measures, or when certain supportive elements (e.g., relaxation training; the directions specifying context details) were favorable, but not otherwise. This is because both types of surrogate approach share many common features (e.g., interacting calmly with stressors) and are mediated by similar cognitive processes. Demonstrations may typically prove more vivid and under better therapist control than fantasied scenes (Rosenthal, Rosenthal, & Chang, 1977), but often observed and imagined episodes yield similar outcomes.

Thus, test-anxious students either (1) heard audio modeling tapes of peers who role-played taking tests calmly, or (2) underwent prototypic imaginal desensitization, or (3) were guided in such relevant study skills as how to take notes and to budget one's time, or (4) were given *flooding*—a variant of desensitization wherein the practice scenes are high in fear value, rather than of low intensity, or (5) received no treatment. Overall, the numbers in parentheses are in descending order of therapy benefits that resulted.

Modeling proved clearly the best method on a self-report measure of test anxiety, and in clients' satisfaction with treatment; desensitization was the next-best therapy; and both these symbolic treatment strategies were equivalent on other measures of progress, but they usually surpassed the remaining conditions (Horne & Matson, 1977). Likewise, to develop assertiveness in submissive clients, brief videotaped demonstrations of forceful conduct were combined with one of two types of role-playing practice. Another, "consciousness-raising" method instead presented a videotape of peers discussing their assertion difficulties, and all treatment was withheld from a last, control group. Both groups which observed illustrations of assertive behavior increased assertion more than the "consciousness-raising" clients, who failed to outperform the untreated controls (Wolfe & Fodor, 1977). Must clients witness other persons as models? Not necessarily. When used properly, playback of one's own efforts and therapeutic guidance to eliminate mistakes and improve one's subsequent attempts can be very helpful (Hung & Rosenthal, 1978). In such applications, the client's own performance serves as the basis to illustrate aspects of conduct needing further refinement. By carefully editing videotapes of client behavior, it was possible to compose a scenario that produced therapeutic gains (Dowrick & Raeburn, 1977). As a means to inform clients about progress accomplished and changes still needed, such techniques have surpassed verbal feedback methods (Edelson & Seidman, 1975). Because clients learn from observing their own behavior, these procedures are sometimes labeled self-modeling techniques. In any case, the cognitive representations and guidelines for action that are derived from alternative forms of symbolic approach to feared events have much in common. This is shown most clearly when clients imagine modeling scenarios rather than witnessing the sensory cues provided by live or recorded models.

Covert Modeling.   Treatment by means of modeling sequences rehearsed in fantasy is called covert modeling, a strategy quite similar to systematic desensitization. Using scripts much like those followed when therapeutic models perform, but visualizing others enact approach episodes, has proven clinically helpful. It has reduced snake fears (Kazdin, 1973, 1974a) and enhanced assertiveness in college students, especially if forceful conduct was imagined as leading to favorable consequences (Kazdin, 1974c, 1975, 1976). For both fear and assertion, there were no outcome differences between mental images of self versus another person executing the steps of approach behavior (Kazdin, 1974b; Rosenthal & Reese, 1976). Some research has compared covert with overt symbolic modeling. One study found minor, clinically negligible advantages for observed over fantasied models to treat fear of rats (Cautela, Flannery, & Hanley, 1974). A second study found equal assertion gains in overt and two covert modeling variations (Rosenthal &

Reese, 1976). Because both these tests involved college populations, it remains to confirm whether the methods are interchangeable with less sophisticated clients, e.g., children—who may have difficulty in correctly imagining the required therapy scripts. Yet, tallying the outcome results across surrogate approach formats (with several versions of each) suggests this conclusion for practical purposes: covert = overt symbolic modeling $\geq$ systematic desentization. Such rough equivalence seems to stem from (1) identical mediating processes operating on (2) largely the same meanings cast into alternative surrogate scenarios. If so, where next?

Enacted Approach Scenarios

Much treatment research on diverse avoidance problems suggests that making in vivo approach to feared events rehabilitates clients better than symbolic contacts (Bandura, 1977a, b). Is this because new response patttterns or rules for their use are better acquired from making overt responses? Not usually. Data from difficult, abstract tasks show that direct practice often interferes with basic *learning* (Rosenthal & Zimmerman, 1978). However, most clinical fears prevent rather simple acts (e.g., enduring open, dark, high, or confined places), which are known but inhibited by forebodings. Such familiar conduct is largely regulated by central plans, not by movement-produced feedback (Kelso, 1977). The virtues of overt approach practice instead seem to lie in its clear confirmation of restored capacity to *perform*. Clients may distrust "counting chickens until hatched." Our conception or definition of Self weights information by its certainty (Markus, 1977). Before in vivo success proves restored mastery, people may doubt symbolic gains as less relevant evidence of progress. Actual feats will more likely shift one's self-view from vulnerable to able. Hence, there is reason to expect that clinical outcomes will depend on how well treatment scenarios validate naturalistic competence.

Simulated Episodes.   Therapies for test-taking and similar performance anxieties have made limited strides toward giving in vivo practice. Rehearsal is mainly simulated in facsimiles of natural contexts. Many programs to develop assertion skills include modeled illustrations of apt conduct which clients then emulate and discuss in groups or dyads (e.g., Galassi, Galassi, & Litz, 1974; Trower et al, 1978). Discussions themselves have value, but demonstrations often enhance benefits (Linehan & Rosenthal, 1979; Sarason & Ganzer, 1973; Schinke & Rose, 1976). The rule of thumb is that if alternative methods convey distinct skill elements, combining techniques will surpass any one option (Hollandsworth, Dressel, & Stevens, 1977). Research must still clarify when and which tactics complement each other and when particular methods are not better combined than if used alone. Thus, various means to treat communication fears proved equivalent when simulated practice trials were provided (Deffenbacher & Payne, 1977; Trussel, 1978). Yet simulating relaxed conversation with fellow counselees was the closest approximation to real-life settings.

In Vivo Episodes. New behavior is most durable if refined under conditions that closely match future demands (cf. MacNeil & Sherif, 1976). Worksample tests have been used to assess clients' progress but rarely, if ever, for therapy per se. This neglect of giving repeated exams under protected conditions in order to reduce groundless fears contrasts with current treatments for other problems. Overt exposures typify such methods as (avoidant) *response prevention* and *participant modeling*—where the therapist and clients take alternate turns at making in vivo approaches to scarey events—which consistently surpass techniques using simulated exposures. Bandura (1977b) proposes a cognitive mechanism to explain both (1) the gains common to all fear-removal methods, and (2) why overt exposures have special merit. Clients' expectations about *self-efficacy,* i.e., their ability to perform some specific act, regulate their zeal and persistence on "dangerous" tasks. Many types of guidance can enhance self-efficacy, but only actual contacts assure in vivo competence. Simulated encounters are less convincing evidence of progress and have less impact in raising one's estimated competence and willingness to strive. Thus, real trials increase self-efficacy more than surrogate episodes, but the reciprocity between self-expectations and coping efforts remains similar: Research finds that as self-efficacy rises, clients will undertake and complete progressively harder approach tasks (Bandura & Adams, 1977; Bandura, Adams, & Beyer, 1977). Participant modeling need not involve expert staff. Friends and peer stangers who were taught its essentials then aided clients as much as did trained therapists (Moss & Arend, 1977). It hence appears the modeling treatment of choice, and from the outset brings the client into as close contact with actual feared stimuli as can be tolerated, unlike symbolic modeling.

A caveat is required. The foregoing sketch of in vivo exposure options rests just on recent data from simply organized goal responses, e.g., moving close to or touching such phobic stimuli as spiders. With test-taking and communication fears, skilled performance demands finer integration, which potentially might be more disrupted by arousal decrements of the Yerkes–Dodson law type.[1] Thus, major disruptions coming early in an overt practice trial might so impair composure or tax behavioral harmonies that the

---

[1]Namely, performance (and cognition) is a curvilinear function of arousal (motivation). As arousal mounts, performance improves, rising to asymptote, and then declines. The more complex or abstract the competency at issue, the sooner it reaches asymptote and the more sharply it declines in the face of stress.

whole episode is ruined, with more harm than help to the client, as sometimes is found in severe stuttering patterns. If so, slowing the pace of graded approach steps seems indicated. Perhaps an initial course of symbolic approach should precede overt enactments, or they should mount very gradually upward from the easiest. Research has not yet addressed such subtleties. In any case, there seems good reason to *conclude* fear-removal treatment programs with direct performance experiences so that clients can verify their independent mastery of the criterion demands. Guided overt practice techniques surely invite further study, but the existing modeling literature on examination-relevant fears mainly concerns means to bolster symbolic scenarios (below).

TREATMENT FORMATS

The medium in which fear-removal information is conveyed aside, some data bear on client composition at guidance sessions, and some on attributes of therapeutic models.

Audience Arrangements

Lay persons assume the burdened client will earn a counselor's undivided solace for 50 minutes. This surmise is a legacy of interview therapy and is costly to implement. Group formats can work as well, yet allow options precluded by individual sessions. Group economies may hinge on member characteristics suitable for specific features of content and method, but data on such variables are sparse with both child (Kirkland & Thelen, 1977) and older (Linehan & Rosenthal, 1979) clienteles.

Individual or Group Contexts. When relevant for multiple clients, exemplary guidance can usually be given conjointly. Demonstrations to allay test anxiety serve well if observed by adult or adolescent groups (e.g., Horne & Matson, 1977; Mann, 1972). Clients reduced examination fears equally well whether treated singly or in quintets (Mann & Rosenthal, 1969), and no evidence shows any intrinsic advantages for solo observation. Efforts at personalized tuning of therapy, easier done individually, may add nothing to standardized scenarios amenable to groups (Rosenthal & Reese, 1976). The main limiting conditions seem to require (1) that group numbers do not interfere with rapport, sensory access to stimulus events, or therapist monitoring of client reactions, and (2) that members can attend to and correctly interpret the same message without undue detriment from ideosyncratic factors. In such cases, a group of six or eight may require little more effort than just one client.

Further, groups permit social rehearsal options that are not possible with individual clients. These tactics include: (1) group feedback, discussion, and multiple role-taking to clarify better ways to implement modeled guidance; (2) shared in vivo task assignments between therapy sessions; and (3) "buddy system" monitoring plus social support among members to assure that all complete their assigned homework. Such cooperative arrangements are being explored for many academic and social handicaps. Neglect of coursework invites valid student worries about facing tests. Thus, research finds that team formats can promote regular studying and raise college grades better than solo guidance (Beaman, Fraser, Diener, & Endreson, 1977; Fraser, Diener, Beaman, & Kelem, 1977). Likewise, buddy formats could also assist diligent but fearful students. Together, they can rehearse modeled guidance steps for maintaining poise just before taking exams. This would provide scrutiny of the client's coping practice, corrective feedback, and encouragement from the partner. In this vein, reciprocal benefits were found when children were taught via modeling how to deliver constructive feedback to their peers (Blaney, Stephan, Rosenfield, Aronson, & Sikes, 1977).

Severity of Problem.   Clients range widely in their degree of avoidance and the disruptions it creates. This diversity raises two questions: First, do fear removal methods that are developed with milder cases—more numerous and available for study—apply to severe handicaps? And also, should the same modeling treatment be given to a group if its members' problems vary in severity? Both tentative answers seem "Yes" given some caution: Thus, strategies to spur zealous efforts may aid mildly but overmotivate highly anxious clients. This was found when arousing directions were part of treatment for test fears. The less worried group earned higher scores if instructions defined the task as academically vital. But very fearful students performed best if the task was not portrayed as so critical (I. Sarason, 1975). In general, the more arousal present in clients, the more likely that further stress will impair response (see Footnote 1).

Methods that reduce moderate avoidance usually aid graver cases, but do so more slowly. Some data suggest that clients recruited from the general community may be more fearful than college research samples, but for speech anxiety the differences were not great and only emerged on certain dependent measures (Maiuro & Talent, 1977). Effective treatments seem able to assist clients with more and less severe handicaps, sometimes largely negating any initial fear differences. In contrast, weak and "placebo" therapies may overcome mild problems but work much less well in serious cases, as has been found with examination and other fears (Bernotas, Ribordy, & Tracy, 1977; Feist & Rosenthal, 1973). Therefore, diverse modeling techniques have aided severely distressed psychotic inpatients and other clients with profound handicaps (see Rosenthal, 1979; Rosenthal & Bandura, 1978). One study assessed treatment gains in the ability to meet stressful social demands when demonstrations were or were not included in the therapy program. Although both versions of therapy helped nonpsychotics, modeling proved essential to help the less skillful schizophrenic patients (Eisler, Blanchard, Fitts, & Williams, 1978). Those results suggest there may be reason to keep groups fairly homogeneous when handicaps are extreme—in part so that group members will see each other as plausible companions and references figures. However, within the range of severity typical for fearful outpatients, greater variability can be tolerated among group members.

Indeed, research is only starting to explore how much diversity in client composition and teaching content will still lead to comparable outcomes. With college students, and depending on specific mode of guidance, giving four of 21 total episodes dealing with test anxiety problems worked about as well as confining all treatment items to examination fears (Speigler, Cooley, Marshall, Prince, Puckett, & Skenazy, 1976). In another test, college groups composed of members having distinct fears observed modeling treatment episodes that spanned several types of problems. This format created as much progress as was made by other clients, who instead met in homogeneous-problem groups, where triple the time was spent on the shared common fear (Linehan, Rosenthal, Kelley, & Theobald, 1977).

Source Characteristics

Observers' interpretations and active contributions determine the net value of guidance. Clients' perspectives influence treatment, whether problem solutions, nuances of interpersonal style, or fearless deeds are exemplified. It remains difficult to foresee which cue features will alter subjective reactions. Some distinctions, e.g., between live versus filmed (Mann, 1972; Weissberg, 1977) or imagined (Kazdin, 1974b; Rosenthal & Reese, 1976) tutors, have not proved very critical perhaps because adults perceived all the models as agents of the therapist. Yet some criteria e.g., physical attractiveness (Farina, Fischer, Sherman, Smith, Groh, & Mermin, 1977), which seem of minor relevance, may count heavily. In any event, people do not seize modeled exemplars uncritically, retain them passively, nor match them by rote The same actions and rhetoric adopted to end a strike will have quite different meaning to workers if coming from their national union, local leaders, the White House, or management. All these sources may have less impact than the precedent of fellow-strikers elsewhere in response to a contract proposal. Likewise, the frame of reference created by recent wage settlements in allied trades or the history of specific grievances and demands under dispute may qualify response to a message from any source. Adopting modeled conduct thus rests on decisions about how pertinent and trustworthy are others' practices as guides for one's own situation.

Single or Multiple Mentors. Even well-conceived demonstrations, given by a trusted source, must overcome clients' doubts and pessimism based on previous experience. People will more likely discount guidance from any single source than if basically the same information is endorsed by a range of sponsors whose standpoints might, in principle, differ. First, stability across models lends credence to the common theme—it applies to various people and cannot be dismissed as any one person's bias or ideosyncracy. Therefore, the measage gains in plausibility. Second, therapeutic modeling episodes are normally repeated several times in modified form to assure understanding. Thus, diversity among protagonists may better sustain attention and prevent satiation. Third, research on social influence (e.g., Asch, 1958) suggests that private doubts or reservations about the value of some treatment element should more readily yield to consensus perceived among others than to the stance of an isolated source. In effect, it is easier to ignore one person than several.

Such reasoning clearly argues for the use of multiple teaching models. Their treatment advantages were first proposed and tested in a study with dog-phobic children. Those who saw tapes of one peer demonstrating approach made major gains, but they then partly declined from the end of treatment to eventual follow-up. Other youngsters instead observed films of various girl and boy age-mates, who all modeled approaching dogs. Those clients were able to cope with more intimate canine contacts at the end of therapy, and they achieved further progress between that point and the time of follow-up (Bandura & Menlove, 1968). Despite these encouraging outcomes, surprisingly few later studies have exploited the potentialities of diversified modeling. Although few in number, the results from such tests continue to be positive. With children, multiple televised models successfully taught American Indian preschoolers a difficult size-seriation task (Henderson, Swanson, & Zimmerman, 1975). Retarded youngsters who observed several models were able to generalize newly learned behavior some eight times as well as did peers who watched a single model exemplify the same content (Marburg, Houston, & Holmes, 1976).

With adults, the benefits are similar. Some research on covert modeling has assessed the effects of variety among mentors to promote assertiveness. College students imagined an individual much like themselves in age and sex epitomize forceful conduct during a series of social encounters. Other timid students instead visualized a range of models—both similar to and different from themselves (older and younger; of the opposite sex) in status—who executed the same uninhibited behavior. In each experiment, clients who fantasied several protagonists overcame submissiveness better than their solo model counterparts (Kazdin, 1975, 1976). Thus far, one study has applied plural modeling to test anxiety. No direct comparison was made with a single model scenario. However, contrasting treatment methods were assessed after each was given for 10 hourly group sessions:

1. Some college students listened to audiotapes in which multiple peers learned to face examinations calmly. During early tapes, the models

expressed considerable test anxiety, but they became progressively calmer in later tapes.

2. A second group was given traditional systematic desensitization, using a standard hierarchy of test-taking scenes.

3. Another group instead received flooding, starting with the same scene hierarchy. Rather than visualizing calm behavior on items that gradually rose in difficulty, however, these clients were asked to imagine failing the tests. To further increase arousal, students were told to embellish the failure situations with personal details and to monitor their inward anxious feelings.

4. The fourth treatment provided specific study skills, e.g., how to pay attention during lectures, take notes, and budget their study time. Information to assist in analyzing and answering tests was also supplied.

5. All guidance was withheld from a last, control group until the research was completed.

In terms of reducing test anxiety, the results from best to worst fell in the foregoing numerical order. Modeling was significantly better than desensitization, which exceeded all other groups, and flooding proved more effective than both the study skills and control conditions. In terms of course grades, desensitization and modeling were superior to any other group. However, study-skills clients surpassed the controls but the flooding group did not. Further, a majority of flooding clients disliked their therapy and would not recommend it to others. In contrast, half the desensitization and nearly all the modeling clients endorsed their treatments. The modeling therapy also produced the most favorable client perceptions of the counselor's concern for their welfare (Horne & Matson, 1977).

Hence, there seems a good basis to invite further extensions of multiple modeling procedures for test anxiety and related problems. Such thrusts might well take account of the potential advantages permitted by group treatment formats, as noted earlier. Not only can a number of clients simultaneously observe any teaching episodes that "outsiders" perform, but group members can also aid each other as cooperative mutual tutors. For example, it would be possible to establish remedial classes for test-anxious students under school or college auspices. There, they might start with a phase of observing live or filmed demonstrations by diverse models, showing how to prepare for and cope with exams. The "course" content might also include study skills. At this initial stage of guidance, members would be helped to consolidate the key points demonstrated by means of additional group discussion and shared role playing. They would offer feedback and correction to one another and would continue to exchange advice and self-help hints drawn from personal discoveries as therapy advanced. Further, practice examinations could be given frequently. Such class-like settings would better approximate the in vivo conditions of eventual test taking than do settings defined in more "clinical" (and possibly stigmatizing) terms. Rather than paying assistants or recruiting sophomore volunteers to serve as pseudoclassmates, therapists would have an ongoing worksample of an academic environment. This would also spare the need for devising pretexts to arrange repeated tests in actual courses without alerting the instructors to the clients' personal difficulties. Interference or excessive arousal experienced before and during such practice tests could be dealt with in a manner not feasible when competative grades must be awarded. Yet, in most respects, close parallels to the context of actual scholastic exams could be maintained. In later stages of treatment, mutual self-help partnerships would be formed; as mentioned earlier, partners would aid each other on assignments given between group sessions and when either was facing a real life exam. Finally, clients who showed special aptitude for resolving their avoidance problems or "graduates" who have successfully overcome their original difficulties could then be enlisted as teaching models for new clients and for recordings to be used with future classes. Organized programs using similar modeling strategies have led to encouraging progress when applied to other types of skill deficiencies (Rosenthal, 1979; Rosenthal & Bandura, 1978).

Who Can Be Believed These Days?   In matters familar to us or if meanings are self-evident, we typically favor our own determinations of reality. For this reason, therapeutic progress is better validated when clients master naturalistic rather than simulated tasks. However, many urgent problems require us to rely on others' decisions, e.g., about the state of our economy, military preparedness, or liver functions. Other things equal, audiences judge the worth of a message by who sends it. This dependence on external authorities has prompted considerable research, for several decades, on how the cultural status and personal attributes of models affect the influence they exert on observers (see Bandura, 1977a; Rosenthal & Bandura, 1978). For the most part, that voluminous literature can be summarized in terms of the credibility and relevance of social communications.

People are more disposed to accept the views of sources (1) who are experienced rather than novices, (2) who have expert credentials rather than happenstance knowledge, (3) who have proven correct rather than misleading in the past, (4) who are recognized as leaders rather than nonentities in their fields, (5) who in general enjoy high prestige rather than reflecting low status, (6) who are perceived to practice rather than ignore their own exhortations, (7) who are known or reputed to be veracious rather than mendacious, (8) who exemplify modal rather than deviant conduct and values, and (9) who appear impartial rather than biased or self-serving, etc. In sum, the more credible the communicator, the more likely that a message will create its intended effects on the audience.

Given trust in the truth of a message, its impact will further depend on how clients judge its relevance. People actively seek out information that seems pertinent to serve their needs (Halisch & Heckhausen, 1977; Yussen, 1974). But, depending on context, they may strive to disregard cues that appear to digress from main concerns (Neill, 1977). Both clients' acceptance and cognitive processing of content will depend on how relevant it seems. Thus, the degree of similarity between model and observer is one criterion for judging the worth of teaching demonstrations, especially when clients lack other judgmental criteria. People discount or dismiss guidelines conveyed by others who are perceived as too alien for meaningful comparisons with self. Under some conditions, people will disregard a source who is deviant in attitudes (Cartwright, 1968) or demographic characteristics, e.g., age and sex (Kazdin, 1974a), which are actually irrelevant to the task at hand. This problem is more likely to arise when all modeling is done by just one individual, who is viewed as alien in some respect. As earlier noted, diversity among multiple models did not reduce their impact. Nor did covert modeling clients who imagined themselves enact episodes (maximum similarity) surpass those who instead visualized another person (less similarity). Likewise, sheer similarity does not assure that clients will draw beneficial conclusions from episodes of low information value. Thus, a condition in which clients observed a model who expressed high test anxiety, but failed to illustrate tactics for coping with arousal, brought no benefits. Instead, those clients earned the poorest scores among five groups studied, including no modeling controls (I. Sarason, 1975). Through social comparison processes, people gauge their own chances of success in a situation from the attainments of others who are judged to have similar ability. When a peer of equal skill failed an intellectual task, observers surrendered quickly during later testing. When failure could instead be attributed to the model's relative incompetence, observers persevered much longer (Brown & Inouye, 1978). Reciprocally, reference persons who are perceived as comparable to self, who have first-hand knowledge of the client's problem *and* have learned ways to overcome it are particularly relevant and credible as tutors.

Coping and Mastery Models. The extent to which modeling depicts persons who are sophisticated versus uninformed about the client's own plight will influence the value of treatment. To indecisive, worried clients, guidance from a carefree model may lack personal relevance. For one who is socially inept, the cinema exploits of a Robert Redford will seem less useful guides to romance than gains made despite adversity by a Woody Allen or Dustin Hoffman character. Likewise, research shows that *coping* models— who have shared the client's problem but can illustrate strategies to resolve it—are more efficient than *mastery* models—who portray fearless behavior from the outset. Thus, films of multiple models who at first manifested snake fear but slowly grew bolder until performing confidently were more helpful to college women clients than were scenarios in which models never disclosed any fear. When models verbalized their thoughts and behavior while interacting with the snake, observers progressed further than those given silent approach demonstrations (Meichenbaum, 1971). The advantages of coping over mastery formats were confirmed in two studies using covert modeling. Even though snake approach was imagined rather than witnessed, clients directed to visualize scenarios in which the model overcame fear surpassed others whose scripts only specified calm demonstrations. Similarity in age and sex between model and client enhanced progress, and dissimilarity interfered. Thus, clients who imagined similar coping models improved the most, both when measured at the end of treatment and several weeks later (Kazdin, 1974a,b).

Having models portray but surmount their fears has proven beneficial in treating examination anxiety. After brief guidance, undergraduates scored somewhat higher on an intelligence test and earned better course grades if their model displayed arousal rather than calm mastery while performing (Jaffe & Carlson, 1972). The interplay between a model's social stimulus value and providing concrete suggestions for guidance purposes was shown by varying the modeled role for women students who were either high or low in test anxiety. Before administering a verbal learning task, the model informed clients in one condition that she dreaded tests but then proceeded to share her rules for coping with fear. This counter-arousal strategy was withheld from the other groups. For them, the model either presented herself as (1) high, or (2) low in test anxiety, or (3) alluded to neutral material instead of tests, or (4) omitted any self-disclosure for the control subjects. Overall, the coping anxious model surpassed every other format, and the normal students outperformed their very fearful counterparts. Nonetheless, the hightly anxious clients who were exposed to the coping anxious model proved best of *all* groups: Although they were potentially prone to suffer arousal decrements when performing, as shown by their highly anxious peers who were not taught the self-help strategy, relevant modeling reversed the usual pattern of results (I. Sarason, 1975). In contrast, consider situations in which new behavior to be taught does *not* raise fearful apprehensions or exceed observers' self-expectations. Then, poised and expert (i.e., mastery) models may be preferable as teachers. For such nonthreatening guidance purposes, portraying possible hazards can divert learners from grasping the main principles (Rosenthal & Zimmerman, 1978). In the same vein, a model who appears to perform reluctantly when no threat is evident can cast doubt on the social desirability of the conduct demonstrated (Smith & Lewis, 1974).

THERAPEUTIC CONTENT

The meanings that people derive from vicarious episodes and other treatment experiences jointly depend on: (1) the information exemplified in guidance scenarios; (2) on the directions given to specify what perspective the client should adopt; and (3) on observers' personal interpretations and reconstructions of what they witness. When people were told to assume a detached stance, they shared in events less than when told to empathize with the model (Aderman, Brehm, & Katz, 1974; Regan & Totten, 1975). Likewise, setting instructions can alter which facets of a situation people assume to be determining the behavior they observe. For example, subjects directed to focus on the model's point of view and those instead told to focus on the objective nature of the situation attributed very different motives to the model in explaining the conduct they observed (Wegner & Finstuen, 1977). Nor will observers necessarily attend to the more important features of guidance content unless they are aided to discern them. Thus, if clients hear a model state rules for dealing with exams in a calm and organized manner, they may overlook the need to emulate such planning unless they are set to appreciate its integral part in the test-taking demonstration. Judgments about the relative priority of content units, and the eventual recall of key material both depended on what perspective was specified for learners (Pichert & Anderson, 1977). Unless one defines the vantage points or emphases clients should adopt, one cannot assume they will construe teaching episodes in the manner intended.

There is evidence that making clients active participants in the treatment process enhances benefits. For example, among college adults fearful of public speaking, therapeutic content had more impact when there was need to transmit it to others. Clients given training in anxiety-reduction techniques that they then taught to anxious peers made greater progress than their pupils (Fremouw & Harmatz, 1975). In general, guidance that establishes new skills in adaptive self-control surpasses formats in which clients take more passive roles as the recipients of others' service efforts. Giving clients an active part in helping themselves, e.g., by assigning homework tasks for them to execute, has merit for most therapy programs, whatever their specific methods. Such issues are further discussed by Denney, (see Chapter 10, this volume).

Also, modeling components enter into many cognitive-behavioral treatment composites: The cumulative impact of such combined therapy programs stems from multiple elements. Thus, a *self-instructions* technique combines demonstrations with verbal guidelines for appropriate conduct and with other procedures. It leads the client to attain independent self-regulation in a series of progressive steps. That composite strategy has effectively resolved test anxiety problems (see Meichenbaum and Butler, Chapter 9 in this volume). Just as demonstrations can assist programs that are not primarily vicarious in nature, a range of supplementary methods can aid modeling approaches. For example, teaching clients progressive relaxation skills has improved symbolic modeling therapy with various fear problems (Bandura et al., 1969; Wroblewski et al., 1977). Despite the architecture of guidance, clinical impact depends on what is ultimately learned and applied. The need to assure clients' understanding and continuing involvement and to provide them with corrective feedback until competence is fully achieved transcends particular methods. The clarity and appropriateness of treatment information count more than its form of transmission.

Devising Guidance Messages

Psychology has begun to make major advances toward explaining how people grasp and organize knowledge. These developments portend a vigorous applied science that will assist clinicians and educators to structure information efficiently for practical purposes. Although promising, such applications are still in early stages of evolution (Rosenthal & Zimmerman, 1978). But a basis exists for sketching some tentative guideposts for enhancing the comprehension and retrieval of therapy content.

People typically attend to and extract the central meanings of messages rather than minute details. This is especially likely when learners are only alerted to the main focus or recurring common themes contained in a message. If a subtle point is crucial, it had best be emphasized and reviewed by the therapist or clients will likely miss it. Information is rarely preserved in its initial, raw form. It is reworked, summarized, and classified into categories, which are often defined and organized by means of familiar prototypes, pattern relationships, or capsule principles. An exemplar whose features are representative and familiar may typify—i.e., sum up and stand for—an entire semantic category, much as "apple" may subjectively exemplify all fruit (Rosch, Simpson, & Miller, 1976). This means that obvious examples using content elements that are already familiar are the easiest to cognize. Messages that draw remote parallels between events or rely on esoteric material to make conceptual points are likely to be confusing and misunderstood. Guidance that makes use of lucid exemplars and the summary concepts that chunk or integrate them will surpass rote-like or piecemeal teaching formats (Matsuda & Robbins, 1977). Hence, vivid analogies and concrete illustrations support understanding. They make it easier to grasp very abstract or novel content and to tie it to more familiar knowledge (Rigney & Lutz, 1976; Royer & Cable, 1976). This seems a particular advantage of clinical modeling. Clients can perceive events unfold in natural sequence, faithful to real life and teaching priorities, but pruned of inessential features which might be distracting. Observers can acquire an organized gestalt or overview of the essential content economically and safely. For example, they can learn appropriate limits for self-assertiveness without repeatedly offending real-life interaction partners. Demonstrations often convey the points at issue faster and better than alternative content formats, such as prose discourse. Thus, a film depicting how to cope with the problems of abstaining from heroin was more helpful to addicts than a lecture about coping behavior (Reeder & Kunce, 1976). Some technical advice for preparing modeling displays is provided elsewhere (Rosenthal, 1976, 1979).

Whatever the mode of guidance, it is important that enough scope and opportunity are allowed for clients to mediate the message properly. This can be checked by asking clients to paraphrase the content as perceived, to relate it to their personal situations (e.g., "Think about how this applies to your own life and tell me about how it fits in!"), by questions to assess their comprehension, and by other types of review. Likewise, clients can be oriented to key points before the main episodes begin. Giving concept definitions and providing several examples to illustrate them was more helpful to learners than were fewer examples or abstract definitions alone (Klausmeier & Feldman, 1975). A topical outline that served as an orderly map of an upcoming prose reading passage increased retention and further elaboration of the material compared to outlines less adequate in structure or given after the content had been presented (Glynn & Di Vesta, 1977). Usually, any content aids should prove beneficial if they lead clients (1) to comprehend messages clearly and accurately, (2) to organize the information into meaningful frameworks that are familiar or salient, and (3) to further rehearse and actively reformulate the content in subjectively compelling terms. In practice, the prerequisites for improving communication may be as simple as assuring sufficient exposure time and a slow enough pace of introducing and reviewing the points to be learned, so that clients can process the information without loss or confusion (Hung & Rosenthal, 1978). Effective communication may instead demand complex message aids such as mnemonic schemes or superordinate plans to subsume and harmonize the separate elements of multifaceted guidance. A case in point would be the detailed contracts which have aided marital and family therapies by specifying the behavior that participants have agreed to adopt after mutual negotiations (Linehan & Rosenthal, 1979). To improve the utilization of therapy content, several interrelated techniques deserve special mention.

Rules and Rationales. Knowledge is retained and applied more efficiently when it is organized conceptually. One precept can then encompass a host of specific instances, with sharp gains in learning, retention, and transfer. For example, teaching shy clients to watch for topics of which they have first-hand knowledge will ease conversations with strangers who differ in age, sex, or social status. The same rule will apply whether gardening, politics, or sports is the topic of discussion. Modeling episodes can convey general principles as well as discrete acts, with resultant benefits to clients. This was illustrated in a study that compared students high and low in test anxiety when exposed to alternative teaching formats. In the first, a model merely solved a set of problems while observed. In another, the model both solved the problems and described his actions in so doing. In the last, the model solved problems, described actions, and also commented on the principles underlying solution. Overall, low surpassed high-anxiety subjects, and supplying principles and descriptive verbal cues aided performance. However, the very anxious subjects who observed the solution principles outperformed all other groups. Access to informative rules reversed their typically inferior problem-solving scores (I. Sarason, 1973). This recalls a similar pattern of results when the coping anxious model supplied a cognitive blueprint for warding off arousal, as mentioned earlier. Likewise, modeling and rehearsal to foster more expressive covert guidelines improved clients' social spontaneity (Cabush & Edwards, 1976).

The orientations given to prepare learners for future steps can dictate how those events are interpreted (Finke & Schmidt, 1977; Galassi et al., 1974). People seldom comply with therapeutic directives unthinkingly and will dismiss demands that seem arbitrary. When clear rules and justifications are lacking, people usually evolve their own explanatory premises for what is asked of them and then interpret their options accordingly. But false inferences about the purpose, structure, or priorities of guidance can promote systematic errors which continue unless detected by the counselor. Conversely, appropriate rationales are helpful in themselves and spur clients' zeal and cooperation (Chang-Liang & Denney, 1976; Wein, Nelson, & Odom, 1975). Progress was fastest and most stable when a congruent rationale supported demands for clients' active involvement in therapy (Denney & Rupert, 1977; and see Denney, Chapter 10 in this volume). Thus, akin to other rules, accurate explanations and orientations can (1) prevent misperception or attrition of guidance content, (2) reduce situational ambiguities, (3) enhance rapport and motivation, and (4) protect clients from inventing and then following erroneous hypotheses.

Self-Regulatory Strategies and Plans. In most situations, a range of potential cognitive standards and overt behavior is accessible to us. For example, should one attempt to answer test questions in the order listed, first respond to easy and then go back to harder items, or quickly read over the entire test to gauge its nature before starting to answer it? In order to simplify living, executive processes must coordinate the route to be taken from a myriad of options. People estimate the utility of competing paths and then synchronize the steps of what is chosen. They assign priorities about sequence and importance to multiple guidelines, decide among alternative courses of action, and then order and integrate the execution of component responses. Rather than performing linear chains of discrete acts, people apply structured molar strategies. Those, in essence, are organized systems of rules (Rosenthal & Zimmerman, 1978).

Such premises imply that guidance content that sets forth a coherent map for enacting available behavior will often aid clients more than teaching concrete deeds alone. For example, appropriate assertiveness requires grasping the contextual variables which qualify and delimit the propriety of forceful conduct. Whether conveyed through modeling or other means, superordinate plans improve therapy outcomes. Therefore, providing generic strategies for coping with interfering arousal has surpassed other content emphases to treat test-anxious clients both individually and in groups (e.g., Goldfried & Goldfried, 1977; Holroyd, 1976; I. Sarason, 1975). Although guiding clients in handling test-specific stressors has been found superior to preparing them to deal with more global arousal, the common strategy dominated over the specific source of stress. Thus, some test-anxious college students were helped to replace their usual self-hampering worries with covert self-instructions applicable to any performance demands, e.g., (just take) "One step at a time, I can handle the situation." For another group, the therapeutic self-instructions directly pertained to examinations, e.g., "I know I'm well prepared for this test, so just relax." The latter, more concrete guidance surpassed control groups more strongly than did the global counterarousal content. But the alternative treatment directions did not differ significantly from each other. Both the global and the specific self-control strategies led to reductions in test anxiety that were maintained at a follow-up eight months after treatment (Hussian & Lawrence, 1978a, b).

Research with children has shown the value of preparing them to resist positive temptations. Guidance plans that enabled the child to ignore arousing lures maintained goal-oriented behavior best in the face of distracting opportunities (Mischel & Baker, 1975; Moore, 1977). Spelling out in detail how to apply self-regulatory strategies created better resistance to temptation and more self-generated refinements of the guidelines than did less adequately structured plans (Mischel & Patterson, 1976). Likewise, test-anxious adults benefited when aided to disregard fear cues. They observed coping models who first manifested distress but then exemplified how to redirect attention toward task-oriented events. After each demonstration, clients role-played the adaptive solution, with favorable outcomes (Malec, Park, & Watkins, 1976). The critical impact of systematic planning was confirmed by efforts to enhance studying and scholastic achievement among college students. In a hierarchical design, the following components were successively added to create five therapy conditions: (1) training in study and test-taking skills; (2) optimistic expectancies about the progress clients would make; (3) self-monitoring and recording acts of study; (4) rewarding oneself for studying; and (5) strategic planning—how to break large task units into manageable substeps, how to schedule time for study, etc. There were few outcome differences among the first four conditions. In contrast, the strategic planning clients proved by far the best on most measures of studying activity, test performance, and course grades (Greiner & Karoly, 1976). Thus, providing guidance in how to organize and apply other information can be essential for that knowledge to be utilized. Communicating integrative strategies, which facilitate the structuring of subordinate content, promises to amplify the impact of guidance information and to better assure that therapeutic messages are correctly interpreted and applied.

RETROSPECT AND PROSPECT

One can see that the foregoing overview of modeling approaches reveals a somewhat sketchy, adventitious penetration of the test anxiety realm. This is because various thrusts have been made, often with encouraging results, to explore the shared "*g*" common to treating most avoidance problems. However, little systematic work has explicitly pursued modeling techniques with the major goal of developing a complete treatment for examination (or speech) anxiety as a target clinical category. Thus, the specific factors that may set test-taking fears apart from other performance problems have received little attention. For purposes of delivering efficient clinical services, it is unlikely that any one channel for transmitting information or any single technique to restore calm performance will best aid clients if used in isolation. Composite programs, in which multiple elements are harmonized to address multiple problem facets, appear more realistic. In the larger sphere of teaching social competencies, diverse syntheses of guidance components are under active study. For example, instructions about principles to follow, demonstrations of apt cognitive and overt response to illustrate simulated episodes, client practice of those coping examples, feedback to correct rehearsal efforts, and further group role-playing and discussion may all be combined to prepare the client before actual in vivo practice. Then, participant modeling, peer monitoring, "buddy system" task assignments, and related methods can be introduced when clients begin performing under largely naturalistic conditions.

The future invites empirically validated amalgams of guidance techniques rather than fixation on any single method. A possible exception may involve the economy of observational learning for mass-media purposes. Filmed programs to prevent or correct test fears and other frequent handicaps could reach vast numbers of children and adults at little cost—quite unlike the economic limitations that attend face-to-face interventions in clinical service settings. Modeling approaches are yielding benefits in preventing physical illness through mass-media educational programs. But plausible applications to better serve humanity have barely begun (see Bandura, 1978; Rosenthal & Bandura, 1978). It would be relatively easy, for example, to develop filmed "courses" that could teach children strategies for coping adaptively with tests, public speaking, and related stresses. Such guidance might be made part of the school curriculum during the primary grades—before performance difficulties had become deeply engrained. Likewise, videotaped modeling could serve as the core of lessons in productive thinking. Educative scenarios might illustrate plans for organizing information, for solving problems efficiently, or for devising personal study schedules. Teaching these types of skills would benefit many students' academic development. Such modeling possibilities clamor for trial.

REFERENCES

Aderman, D., Brehm, S. S., & Katz, L. B. Empathic observation of an innocent victim: The just world revisited. *Journal of Personality and Social Psychology*, 1974, *29*, 342–347.

Asch, S. E. Effects of group pressure upon the modification and distortion of judgments. In E. E. Maccoby, T. M. Newcomb, & E. L. Hartley (Eds.), *Readings in social psychology* (3rd ed.). New York: Henry Holt, 1958.

Bandura, A. *Social learning theory.* Englewood Cliffs, N. J.: Prentice-Hall, 1977. (a)

Bandura, A. Self-efficacy: Toward a unifying theory of behavioral change. *Psychological Review,* 1977, *84,* 191–215. (b)

Bandura, A. On paradigms and recycled idealogies. *Cognitive Therapy and Research,* 1978, *2,* 79–103.

Bandura, A., & Adams, N. E. Analysis of self-efficacy theory of behavioral change. *Cognitive Therapy and Research,* 1977, *1,* 287–310.

Bandura, A., Adams, N. E., & Beyer, J. Cognitive processes mediating behavior change. *Journal of Personality and Social Psychology,* 1977, *35,* 125–139.

Bandura, A., Blanchard, E. B., & Ritter, B. The relative efficacy of desensitization and modeling approaches for inducing behavioral, affective, and attitudinal changes. *Journal of Personality and Social Psychology,* 1969, *13,* 173–199.

Bandura, A., & Menlove, F. L. Factors determining vicarious extinction of avoidance behavior. *Journal of Personality and Social Psychology,* 1968, *8,* 99–108.

Baum, D. D. Equivalence of client problems perceived over different media. *Journal of Counseling Psychology,* 1974, *21,* 15–22.

Beaman, A. L., Fraser, S. C., Diener, E., & Endreson, K. L. Effects of voluntary and semivoluntary peer-monitoring programs on academic performance. *Journal of Educational Psychology,* 1977, *69,* 109–114.

Bernotas, T. D., Ribordy, S. C., & Tracy, R. J. *Attentional training for test anxious children.* Paper presented at the Association for the Advancement of Behavior Therapy Convention, Atlanta, December 1977.

Blaney, N. T., Stephan, C., Rosenthal, D., Aronson, E., & Sikes, J. Interdependence in the classroom: A field study. *Journal of Educational Psychology,* 1977, *69,* 121–128.

Brown, I., Jr., & Inouye, D. K. Learned helplessness through modeling: The role of perceived similarity in competence. *Journal of Personality and Social Psychology,* 1978, *36,* 900–908.

Cabush, D. W., & Edwards, K. J. Training clients to help themselves: Outcome effects of training college student clients in facilitative self-responding. *Journal of Counseling Psychology,* 1976, *23,* 34–39.

Caird, W. K., & Wincze, J. P. Videotaped desensitization of frigidity. *Journal of Behavior Therapy and Experimental Psychiatry,* 1974, *5,* 175–178.

Cartwright, D. The nature of group cohesiveness. In D. Cartwright & A. Zander (Eds.), *Group dynamics: Research and theory* (3rd ed.). New York: Harper & Row, 1968.

Cautela, J. R., Flannery, R. B., & Hanley, S. Covert modeling: An experimental test: *Behavior Therapy,* 1974, *5,* 494–502.

Chang-Liang, R., & Denney, D. R. Applied relaxation as training in self-control. *Journal of Counseling Psychology,* 1976, *23,* 183–189.

Curran, J. P. Social skills training and systematic desensitization in reducing dating anxiety. *Behaviour Research & Therapy,* 1975, *13,* 65–68.

Curran, J. P., & Gilbert, F. S. A test of the relative effectiveness of a systematic desensitization skills training program with date anxious subjects. *Behavior Therapy,* 1975, *6,* 510–521.

Dalton, R. F., & Sundblad, L. M. Using principles of social learning in training for communication empathy. *Journal of Counseling Psychology,* 1976, *23,* 454–457.

Dalton, R. F., Sundblad, L. M., & Hylbert, K. W. An application of principles of social learning to training in communication of empathy. *Journal of Counseling Psychology,* 1973, *20,* 378–383.

Deffenbacher, J. L., & Payne, D. Two procedures for relaxation as self-control in the treatment of communication apprehension. *Journal of Counseling Psychology,* 1977, *24,* 255–258.

Denney, D. R. Active, passive, and vicarious desensitization. *Journal of Counseling Psychology,* 1974, *21,* 369–375.

Denney, D. R., & Rupert, P. A. Desensitization and self-control in the treatment of test anxiety. *Journal of Counseling Psychology*, 1977, *24*, 272–280.

Denney, D. R., & Sullivan, B. J. Desensitization and modeling treatments of spider fear using two types of scenes. *Journal of Consulting and Clinical Psychology*, 1976, *44*, 573–579.

Dowrick, P. W., & Raeburn, J. M. Video editing and medication to produce a therapeutic self model. *Journal of Consulting and Clinical Psychology*, 1977, *45*, 1156–1158.

Edelson, R. I., & Seidman, E. Use of videotaped feedback in altering interpersonal perceptions of married couples: A therapy analogue. *Journal of Consulting and Clinical Psychology*, 1975, *43*, 244–250.

Eisler, R. M., Blanchard, E. B., Fitts, H., & Williams, J. G. Social skill training with and without modeling on schizophrenic and non-psychotic hospitalized psychiatric patients. *Behavior Modification*, 1978, *2*, 147–172.

Eskedal, G. A. Symbolic role modeling and cognitive learning in the training of counselors. *Journal of Counseling Psychology*, 1975, *22*, 152–155.

Farina, A., Fischer, E. H., Sherman, S., Smith, W. T., Groh, T., & Mermin, P. Physical attractiveness and mental health. *Journal of Abnormal Psychology*, 1977, *86*, 510–517.

Feist, J. R., & Rosenthal, T. L. Serpent versus surrogate and other determinants of runway fear differences. *Behavior Research and Therapy*, 1973, *11*, 483–489.

Finger, R., & Galassi, J. P. Effects of modifying cognitive versus emotionality responses in the treatment of test anxiety. *Journal of Consulting and Clinical Psychology*, 1977, *45*, 280–287.

Finke, R. A., & Schmidt, M. J. Orientation-specific color aftereffects following imagination. *Journal of Experimental Psychology: Human Perception and Performance*, 1977, *3*, 599–606.

Fisher, T. J., Reardon, R. C., & Burck, H. D. Increasing information-seeking behavior with a model-reinforced videotape. *Journal of Counseling Psychology*, 1976, *23*, 234–238.

Fraser, S. C., Diener, E., Beaman, A. L., & Kelem, R. T. Two, three, or four heads are better than one: Modification of college performance by peer monitoring. *Journal of Educational Psychology*, 1977, *69*, 101–108.

Fremouw, W. J., & Harmatz, M. G. A helper model for behavioral treatment of speech anxiety. *Journal of Consulting and Clinical Psychology*, 1975, *43*, 652–660.

Galassi, J. P., Galassi, M. D., & Litz, M. C. Assertive training in groups using video feedback. *Journal of Counseling Psychology*, 1974, *21*, 390–394.

Glynn, S. M., & Di Vesta, F. J. Outline and hierarchical organization as aids for study and retrieval. *Journal of Educational Psychology*, 1977, *69*, 89–95.

Goldfried, M. R., & Goldfried, A. P. Importance of hierarchy content in the self-control of anxiety. *Journal of Consulting and Clinical Psychology*, 1977, *45*, 124–154.

Greiner, J. M., & Karoly, P. Effects of self-control training on study activity and academic performance: An analysis of self-monitoring, self-reward, and systematic planning components. *Journal of Counseling Psychology*, 1976, *23*, 495–502.

Guidry, L. S., & Randolph, D. L. Covert reinforcement in the treatment of test anxiety. *Journal of Counseling Psychology*, 1974, *21*, 260–264.

Halisch, F., & Heckhausen, H. Search for feedback information and effort regulation during task performance. *Journal of Personality and Social Psychology*, 1977, *35*, 724–733.

Henderson, R. W., Swanson, R., & Zimmerman, B. J. Training seriation responses in young children through televised modeling of hierarchically sequenced rule components. *American Educational Research Journal*, 1975, *12*, 479–489.

Hollandsworth, J. G., Dressel, M. E., & Stevens, J. Use of behavioral versus traditional procedures for increasing job interview skills. *Journal of Counseling Psychology*, 1977, *24*, 503–510.

Holroyd, K.A. Cognition and desensitization in the group treatment of test anxiety. *Journal of Consulting and Clinical Psychology*, 1976, *44*, 991–1001.

Horne, A. M., & Matson, J. L. A comparison of modeling, desensitization, flooding, study skills, and control groups for reducing test anxiety. *Behavior Therapy*, 1977, *8*, 1–8.

Hung, J. H., & Rosenthal, T. L. Therapeutic videotaped playback: A critical review. *Advances in Behaviour Research and Therapy*, 1978, *1*, 103–135.

Hussian, R. A., & Lawrence, P. S. The reduction of test, state, and trait anxiety by test-specified and generalized stress inoculation training. *Cognitive Therapy and Research*, 1978, *2*, 25–37. (a)

Hussian, R. A., & Lawrence, P. S. *Modification of test anxiety by self-administered stress inoculation training: Extinction versus cognitive restructuring.* Unpublished manuscript, University of North Carolina at Greensboro, 1978. (b)

Jaffe, P. G., & Carlson, P. M. Modeling therapy for test anxiety: The role of modeled affect and consequences. *Behavior Research & Therapy*, 1972, *10*, 329–339.

Kazdin, A. E. Covert modeling and the reduction of avoidance behavior. *Journal of Abnormal Psychology*, 1973, *81*, 87–95.

Kazdin, A. E. Covert modeling, model similarity, and reduction of avoidance behavior. *Behavior Therapy*, 1974, *5*, 325–340. (a)

Kazdin, A. E. The effect of model identity and fear-relevant similarity on covert modeling. *Behavior Therapy*, 1974, *5*, 624–635. (b)

Kazdin, A. E. Effects of covert modeling and model reinforcement on assertive behavior. *Journal of Abnormal Psychology*, 1974, *83*, 240–252. (c)

Kazdin, A. E. Covert modeling, imagery assessment, and assertive behavior. *Journal of Consulting and Clinical Psychology*, 1975, *43*, 716–724.

Kazdin, A. E. Effects of covert modeling, multiple models, and model reinforcement on assertive behavior. *Behavior Therapy*, 1976, *7*, 211–222.

Kelso, J. A. S. Motor control mechanisms underlying human movement reproduction. *Journal of Experimental Psychology: Human Perception and Performance*, 1977, *3*, 529–543.

Kirkland, K. D., & Thelen, M. H. Uses of modeling in child treatment. In B. B. Lahey & A. E. Kazdin (Eds.), *Advances in child clinical psychology* (Vol. 1). New York: Plenum, 1977.

Kirsch, I., & Henry, D. Extinction versus credibility in the desensitization of speech anxiety. *Journal of Consulting and Clinical Psychology*, 1977, *45*, 1052–1059.

Klausmeier, H. J., & Feldman, K. V. Effects of a definition and a varying number of examples and nonexamples on concept attainment. *Journal of Educational Psychology*, 1975, *67*, 174–178.

Kostka, M. P., & Galassi, J. P. Group systematic desensitization versus covert positive reinforcement in the reduction of test anxiety. *Journal of Counseling Psychology*, 1974, *21*, 464–468.

Kunce, J. T., Bruch, M. A., & Thelen, M. H. Vicarious induction of academic achievement behavior in disadvantaged adults. *Journal of Counseling Psychology*, 1974, *21*, 507–510.

Levine, M., Rotkin, L., Jankovic, I. N., & Pitchford, L. Impaired performance by adult humans: Learned helplessness or wrong hypothesis? *Cognitive Therapy and Research*, 1977, *1*, 275–285.

Linehan, K. S., & Rosenthal, T. L. Current behavioral approaches to marital and family therapy. *Advances in Behaviour Research and Therapy*, 1979, *2*, 99–143.

Linehan, K. S., Rosenthal, T. L., Kelley, J. E., & Theobald, D. E. Homogeneity and heterogeneity of problem class in modeling treatment of fears. *Behaviour Research & Therapy*, 1977, *15*, 211–215.

MacNeil, M. K., & Sherif, M. Norm change over subject generations as a function of arbitrariness of prescribed norms. *Journal of Personality and Social Psychology*, 1976, *34*, 762–773.

Mahoney, M. J. *Cognition and behavior modification.* Cambridge, Mass.: Ballinger, 1974.

Maiuro, R. D., & Talent, B. *Evidence on the validity of "analogue populations" in anxiety reduction research.* Paper presented at the Association for the Advancement of Behavior Therapy Convention, Atlanta, December 1977.

Malec, J., Park, T., & Watkins, J. T. Modeling and role playing as a treatment for test anxiety. *Journal of Consulting and Clinical Psychology,* 1976, *44,* 679.

Mann, J. Vicarious desensitization of test anxiety through observation of videotaped treatment. *Journal of Counseling Psychology,* 1972, *19,* 1–7.

Mann, J., & Rosenthal, T. L. Vicarious and direct counterconditioning of test anxiety through individual and group desensitization. *Behaviour Research & Therapy,* 1969, *7,* 359–367.

Marburg, C. C., Houston, B. K., & Holmes, D. S. Influence of multiple models on the behavior of institutionalized retarded children: Increased generalization to other models and other behaviors. *Journal of Consulting and Clinical Psychology,* 1976, *44,* 514–519.

Markus, H. Self-schemata and processing information about the self. *Journal of Personality and Social Psychology,* 1977, *35,* 63–78.

Matsuda, N., & Robbins, D. Prototype abstraction and distinctive feature learning: An application to learning Chinese characters. *Journal of Educational Psychology,* 1977, *69,* 15–23.

Meichenbaum, D. Examination of model characteristics in reducing avoidance behavior. *Journal of Personality and Social Psychology,* 1971, *17,* 298–307.

Mischel, W., & Baker, N. Cognitive appraisals and transformations in delay behavior. *Journal of Personality and Social Psychology,* 1975, *31,* 254–261.

Mischel, W., & Patterson, C. J. Substantive and structural elements of effective plans for self-control. *Journal of Personality and Social Psychology,* 1976, *34,* 942–950.

Moore, B. S. Cognitive representation of rewards in delay of gratification. *Cognitive Therapy and Research,* 1977, *1,* 73–83.

Moss, M. K., & Arend, R. A. Self-directed contact desensitization. *Journal of Consulting and Clinical Psychology,* 1977, *45,* 730–738.

Neill, W. T. Inhibitory and facilitatory processes in selective attention. *Journal of Experimental Psychology: Human Perception and Performance,* 1977, *3,* 444–450.

Perry, M. A. Modeling and instructions in training for counselor empathy. *Journal of Counseling Psychology,* 1975, *22,* 173–179.

Pichart, J. W., & Anderson, R. C. Taking different perspectives on a story. *Journal of Educational Psychology,* 1977, *69,* 309–315.

Rachman, S. The conditioning theory of fear-acquisition: A critical reexamination. *Behaviour Research & Therapy,* 1977, *15,* 375–387.

Reeder, C. W., & Kunce, J. T. Modeling techniques, drug-abstinent behavior, and heroin addicts: A pilot study. *Journal of Counseling Psychology,* 1976, *23,* 560–562.

Regan, D. T., & Totten, J. Empathy and attribution: Turning observers into actors. *Journal of Personality and Social Psychology,* 1975, *32,* 850–856.

Rigney, J. W., & Lutz, K. A. Effect of graphic analogies in chemistry on learning and attitude. *Journal of Educational Psychology,* 1976, *68,* 305–311.

Romano, J. L., & Cabianca, W. A. EMG biofeedback training versus systematic desensitization for test anxiety reduction. *Journal of Counseling Psychology,* 1978, *25,* 8–13.

Rosch, E., Simpson, C., & Miller, R. S. Structural bases of typicality effects. *Journal of Experimental Psychology: Human Perception and Performance,* 1976, *2,* 491–502.

Rosenthal, T. L. Modeling therapies. In M. Hersen, R. M. Eisler, & P. M. Miller (Eds.), *Progress in behavior modification* (Vol. 2). New York: Academic Press, 1976.

Rosenthal, T. L. Applying a cognitive behavioral view to clinical and social problems. In G. R. Whitehurst & B. J. Zimmerman (Eds.), *The functions of language and cognition.* New York: Academic press, 1979.

Rosenthal, T. L., & Bandura, A. Psychological modeling: Theory and practice. In S. L. Garfield & A. E. Bergin (Eds.), *Handbook of psychotherapy and behavior change* (2nd ed.). New York: John Wiley, 1978.

Rosenthal, T. L., Hung, J. H., & Kelley, J. E. Therapeutic social influence: Sternly strike while the iron is hot. *Behaviour Research & Therapy,* 1977, *15,* 253–259.

Rosenthal, T. L., & Reese, S. L. The effects of covert and overt modeling on assertive behavior. *Behaviour Research & Therapy*, 1976, *14*, 463-469.

Rosenthal, T. L., Rosenthal, R. H., & Chang, A. F. Vicarious, direct, and imaginal aversion in habit control: Outcomes, heart rates, and subjective perceptions. *Cognitive Therapy and Research*, 1977, *1*, 143-159.

Rosenthal, T. L., & Zimmerman, B. J. *Social learning and cognition.* New York: Academic Press, 1978.

Royer, J. M., & Cable, C. W. Illustrations, analogies, and facilitative transfer in prose learning. *Journal of Educational Psychology*, 1976, *65*, 205-209.

Sarason, I. G. Test anxiety and cognitive modeling. *Journal of Personality and Social Psychology*, 1973, *28*, 58-61.

Sarason, I. G. Test anxiety and the self-disclosing coping model. *Journal of Consulting and Clinical Psychology*, 1975, *43*, 148-153.

Sarason, I. G., & Ganzer, V. J. Modeling and group discussion in the rehabilitation of juvenile delinquents. *Journal of Counseling Psychology*, 1973, *20*, 442-449.

Schinke, S. P., & Rose, S. D. Interpersonal skill training in groups. *Journal of Counseling Psychology*, 1976, *23*, 442-448.

Smith, J. A., & Lewis, W. A. Effect of videotaped models on the communications of college students in counseling. *Journal of Counseling Psychology*, 1974, *21*, 78-80.

Spiegler, M. D., Cooley, E. J., Marshall, G. J., Prince, H. T., Puckett, S. P., & Skenazy, J. A. A self-control versus a counterconditioning paradigm for systemic desensitization: An experimental comparison. *Journal of Counseling Psychology*, 1976, *23*, 83-86.

Trower, P., Yardley, K., Bryant, B. M., & Shaw, P. The treatment of social failure: A comparison of anxiety-reduction and skills-acquisition procedures on two social problems. *Behavior Modification*, 1978, *2*, 41-60.

Trussell, R. T. Use of graduated behavior rehearsal, feedback, and systematic desensitization for speech anxiety. *Journal of Counseling Psychology*, 1978, *25*, 14-20.

Wegner, D. M., & Finstuen, K. Observers' focus of attention in the simulation of self-perception. *Journal of Personality and Social Psychology*, 1977, *35*, 56-62.

Wein, K. S., Nelson, R. O., & Odom, J. V. The relative contributions of reattribution and verbal extinction to the effectiveness of cognitive restructuring. *Behavior Therapy*, 1975, *6*, 459-474.

Weissberg, M. A comparison of direct and vicarious treatments of speech anxiety: Desensitization, desensitization with coping imagery, and cognitive modification. *Behavior Therapy*, 1977, *8*, 606-620.

Wincze, J. P., & Caird, W. K. The effects of systematic desensitization and video desensitization in the treatment of essential sexual dysfunction in women. *Behavior Therapy*, 1976, *7*, 335-342.

Wolfe, J. L., & Fodor, I. G. Modifying assertive behavior in women: A comparison of three approaches. *Behavior Therapy*, 1977, *8*, 567-574.

Woodson, M. I. C. E. Seven aspects of teaching concepts. *Journal of Educational Psychology*, 1974, *66*, 184-188.

Wright, J. C. A comparison of systematic desensitization and social skill acquisition in the modification of a social fear. *Behavior Therapy*, 1976, *7*, 205-210.

Wroblewski, P. F., Jacob, T., & Rehm, L. P. The contribution of relaxation to symbolic modeling in the modification of dental fears. *Behavior Research & Therapy*, 1977, *15*, 113-117.

Yussen, S. R. Determinants of visual attention and recall in observational learning by preschoolers and second graders. *Developmental Psychology*, 1974, *10*, 93-100.

12 Mathematics Anxiety

Frank C. Richardson
University of Texas at Austin

Robert L. Woolfolk
Rutgers University

Mathematics anxiety can be viewed as a form of test anxiety. Attempting to solve a mathematical problem resembles taking a test. And mathematics-anxious high school and college students report much of their anxiety in terms of apprehension about their performance on mathematics quizzes and tests. The cognitive and emotional dynamics of mathematics anxiety are quite similar to those of test anxiety, making it a fruitful area of investigation for researchers, clinicians, and educators interested in performance anxieties and their effects upon students' learning and emotional welfare. An advantage, for the researcher, of studying mathematics anxiety is that it is relatively easy to construct a convincing behavioral measure of this problem. Taking a mathematics test with a time limit under instructions to do as well as possible appears to be nearly as threatening as a real-life test for most mathematics-anxious individuals. Perhaps only an ischemic pain situation, produced by temporarily depriving tissue of its blood supply (Beecher, 1966; Meichenbaum & Turk, 1976), comes closer than a math test to reproducing a clinical problem in a laboratory setting.

But mathematics anxiety is something more or different than test anxiety when mathematics is involved. Math anxiety appears to be a reaction to mathematical *content*, to some of its distinctive features as an intellectual activity and its connotative meanings for many persons in our society as well as a reaction to the evaluative *form* of mathematics tests and problem-solving activities. The science of mathematics, "being good" at math or liking it connotes certainty, perfection, high intelligence, genius, arcane wisdom, highly specialized knowledge remote from common sense, monotonous and mechanical problem solving, the key to ultimate truth, something antagonistic to humanistic values, the essence of practicality, something essentially irrelevant to everyday life, a characteristically masculine activity, or a decidedly unfeminine activity—in varying and more or less consistent combinations of meanings. The nature and extremity of these meanings make it evident that mathematics and math tests have considerable potential for triggering debilitating emotional arousal. They invite perfectionism, feelings of inferiority, and intense concerns about social and sexual acceptability, all reliable producers of anxiety and stress. Presumably, we do not hear very much about "biology anxiety" or "English-literature anxiety" because these areas of study do not have such disturbing associations for very many persons. The source of these anxiety-producing connotations and how best to remedy them are issues that have received thoughtful attention from a number of mathematics educators and educational researchers.

In social scientific circles, mathematics anxiety is but one of test anxiety's poor relations. It is, however, a flashy cousin that has caught the public's eye in recent years. Articles about math anxiety, sex-related differences in confidence and anxiety about mathematics, and ways to meliorate the problem have appeared in *McCall's, Saturday Review, MS, Time, Parade,* and a variety of newspapers across the country. The *Chronical of Higher Education* and numerous journals and magazines for professional educators at all levels have published discussions of these topics. Russell Baker responded in his column to one of these articles by wishing (tongue-in-cheek) that college women would not blame their anxiety on men. He confessed to a long-standing incapacity with, and fear of, even simple math that began in the seventh grade with an "adolescent male terror of women who snorted like war horses while raving about isosceles triangles." Presumably, there has been suffering enough on all sides. Clearly, there is a widespread acknowledgment of the problem and interest in doing something about it.

THE ASSESSMENT OF MATHEMATICS ANXIETY

Numerous investigations over the last 25 years into the relationships between attitudes toward mathematics and math performance, reviewed by Aiken (1970, 1976), have utilized a variety of one-item or brief questionnaires to assess mathematics anxiety. Reliability or validity data have not been presented for any of these scales, and their use rarely extends beyond one or two studies.

Fennema and Sherman (1976) have developed nine 12-item scales designed to measure a number of different attitudes and feelings about the learning of mathematics by female and male high school students. These scales assess students' confidence in learning math, view of mathematics as a male domain, usefulness of math, attitudes of mother, father, and teachers toward the student's learning of math, and several other factors. One of the scales measures mathematics anxiety. Students respond to a five-point Likert-type scale in order to indicate the extent to which they agree or disagree with 12 statements that express feeling anxious, tense, or at ease with mathematics problems and tests. Six items are scored negatively and six positively. Male and female norms based on two large high school samples are presented, and a split-half reliability coefficient of .89 is reported for the scale. The wording of several of the items may be less appropriate for college students or adults. No information is given concerning test–retest stability or validity of the scale. And it would be desirable to have more precise information than given about internal consistency reliability to ensure that each item of this very brief scale correlates substantially with total scores on the instrument. Nevertheless, this battery of scales and their rationale deserve close study by anyone interested in mathematics anxiety treatment or research.

Richardson and Suinn (1972) and Suinn, Edie, Nicoletti, and Spinelli (1972) report psychometric data on the Mathematics Anxiety Rating Scale (MARS). The MARS is a 98-item scale composed of brief descriptions of ordinary life and academic situations involving the manipulation of numbers or solving of mathematical problems that may arouse anxiety. A total mathematics anxiety score is calculated by assigning a value of from 1 to 5, corresponding to the level of anxiety checked (with 1 assigned to "not at all" anxious and 5 to "very much" anxious), and then summing all the values.

An internal consistency reliability coefficient, coefficient alpha (Nunnally, 1967), calculated from the MARS scores of 397 college students by Richardson and Suinn (1972), was .93. A test–retest reliability coefficient for the MARS of .85 was computed from the scores of two complete classes (n = 35) of students from the original sample who were retested 7 weeks later. Suinn et al. (1972) also found a test–retest correlation of .78 between the MARS scores of 119 college students at two testings 2 weeks apart.

Richardson and Suinn (1972) and Suinn et al. (1972) both obtained data concerning the validity of the MARS by correlating MARS total scores with scores on the mathematics form of the Differential Aptitude Test (DAT), administered with a 10-minute time limit. These studies found a correlation of −.35 (p < .05) and −.64 (p < .01) for samples of 119 and 30 students, respectively. Other information bearing on the validity of the MARS is reported in following sections of this chapter.

The authors recently performed a principle components factor analysis with a varimax rotation of the factors on the 397 students' MARS scores from the Richardson and Suinn (1972) study and also determined the item-total correlations for each MARS item. Only one clear factor, accounting for 76% of the variance, emerged from the analysis. Brush (1976) reports a similar factor analysis of MARS scores of a smaller group of 109 college upperclassmen that indicated the presence of two factors. One factor was dominated by items describing everyday, nonacademic, relatively simple calculations, such as "Figuring the sales tax on a purchase that costs more than $1.00." The other factor was composed of items mainly describing academic, evaluative mathematics problem-solving and test-taking situations, such as "Taking an examination (final) in a math course." Although there is some discrepancy between the results of these two studies, our results with a large sample indicate that almost all MARS items correlate with total scores above .40 and that almost all the items describing evaluative academic and problem-solving situations correlate more highly with total MARS scores than do the items concerning everyday, nonevaluative number manipulations. Table 12.1 presents the 40 MARS items with the highest item-total correlations according to our data, excluding five items that refer to nonacademic situations or might not apply to a number of students. This 40-item scale is presumably at least as reliable, stable, and valid as the original AMRS and is almost certainly dominated by a single homogeneous factor of anxiety concerning evaluative test-taking and problem-solving mathematics situations. We recommend its use in clinical assessment and mathematics anxiety research. The 40 items are listed in order from high (.74) to low (.56) in terms of their correlations with original MARS total scores.

MATHEMATICS ANXIETY AND TEST ANXIETY

Suinn (1970) reported that over one-third of students applying for a behavior therapy program to reduce test anxiety indicated that their primary difficulty was connected with mathematics. Suinn and Richardson (1971) found that students requesting assistance specifically for math anxiety scored significantly higher than a control group on the Suinn Test Anxiety Behavior Scale (STABS), a measure of test anxiety (Suinn, 1969), at a level comparable to that of students requesting test anxiety treatment. To what extent, then, is math anxiety a matter of test anxiety experienced in mathematics situations? Do feelings of apprehension and aversion about mathematics concern anything more or different than fear of evaluative or test-taking situations involving numbers and math?

Brush (1976) found a strong positive relationship ($r = 65$, $p < .001$) between STABS and MARS total scores in a sample of 80 university students, 48 females and 32 males. But when students were divided into (approximately equal) groups of Physical Science, Social Science, and Humanities majors, it was found that although the mean STABS group scores were virtually identical, the groups differed significantly on the MARS ($F(2,74) = 5.63$, $p < .01$). Physical science majors showed the least and Humanities majors the most mathematics anxiety. An analysis of covariance performed on the three groups' MARS scores, with STABS scores as

TABLE 12.1
Mathematics Anxiety Scale

	A Not at All	B A Little	C A Fair Amount	D Much	E Very Much
1. Thinking about an up- coming math test one day before					
2. Picking up a math text- book to begin a dif- ficult reading assignment					
3. Opening a math or stat book and seeing a page full of problems					
4. Studying for a math test					
5. Thinking about an up- coming math test one week before					
6. Taking an examination (quiz) in a math course					
7. Listening to a lecture in a math class					
8. Starting a new chapter in a math book					
9. Signing up for a math course					
10. Picking up the math text- book to begin working on a homework assignment					
11. Thinking about an up- coming math test one hour before					
12. Realizing that you have to take a certain num- ber of math classes to fulfill the requirements in your major					

(continued)

TABLE 12.1 *(contd.)*

	A Not at All	B A Little	C A Fair Amount	D Much	E Very Much
13. Not knowing the formula needed to solve a particular problem					
14. Taking the math section of a college entrance exam					
15. Being given a homework assignment of many difficult math problems which is due the next class meeting					
16. Being given a "pop" quiz in a math class					
17. Listening to another student explain a math formula					
18. Working on an abstract mathematical problem, such as: "If x = outstanding bills, and y = total income, calculate how much you have left for recreational expenditures."					
19. Getting ready to study for a math test					
20. Hearing a friend try to teach you a math procedure and finding that you cannot understand what he is telling you					
21. Walking on campus and thinking about a math course					
22. Taking an examination (final) in a math course					

TABLE 12.1 *(contd.)*

	A *Not at* *All*	B *A* *Little*	C *A Fair* *Amount*	D *Much*	E *Very* *Much*
23. Reading a formula in chemistry					
24. Watching a teacher work an algebraic equation on the blackboard					
25. Looking through the pages of a math text					
26. Solving a square root problem					
27. Walking into a math class					
28. Having to use the tables in the back of a math book					
29. Walking to math class					
30. Talking to someone in your class who does well about a problem and not being able to understand what he is explaining					
31. Thinking about an up-coming math test 5 minutes before					
32. Being asked to explain how you arrive at a particular solution for a problem					
33. Receiving your final math grade in the mail					
34. Reading and interpreting graphs or charts					
35. Tallying up the results of a survey or poll					

(continued)

TABLE 12.1 *(contd.)*

	A *Not at* *All*	B *A* *Little*	C *A Fair* *Amount*	D *Much*	E *Very* *Much*
36. Doing a word problem in algebra					
37. Sitting in a math class and waiting for the instructor to arrive					
38. Being called upon to recite in a math class when you are prepared					
39. Buying a math textbook					
40. Asking your math instructor to help you with a problem that you don't understand					

covariate, showed an even more pronounced difference among groups ($F(2,73) = 9.59$, p $<$ .001). Clearly, math anxiety is related to test anxiety, but the two are by no means equivalent phenomena.

WOMEN AND MATHEMATICS

A survey by sociologist Lucy Sells carried out in 1973 at the University of California at Berkeley determined that 57% of the entering males had had four years of high school math, the prerequisite for college math, science, and statistics courses, whereas only 8% of the incoming females had such preparation (Sells, 1976). A similar survey by statistician and mathematics educator John Ernest (1976) confirmed that "mathematics is a 'critical filter' tending to eliminate women from many fields, from chemistry, physics and engineering to architecture and medicine [p. 23]." In this extensive and carefully executed survey, Ernest determined that, in the elementary school years, girls as well as boys tend to think that their own sex does better in all subjects. But by high school, both males and females assume that males do better in math. Most interesting, when asked why they did poorly on a math exam, high school females tend to attribute their failure to lack of ability, whereas males with the same intellectual ability attribute their failure to lack of effort. These attitudes are reinforced by both male and female teachers (even when they like and have specialized in math), who generally report that they believe girls do less well than boys in math.

Interest in the problem of math anxiety resulting in restricted educational and occupational opportunities for women has prompted the Education for Work Group of the National Institute of education to develop a program of research in the area of women and mathematics. They initially asked three researchers to determine what was known about the major influences affecting women's participation and achievement in mathematics and their preferences for mathematics-related careers. These papers (Fox, Fennema, & Sherman, 1977) have served as the foundation for a national planning conference and an ongoing research grants program.

Fox (1977) concludes that sex differences in math achievement, which only emerge around grade eight or nine, are primarily the result of differential course taking rather than any female inability to learn mathematics. She finds that math tests that show sex differences usually fail to control for number of courses taken. Sherman (1977) argues that differences between males and females in math achievement do not appear to be linked to biological differences. She concludes that only one such notion has any supporting evidence—the idea that earlier left cerebral dominance in females or reliance on left cerebral functions that are linked to verbal, analytical modes of learning could lead to a preference or reliance on verbal learning rather than spatial-gestalt learning associated with the right half of the brain and increasingly thought to play a strong role in mathematical learning beyond simple computation.

Fennema (1977) also underscores the importance of the ability to visualize spatially as related to sex differences in math achievement. It has often been speculated that the more aggressive, manipulative approach to objects and the environment that characterizes the play of young boys as opposed to girls may foster superior spatial visualization in males. Fennema (1977) notes, however, that current evidence indicates that male superiority on tests of spatial visualization emerges during early adolescence, at the same time when differences in mathematics achievement begin to appear. Also, at this time, certain attitudes and values of students, parents, and teachers may begin to affect mathematics participation and achievement in young women. Mathematics is stereotyped as a male domain. Both boys and girls for the first time begin to consult their fathers more frequently than their mothers for assistance with math homework. And, traditionally, girls begin to perceive math as less useful to their future adult roles. Weitzman and Rizzo (1974) have exhaustively documented the fact that, in elementary school textbooks, males were represented in more than two-thirds of pictures showing science or math activities and that texts often portrayed women and girls in the statement of math problems in ways that emphasize their "stupidity." The cumulative effects of negative stereotyping, lack of expectations or reinforcement for math achievement, and deficient educational and career guidance appear to have created in many women low confidence and a tendency to internalize failure and attribute success to luck in dealing with mathematics.

SEX DIFFERENCES IN MATHEMATICS ANXIETY

Richardson and Suinn (1972) found no significant difference between the mean total MARS scores of men and women college students in a large sample of freshman and sophomore undergraduate education majors. Brush (1976) found a significant difference (p < .01) between male and female MARS total scores in a sample of 109 university upperclassmen, with females scoring higher than males. She failed to find a sex difference in math anxiety, however, in a second sample of 80 upperclassmen from the same university a year later. Further inquiry determined that there was a highly significant difference between number of years of high school mathematics completed by the two sexes in the first sample but that no such difference occurred in the second sample. This interesting finding suggests strongly that amount of interaction with math, not the variable of sex, predicts level of mathematics anxiety in college students.

CRITIQUES OF MATHEMATICS CURRICULA

This is no place to recapitulate or involve oneself in the widespread debate concerning "old" versus "new" math or to attempt to make sense out of the endless stream of new "techniques" for teaching math to school children that issue forth each year from the educational establishment. None of these innovations has had much impact on the negative sex-role stereotypes and deficient educational advisement that seem to have drastically hindered women's participation in and enjoyment of mathematics and math-related careers. Furthermore, it is clear from the results of studies employing the MARS and other math anxiety scales that a large number of males as well as females have a great deal of apprehension about mathematics activities. Nevertheless, we feel a few of the comments of mathematics educator Mitchell Lazarus are especially astute and may be of interest to test anxiety researchers.

M. Lazarus (1975a, 1975b) reminds us that fear of mathematics is widespread and speculates about the etiology of what he terms "mathophobia." One factor he suggests is that difficulty at any level spells trouble for all the years to come. Mathematics curricula rely heavily on a "memorize-what-to-do" approach that makes it difficult to make up deficiencies in skills no longer taught at the current level. It also discourages the kinds of divergent thinking and higher-order problem solving that are necessary for success at more advanced levels of mathematics. Second, math anxiety, he notes, has a peculiar social acceptability. Persons otherwise proud of their educational attainments shamelessly confess to being "no good at math." Third, and most important, there appears to be a pervasive lack of meaningful connection between school mathematics and the rest of a student's life. According to M. Lazarus (1975a), math is widely viewed as either the arcane province of a few select geniuses or equated with the "tedious, boring exacting routines of school arithmetic [p. 37]."

M. Lazarus argues that mathematics and mathematical modeling are an intimate part of contemporary life, and that a new approach to math education should take as its starting point the idea that mathematics is useful to people. He suggests that topics should be stressed that exhibit the most direct links between math and the real world. According to M. Lazarus (1975a):

> Instead of trying to teach mathematics for its own sake, colleges should teach it for their students' sakes. Not elaborate arithmetic, which is quickly becoming obsolete thanks to pocket calculators. Not the beauty of mathematics, which leaves all but a few students cold. The focus should be on mathematics that can open the eyes and equip the hands, letting students look upon the world in new and fruitful ways . . . . The stress should be on the relationships between reality and mathematics, encouraging the idea of mathematical modeling to the point where it becomes almost automatic and intuitive [p. 38].

A behavioral scientist might add that an intuitive, deeply ingrained sense of mathematical modeling of everyday realities could greatly improve individual and collective economic decision making in a democracy and might also enhance individual problem-solving skills in dealing with many of the problems and challenges of everyday life (D'Zurilla & Goldfried, 1971).

NEW PROGRAMS AND SERVICES FOR MATHEMATICS-ANXIOUS COLLEGE STUDENTS

Spurred by a growing awareness of the math anxiety problem, especially among women students, and by the research of Sells (1976) and Ernest (1976) mentioned previously, Wellesley College and Wesleyan University are experimenting with new approaches to alleviating math anxiety and avoidance. The project at Wellesley consists of the development of a new "Discovery Course in Mathematics" at the precalculus level, which is nonremedial in nature and emphasizes applications of mathematics in the area of music and design (Schafer, 1977). At Wesleyan, students with an inadequate mathematics background are encouraged to take an explicitly remedial precalculus that has an optional once-a-week "psychological laboratory" associated with it. This laboratory is conducted by the staff of a "Math Clinic" who assists students in overcoming math anxiety through a variety of group discussion and individual counseling methods. Thoughtful presentations of case study material and suggestions for counseling the math-anxious student from the experience of the clinic have been published by Donady and Tobias (1977) and Donady, Kogelman, and Tobias (1976). These papers make interesting reading for clinicians concerned with undertstanding and treating performance anxieties. More extensive evaluations of the effectiveness of the Wellesley and Wesleyan projects, jointly supported by the Fund for the Improvement of Postsecondary Education, should be available in the near future.

Several other universities have initiated similar programs to reduce mathematics anxiety and increase the participation of women students in math courses and math-related careers. Mills College, for example, an all-women's school, has developed a precalculus workshop that emphasizes becoming familiar with graphic representations of algebraic functions in a way that may be tantamount to teaching or perfecting spatial relations ability.

TREATMENT OF MATHEMATICS ANXIETY—
CONTROLLED STUDIES

Controlled investigations of math anxiety treatment are limited to a handful of studies concerned with comparing the effectiveness of relatively traditional behavior therapy methods in treating a common phobia. Suinn, Edie, and Spinelli (1970) found that math-anxious subjects receiving Accelerated Massed Desensitization, utilizing only the top one-third of a standardized math anxiety heirarchy, showed as much improvement on the MARS and a behavioral measure of math anxiety, the DAT, with a 10-minute time limit, as did subjects receiving a standard systematic desensitization procedure using the entire hierarchy and twice the treatment time of the accelerated group. No control group was included in this study, so significant pre- to posttest changes on both measures are difficult to evaluate. Suinn and Richardson (1971) found that Anxiety Management Training, a nonspecific anxiety-reduction program involving alternating instructions to self-generate thoughts and feelings associated with anxiety with instructions to relax physically and mentally, was as effective as standard systematic desensitization in reducing math anxiety as assessed by the same MARS and DAT measures. The control group in this study had comparable pretest scores on both instruments but had not requested treatment for math anxiety.

Richardson and Suinn (1973) found that accelerated massed and standard systematic desensitization were comparably effective in reducing self-reported mathematics anxiety, as assessed by the MARS, when compared with wait-list and no-treatment control groups. Differences between treatment and control groups only approached statistical significance on the behavioral measure, against the DAT with a 10-minute time limit. These three studies encouraged the belief that behavior therapy programs of this type have an impact on math anxiety, but they do not clearly demonstrate effectiveness in improving math performance, in maintaining this improvement, or in modifying other attitudes that may mediate participation and pleasure in mathematics-related activities. A recent study by Olson and Gillingham (1977), for example, found that systematic desensitization significantly lowered MARS scores but did not alter scores on scales pertaining to the "enjoyment" and the "value" of mathematics.

SOME CLINICAL OBSERVATIONS AND COMMENTS

Since completion of the studies mentioned in the previous section, a cognitive-attentional view of test anxiety has matured and found extensive empirical support (Wine, Chapter 16, this volume). Effective treatment of anxiety problems, such as test and mathematics anxiety, has come to center around techniques for restructuring cognitive and attentional processes (Meichenbaum, Chapter 9, this volume). And many writers (A. Lazarus, 1976; Rosenthal, Chapter 11, this volume) have emphasized the desirability of multifaceted treatment approaches to enhance both the magnitude and durability of change. Over the last two years, we have adopted this view and approach in the individual treatment of a number of severe cases of mathematics anxiety and the group treatment of one mixed-sex group of math-anxious college students. Some observations from this experience may be of interest.

In all cases, treatment followed the general outline for "multimodal anxiety management training" described by Richardson (1976), which is similar to Meichenbaum's "stress innoculation training" (Meichenbaum & Turk, 1976). Such an approach, first of all, does not focus narrowly upon mathematics situations but discusses coping with anxiety and stress in a wide variety of life circumstances. This seems to facilitate isolating and restructuring the many strains of immature and perfectionistic thinking that are present and seem often to play an important role with even such relatively situation-specific problems as test and math anxiety. It also seems to increase client interest and enhance client perceptions of the program as plausible and potentially beneficial.

Second, this approach systematically educates clients in the use of several overt behavioral and cognitive self-control techniques for managing stress and anxiety. It attempts, also, to increase benefits and their durability by dealing explicitly with the different zones or modalities of functioning, including overt behavior, affect, sensation, cognition and problem solving, and imagery. Some clients will have fairly rational perspectives and cognitive skills for coping with math problems and tests in their "mental repertoire" but be unable to adopt or apply them when faced with actual math situations. Such individuals often find self-control relaxation skills, combined with training in "positive self-talk," sufficient to turn the corner on mathematics anxiety. For other clients, mathematics anxiety seems to have become a focus for distinctly perfectionistic or self-critical tendencies in their personality and behavior. Progress in these cases seems to be impossible without restructuring basic irrational beliefs about the sources of self-esteem and attempting to disconnect the client's sense of self-worth from external standards for their performances in different life roles (Ellis & Harper, 1975; Woolfolk & Richardson, 1978). It is difficult to predict in advance which facet of training will trigger needed insights or change, but utilizing multiple techniques and perspectives seem to increase clients' self-confidence and produce more durable change.

Third, undoing math anxiety seems regularly to involve detailed cognitive restructuring of certain faulty beliefs or misconceptions concerning mathematical problem solving and sometimes problem solving in general. Donady and Tobias (1977) may be referring to the same phenomenon when they write that in their Math Clinic "Much of our effort is spent on dealing with how people see math, and on how their feelings about the subject have affected their method of attacking problems [p. 17]." To give one common example, clients routinely operate from the assumption that there is one and only one correct way or preordained path to a correct solution. It comes as a shock and revelation to them to find out that there are as indefinitely large a number of routes to mathematical discovery and problem solving as there are valid or partially valid perspectives concerning the causes of World War II. Math seems to be associated with a kind of absolute certainty and unimpeachable correctness that is, of course, never present at the outset of dealing with a problem. Math's abstractness, the many "dead ends" often involved in searching for solutions to problems, and the kind of divergent thinking relatively divorced from any familiar worldly content that is often required by mathematical thinking become for most math-anxious individuals a painful and helpless reckoning with overwhelming uncertainty. It seems helpful to repeatedly emphasize with clients that "You are *supposed* to be completely in the dark at that point in the process. *Everyone* is. Now, what can you do about it?" Also, it usually is fairly easy to draw convincing parallels to other areas of life, preferably ones in which the client functions with confidence or a sense of achievement, in which tolerating and even enjoying temporary uncertainty and ambiguity about what is "right" is a regular occurrence.

Finally, mathematics-anxious students like test-anxious counterparts (Spielberger, 1978), usually require some restructuring of their study habits if rewarding and successful work in mathematics is to be ensured. Remedial work in math may also be necessary if, for example, a student wishes to perform up to his or her ability on standardized ability or achievement tests, such as the LSAT or GRE. Obviously, the availability of courses like those developed at Wellesley and Mills College would be of great assistance to such a student.

FUTURE DIRECTIONS

Our review of mathematics anxiety treatment and research has crystalized a few firm opinions and several less solid speculations concerning fruitful directions for future effort. In general, it does seem clear that revisions of mathematical curricula along the lines suggested by M. Lazarus (1975a, 1975b), remedial or developmental coursework like that being experimented with at Wellesley, Mills, and other colleges, and newer treatment approaches for test, math, and general anxiety (Meichenbaum, and Butler, Chapter 9, this volume; Richardson, 1976) that center around the cognitive restructuring of faulty beliefs and maladaptive deployment of attention are intimately compatible and have much to offer one another on practical and theoretical levels. All three lines of development may be needed in order to make a significant dent in the lack of interest in math, fear of and aversion to math actvities, and low math ability that characterize many college students and are a distinct barrier to desirable career opportunities for many women students.

Mathematics educators and educational researchers have acquired a great deal of information concerning the development and change of attitudes toward mathematics, including anxiety, from the early grades through college (Aiken, 1970; Fox et al., 1977). Charting the evolution of attitudes toward and skills in coping with test-taking over the span of school years might prove interesting as well. It could both expand our understanding of the sources of test anxiety and help identify critical points for intervention to prevent its occurrence in many students.

Systematic evaluation of programs to remediate math anxiety, both counseling and innovative educational programs, are sorely needed. Such efforts should include long-term follow-up concerning changes in anxiety, attitudes toward mathematics, educational and occupational choices, and possible generalized benefits to students' positive mental health or coping skills in other areas of living. Perhaps such research could most profitably emphasize the evaluation of ongoing counseling or educational programs in their natural environment, like the Wellesley and Wesleyan projects, rather than familiar, "one-shot" treatment studies that pit artificially truncated treatment procedures against each other and rarely investigate the longer-term durability of effects.

Cubberly, Weinstein, Richardson, and Hukill (1978) attempted to explore some of the specific processes or mechanisms by which anxiety disrupts cognitive performance. They found a highly significant interaction between level of test anxiety, measured by the Test Anxiety Scale, and the level of cognitive processing, "superficial" versus "deep" (Craik & Lockhart, 1972), required of subjects in a test-like situation. High-test-anxious subjects performed much more poorly than low-test-anxious subjects when deep processing of certain materials was demanded but performed slightly better than their low-anxious counterparts when superficial processing of the same materials was required. It was found difficult in this research to devise effective stress instructions for tasks that lasted for more than a few minutes, and hard to identify laboratory task activities that clearly resembled important, real-life intellectual work. However, mathematical reasoning is an important and socially valued activity, it has a discernable structure that remains much the same while problem content varies, and math activities reliably produce anxiety in mathematics-anxious subjects. Thus, math anxiety might prove useful in this type of laboratory research.

REFERENCES

Aiken, L. R. Attitudes toward mathematics. *Review of Educational Research,* 1970, *40,* 551–596.

Aiken, L. R. Update on attitudes and other affective variables in learning mathematics. *Review of Educational Research,* 1976, *46,* 293–311.

Beecher, H. Pain: One mystery solved. *Science,* 1966, *151,* 840–841.

Brush, L. *Mathematics anxiety in college students.* Unpublished paper, Wesleyan University, 1976.

Craik, F., & Lockhart, R. Levels of processing: A framework for memory research. *Journal of Verbal Learning and Verbal Behavior,* 1972, *11,* 671–684.

Cubberly, W., Weinstein, C., Richardson, F., & Hukill, H. *Levels of processing and effects of anxiety on the use of cognitive strategies.* Paper presented at the annual meeting of the American Educational Research Association, Montreal, March 1978.

Donady, B., Kogelman, S., & Tobias, S. *Math anxiety and female mental health: Some unexpected links.* Paper presented at the annual meeting of the National Advisory Committee on Mental Health Services and Women, Cambridge, Massachusetts, August 1976.

Donady, B., & Tobias, S. Math anxiety. *Teacher,* November 1977.

D'Zurilla, T., & Goldfried, M. Problem solving and behavior modification. Journal of Abnormal Psychology, 1971, *78,* 107–126.

Ellis, A., & Harper, R. *A new guide to rational living.* Englewood Cliffs, N.J.: Prentice-Hall, 1975.

Ernest, J. Mathematics and sex. *American Mathematical Monthly,*1976, *83,* 595–614.

Fennema, E. Influences of selected cognitive, affective, and educational variables on sex-related differences in mathematics learning and studying. In L. Fox, E. Fennema, & J. Sherman (Eds.), *Women and mathematics: research perspectives for change.* NIE Papers in Education and Work (No.8). Washington, D. C.: U.S. Department of Health, Education and Welfare, 1977.

Fennema, E., & Sherman, J. A. Fennema–Sherman mathematics attitudes scales: Instruments designed to measure attitudes toward the learning of mathematics by females and males. JSAS *Catalog of Selected Documents in Psychology,* 1976, *6,* 31. (Ms. No. 1225)

Fox, L. The effects of sex role socialization on mathematics participation and achievement. In L. Fox, E. Fennema, & J. Sherman (Eds.), *Women and mathematics: Research perspectives for change.* NIE Papers in Education and Work: (No. 8). Washington, D.C.: U.S. Department of Health, Education and Welfare, 1977.

Fox, L., Fennema, E., & Sherman, J. (Eds.). *Women and mathematics: research perspectives for change.* NIE Papers in Education and work: (No. 8). Washington, D.C.: U.S. Department of Health, Education and Welfare, 1977.

Lazarus, A. (Ed.). *Multimodal behavior therapy.* New York: Springer, 1976.

Lazarus, M. Rx for mathophobia. *Saturday Review,* June 28, 1975, *46.* (a)

Lazarus, M. The elegance and relevance of math. *The Chronicle of Higher Education,* December 1, 1975. *24.* (b)

Meichenbaum, D., & Turk, D. Cognitive-behavioral management of anxiety, anger, and pain. In P. Davidson (Ed.), *The behavioral management of anxiety, depression, and pain.* New York: Brunner/Mazel, 1976.

Nunnally, J. *Psychometric theory.* New York: McGraw-Hill, 1967.

Olson, A., & Gillingham, D. *Systematic desensitization of mathematics anxiety.* Unpublished paper, University of Alberta, Canada, 1977.

Richardson, F. C. Anxiety management training: A multimodal approach. In A. Lazarus (Ed.), *Multimodal behavior therapy.* New York: Springer, 1976.

Richardson, F. C., & Suinn, R. M. The Mathematics Anxiety Rating Scale: Psychometric data. *Journal of Counseling Psychology,* 1972, *19,* 551–554.

Richardson, F. C., & Suinn, R. M. A comparison of traditional systematic desensitization, accelerated massed desensitization, and anxiety management training in the treatment of mathematics anxiety. *Behavior Therapy,* 1973, *4,* 212–218.

Schafer, A. *Wellesley College–Wesleyan University Mathematics Project: Interim Report.* Unpublished paper, Wellesley College, 1977.

Sells, L. W. *The mathematics filter and the education of women and minorities.* Paper presented at the annual meeting of the American Association for the Advancement of Science, Boston, February 1976.

Sherman, J. Effects of biological factors on sex-related differences in mathematics achievement. In L. Fox, E. Fennema, & J. Sherman (Eds.), *Women and mathematics: Research perspectives for change.* NIE Papers in Education and Work: (No. 8). Washington, D.C.: U.S. Department of Health, Education and Welfare, 1977.

Suinn, R. M. The STABS, a measure of test anxiety for behavior therapy. Normative data. *Behaviour Research & Therapy,* 1969, *7,* 335–339.

Suinn, R. M. *The application of short-term video-tape therapy for the treatment of test anxiety of college students. Progress Report.* Colorado: Colorado State University, 1970.

Suinn, R. M., Edie, C. A., Nicoletti, J., & Spinelli, P. R. The MARS, a measure of mathematics anxiety: Psychometric data. *Journal of Clinical Psychology,* 1972, *28,* 373–375.

Suinn, R. M., Edie, C. A. and Spinelli, P. R. Accelerated massed desensitivation: Innovation in short-term treatment. *Behavior Therapy,* 1970, *1,* 303–311.

Suinn, R. M., & Richardson, F. C. Anxiety management training: Nonspecific behavior therapy control. *Behavior Therapy,* 1971, *2,* 498–519.

Weitzman, L. J., & Rizzo, D. *Biased textbooks: A research perspective.* National Foundation of the Improvement of Education, Wash. D.C., 1974.

Woolfolk, R., & Richardson, F. *Stress, sanity, and survival.* New York: Sovereign/Simon & Schuster, 1978.

13 Anxiety and Instruction

Sigmund Tobias
City University of New York

Anxiety is one of the central problems of our times. Literally hundreds of tons of tranquilizing medications are dispensed each year (Coleman, 1964), and the sale of such preparations is one of the cornerstones of the drug industry. Drug addiction, alcohol addiction, and perhaps even tobacco addiction as well can probably also be seen, in part, as attempts by individuals to obtain relief from the discomfort of anxiety.

Anxiety is no less disruptive in school and other instructional settings. In the 1940s and 1950s, there was an enormous amount of research directed at determining the factors associated with underachievement. Not surprisingly, anxiety was typically seen as one of the variables most commonly associated with underachievement. Similarly, one of the factors leading to the acceptance of psychologists in the schools was, surely, the promise that students who were prevented from functioning adequately in school by anxiety would experience relief through the ministrations of the psychologist.

The importance of test anxiety in the ability of students to profit from instruction has been widely documented by research. Thus, for example, Spielberger (1966) found that whereas more than 20% of a group of high-anxious students left school because of academic failure, the comparable incidence was only 6% for a group of low-anxious students. Similar effects of test anxiety on grade point averages have been reported (Spielberger, 1962; Spielberger & Katzenmeyer, 1959). In general, high -anxious students have lower grade point averages than those with less anxiety. Anxiety has been found to be equally debilitating in elementary school contexts. Lunneborg (1964) found that high anxiety was associated with poor achievement in both reading and mathematics. In a review of a number of studies relating anxiety to academic achievement, Gaudry and Spielberger (1971) concluded that the most consistent findings were that low achievement was associated with high anxiety at all academic levels.

The aim of this chapter is to review the effects of anxiety on achievement in instructional contexts. Specifically, different models by which anxiety can be studied in instructional contexts are discussed. The problem of making instructional adaptations designed to enable high-anxiety students to do as well as their low-anxiety counterparts is then reviewed in some detail, and a previously proposed model for research on the effects of anxiety on instructional contexts is discussed. Research data accumulated since this model was proposed is reviewed in terms of the model. Finally, some research in which high-test-anxious students learned more than individuals low in anxiety is reviewed in detail, and a hypothesis is advanced to account for those results.

APPROACHES TO THE STUDY
OF ANXIETY AND INSTRUCTION

There are two different ways of studying anxiety in instructional contexts. Simultaneously, these approaches lend themselves to practical attempts to ameliorate the effects of anxiety in instructional contexts. The different approaches are: (1) attempting to reduce anxiety directly; (2) adapting instruction in order to be differentially more effective for high-anxiety students than those lower in anxiety.

Anxiety Reduction

One way of studying anxiety and coping with its debilitating effects in instructional contexts is to attempt to reduce anxiety directly. The results of these approaches are reviewed in Chapters 11 through 15 in this volume and hence are not described here. A reasonably accurate generalization regarding the effects of the different anxiety-reduction treatment programs would be that they have typically succeeded in reducing feelings of anxiety. Frequently, however, the reduction in anxiety has not been accompanied by a concomitant increase in student achievement or test performance. Although the specific details of these various treatment programs are discussed in the prior chapters, another approach to improving the achievement of anxious students would be to study ways in which instructional materials can be appropriately modified so that the achievement of anxious students is improved.

Instructional Adaptations to Anxiety

There are a number of variables in the conventional instructional context that are likely to be especially debilitating to test-anxious students. Leading among those, of course, are the periodic examinations which are administered in instructional contexts. There is abundant evidence (Tobias, 1977a; Hedl & O'Neil, 1977) that anxiety increases significantly during examinations. There are, of course, other types of evaluative threat in instructional situations which are anxiety-arousing to students. Being required to hand in a product to an instructor, whether a paper, an experiment, or any other kind of homework assignment, clearly constitutes something of an evaluative threat. Similarly, being called on in class and participating in class discussions has evaluative consequences. The uncertainty among students regarding whether a particular instructional objective has been mastered is also likely to be anxiety-arousing to students.

It is possible to make some adaptations to the instructional environment that would have the effect of reducing the debilitating effects of anxiety. The literature has suggested such instructional variables as having a well-organized instructor-centered classroom organization, permitting students to rewind instruction delivered via tapes, and a variety of other instructional adaptations as being differentially beneficial to high-anxiety students. The next section of this chapter discusses this research in greater detail.

ANXIETY TREATMENT INTERACTIONS

The study of the interaction between differences in student aptitudes and different instructional treatments dates back to Cronbach's (1957) call for a rapprochement between experimental and correlational psychologists. Comprehensive reviews of the literature in this area in general have been made by Cronbach and Snow (1977) and by Snow (1976, 1977). Detailed reviews of such research dealing specifically with anxiety are also available in Cronbach and Snow (1977, Chapter 12) and in Sieber, O'Neil, & Tobias (1977). The aim of this section will be to review these sources in general and update them by reference to more recent studies.

Much of the prior research on the interaction between anxiety and instructional treatments, or anxiety treatment interactions, utilized essentially two instructional environments: 1) individualized instructional systems, such as programmed instruction, computer-assisted instruction, and computer managed instruction; 2) Conventional types of classroom-based instruction. The research strategy in the individualized instructional contexts consisted of assigning low- and high-anxiety students to an instructional program presented in what was considered a most effective form. Other groups were then assigned to the same instructional material which had been altered in some way. The alteration was presumed, in general, to reduce the efficiency of the instructional program and presumably make it especially debilitating to the performance and achievement of high-anxiety students. For example, when the instructional program in its original version required overt responses to the program, and feedback concerning their accuracy was provided, in the altered version the feedback may have been eliminated and/or the requirement for overt responses removed.

In other studies, students may have been exposed to materials like those described previously except that they were prepared in high, or low difficulty formats. Many other variations of these individualized instructional programs were studied. In general, expectations of the researchers were that the altered program would pose greater evaluative threat to the students by raising the amount of uncertainty experienced, increasing the difficulty and in general reducing the amount of support the students received from the instructional materials, hence raising the probability of student error. Because the results of this research have been described in detail elsewhere (Sieber et al., 1977; Cronbach & Snow, 1977), there is little need to repeat those reviews here. Instead, the general conclusions drawn in these prior sources are summarized and the results of newer studies in this area are reviewed in some detail.

Detailed analysis of the prior research led to the formulation of a model (Tobias, 1977b) that attempted to identify specifically where the debilitating effects of anxiety in instructional situations could be most easily observed. The model, illustrated in Fig. 13.1, divides the instructional process into three basic information-processing components: input, processing, and output. The input section is synonymous with any instructional method and describes the presentation of instructional materials to students. The processing section represents all operations performed by the student to register, record, organize, and store the instructional input. The output section of the model denotes students' performance on any measure or situation to demonstrate that the instructional objectives have been attained. Because anxiety is an affective state, it affects performance indirectly by impacting on the cognitive processes utilized in the instructional sequence. The model suggests that there are three possible points where anxiety can have its greatest effects: (1) at the preprocessing stage, between input and processing; (2) during processing; (3) postprocessing, and just before output.

Preprocessing

This effect is meant to represent any interference by anxiety in registering and internally representing the instructional input that, until this point, has been a

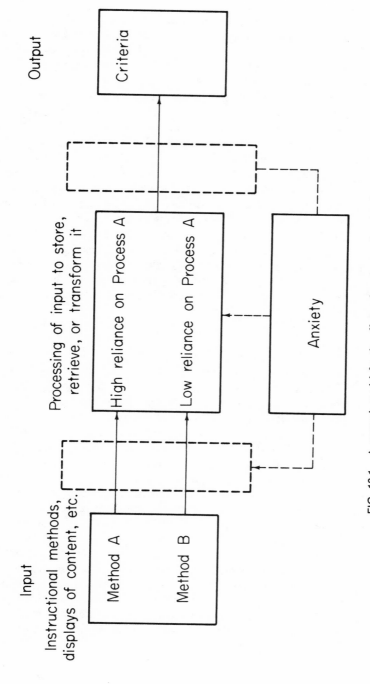

FIG. 13.1. A research model for the effects of anxiety on learning from instruction.

source of external stimulation to the student. It is reasoned that anxious students, probably by virtue of the diversion of attention discussed by Wine in this volume (Chapter 16) and by I. Sarason (1972a), are likely to experience greater difficulty than their low-anxiety counterparts in making nominal input materials effective stimuli. This source of interference is most debilitating to students because, if input is restricted, a smaller proportion of the content is subjected to processing, and some portion of processing energy and time has to be devoted to figuring out the proportion of the input originally missed. Therefore, interference at this stage is likely to be cumulative with that of other stages.

It was suggested that any operation that permits students to reinstitute some segment of input would be beneficial to the achievement of high-anxiety students and would leave the performance of low-anxiety individuals relatively unaffected. Such procedures as being able to rewind a video- or audiotape to catch aspects of the input previously missed or being branched back to a prior segment of instruction is likely to be especially effective in improving the performance of high-anxiety students. There is some support for this effect in research on instructionally relevant situations, though, typically, this potential source of interference has received relatively little systematic attention in this literature.

Processing Effect

At this point, anxiety exercises its effect on instruction by directly impacting on the cognitive operations performed to process the input. During processing, three types of manipulations are likely to have the largest effect on learning. (1) *Difficulty.* Research suggests that the performance of anxious individuals is poorer on difficult than on easy content. Any efforts to reduce the difficulty of materials should, therefore, be differentially effective for anxious students. The whole area of the difficulty of subject matter is discussed in greater detail later in this chapter. (2) *Reliance on memory.* It has been found (Tobias, 1977a) that instructional methods in which students are required to rely on short and intermediate term memory are more debilitating to anxious students than to those low in anxiety. Any implimentation, therefore, which reduces the degree to which students have to rely on memory, such as making prior material available to them, would improve the achievement of high-anxiety students. (3) *Organization of the task.* A number of studies (Tobias, 1977a) have indicated that material which is well organized tends to improve the achievement of high-anxiety students to a greater degree than that of low-anxiety individuals. Any adaptations which assure a tight and clear organization of instructional material would be likely to improve the achievement of anxious students.

Postprocessing Effect

The type of effect designated by this category occurs when students appear to have mastered the content during the course of instruction, yet experience some difficulty reproducing it on some subsequent occasion, such as on a posttest. When curriculum-embedded tests indicate that instructional material has been mastered during acquisition, yet students are unable to pass a summative evaluation at a later point in time, this type of interference is implied. There were no studies of this type of effect, though the model suggests that this type of interference should logically be evident under the appropriate experimental manipulations.

SUMMARY OF PRIOR FINDINGS

Analysis of research findings in individualized instructional contexts (Tobias, 1977a) has indicated that there were relatively few replicated interactions between instructional manipulations and anxiety in individualized instructional contexts. Main effects with anxiety, indicating that the performance of high-anxious students was poorer than those with lower anxiety, have frequently been reported; however, in individualized instructional contexts, there have been few well-established, replicated interactions. Generally, an ordinal interaction was sought in which the performance of high-anxiety individuals was improved by a particular instructional manipulation, whereas that of low-anxiety students was left relatively unaffected. It was reasoned that the failure to find a greater number of replicated interactions in individualized instructional contexts could be attributed to the fact that, by and large, the instructional manipulations attempted in those experiments may not have been as relevant to anxiety as first assumed. Thus, whether a student made an overt response to the instructional material or a more covert response was probably not differentially affected by anxiety. It was suggested that when individualized instructional studies would rigorously vary the types of manipulation suggested by the model that more consistent findings could be expected.

In more conventional, classroom-based instructional situations, a number of findings consistent with the model proposed earlier have been reported. Thus, it has been found (Oosthoek and Ackers, 1973) that the performance of anxious students who could rewind an audiotape was facilitated; furthermore, anxious students tended to use the rewind option more frequently than those lower in anxiety. Similarly, a number of findings (Dowaliby & Shumer, 1973; Domino, 1974) demonstrated that a tightly organized instructor-centered class yielded higher achievement for high-anxiety students than a more loosely organized student-centered, discussion-oriented type of classroom presentation.

RECENT RESEARCH FINDINGS

Peterson (1977) reported an ambitious and complicated study attempting to extend the Domino (1974) and Dowaliby and Schumer (1973) findings. Students were randomly assigned to a 2 × 2 matrix of treatments with two levels of structure, defined as the degree to which the instructor made lesson structure explicit to students, and two levels of student participation so that four instructional treatments were created: high structure/high participation, high structure/low participation, low structure/high participation, and low structure/low participation. In addition, anxiety, represented by the Children's Manifest Anxiety Scale and Spielberger's Trait Anxiety Scale (which were converted to standard scores and added to one another), achievement via independence and achievement via conformity, from the California Psychological Inventory, and verbal ability also were part of this research design. Peterson trained the teachers in the four different teaching styles and checked to assure that the differences were actually implemented during the conduct of this investigation. The major outcome measures consisted of a multiple-choice test designed to assess recall of the course material covered in the classes and an essay test consisting of five questions. The tests were administered at the end of the unit and again three weeks later.

Peterson found that there were a number of significant interactions among ability, anxiety, and the instructional treatments. The low-structure/low-participation treatment yielded poorest performance for students who were either high, or low, on *both* anxiety and ability. On the other hand, students who were high on one of these variables and low on the other performed best with the same low-structure/low-particiaption treatment and most poorly with the high-structure/low-participation treatment. The regression results for the essay achievement tests were similar to that of the multiple-choice posttest. Results for the retention test administered three weeks later indicated reduced interactions. Finally, the results for student attitudes exhibited no significant interactions. Interestingly, however, the pattern of interactions for attitude was the opposite of a pattern in the interactions for achievement.

Peterson (1978) attempted to replicate the earlier study, which was conducted with ninth-grade students, by using four classes of college undergraduates in a 5-week educational psychology course. In the college sample, the low-structure/low-participation treatment was again most important; however, the results were essentially the opposite of those reported for ninth-grade students. The low-structure/low-participation treatment resulted in the highest achievement for students who were either high or low on *both* anxiety and ability. For students high on the ability variable and low on anxiety, or vice versa, the low-structure/low-participation treatement was poorest. One possible explanation for these contradictory findings advanced by Peterson was the fact that the college sample represented considerably higher ability than the ninth-grade population.

It is difficult to discuss Peterson's findings in terms of the research model advanced previously. The inclusion of verbal ability as a variable is clearly a worthwhile procedure because able anxious students can certainly be expected to perform differently from anxious students lower in ability. This had not been anticipated in the model.

Second, the inclusion of student participation as a variable raises even more serious interpretive problems. There is some research, to be reviewed later, suggesting that high-anxiety individuals can be expected to perform well in situations in which attention to social cues is important. Participation clearly falls within that class of variables, as does the structure variable because it was implemented within the social organization of an intact classroom. Although these studies make valuable contributions to the study of aptitude treatment interactions in general, more conservative unpacking of these variables would be required in order to determine the implications of these studies for the anxiety model advanced earlier.

In a similar study, Porteus (1976) studied the achievement of 56 students in a private high school in two subjects: Economics and Educational Philosophy. Porteus used two instructional treatments: a teacher-centered and a student-centered instructional method. A variety of individual difference variables was available on the subjects. Most important for present purposes was the anxiety measure and a measure of general verbal ability. Among the outcome measures were three multiple-choice tests spread throughout the year and an essay test. The findings were partially consistent with those reported by Peterson. Students who were high on *both* anxiety and ability, or low on both, achieved most in the teacher-centered instructional strategy; those who were high on one of these variables and low on the other tended to achieve most in the student-centered instructional method. These findings could be seen most clearly in outcomes of the first test in Economics and on the essay test of Educational Philosophy.

Tsao (1977) studied the effects of error rate and feedback on achievement from programmed instruction. He employed the 55 easy frames (error rate = 6.5%) and 60 moderately difficult frames (error rate = 24.7%) of a program developed by Tobias (1968). Feedback was removed for half of the students who were selected after scoring in the top and bottom third on the debilitating anxiety scale. Tsao found no main effects or interactions for anxiety on either program. It should be noted that no ego-arousing instructions were employed in this study, and students were apparently free to go back and reread any part of the material previously read in order to figure out whether their answers were correct.

Oner (1977) assigned 160 sixth graders to learn some material on decimals via programmed instruction. Feedback regarding correctness of responses and teacher support were varied in this experiment. The expected interaction between test anxiety and feedback as well as anxiety and teacher support were not obtained, and low-anxiety students outperformed their high-anxiety counterparts.

Studies varying feedback with programmed materials are generally inconsistent in their results (Campeau, 1968; Tobias & Abramson, 1971) because students can easily look back or ahead to check the accuracy of their responses. In view of this fact, no achievement differences would be expected in terms of the model advanced previously. The failure to obtain interactions between anxiety and teacher support could be attributed to the fact that, in this context, teacher support may have been irrelevant to learning from materials designed to be self-instructional.

Crawford (1976) investigated the effects of a number of variables on achievement from programmed instruction. A brief instructional program dealing with physiological psychology was prepared in a form either requiring constructed responses with feedback or reading the material cast in the form of completed sentences. In addition, the program was prepared in three levels of difficulty for constructed responding and in two difficulty levels for the reading mode. Half the subjects received a pretest on the instructional content that was presumed to familiarize them with the material, and another half of the subjects received no pretest. In addition, data on the students' test anxiety, achievement motivation, and scholastic aptitude were also available.

Among the results which were most relevant for present purposes was the finding that students high in test anxiety and low in need for achievement obtained the highest posttest scores on easy versions of the material. Students who were high on need for achievement and low on test anxiety, on the other hand, achieved best on difficult materials. When the interaction between test anxiety and the different instructional manipulations was examined without simultaneously taking into account need for achievement, no significant interactions emerged. Similarly, when the interactions between treatments and need for achievement were examined in the absence of test anxiety, they were also nonsignificant. This study clearly suggests that, especially in instructional situations, it may be profitable to investigate the effects of test anxiety in interaction with achievement motivation. The Atkinson and Feather (1966) research on motive to avoid failure and motive to achieve success has been widely employed in social psychology and personality research. The present findings strongly suggest that use of this paradigm in the instructional area may be very valuable as well.

In the review of prior research in this area (Tobias, 1977a, b), it was suggested that interactions with anxiety could be expected largely when students viewed performance on the research task as being similar in importance to achievement in situations having real-life importance to them. In research contexts having little personal involvement for the student, there is little reason to expect anxiety to be engaged during the instructional task (Tobias, 1969); hence, it is not surprising to find nonsignificant results in such a situation. This interpretation is in accord with the frequent finding that anxiety effects emerge in those situations where instructions are used stressing the importance of the task for the student (commonly called ego-involving instructions) and not with more neutral task directions (I. Sarason, 1960, 1972a; Wine, 1971). It may be that for students with strong achievement needs any situation in which outcome measures are administered is of importance to the students, enlists their best efforts, and engages the variety of individual difference variables, including anxiety, relevant to performing on the task.

Mayer (1976) performed some experiments varying whether the students or the experimenter had control over the sequence in which they worked on a number of problem-solving puzzles. Students working in the self-paced mode could switch from one problem to the other at any time, with the restriction that no more than ten minutes could be spent on any one problem. In the other group, the order of presentation was determined by the experimenter who would stop students when the time allotted for one problem had been exhausted and switch them to another problem. Unexpectedly, high-anxious students solved significantly more problems than the low-anxious group in both modes. In addition, there was an anxiety by pacing interaction indicating that self-pacing greatly improved performance of high-anxious subjects but had little effect on individuals lower in anxiety. Because only 24 subjects were utilized in this experiment, eight additional subjects were run in the self-paced group. Again, the higher anxious students outperformed their low-anxiety counterparts.

Mayer ran another experiment (Experiment 3) utilizing 40 subjects in a self-versus-experimenter-paced group; subjects performed on both rote and cognitive tasks. In this study, the low-anxiety students outperformed those with higher anxiety, but the same pacing by anxiety interaction was found with the performance of high-anxious subjects superior in the self-paced condition compared to the experimenter-paced condition. There were no differences between the conditions for the low-anxiety subjects. Finally, an anxiety by type of task interaction was also found indicating that high-anxious subject performed more poorly than low-anxious subjects on cognitive tasks. There were no differences on the tasks for rote memory. These findings are generally in accord with the model because self-paced subjects are free to reinstitute any part of the input temporarily not attended to.

Papay, Costello, Hedl, and Spielberger (1975) compared children enrolled in traditional classrooms to those enrolled in an individualized multi-aged program on a number of indices. Two groups of students drawn from the first and second grade were used in this study. It was found that students from the individualized curriculum were significantly lower in trait anxiety than those from the traditional classroom. Furthermore, second graders from the individualized curriculum had significantly lower state anxiety scores than their traditional counterparts. These findings confirm the expectations in the model that individualized classrooms would be beneficial to high-anxiety students by virtue of the ability to repeat material not mastered at first, adjustment of difficulty of the material to the students' level of functioning, and a number of other variables. The students in this study were also administered mathematics tasks away from their classrooms. Posttests on these tasks, consisting of abstract and concrete material, were administered, but the concrete posttests suffered from a ceiling effect. A disordinal interaction between anxiety and type of classes from which the student came was found in which students with high anxiety achieved more if they came from the individualized rather than the traditional setting, whereas the opposite occurred for individuals low in anxiety. Although this experiment was not conducted within the classroom context, this finding may be attributable to the fact that the high-anxiety students in the individualized classroom had learned to function capably despite their anxiety and, hence, adapted easily to the mathematical task.

Moore (1974) compared the differences between open and traditional third and fourth grade classes on a number of variables, including general and test anxiety. It was found that third and fourth graders attending open classes expressed more general anxiety than did the students attending traditional classes. Furthermore, females in open classes expressed more test anxiety than their counterparts in traditional classes. These results are in general accord with the model because traditional classes can be expected to be more tightly organized with respect to the sequence in which different types of subject matter are taken up.

Summary

The findings with respect to the research model are somewhat confusing. When procedures in experiments manipulated variables similar to those proposed in the model, the results were generally supportive of predictions. When the manipulations were different from those advocated, the results were nonsignificant, again as expected. When researchers studied a combination of variables, some of which were not directly related to the model, the relevance of those results to the model were difficult to interpret.

Research that systematically varies the parameters recommended in the model is needed in order to determine its usefulness for clarifying the interaction between anxiety and instructional contexts.

ANXIETY, DIFFICULTY, AND ACHIEVEMENT

A good deal of research on anxiety in learning has been stimulated by the Spence-Taylor drive theory (Spence & Spence, 1966). It will be recalled that drive theory predicts that the performance of individuals high in anxiety will be facilitated on simple tasks and impaired on more complex tasks. The results of research testing this hypothesis in meaningful instructional contexts generally failed to support it. Spence & Spence (1966) expressed some reservations about generalizing their formulation to meaningful instruction. They indicated that, even in highly limited experimental settings, deriving hypotheses about the interaction between anxiety and performance was a major undertaking. Generalizing these predictions to the type of complex learning occurring in most instructional situations may well have been an attempt to extend the theory beyond the bounds its originators had intended.

In general, results have supported drive theory in experiments using simple learning tasks such as eyelid conditioning (Spence, 1964) and similar tasks. Reviews of such research on the effects of anxiety on instruction (Sieber et al., 1977) have found a few studies in which high-anxiety individuals outperform individuals low in anxiety.

In the aforementioned research model (Tobias, 1977b), difficulty was presumed to exert an effect during the processing stage. It should be noted, however, that an essentially ordinal interaction is expected in such instructional contexts. Specifically, the performance of high-anxiety students is expected to be impaired by difficult materials, compared to that of low-anxiety individuals. For easy materials, however, little difference attributable to anxiety is expected. These results are generally in accord with most of the findings in meaningful instructional situations (Sieber et al., 1977). Nevertheless, there are occasional findings in the literature suggesting that the performance of individuals high in anxiety is superior to that of their low-anxiety counterparts. It is the purpose of this section to review some of these studies and to suggest a hypothesis to guide future research regarding this aspect of the model.

Anxiety Facilitating Performance

In a study by Nottelmann and Hill (1977), it was found that fourth and fifth graders who were high on test anxiety performed more poorly on an anagram task than did medium- and low-test-anxious students. It was especially interesting that high-anxious children glanced away from their task significantly more frequently than medium- and low-anxiety students and that high-anxiety children glanced significantly at the experimenter, who was also working on an anagram task, than did the other two anxiety groups.

Potter (1974) studied the correlates of a number of variables on classroom participation in elementary schools. He found that anxiety, as measured by the *Test Anxiety Scale for Children,* was positively related to classroom participation. Specifically, test anxious scores were positive predictors of the number of times children raised their hands in class and of how often they initiated private seat work conversations with the teacher. Detailed analysis of this relationship indicated that children who were within one standard deviation above the mean on test anxiety tended also to be the above mean with respect to raising their hands in class. This relationship did *not* hold for those children scoring above one standard deviation on anxiety. Potter suggests that these results may be attributed to the fact that regression analysis was used in this study and, consequently, the full range of anxiety scores employed, compared to the more conventional extreme groups design that is analyzed by the analysis of variance.

Anxiety Research and Regression Analysis. It may be observed parenthetically that, in anxiety research in which a test score of any kind is employed, multiple linear regression analysis is the treatment of choice, compared to the analysis of variance. In regression analysis, the anxiety test score is entered into the statistical analysis in its continuous form rather than having to be dichotomized into a high- and low-anxiety group, or trichotomized in a situation where the medium-anxiety group is used as well. Such data analysis yields a number of advantages. First of all, it has been estimated (Cohen, 1968) that using the data in continuous form increases the size of the effect and, hence, the statistical significance of the findings by 36%. Second, it is possible to save some degrees of freedom in designs in which the groups are trichotomized or split into even more groups by the use of regression analysis. Because the data exist in continuous form, only one degree of freedom is used to test for the main anxiety effect, and similarly, anxiety contributes only one degree of freedom in any double or triple interactions investigated in such a study. Furthermore, with the possible exception of repeated measures analysis of variance, any effect investigated by analysis of variance can be similarly investigated by regression analysis with considerably greater flexibility and rigor. Extensive treatments of regression analysis are available in Cohen (1968), and Kerlinger and Pedhazur (1975). An extended discussion of problems in the analysis of research designs in which a continuous test score is examined in interaction with different experimental treatments is available in Cronbach and Snow (1977).

Anxiety and Attention to Social Cues

The findings reported earlier in which high-anxiety students outperformed their low-anxiety counterparts, plus those to be reviewed in the next few pages, suggest a hypothesis to account for these results. Perhaps students high in anxiety perform more effectively on tasks in which attention to social cues is important as compared to people lower in anxiety. High-anxiety students may scan the environment for cues to reassure themselves regarding their performance. When positive social cues are available, these can be expected to be extremely reinforcing to high-anxiety individuals. When neutral cues are present, such as in the Nottelmann and Hill study, these are also likely to be interpreted as reinforcing to those high in anxiety because they fear a negative evaluation, and neutral social feedback cues are more positive than those they expect. If this reasoning is correct, low-anxiety students, on the other hand, will not be facilitated by neutral feedback or by tasks in which attention to social cues is of importance because they do not expect a negative evaluation and, hence, are not as busy scanning the interpersonal social milleu as their high-anxiety counterparts.

Two types of predictions can be made from this formulation. First, on tasks in which positive and neutral social feedback are available, high-anxiety individuals are likely to be more responsive to neutral feedback than those lower in anxiety, with little difference to be expected between anxiety groups for positive feedback. Negative feedback can be expected to be more debilitating to high-anxiety students because it confirms their worst expectations and probably makes attending to task demands even more difficult than it was before, resulting in consequent increased disruption of performance.

Second, this formulation predicts that, on those tasks in which attention to social cues facilitates task performance, persons high in anxiety can be expected to outperform their low-anxiety counterparts. This expectation is based on the reasoning that high-anxiety individuals are scanning the social environment for cues to determine how they are doing and, in this process, can be expected to observe more social and interpersonal stimuli that those lower in anxiety. Where this scanning is *not* related to task demands, performance by those high in anxiety is likely to be lower than for less anxious students because less attention is being devoted to task demands by high than by low-anxiety individuals. Deffenbacher (1978) reported results confirming this hypothesis originally advanced by Wine (1971) and by I. Sarason (1972a). There is some support for these hypotheses in a number of studies using both anxiety and modeling as variables.

Modeling Studies. Sarason, Pederson, and Nyman (1968) studied the effects of modeling and test anxiety on learning paired associates from a memory drum. The rationale for that experiment by I. Sarason et al. (1968) was strikingly similar to the hypothesis suggested earlier that "test anxiety may contribute to increased vigilance with regard to possibly helpful cues in the environment.... Because high anxious individuals are more insecure than other persons, they may be relatively more interested and active in attending to cues in strange situations and in 'borrowing' behaviors and attitudes from models [pp. 496–497]."

In the experiment, seven conditions were used and students had to learn two serial lists. In some of the conditions the subjects had the opportunity to observe a model working on one of the two lists; under those conditions high and middle test anxiety groups were significantly superior to the low-anxiety groups. A significant anxiety by conditions interaction indicated that the superiority of the high and middle test anxiety groups was due largely to the two conditions in which subjects could observe models learn these lists, rather than the conditions for groups in which such observation was not possible. In addition, high and middle test anxiety groups showed more improvement in moving from a list on which they had *not* observed the model working to a list in which the model had been observed.

Sarason (1975) examined the degree to which high- and low-anxiety students profited from experimenters serving as models. Of special relevance to the present discussion was the finding of an interaction between test anxiety and type of model behavior. Specifically, on a serial learning task, high-anxiety students profited most from interacting with an experimenter-model who admitted to experiencing high anxiety and verbalized a variety of ways of coping with it effectively. The high-anxiety groups' performance under this condition was the highest of any of 10 groups.

Two studies by Sarason are also pertinent here. In one of these (Sarason, 1972b), students of different anxiety levels performed on a verbal learning task under three different conditions: (1) observing a model perform the task; (2) observing a model described as doing poorly on the task; and (3) a control group in which a model was not utilized. There was a significant anxiety by treatment interaction, indicating that the performance of high-test-anxious subjects was superior to the low and middle groups in the modeling condition. In another experiment (Sarason, 1973), subjects observed a model working on anagram tasks under three different conditions: (1) observing the performance of the model; (2) observing the performance and being able to hear the model verbalize the reasons for responses; and (3) in addition to the second condition, verbalizing the principles underlying the model's behavior. A no-model control group was also used in this experiment. The performance of the high-anxiety group was significantly superior to that of the low-anxiety group in the condition where the model verbalized the responses and the reasons underlying them.

Evidence that high-anxiety subjects were more responsive to reinforcement in a verbal conditioning situation was obtained in two experiments by Sarason and Ganzer (1962, 1963). In the first experiment, subjects high in test anxiety who were reinforced for negative self-references showed greater increases in these responses under stress conditions than under nonstress and greater increases in negative self-references than all other subjects combined for this response class. In the second experiment (Sarason and Ganzer, 1963), further evidence for high-anxiety students' reliance on experimental cues was found. High-test-anxious subjects who had been reinforced for negative self-references on the first day of a 2-day experiment showed a drop in this response class during an operant period on the second day. The researchers interpreted this finding as follows: High-anxiety subjects may have been switching from one response class to another to seek the reinforcement to which they had become accustomed on day one and missed on the second day of the experiment.

These experiments support the contention that high- compared to low-anxiety individuals are more responsive to social cues and can be expected to do better on those tasks in which such responsiveness facilitates performance. Some similar evidence can be found in studies in the area of persuasiveness.

Persuasion and Conformity Studies. The hypothesis advanced earlier suggests that high-anxiety individuals are more likely to yield to persuasion and to conform than those lower in anxiety. This expectation is similar to Sarason's (1960) hypothesis that high- compared to low-anxious individuals may have "a greater susceptibility to persuasion and opinion change [p. 410]." There are several studies addressed to this question.

Meunier & Rule (1967) exposed high- and low-test-anxious persons to a situation in which they were required to make judgments and indicate their confidence concerning these in a group-pressure situation. High-test-anxious individuals conformed more to others' judgment than did those lower in test anxiety. Furthermore, those high in test anxiety expressed little confidence in their judgment in two types of situations: when no feedback about their performance on prior trials was provided, and when feedback indicating poor performance was provided. On the other hand, low-test-anxious individuals expressed high confidence when provided no information about prior performance, and this confidence level corresponded to the level of confidence expressed when feedback regarding good performance was provided. It seemed, therefore, that high-test-anxious individuals interpreted the lack of information in the same way they did information indicating poor performance, whereas those low in anxiety interpreted the lack of information in the same way as they did information indicating success. This study confirms the high reliance on social support by those high in anxiety and is quite consistent with the hypothesis that high-anxious individuals will go out of their way to seek such social support and achieve better on tasks including such an element.

Rule and Sandilands (1969) studied the effects of confidence and public commitment on conformity for persons varying in test anxiety. Test anxiety and commitment interacted significantly on conformity, with high-test-anxious persons conforming more under high than low commitment conditions and the reverse being true for low-test-anxious persons.

These studies are clearly consistent with the hypothesis of superior performance by high-anxiety students on tasks having a social dimension. Although most of these studies come from the personality and social area, rather than from instructional psychology, they nevertheless suggest that similar investigations more directly relevant to instructional concerns may well prove enlightening about the performance of individuals differing in anxiety on tasks involving either responsiveness to different types of reinforcement or attention to social cues.

Summary

Recent research and theory in the area of adapting instruction to individual differences in anxiety were reviewed in this chapter. An information-processing research model intended to summarize this research was briefly described and recent studies were reviewed in terms of the model. In general, when researchers varied conditions similar to those suggested in the model, the results were consonant with predictions. A number of researchers studied a combination of variables which were difficult to interpret in terms of the model.

Research dealing with the performance of anxious individuals in situations involving attention to social factors or susceptibility to persuasion was reviewed, and a hypothesis was offered that high- as compared to low-anxiety persons can be expected to perform more effectively in such situations.

ACKNOWLEDGMENTS

Gratitude is expressed to Judith Butt, Toni Deutsch and Howard Everson for their assistance with the preparation of this chapter.

Completion of this manuscript was supported, in part, by the Institute for Research and Development for Occupational Education, Center for the Advanced Study of Education, City University of New York.

REFERENCES

Atkinson, J. W., & Feather, N. T. (Eds.). *A theory of achievement motivation.* New York: John Wiley, 1966.

Campeau, P. L. Test anxiety and feedback in programmed instruction. *Journal of Educational Psychology,* 1968, *59,* 159–163.

Cohen, J. Multiple regression as a general data analytic system. *Psychological Bulletin,* 1968, *70,* 426–443.

Coleman, J. C. *Abnorml psychology and modern life* (3rd ed.). Glenview, Ill.: Scott Foresman, 1964.

Crawford, J. *An investigation of internally and externally operative variables in an interactive learning model.* Unpublished manuscript. (Report No. 76–8) Austin, Tex.: Research and Development Center for Teacher Education, 1976.

Cronbach, L. J. The two disciplines of scientific psychology. *American Psychologist,* 1957, *12,* 671–684.

Cronbach, L. J., & Snow, R. E. *Aptitudes and instructional methods.* New York: Irvington Press, 1977.

Deffenbacher, J. L. Worry, emotionality, and task-generated interference in test anxiety: An empirical test of attentional theory. *Journal of Educational Psychology,* 1978, *70,* 248–254.

Domino, G. *Aptitude by treatment interaction effects in college instruction.* Paper presented at the American Psychological Association Convention, New Orleans, September 1974.

Dowaliby, F. J., & Schumer, H. Teacher-centered vs. student-centered mode of college instruction as related to manifest anxiety. *Journal of Educational Psychology,* 1973, *64,* 125–132.

Gaudry, E., & Spielberger, C. D. *Anxiety and educational achievement.* Sydney, Australia: John Wiley and Sons, 1971.

Hedl, J., Jr., & O'Neil, H. F., Jr. Reduction of state anxiety via instructional design in computer based learning environments. In Sieber, J., O'Neil, H. F., Jr., & Tobias, S., *Anxiety, learning, and instruction.* Hillsdale, N.J.: Lawrence Erlbaum Associates, 1977.

Kerlinger, F. N., & Pedhazur, E. J. *Multiple regression in behavioral research.* New York: Holt, Rinehart & Winston, 1973.

Lunneborg, P. W. Relations among social desirability, achievement and anxiety measures in children. *Child Development,* 1964, *35,* 169–182.

Mayer, R. E. *Interactive effects of trait anxiety and self pacing in problem solving.* Paper presented at the annual meeting of the Western Psychological Association, Los Angeles, 1976.

Meunier, C., & Rule, B. G. Anxiety, confidence and conformity. *Journal of Personality,* 1967, *35,* 498–504.

Moore, A. *A comparison of school achievement, self-esteem, anxiety, and trust in open and traditional classes at the third and fourth grades.* Unpublished doctoral dissertation, Northern Illinois University, 1974.

Nottelmann, E. D., & Hill, K. T. Test anxiety and off-task behavior in evaluation situations. *Child Development,* 1977, *48,* 225–231.

Oner, N. P. Impact of teacher behavior and teaching technique on learning by anxious children. In Speilberger, C. D., & Sarason I. G. (Eds.), *Stress and anxiety: (Vol. IV).* Washington, D.C.: Hemisphere, 1977.

Oosthoek, H., & Ackers, G. The evaluation of an audio-tape mediated course II. *British Journal of Educational Technology,* 1973, *4,* 54–73.

Papay, J. P., Costello, R. J., Hedl, J. J., Jr., & Spielberger, C. D. Effects of trait and state anxiety on the performance of elementary school children in traditional and individualized multi-age classrooms. *Journal of Educational Psychology,* 1975, *5,* 840–846.

Peterson, P. L. Interactive effects of student anxiety, achievement orientation, and teacher behavior on student achievement and attitude. *Journal of Educational Psychology,* 1977, 69, 770–792.

Peterson, P. L. Interactive effects of student anxiety, achievement orientation, and teacher behavior on student achievement and attitude. *Journal of Educational Psychology,* 1977, 69, 779–792.

Porteus, A. W. *Teacher-centered versus student-center instruction: Interactions with cognitive and motivational aptitudes.* Unpublished doctoral dissertation, Stanford University, 1976.

Potter, E. F. *Correlates of oral participation in classrooms.* Unpublished doctoral dissertation, University of Chicago, 1974.

Rule, B. G., & Sandilands, M. L. Test anxiety, confidence, commitment, and conformity. *Journal of Personality,* 1969, *37,* 460–467.

Sarason, I. G. Empirical findings and theoretical problems in the use of anxiety scales. *Psychological Bulletin,* 1960, *57,* 403–415.

Sarason, I. G. Experimental approaches to test anxiety: Attention and the uses of information. In Spielberger, C. D. (Ed.), *Anxiety: Current trends in theory and research (Vol. 11).* New York: Academic Press, 1972. (a)

Sarason, I. G. Test anxiety and the model who fails. *Journal of Personality and Social Psychology,* 1972, *22,* 410–413. (b)

Sarason, I. G. Test anxiety and cognitive modeling. *Journal of Personality and Social Psychology,* 1973, *28,* 58–61.

Sarason, I. G. Test anxiety and the self-disclosing, coping model. *Journal of Consulting and Clinical Psychology,* 1975, *43,* 148–153.

Sarason, I. G. and Ganzer, V. J. Anxiety, reinforcement and experimental instructions in a free verbalization situation. *Journal of Abnormal and Social Psychology,* 1962, *65,* 30–307.

Sarason, I. G., and Ganzer, V. J. Effects of test anxiety and reinforcement history on verbal behavior. *Journal of Abnormal and Social Psychology,* 1963, *67,* 87–91.

Sarason, I. G., Pederson, A. M. & Nyman, B. Test anxiety and the observation of models. *Journal of Personality,* 1968, *36,* 493–511.

Sieber, J., O'Neil, H. F. Jr., & Tobias, S. *Anxiety, learning and instruction.* Hillsdale, N.J.: Lawrence Erlbaum Associates, 1977.

Snow, R. E. Research on aptitude for learning: A progress report. In Shulman, L. S. (Ed.), *Review of Research in Education (Vol. IV).* Itasca, Ill.: Peacock, 1976.

Snow, R. E. Individual differences and instructional theory. *Educational Researcher,* 1977, *6,* 11–15.

Spence, K. W. Anxiety (drive) level and performance in eyelid conditioning. *Psychological Bulletin,* 1964, *61,* 129–139.

Spence, J. T., & Spence, K. W. The motivational components of manifest anxiety: Drive and drive stimuli. In Spielberger, C. D. (Ed.), *Anxiety and behavior.* New York: Academic Press, 1966.

Spielberger, C. D. The effects of manifest anxiety on the academic achievement of college students. *Mental Hygiene,* 1962, *46,* 420–426.

Spielberger, C. D. Complex learning and academic achievement. In Spielberger, C. D. (Ed.), *Anxiety and behavior.* New York: Academic Press, 1966.

Spielberger, C. D., & Katzenmeyer, W. G. Manifest anxiety, intelligence, and college grades. *Journal of Consulting Psychology,* 1959, *23,* 278.

Tobias, S. *The effect of creativity, response mode, and subject matter familiarity on achievement from programmed instruction.* New York: MSS Educational Publishing Co., 1968.

Tobias, S. *Research strategy on the effect of individual differences on achievement from programmed instruction.* Paper presented at the annual convention of the American Psychological Association, Washington, D.C., September 1969.

Tobias, S. Anxiety-treatment interaction: a review of research. In Sieber, S., O'Neil, H. F., Jr., & Tobias, S., *Anxiety, learning, and instruction.* Hillsdale, N.J.: Lawrence Erlbaum Associates, 1977a.

Tobias, S. A model for research on the effect of anxiety on instruction. In Sieber, J., O'Neil. H. F., Jr., & Tobias, S. *Anxiety, learning, and instruction.* Hillsdale, N.J.: Lawrence Erlbaum Associates, 1977b.

Tobias, S., & Abramson, T. The relationship of anxiety, response mode, and content difficulty to achievement in programmed instruction. *Journal of Educational Psychology, 1971, 62,* 354–357.

Tsao, P. *The effect of error rate, knowledge of correct response and test anxiety in linear programs.* Unpublished doctoral dissertation, University of Oklahoma, 1977.

Wine, J. Test anxiety and direction of attention. *Psychological Bulletin, 1971, 76,* 92–104.

14

Test Anxiety Reduction and Computer-Based Learning Environments

Harold F. O'Neil, Jr.
*Army Research Institute for
the Behavioral and Social Sciences*

Frank C. Richardson
The University of Texas at Austin

This chapter summarizes some of our research and that of our colleagues to date that focuses on the measurement and remediation of test anxiety in computer-based learning environments. One result of these efforts was the development and validation of a semiautomated test anxiety reduction program. The chapter also presents our ideas and design—not yet implemented—for a "second generation" stress and anxiety reduction program that might be made available to almost any student through home computer-based education systems that probably, in just a few years, will become as commonplace as color television.

Initially, we were struck by apparent parallels between "automated," instructor-free computer-based instruction and partially automated desensitization-like treatment programs (Donner & Guerney, 1969; Suinn & Richardson, 1971) for the treatment of common phobias. It seemed desirable to combine intellectual and emotional skills training in an ideal computer-based learning environment. Upon continued reflection, we suggested a deeper parallel between emerging views of the potential for computers in education (Levien, 1972) and a rapidly maturing cognitive-attentional view of test anxiety (Meichenbaum, 1972; Wine, 1971). Both emphasized instructional or treatment approaches that exploited and attempted to enhance *self-directed* learning and coping. Therefore, rather than trying merely to stuff learners full of more facts or mechanically decondition anxiety reflexes, these approaches, generally speaking, encourage and enable students to become more effectively active in self-managing their own participation in the learning process.

COMPUTER-BASED LEARNING ENVIRONMENTS

Computer-based learning situations seemed to us to represent not only a promising educational technology for the future, but an especially promising vehicle for relevant educational research. The learning tasks administered to students in the research described later, for the most part, were actual coursework in the students' academic specialization. They almost certainly engaged students' real-life motivations and interests to a greater degree than experiments utilizing traditional laboratory learning tasks. The context of this research represented an inevitable compromise between relevance and rigor but may have preserved many of the advantages of each.

It may be argued that American education will be caught soon in a dilemma similar to that faced now by other manpower/technology-intensive organizations. On the one hand, greater technological complexity induces knowledge obsolescence at an increasing rate. At the same time, competition for needed resources to meet the demands of change is heightening and is exacerbated by increasing manpower costs. In the field of education, powerful teachers' unions, the incipient taxpayers' revolt, and a projected decrease in student enrollment further limit one's freedom to maneuver. While these pressures mount, we discover that both aptitude and achievement standardized test scores of college-bound students have dropped dramatically over the past 10 years (National Institute of Education, 1977).

Computer-based learning technology may represent a partial solution to the problem of dealing with these harsh economic realities without sacrificing educational opportunity. This technology may permit us to distribute a uniformly high quality of many types of education or training to large numbers of students in an economical manner. Many problems of logistics and time could be solved through the centralized updating of curriculum. Furthermore, in the 1980s, the transmission of information may be cheaper by electronic than by paper means.

We seem to be entering an era of computational plenty fostered by the explosion of silicon integrated-circuit technology. A recent conference on computers in education (Seidel, 1975) projected that, by 1985, an intelligent terminal capable of the computing power of a medium-size 1975 computer will retail for under $1,000. The technology for storage of information will progress to the point where, in a few years, entire libraries will be available at low cost, not only in educational settings, but also in the home. Color, videotapes, random-access slides, and interactive computing will be major features of these new low-cost systems.

Research and experience with computer-based instruction in recent years have suggested that it may have several advantages over other instructional methods. The computer can be programmed to adapt the learning environment precisely to each individual's strengths and weaknesses along many dimensions, thus allowing for true individualization of learning. In addition, computer-based learning programs require less time to convey the same amount of material than traditional instructional methods. This saving in time is especially important in situations in which students are paid, as in military and industrial training systems.

Compared with traditional instruction, the major disadvantages of computer-based instruction include the greater time and cost required for course development, higher initial outlay of funds, and higher total costs— although new technologies and widespread use of initially expensive programs may soon alter this picture. The advantages and disadvantages of computer-based instruction with respect to different types of cognitive learning are reviewed elsewhere (e.g., Atkinson & Wilson, 1969; Holtzman, 1970; Levien, 1972). We are assuming only that computer-based learning environments are appropriate and efficient means for reaching some educational and training goals in today's society. To date, these environments have been mainly one of two types, computer-assisted or computer-managed instruction.

COMPUTER-ASSISTED INSTRUCTION

Computer-assisted instruction is a form of human–computer interaction designed to make the learning process and materials more efficient. It is a general rubric covering a number of instructional methods in which a computer is programmed to accomplish the teaching functions of conveying information to the student, evaluating the student's understanding of this information, and providing the student with feedback and guidance through the learning program. Programs vary in complexity and sophistication, and they may play a variety of different instructional roles. In all cases, the instruction is stored within the computer system.

Computer-assisted instruction involves intensive interactions between the students and the computer. Because of the amount of effort required to carefully specify these interactions, the design, development, implementation, and evaluation of these instructional programs is a very expensive and time-consuming endeavor. As a result, most of the computer-assisted instruction programs currently available are fairly short and cover only a small part of a total course. Most commonly, one finds short segments of highly individualized computer-assisted instruction embedded in a course that otherwise is taught in a traditional, nonindividualized way.

COMPUTER-MANAGED INSTRUCTION

Using a computer to manage the instructional process is one alternative to relatively expensive computer-assisted instructional programs. In computer-managed instruction, the instruction itself is not presented by means of the computer. Rather, instructional materials consist of conventional printed or audiovisual materials. The computer is used to monitor and, to some extent, direct students' progress through the use of noncomputerized instructional materials. The computer tests students at frequent points in the learning program in order to assess progress and diagnose various strengths and weaknesses, provides prescriptions for remedial work, and schedules the students' use of available instructional resources. Short segments of computer-assisted instruction, of course, might be one of the resources available for assignment by the computer-managed instructional system.

The equipment or hardware needed to implement computer-assisted or computer-managed instruction systems varies concerning: (1) the type of terminal (such as typewriters, cathode-ray tubes, film projectors, audiotape players, or combinations of these); (2) the response devices (such as keyboards, light pens, and touch-sensitive surfaces); and (3) the number of terminals (typically one to 60). The instructional materials and response recordings are usually stored on random-access disks or magnetic tapes. The control of each student's program is implemented in a central processing unit. This unit is the "brain" of the systems and controls its other elements. These units of equipment are essential to a computer-based instructional system, although it may include other devices as well.

ANXIETY AND COMPUTER-BASED LEARNING

The authors and their colleagues have carried out a number of studies in computer-based learning environments in which instructional procedures were modified in attempts directly to reduce state anxiety (reviewed in Hedl & O'Neil, 1977). A number of previous studies had investigated instructional modifications designed to improve the performance of high-anxious students, including the provision of feedback in programmed instruction (Campeau, 1968), reassurance instructions to students that their performance will not be used in evaluations (I. Sarason, 1972), and relaxation instructions prior to completing a paired-associate learning task (Straughan & Dufort, 1969). Despite the long-standing recognition that anxiety can interfere with the learning process (I. Sarason, 1960; Spielberger, 1966, 1972), there has been relatively little research concerned with reducing anxiety per se, in which levels of state anxiety are assessed directly, in realistic learning situations. Computer-based learning situations make it possible to correct this deficiency with relative ease because they permit the presentation of well-controlled treatments and the acquisition of detailed response data, at almost any point in time, concerning learning to date, performance capability, or momentary state anxiety.

The results of these studies were, in many respects, both surprising and disappointing (Hedl & O'Neil, 1977). Four studies concerned with the presence of behavioral objectives indicated that, in general, they neither facilitated achievement nor reduced anxiety. Another series of studies showed that a modification which provided students with presumably optimal response mode involving active responding and immediate feedback, as compared with simple reading conditions, led to higher levels of state anxiety. In fact, the mean state-anxiety scores within the computer learning task match the expected level of anxiety in a difficult examination. Several studies investigating the effects of providing students with learner control over some instructional variables yielded mixed results concerning learner control's ability to reduce anxiety and improve performance. Studies concerning the effects of interactive computer testing, compared with traditional testing on state anxiety, indicated no lower anxiety during computer testing. Two large-scale studies in a computer-managed instruction setting showed that state-anxiety levels were relatively high, indicating a stressful situation, during test taking even though the type of tests and other features of the situation were designed to minimize anxiety and stress.

The results of these studies, viewed collectively, indicated that high anxiety often interferes with effective learning and performance on tests in computer-based learning situations but discouraged belief that available modifications in instructional design or presentation of test material would substantially reduce test anxiety, especially in that sizeable minority of highly test-anxious individuals who appear in any student population.

A SEMIAUTOMATED TEST ANXIETY REDUCTION PROGRAM

Partly in response to these difficulties in reducing anxiety through modification of instructional procedures, the authors developed and validated a semiautomated, media-based program to teach anxiety management skills to interested, highly anxious students completing a series of computer-managed instructional modules that formed the major part of an undergraduate educational psychology course (Richardson, O'Neil, & Grant, 1977). The program was developed within the framework of a cognitive-attentional view of test anxiety and its effects on learning and performance. It was automated to a large degree in order to reduce dramatically the demand on relatively scarce professional time and energies and to make it potentially available to large numbers of students. The apparent success of a number of semiautomated desensitization programs, utilizing audiotape or videotape (Richardson & Suinn, 1973; Suinn & Hall, 1970), and the large amount of literature demonstrating the vicarious desensitization of fear through observation of live or symbolic models (Bandura, 1969) encouraged belief in the possibility of an effective automated program.

The literature on test anxiety and its treatment was surveyed for techniques and approaches that might be incorporated into or modified for the automated format. In addition, some new approaches were developed. The four principal components of the program were as follows:

1. Reading and completing written exercises in special manual, written for the program, on coping with test anxiety. The text of this 75-page manual is available in a separate technical report (Richardson, 1973) and is described in greater detail later.

2. A symbolic modeling component consisting of a half-hour videotape of a female student modeling effective and ineffective management of anxiety (including verbalized self-talk) while completing intelligence tests questions presented on the cathode-ray tube of a terminal in a computer-based learning situation.

3. A brief, modified desensitization procedure in which subjects are given half an hour of deep muscle relaxation instructions by a therapist on videotape and, at a later date, are instructed by videotape to visualize themselves, while relaxed, coping with anxiety in a graded series of test-taking scenes by means of slow, deep breaths plus the use of appropriate self-instructions to relax and pay attention to the test.

4. A practice test-taking component in which students respond for about 45 minutes to test-like questions at a computer terminal. Periodic reminders presented by the terminal instruct them to practice various anxiety-management techniques they have learned in the program.

In each of the three validation studies (Richardson et al. 1977), the treatment procedure was completed for each student during a 2-week period early in a given semester. All students (between 400 and 500 each semester) completed the 27-item Test Anxiety Scale (Sarason, 1972) at the outset of the course. Those with scores in the upper 20% of the scale were contacted and invited to participate in the program. Those choosing to do so (about four out of five, on the average) were given a copy of the manual and then completed a five-part treatment procedure consisting of: (1) reading the first two parts of the manual over the weekend; (2) attending the first scheduled individual session, consisting of watching a 1-hour videotape (the first half-hour was the modeling sequence, and the second half-hour features deep muscle and slow deep breathing relaxation instructions); (3) reading the third part of the manual and completing the written exercises it contained; (4) attending a second scheduled session, consisting of viewing a second videotape presenting the modified desensitization component of the program; and (5) attending the last scheduled session of the program, the practice test-taking session at a computer terminal.

The test anxiety manual used in these studies may be a promising means of communicating useful information and skills to interested learners. A number of prominent writers in the fields of psychotherapy and behavior modification have stressed that the straightforward provision of new information about behavior and the environment may be an overlooked, but perhaps basic, ingredient in most behavior change procedures (Lazarus, 1971; Murray & Jacobson, 1971; Sarason, 1972; Urban & Ford, 1971), one that could profitably be expanded and utilized in a more systematic manner (Sarason, 1972). Students who receive a test anxiety treatment are usually *treated* in a manner based on some reasonably well-developed theory about test anxiety and its alleviation. However, they are not usually provided systematically with the full extent of available *information* about the behavioral and emotional dynamics of test anxiety and techniques for coping with it. In some cases, simply the provision of new and useful information about these matters and the resulting increased awareness regarding their own functioning may enable students to modify their test-anxious behavior. Also, conveying this information in a permanent written form may be not only an economical means of communication, but an effective way to make this information available as a continuing resource to students.

The manual developed for this program was an attempt to present comprehensive information about test anxiety and coping with it to anxious students in a manner most likely to assist them in implementing new coping strategies in the testing situation. The manual included:

1. Guidelines for use of the manual, stressing the use of imagination and fantasy to relate the ideas to personal experience.

2. Several detailed sample "case histories" of test anxiety in college students.

3. A relatively lengthy discussion of different sources of anxiety on tests, namely: (a) lack of ability or preparation; (b) lack of motivation or interest; (c) other emotional or behavioral concerns; or (d) test anxiety proper, defined in terms of habitual autonomic reactions and self-oriented, panicky thinking about oneself and one's performance on tests. Some written exercises provide a self-screening procedure whereby students assess the relative contributions of these factors to their situation and decide about the appropriateness of the program for their current needs.

4. Detailed information about the behavioral and emotional dynamics of test anxiety and about a number of strategies for coping with it. Descriptions,

examples, and diagrams are used to convey techniques for coping with test anxiety that are grouped under four general headings: (a) emotional state; (b) self-oriented versus task-oriented direction of attention; (c) anxiety-arousing self-talk; and (d) the overall management of preparation, time, and other pressures before and during tests.

5. A series of written exercises in which the student outlines personalized strategies for coping with test anxiety in the future. The results of some of these exercises—for example, a personal list of panicky and alternative, calming self-talk—are used in other parts of the semiautomated program.

Three studies were undertaken over a period of two years to investigate the effects of this program. A preliminary study found very promising results in terms of reducing self-reported test anxiety, with some indications of improved performance on module tests for treated students. A second larger-scale study found only very weak treatment effects for students who completed the program as compared with a control group that did not. However, it appeared that certain aspects of the procedure in this study may have led students to feel depersonalized and thus may have reduced the effectiveness of the program. Steps were taken—including a brief initial and concluding interview with a paraprofessional counselor—in a third study to personalize the procedure of completing the program without altering the content of the semiautomated program itself. The results of this study showed very substantial treatment effects, similar to the results of the first study.

The marginally significant improvement in module test scores obtained in the first and third studies might be improved by adding some training in study skills to the program. There is evidence (Allen, 1972) that such training may be necessary if a reduction of test anxiety is to be followed by improved academic performance. This program also might be modified to apply broadly to most types of academic testing situations. It is inexpensive, and a program of this type could be used to impart valuable knowledge and coping skills to an almost unlimited number of interested persons in a wide variety of academic and training settings.

THE POSSIBLE NEAR FUTURE
OF COMPUTER-BASED EDUCATION

One of the major barriers to the implementation of computer-based education is the fragmented nature of the educational market. The financial, marketing, planning, and dissemination expertise of industry have not been brought to bear on the problem. Computer-based educational systems of the future, however, may be able to make progress in the wake of the sophisticated home entertainment video systems that may soon be within the financial reach of most American families.

The embedded microprocessors that make today's video games possible and new video disc systems will make available a sophisticated entertainment and computer-based education system for the home. A video disc, which looks something like a phonograph record, stores both audio and video information. It functions like a random-access videotape. Information is written on the master video disc by a process involving a laser and is read from an inexpensively produced copy by a device also using a laser. Any information that can be represented in binary form can be stored on the disc. Possible applications include: linear video in place of movie films, archival storage with large capacity; and low cost, "books" that include audio, video as well as text, and interactive use with computers. When inexpensive storing of digital information is joined with cheap microprocessing technology (the "computer on a chip" in the now-familiar hand calculator), we will have reached a situation where, in 5 to 8 years, all the components of a first-rate computer-based educational system will be commercially available for less than $500. Only a television screen for display and telephone for a communications link are required to complete the system.

STRESS MANAGEMENT— A COMPREHENSIVE APPROACH

A home (or school) computer-based education system might offer, besides entertainment, an almost indefinitely large array of educational programs. A version of the test anxiety reduction program described earlier might be made widely available through such a system. However, the passage of time, progress in understanding behavior change and the awesome opportunity possibly to influence so many persons make us want to reconsider what sort of programs we might choose to offer students and the public. It occurs to us that many different types of potentially useful programs designed to enhance emotional skills or skills for living might be viewed usefully as facets or dimensions of coping with stress in contemporary society. A basic or introductory program on stress management, which would have a broader and deeper focus than test anxiety as it is usually discussed, might be followed by programs designed to facilitate the application of these principles in particular problem areas.

Many emotional and behavioral difficulties in living (including anxiety about tests) can be viewed as assorted failures in coping effectively with psychological stress. A stress management program (which we might call STRESS for eye-catching purposes) would take advantage of a convergence of ideas around the concept of stress, which makes as much sense to the layperson nowadays as it is beginning to make sense reflectively to medical and social science researchers. Many pernicious influences, from noise to neurosis, can be viewed as putting persons under stress. The stress reaction in psychologically and physiologically similar across individuals, although the symptoms of chronic stress may vary considerably from person to person because of differences in psychological make-up, physical constitution, or current environment.

The STRESS program as we envision it would consist of two main parts or phases. The first of these would attempt to convey information about stress and stressful emotions, especially concerning the recurrent patterns of faulty thinking and defective coping that are the source of those unwanted reactions. The second part of the program would make available to students a variety of training modules designed to teach skills in the self-assessment of problems with stress and in coping with stress more effectively in daily life.

A cognitive-attentional view of test anxiety served as a framework for the development of the semiautomated test anxiety reduction program described earlier. The rationale and much of the content of the STRESS program would derive from a cognitive-behavioral analysis of stress and coping of the sort set forth in *Stress, Sanity,* and *Survival* (Woolfolk & Richardson, 1978). This book is written for laypersons and conveys information and skills for coping with stress.

The first portion of the STRESS program would attempt to convey some key facts about stress and present a relatively simple, easily comprehensible model of the dynamics of stress. This part of the program would most likely consist of a series of video or audio presentations accompanied by a written manual, similar to the test anxiety manual described earlier, that summarizes the information, with diagrams and exercises, for the students' permanent reference and use. An initial tape or series of tapes would present the basic model of stress and cover such points as the following:

1. The adaptive capacities of people create the potential for intellectual and technological achievements that also carry the risk of medical and psychological difficulties relatively unknown in the animal kingdom.

2. The contemporary stress problem consists of low to moderate levels of chronic arousal or tension that often lead to physical illness or psychological distress. Common physical, psychosomatic, and psychological effects are catalogued and described.

3. The psychophysiology of the stress reaction or "fight or flight" response is reviewed. The stress problem is discussed in terms of the body's periodic or chronic preparation for coping with physical dangers that do not any longer exist in most human environments. This response, though inappropriate and dysfunctional, produces chemical and physical alterations that often

eventuate in physical breakdown, psychomatic disease, or debilitating psychological tension.

4. A brief summary of some of the more interesting dimensions of the environment associated with high levels of stress, such as high noise levels and rapid social change, are discussed. It is emphasized, however, that these debilitating environments were created by human beings who may have misperceived their needs or how to most effectively go about meeting them.

5. It is emphasized that stress is not primarily a matter of the automatic pressure of events or physiological reflexes. We are *not* victims of outside events or our own emotional response to them. Rather, the stress response is triggered by *perceptions* of threat, and stress must be defined in terms of our *appraisals* of events. Once the stress reaction is triggered by a perception of threat, it unfolds fairly automatically. But it is possible to prevent the initial triggering of stress by changing the early perceptions of threat and the mistaken beliefs about events or their underlying significance for the individual.

This initial presentation would be followed by tapes or tape series explaining the dynamics of the two primary stressful emotions, anger and anxiety. The presentation on anger would explain and illustrate how anger, especially the kind of chronic irritation that is a prime danger to physical and emotional well-being and adversely affects close relationships, results from perceiving events (usually the action of others) as an infringement upon our "territory" or status, from frustration in terms of reaching urgent goals, or from wrong intentions that in some ways relate to our interests. Thus, anger is caused by perceptions of infringement, frustration, or wrongful intentions on the part of others. The presentation, then, would go on to explore certain styles of living and thinking that predispose persons to such perceptions and resulting angry arousal. These include:

1. *Competitiveness.* Adopting a competitive, win–lose orientation that makes living into a series of contests and tends to put one's self-esteem "on the line" in many life situations.

2. *Moralistic thinking.* Moralizing about how others "should" and "should not" behave; this leads to feelings of anger, frustration, and moral indignation.

3. *Attributional thinking.* Attributing the negative or disappointing behavior of other people to their enduring intentions or basic personality traits, leading to condemnation of others, anger, and moral intolerance.

4. *Low frustration tolerance.* Believing that one has a right to be free from discomfort or deserves to get what one wants, which produces a low tolerance for life's inevitable frustrations and undermines self-discipline.

The next portion of the program would attempt to portray the sources of maladaptive anxiety and tension. Feelings of anxiety would be shown to derive from perceptions of events as threatening to one's self-esteem or emotional security in a relatively immediate and overwhelming manner. Pertinent dimensions of anxious functioning, such as negative self-talk, inappropriate direction of attention, ineffective response to bodily signs of tension, and overevaluative basic beliefs about oneself and the world, would be illustrated and discussed. Certain fundamental mistaken beliefs or assumptions that inevitably lead to perceptions of threat and anxious arousal would be delineated, including beliefs concerning:

1. *Worry.* Holding superstitious beliefs that worry prevents mistakes or misfortune, helps anticipate the future, or gives one added control over the course of events.

2. *Self-evaluation.* Evaluating oneself as less worthy or deserving a person because one falls short of some standard of performance or expectation of others.

3. *Emotional security.* Believing that one's emotional security and the prospect of rewarding relationships are tied to specific people and situations upon which one depends for affection, support, or love.

4. *Inferiority.* Regarding oneself irrationally as inferior or permanently disadvantaged as compared with some other people, making it difficult or impossible for one to lead a satisfying life.

At this point, the student might be asked to take a multiple constructed response quiz concerning the material covered and, based on his or her score, given feedback about the adequacy of his or her understanding of this analysis of psychological stress and its effects.

The second phase of the program would consist of a variety of skill training modules. In one possible version of such a program, an introductory module would help students to learn certain general skills of self-assessment and to select appropriate modules to enhance their own coping with stress. First, it would be explained that the analysis of stress given in the first part of the program implies a threefold approach to minimizing stress: (1) altering the environment or changing the nature of one's interaction with the environment so that events that give rise to stress do not occur (such as managing one's time more effectively); (2) utilizing such techniques as progressive relaxation or meditation to dampen unwanted arousal in a relatively direct manner; or (3) realigning perceptions, altering faulty beliefs, and changing evaluations of the environment or oneself and one's behavior so that perceptions of threat or infringement do not occur in the first place: usually such a shift in attitude must accompany (1) or (2) if they are to be effective.

At the outset of the STRESS program as we currently envision it, students would complete a number of self-report questionnaires designed to assess their levels of anxiety or stress and their current coping repertoires in various areas of living. These would be administered before the program commenced to assist students in selecting skill training modules. These questionnaires might include available instruments to measure general, test, and social anxiety, assertiveness or irrational beliefs. Improved or new instruments could be added as they became available. With these scores on hand, the sequence of activities in the self-assessment part of this introductory module would be as follows:

1. A brief videotape presentation or symbolic modeling of students going through these steps and electing to complete certain skill training modules.

2. Several detailed presentations of typical students receiving feedback concerning their scores on questionnaires of the type mentioned earlier, completing written exercises to further assist them in assessing particular areas of weakness and strength in coping with stress, and finally preparing a personal "stress profile." This presentation might be simply written descriptions of the process for these typical individuals. Or they might be presentations of data concerning these individuals which students utilize, following guidelines, in preparing a "stress profile" for them. The presentations might be more elaborate, e.g., a computer-assisted instruction program in which students interact extensively with a computer, attempting to correctly describe or diagnose the coping skill repertoires of these typical individuals and gauge their predictable consequences for the imaginary persons' functioning.

3. Feedback is given students concerning the results of the questionnaires they completed at the outset of the STRESS program. Students then follow guidelines in interpreting their test scores and completing certain exercises and combine this information into a personal "stress profile" of their own that identifies areas of strength and weakness in dealing with everyday challenges and stress. This part of the module could include instructions to students to identify and self-monitor certain problem behaviors for a period of time or keep a more or less structured "stress diary" in order to gather relevant information for the profile.

4. Following additional guidelines, students would then select skill training modules to remedy deficiencies or enhance areas of coping they currently wish to address. They would also be asked to consider whether the self-assessment procedures may have turned up any personal concerns that might require the attention of a professional therapist and would be given examples of such concerns and guidelines for deciding whether or not to proceed with training modules at this time.

The possibilities for automated or semiautomated, media-based, informational and skill training modules, presented in a computer-based instructional format, are quite extensive. In some instances, such as the teaching of progressive relaxation skills, a fully automated program may be as effective for most persons as live instruction from a professional. In other cases, such as a program for test anxiety reduction, occasional consultation with a live counselor may be desirable. In still other instances, such as programs for increasing social assertiveness skills or skills in dealing with interpersonal conflict, the program may have limited, but significant, preventive or remedial benefits without pretending to accomplish as much as live psychological consultation or psychotherapy.

The following modules, pertinent to the broad topic of coping with stress, would be relatively easy to prepare at present: (1) progressive relaxation; (2) meditation techniques; (3) self-hypnosis and auto-suggestion; (4) resolving interpersonal conflict—issue identification and conflict resolution strategies; (5) time and lifestyle management; (6) changing stress-related beliefs and attitudes; (7) test anxiety reduction; (8) social anxiety reduction; (9) mathematics anxiety reduction; (10) study and test-taking skills; (11) increasing social assertiveness; and (12) career and life planning.

Obviously, there are many ways to divide up skill domains and problem areas and many ways to structure such an array of module offerings. A considerable overlap, possibly leading to overlearning, may be as desirable as it is inevitable. Specific problems or deficits may call for different combinations of modules. Thus, a typical highly test-anxious student may opt for training in relaxation skills through modules 1 and 2 from the aforementioned list, module 5 because the self-assessment turned up the fact that anxiety has bred bad habits of time management in this person's life, module 7 that focuses on undoing the negative cognitive dynamics of test anxiety, and module 10 because of the accumulating evidence that effective and lasting remediation of test anxiety requires restructuring of study habits.

Modalities for presentation of information and training procedures in this hypothetical STRESS program might include audio- and videotape recordings, written materials and exercises, interactive computer-assisted instruction programs of varying complexity, and assigned "homework" or practice activities away from the learning or training center.

Some of the methods for self-assessment and self-directed behavior change that might be utilized in a program of this type to teach coping skills include:

1. Verbal and symbolic modeling of overt and covert coping behaviors of all types—overt actions, dialogue, self-talk (spoken aloud), overt and covert problem-solving activities, and so forth.

2. Instructions in relaxation, meditation, and related techniques.

3. Diary and record keeping of several different types, including the self-monitoring of positive and negative stress-related behaviors.

4. Written exercises of various kinds to assist in self-assessment, decision making, and planning of new coping approaches.

5. Instructions in the use of imagery techniques to reduce stressful emotions and practice new coping skills (a number are described in Woolfolk & Richardson, 1978).

6. Computer-guided practice in various analytical, problem-solving, and other cognitive activities related to improved coping, including integrated assessing of stress-related difficulties and drafting plans for their remediation.

In summary, we are speculating that a generalized stress management training program can be made available to individuals in the context of computer-based learning environments in the home. Thus the opportunity exists to create a feasible mechanism to cope with stress in our contemporary society.

REFERENCES

Allen, G. The behavioral treatment of test anxiety. *Behavior Therapy*, 1972, *3*, 253–262.

Atkinson, R., & Wilson, H. (Eds.). *Computer-assisted instruction: A book of readings.* New York: Academic Press, 1969.

Bandura, A. *Principles of behavior modification.* New York: Holt, 1969.

Campeau, P. Text anxiety and feedback in programmed instruction. *Journal of Educational Psychology*, 1968, *59*, 159–163.

Donner, L., & Guerney, B., Jr. Automated group desensitization for test anxiety. *Behavior Research & Therapy*, 1969, *7*, 1–14.

Hedl, J., & O'Neil, H. Reduction of state anxiety via instructional design in computer-based learning environments. In J. Sieber, H. O'Neil, and S. Tobias (Eds.), *Anxiety, learning, and instruction.* Hillsdale, N.J.: Lawrence Erlbaum Associates, 1977.

Holtzman, W. (Ed.). *Computer-assisted instruction, testing, and guidance.* New York: Harper and Row, 1970.

Lazarus, A. *Behavior therapy and beyond.* New York: McGraw-Hill, 1971.

Levien, R. *The emerging technology: Instructional uses of the computer in higher education.* New York: McGraw-Hill, 1972.

Meichenbaum. D. Cognitive modification of test-anxious college students. *Journal of Consulting and Clinical Psychology*, 1972, *39*, 370–380.

Murray, E., & Jacobson, L. The nature of learning in traditional and behavioral psychotherapy. In A. Bergin and S. Garfield (Eds.), *Handbook of psychotherapy and behavior change.* New York: Wiley, 1971.

Richardson, F. *A self-study manual on coping with test anxiety.* (Tech. Rep.). Austin: University of Texas, Computer-Assisted Instruction Laboratory, 1973.

Richardson, F., O'Neil, H., & Grant, N. Development and evaluation of an automated test anxiety reduction program for a computer-based learning environment. In J. Sieber, H. O'Neil, and S. Tobias (Eds.), *Anxiety, learning, and instruction.* Hillsdale, N.J.: Lawrence Erlbaum Associates, 1977.

Richardson, F., & Suinn, R. A comparison of traditional systematic desensitization, accelerated massed desensitization, and anxiety management training in the treatment of mathematics anxiety. *Behavior Therapy*, 1973, *4*, 212–218.

Sarason, I. Empirical findings and theoretical problems in the use of anxiety scales. *Psychological Bulletin*, 1960, *57*, 403–415.

Sarason, I. Experimental approaches to test anxiety: Attention and the uses of information. In C. D. Speilberger (Ed.), *Anxiety: Current trends in theory and research* (Vol. 2). New York: Academic Press, 1972.

Spielberger, C. The effects of anxiety on complex learning and academic achievement. In C. D. Spielberger (Ed.), *Anxiety and behavior*. New York: Academic Press, 1966.

Spielberger, C. Anxiety as an emotional state. In C. D. Spielberger (Ed.), *Anxiety: Current trends in theory and research* (Vol. 2). New York: Academic Press, 1972.

Straughan, J., & Dufort, W. Task difficulty, relaxation, and anxiety level during verbal learning and recall. *Journal of Abnormal Psychology*, 1969, *74*, 621–624.

Suinn, R., & Hall, R. Marathon group desensitization. *Behaviour Research & Therapy*, 1970, *8*, 97–98.

Suinn, R., & Richardson, F. Anxiety management training: A non-specific behavior therapy program for anxiety control. *Behavior Therapy*, 1971, *2*, 498–510.

Urban, H., & Ford, D. Some historical and conceptual perspectives on psychotherapy and behavior change. In A. Bergin and S. Garfield (Eds.), *Handbook of psychotherapy and behavior change*. New York: Wiley, 1971.

Wine, J. Test anxiety and direction of attention. *Psychological Bulletin*, 1971, *76*, 92–104.

Woolfolk, R., & Richardson, F. *Stress, sanity, and survival*. New York: Sovereign, 1978.

15

Test Anxiety and
the School Environment

Beeman N. Phillips
Gayle D. Pitcher
Murray E. Worsham
Steven C. Miller
The University of Texas at Austin

This chapter examines selected characteristics of the school environment of the test-anxious student. The review emphasizes the basically evaluative nature of the school environment and delineates the point of view that test anxiety is a reaction to evaluative situations, especially test- and test-like situations. Test anxiety is additionally viewed from a motivational perspective, and the motivational effects of test anxiety on children in school are evaluated. The chapter also focuses on research on tests and testing, teachers and teaching behaviors, characteristics of test-anxious children, and other factors associated with test anxiety and its effects in school-like settings.

THE UBIQUITOUS NATURE OF
EVALUATION IN SCHOOL

Every child experiences evaluation in the home, in school, on the playground, and in other settings, although evaluation in school is different in one important respect: tests are given in school more frequently than anywhere else. But tests are not the only form of evaluation in school. The teacher frequently makes judgments about the student's work and behavior, and peers participate in this process, sometimes evaluating the student's effort in a derisive or humiliating way. While this activity is ubiquitous, students generally are aware of "how things are," i.e., whether things are going right in the eyes of the teacher, or badly. When the student is unable to answer a question or work a problem correctly at the blackboard, he often knows how he has handled the situation without the benefit of overt teacher feedback.

These judgments by teachers are communicated with varying degrees of privacy. Papers which have comments on them from the teacher may be seen by parents and other students. In a more private way, teachers may meet with students to discuss their work. But even these private evaluations are sometimes "shared" with parents and other students, as when a student eavesdrops on such meetings or the student involved "reports" on the meeting in some form.

Although it is focused on academic objectives, evaluation also involves institutional expectations and other behavioral domains, including the student's personal qualities. Parents and peers enter into these nonacademic areas, and the student's reputation is to some extent the result of such evaluation by peers. Popularity and peer status are, in fact, heavily influenced by such assessments.

Because teachers, parents, and classmates participate in school evaluations and because academic, behavioral, and personal qualities enter into them, contradictory judgments are the rule. Behavior in some instances may be praised by the teacher and condemned by classmates, further adding to conflicts and disparities. Such disparities may, on the average, be greater for minorities than middle class whites.

THE PREVALANCE AND SIGNIFICANCE OF TEST ANXIETY IN SCHOOL

Teachers, parents, and psychologists worry about test anxiety, and research has emphasized that there is cause to be concerned. Relatively large numbers of children are highly test-anxious, especially minority children, and test and test-like situations are among the highest anxiety-inducing situations in school (Phillips, 1978). Children also report increased levels of test anxiety across the elementary school years, although age trends may stabilize by the end of the elementary school (Hill, 1972).

Children with learning difficulties and school adjustment problems tend to be more test-anxious than other children, and much research points to a linkage between test anxiety and school performance (Hill, 1972; Phillips, 1978; Phillips, Martin, & Meyers, 1972; Ruebush, 1963). Although the usual interpretation is that test anxiety is the causal influence, the relationship is probably reciprocal in nature. That is, anxiety produces motivational, coping, and school task strategies that interfere with learning and performance with the result that performance suffers, and this leads to further increases over time in test anxiety.

Fear of negative evaluation appears to be a key ingredient of test anxiety, and test-anxious children are highly motivated to avoid disapproval (Hill, 1972). This is accompanied by a general narrowing of the range of cue utilization in test- and test-like situations, and such students become more alert to evaluative cues, less alert to task cues, and more concerned about self-worth (Geen, 1976; Katz, Cole, & Baron, 1976; Nottelmann & Hill, 1977; Wine, 1975). When this generalizes to social behaviors, there is a preference to work alone, to engage in less conversational behavior, and to avoid social situations.

Overall, the school environmental antecedents and consequences of test anxiety are complex, depending on a number of school, teacher, and task characteristics. Although this complexity is a challenge to researchers, there still is convincing evidence that test anxiety interferes with learning and performance in school more often than it facilitates such behavior. It is evident, therefore, that learning to cope with test anxiety is a serious problem for the student and for the school.

TEST ANXIETY AS THE MOTIVE TO AVOID FAILURE AND CRITICISM

Hill (1972) has offered an interpretation of childhood anxiety that combines components of both the S. B. Sarason theory of anxiety (Sarason, Davidson, Lighthall, Waite, & Ruebush, 1960) and the Atkinson approach to achievement motivation (Atkinson & Feather, 1966). According to these interpretations, high test anxiety is equated with strong fear of failure and motives to avoid such failure. Hill's conceptualization agrees with S. B. Sarason's theory in that evaluative reactions from adults are believed to underlie and enhance the effects of success/failure experiences. In addition, however, Hill utilizes Atkinson's theory of emphasizing motives to approach success and avoid failure and attempts to delineate the absolute strength of the two motives. Hill asserts that the high-anxious child has a stronger motive to avoid criticism than to attain praise, but that both motives are stronger in the high-anxious child than in the low-anxious child. Hill further explicates motivational dispositions of children of varying levels of test anxiety and suggests that low-test-anxious children are more concerned about succeeding and obtaining approval, whereas high-test-anxious children are more concerned about avoiding failure and disapproval. Hill also proposes that such differential reactions to evaluation may be at the root of the differences in performance achieved by low- and high-anxious children. According to Hill, low-anxious children are task-oriented, more interested in the adequacy of their performance, and less concerned about external evaluation than high-anxious individuals, who are more oriented toward, and responsive to, evaluation by others.

In his review of the test anxiety literature, Hill (1972) cites research which supports his views. Several studies (Marlett & Watson, 1968; Messer, 1970;

Ruebush, 1960) have indicated that high-anxious children take a more cautious approach to problem-solving tasks (i.e., longer decision times and more redundancy) than low-anxious children. These findings were interpreted in relation to the strong motives of high-anxious individuals to avoid failure and criticism. Another line of research (Dusek & Hill, 1970; Marlett & Watson, 1968; Silverman & Waite, 1969) suggests that high-anxious children are more repetitive and restrictive in their response strategies on a button-pushing task during evaluative conditions than in nonevaluative (nonstressful) conditions. Phillips, Martin, and Meyers (1972) have also shown that high school-anxious children approach problem solving in a rigid, stereotypic manner, which would indicate that anxiety interferes with adaptation to different problem-solving strategies in response to the particular demands of a task. These findings are consistent with the avoidance of failure hypothesis.

Other research (Cox, 1966, 1968; Kozma, 1969; Shelton & Hill, 1969) provides support for the notion that high-anxious children are more sensitive to social reinforcement of adults and peers, purportedly because of a strong fear of negative evaluation by others in test-like situations. Several studies in this area (Cox, 1966, 1968; Lepper & Greene, 1975) indicate that observers have the effect of reducing the adequacy of performance of high-anxious children. Such a result would be expected in light of Hill's assertion that high-anxious, in comparison with low-anxious, individuals are more oriented toward evaluation and less oriented toward task performance. It is likely, then, that the performance of high-anxious children is lowered because they are distracted by the presence of an "evaluative" adult observer. Ganzer (1968) found exactly this—that the presence of an observer produced significantly more task-irrelevant responses in highly anxious college students. More recently, another study (Nottelmann & Hill, 1977) found that off-task behavior (frequency and direction of off-task glancing) of high-anxious children was significantly higher than for low- or middle-anxious children. The findings of a study by Steinke (1973), however, indicate not only that observers affect high- and low-anxious students differently but that perceptions of the observer as either positive or neutral also affect performance differently, depending on the anxiety level of the student. With a neutral observer, low-anxious students performed significantly better than high-anxious students, whereas a positive observer led to the high-anxious students' best performance, but a neutral observer led to the low-anxious students' best performance.

The orientation to failure hypothesis, in summary, is a point of agreement across different theoretical perspectives, and it is consistent with much experimental research. Further, it can be employed as a framework in which to view research that seems potentially related to test anxiety but does not include anxiety specifically as a variable.

TEST-ANXIOUS STUDENTS' RESPONSE TO SCHOOL TESTS AND TESTING

A number of researchers have looked at testing conditions in an effort to influence the performance of test-anxious children. For example, evaluative and nonevaluative testing conditions have been compared, and Hill (1972) points out that high-anxious subjects tend to perform as if they perceive both conditions as evaluative in nature, whereas low-anxious subjects tend to respond differentially, with their performance reflecting, to a greater degree, the essential nature of the task, regardless of instructions. Success/failure experience is another variable that has been studied, and although it may seem paradoxical, both success and failure experience seem to have a similar effect on the subsequent performance of high-anxious students, perhaps because, as Hill (1972) notes, both serve to emphasize that the adequacy of performance is being evaluated.

Another approach to examining the effects of test anxiety has been to modify aspects of the test itself. One such intrinsic characteristic of tests that has sometimes been found to make a difference is sequencing of items by level of difficulty. For example, Lund (1953) gave two untimed administrations of parallel tests, one with items in increasing order of difficulty, the other with some difficult items early in the test. The increasing difficulty order produced better scores, which Lund explained by speculating that difficult items early in the exam raised anxiety. Therefore, some of the easier items that came later were missed as a result of the cognitive impariment brought on by anxiety. However, later research does not provide clear confirmation of this apparent effect for ordering. Kestenbaum and Weiner (1970), for example, did not find significant effects for item sequencing alone or in conjunction with test anxiety or achievement motivation.

Other efforts have been made to optimize testing conditions for the anxious child by investigating variations in test instructions and labeling of evaluative situations. In such studies, it has been assumed that different instructions and labels would modify the evaluative threat of a particular test. Bauer (1975) expected different effects for high- versus low-anxious students, using test instructions to label an intelligence test as "intelligence," "achievement," or "routine." Significant results, however, were not found even though the familiar patterns of better scores for low-anxious students were obtained. Yamamoto and Davis (1966) conducted a similar study using "intelligence," "achievement," "routine," and "regular" test descriptions. They also failed to find instruction by anxiety effects. In the Bauer and Yamamoto studies, the tasks were still clearly tests and varied only along dimensions relating to attempts to modify the test taker's perceptions of the nature of the test and the attribute ostensibly being measured.

Caron (1963) administered a test of reading comprehension under "curiosity" and "examination" conditions and took two measures of retention, one rote and the other comprehension. There was no difference for rote learning between anxiety levels under these conditions. However, for the comprehension measure, low-test-anxious subjects performed better than high-anxious subjects in the examination condition and the same as high-test-anxious subjects in the "curiosity" condition. This study indicates that task difficulty should be included as a variable when assessing instruction by anxiety-level interactions.

As with item sequencing effects, it appears that instructions or labels that attempt to modify the evaluative nature of a task can have interactive effects involving test anxiety, but the relationship is not a simple one. The effects are sometimes slight and seem to be heavily dependent on other factors, such as difficulty of the task involved as well as the test-like characteristics of the task.

Sometimes, in fact probably most of the time, it is not possible to present an evaluative task in a nonevaluative manner. Nevertheless, it is possible that some procedures will lessen the effects of anxiety on performance even in clearly evaluative situations. Gaudry and Spielberger (1971) report a study where it was found that the opportunity to make written comments about test items improved test performance for highly anxious subjects. However, this procedure lowered scores of low-test-anxious subjects.

Memory support procedures (e.g., open book tests) also have been found to benefit highly anxious students (Gaudry and Spielberger, 1971). In fact, with memory support, such as access to previous wrong responses, high-anxious subjects sometimes perform better than low-anxious subjects, possibly because of their characteristic penchant for accuracy and correctness. As Hill (1972) notes, this research suggests differences in how high- and low-anxious students attend to tasks, process information, and encode, store, and retrieve information from memory.

Another test characteristic that has been found to relate to anxiety and performance is scoring schemes which correct for guessing, although writers frequently refer to this as a "penalty" for guessing. An early study by Sherriffs and Boomer (1954) investigated the possibility that students who lacked confidence in their own judgment, had difficulties in making decisions, and were easily threatened by ambiguous situations would be disadvantaged by "penalty" for guessing instructions. They used the A Scale of the MMPI, which may be considered a generalized measure of anxiety, and found that students scoring high on the A Scale performed significantly more poorly under the correction-for-guessing condition. They also found that such students omitted more items, overall, as well as proportionately more that they were capable of answering (when given an opportunity to do so later).

In a related study, Bauer (1971) found that instructions not to guess increased the effect of individual differences in risk-taking behavior, whereas advising students to guess minimized this and other individual differences as sources of variation in test performance. As an alternative to correction for guessing, Bauer recommends advising students to try all items. The situation seems to be more complex than that, however, as when a test is highly timed. In this circumstance, advising students to guess at items may lead to hectic responding, without even reading the items, as time runs out. The point that needs emphasis is that such instructions are a source of information about the testing environment, and what needs to be considered is whether such information affects test-taking strategies and test validity as well as whether test-anxious students may be more likely to interpret such instructions in ways which may adversely affect their test scores.

TEACHERS, TEACHING, AND TEST ANXIETY

Considerable research has been stimulated by the role the teacher plays in influencing children's anxiety, in the school setting in general, and in evaluative situations in particular. S. B. Sarason et al. (1960) have hypothesized that test-anxious children's reactions to the test situation are at least partially a reflection of previous similar experiences at home. He further suggests that test anxiety has unconscious as well as conscious elements that are likely to involve strong feelings about parents. These feelings may be transferred to the teacher, especially when children are placed in the position of having their performance evaluated. Teacher-student relations are likely, therefore, to be an important factor in test anxiety and its influence on school performance.

Zimmerman (1970) and Duffey and Martin (1973) studied students' school-anxiety levels, based on Flanders' (1960, 1967) Interactional Analysis (IA) model that permits analysis of teacher-student verbal interaction in terms of specific categories of behavior and provides a measure of classroom "climate." Zimmerman utilized "accepts feelings," "praises and encourages," and "accepts and uses the ideas of students" as positive reinforcers, in contrast to "giving directions," and "criticizing or justifying authority" as aversive stimuli. His results indicated that the "giving directions" category was the best predictor of the school anxiety of students. He further found that the "accepts feelings" and "criticizing or justifying authority" categories were unstable predictors of school anxiety and suggested (as found by Samph, 1968) that observers had the effect of inhibiting teachers' criticizing behavior. Zimmerman concluded that his overall results indicate clearly that the classroom atmosphere is largely determined by teachers' reinforcing behaviors and is directly related to the school anxiety level of students.

Duffey and Martin investigated the effects of direct and indirect teaching and student anxiety on performance on an academic learning task. Their study was also based on Flanders' Interaction Analysis model, focusing on classroom climate as a result of direct or indirect teacher influence. Their predominant finding has practical implications that strongly suggest that high-anxious students will perform better in an "indirect" classroom than they will in a "direct" classroom and that high-anxious students will do better in an "indirect" classroom than low-anxious students.

Doyal and Forsyth (1973) and H. E. Stanton (1974) studied teacher-student interaction in terms of teacher influence on students' test anxiety from a different perspective. Doyal and Forsyth found that the teachers' own anxiety may have an influence on their students' test anxiety, as evidenced by a weak, but positive, correlation between teachers' MAS scores and students' TASC scores. Stanton's study included male as well as female teachers and included both "conventional" and "open" classrooms. His findings did not support those of Doyal and Forsyth. In fact, his only significant results indicated that "the more anxious a male teacher is, the less anxious the boys whom he teaches seem to be," with a similar finding for anxious female teachers and their female students. He found considerably lower TASC scores among children in conventional classrooms than in open classrooms and interpreted this to be a function of the familiarity, and thereby anxiety-reducing quality, of conventional classrooms as well as a result of the greater noise level, more unstructured nature, and the lack of individual attention in open classrooms.

Sellinger (1972), in a similar study reported in Coates and Thoresen (1976) found that:

Test anxiety was lowest among students of high-anxiety teachers in closed organizational climates and next lowest among students of low-anxiety teachers in open organizational climates. Students of low-anxiety teachers in closed organizational climates and high-anxiety teachers in open organizational climates showed more test anxiety than pupils of high-anxiety teachers in closed organizational climates [p. 169].

In these latter three studies, it should be noted that the behavior of teachers was not reported or even observed. Coates and Thoresen (1976) emphasize the need for data on anxious teachers' behaviors that might affect the test anxiety of students rather than more literature focusing on teachers' characteristics, which has led to generally inconclusive results.

TEST-ANXIOUS CHILDREN'S RESPONSE
TO TEACHER EVALUATIVE REACTIONS

Hill (1976) has summarized research involving individual differences in children's response to adult presence and evaluative reactions. Hill discusses findings from research on the effects of adult presence alone, children's response to nonreaction in a structured (school-like) learning situation, and effects of social aspects of adult evaluation. Our purpose in examining these findings is to see if there are any implications that may help to explain the debilitating effects of test anxiety in school performance.

Several studies (Peterson & Whitehurst, 1971; Steinman, 1971) have suggested that appropriate behaviors are increased by an adult's presence or decreased if an adult leaves the situation. Hill (1976) assumes that when a child has had a positive reinforcement history for behaving in a certain way, the presence of an adult will facilitate performance, which is a form of social compliance. On the other hand, if the child had had a history of adult punishment, the adult's presence should inhibit or suppress behavior. We have already seen that the presence of an adult affects children of varying levels of anxiety differently (Hill, 1971; Meddock, Parsons, & Hill, 1971), and in studies by Cox (1966, 1968), high-test-anxious children's performance was detrimentally affected by adult observers, especially when the adult was their teacher. Because of the teachers' overwhelming "presence," plus the many classroom evaluative activities, further research that takes the school reinforcement history of children into account is suggested.

There is some evidence that adult nonreaction is interpreted differently by children of different anxiety levels. Spence (1966) found, with grade school children, that two-choice verbal list learning is more successful under incorrect-blank feedback (where the adult tells the child when he is wrong but says nothing after correct choices) than under right-blank feedback (where the adult tells the child when he is right but says nothing after an incorrect response). Spence interpreted these findings as indicating that children in the right-blank condition interpreted nonreaction from adults as correct and therefore performed poorly. However, in a more recent study (Hill, Emmerick, Gelber, Lazar, & Schickedanz, 1974), children viewed (through a one-way mirror) an adult providing blank, right, or wrong feedback to another adult working on a learning task. Results indicated that, in a situation such as this (their own task performance was not being evaluated), both low- and high-anxious children interpret blank feedback as meaning the opposite of the overt feedback with which it was paired. Hill (1976) has suggested that children who are apprehensive about negative evaluations, such as those who are highly test-anxious, may be less willing to conclude that adult nonreaction (when their own performance is being evaluated) means that they are wrong and more willing to conclude that they are right. Hill's data concerning wrong-blank feedback could possibly be better understood by a naturalistic analysis of the way in which wrong feedback and no feedback are employed by teachers in the classroom. As previously mentioned, Hill has pointed out that high-anxious children, because of their strong fear of criticism and failure, might not realistically interpret feedback from the teacher. That is, they do not interpret teacher reactions similarly when they are, and are not, being evaluated, and such misinterpretation could contribute to the anxious child's characteristically poor performance in the classroom. Another possibility is that the child's anxiety may be a cue used by teachers in their interactions with children so that teachers use different feedback techniques with low- and high-anxious children (Parke, 1976). Both of these interpretations have implications for test anxiety and its effects, and the latter is developed further in the next section.

In summary, the emphasis in research on test anxiety relating to S. B. Sarason and his colleagues' (1960) ideas of dependency needs and fear of failure is paralled by research on both adult reactions and success/failure experiences in the social reinforcement literature. Such a common emphasis would seem to indicate the importance of both social and nonsocial evaluation in children's academic progress and intellectual development. According to Hill, we seek success because of reactions of others.

INTERACTION OF TEST ANXIETY AND OTHER SCHOOL ENVIRONMENTAL FACTORS

The effects of test anxiety in the classroom need to be examined in terms of mutual or reciprocal influences. From a very early age, children and adults interact causally upon one another, and parent-child relations illustrate this mutual or reciprocal action and influence, as when the child's reaction to particular childrearing practices in turn alters these practices. A child's personal characteristics enter into such interactive relations, thus making a consideration of test anxiety pertinent, particularly since research identifies a number of school behavior differences between low- and high-test-anxious children.

Teachers may respond differently to low- and high-test anxious children, as for example, in the ways they use instructional, disciplinary, and social cues. In the Paris and Cairns (1972) study, it was observed that positive evaluations were used more frequently and indiscriminantly and were less contingent upon children's behavior than negative comments. And if, as Parke (1976) points out, the teacher's utilization of these feedback techniques differs with low- and high-test-anxious children, the test-anxious child's response to positive and negative feedback may to some extent be conditioned by such differences. The general point is that the test-anxious child's response to the teacher's instructional, disciplinary, and social cues may be a function of the child's knowledge and expectations about the ways teachers tend to respond to particular kinds of anxiety-related classroom behaviors. This also speaks to the importance of knowing the history of the child's experiences because the child begins to learn to cope with the experience of anxiety at an early age. What is observed later reflects the consequences of such coping, i.e., cognitive and affective processes and interrelationships that, to a considerable degree, are conditioned by adult reactions to earlier manifestations of anxiety. On the basis of this, evidence relating test anxieties to fear of failure, caution in problem solving, dependency behaviors, perceived differences in causes of success and failure, etc., may need to be examined from a more developmental, historical, or longitudinal perspective.

Other aspects of reciprocity that need exploration require that we take a closer look at some of the assumptions underlying testing. One such assumption is that the meaning of test items, instructions, and answers is shared by respondents and testers. Another is that the influence of the testing situation is minimal, and a third is that the tester plays a passive role. In each case, the assumption is questionable, and there is reason to believe that what actually happens may have some influence on how well test-anxious children do on tests.

For example, on many individually administered tests, prompting by the tester is part of the procedure. Whenever the tester cues the student (e.g., "Can you think of other reasons?"), the student usually provides another answer to the item, and it is likely that the practice of prompting after certain initial replies has the consequence of increasing the student's score. We do not know, however, whether testers tend to prompt high-anxious children less than low-anxious children, and if so, what circumstances lead to less cueing. Of course, testers may prompt anxious children more than other children.

Other forms of cueing which also may be important are compliments like "good" and pauses by testers which might serve to "instruct" students to stop answering, thus cutting off potential answers. At this time, we don't know the net effect of these practices on a student's score or whether such tester behavior differs for low- and high-anxious children. Another potential source of differences in the scores of low- and high-test-anxious children is the interpretive process by which students arrive at answers on tests. In other words, wrong answers do not necessarily result from lack of knowledge and may, instead, result from different interpretations of the meaning of test materials.

In summary, in addition to the interactive process by which testers and test-anxious students "jointly" produce answers, such students may view tests differently and employ different strategies in interpreting test items. We therefore need to know more about such differences (if they exist) and how they influence test performance (if they do).

EVALUATION, TEST ANXIETY, AND LEARNED HELPLESSNESS

There is some indication that differences in how low- and high-anxious children perceive the causes of success and failure may be an important cognitive determinant of the effects of anxiety. Weiner, Frieze, Kukla, Reed, Rest, and Rosenbaum (1972) have posed an interesting question regarding success and failure experiences: Do individuals attribute the causes of their successes and failures to internal factors, such as ability and effort, or to external factors? Dweck (1975) and Dweck and Repucci (1973) address this question, suggesting that children's reactions to failure are related to the way in which they interpret failure (whether they attribute it to factors within their control or beyond their control).

In the Dweck and Repucci (1973) experiment, children were given solvable problems by one experimenter (the "success" experimenter) and insolvable problems by a second experimenter (the "failure" experimenter). Children were subsequently given solvable problems by the failure experimenter that were identical to ones that children had previously solved under the success experimenter. Those children who failed to solve the solvable problems or who showed marked decrements in performance under the failure experimenter were those who tended to attribute failure to external factors (e.g., unfairness of the task) or to a specific internal factor—their lack of ability. Dweck (1976) points out that both of these interpretations of failure reflect the child's belief in his inability to change the situation or attain success. Thus, these children are considered to be examples of a phenomenon called "learned helplessness," which is defined as the perception of independence between one's responses and the occurrence or termination of an aversive stimulus (in this case, failure). If anxious children are especially sensitive to aversive events, failure, or negative evaluation, it seems likely that a large portion of test-anxious children might fall into this learned helplessness category. Thus, such patterns of attribution may be relevant to the poor performance of children who are highly anxious and may at least partially account for the debilitating effects of anxiety. If training alters such attributions, as Dweck (1975) has demonstrated, then research is needed to establish this critical link in school situations.

CONTINUED MOTIVATION, EXTERNAL EVALUATION, AND TEST ANXIETY

Another aspect of test anxiety in school situations is suggested by studies on the question of whether performing an intrinsically interesting task for extrinsic reasons will reduce intrinsic interest. Lepper, Greene, and Nisbitt (1973) demonstrated that children who were told that they would be rewarded for good performance on a learning task (previously determined to be intrinsically rewarding) consequently spent significantly less time on the task during free play than did children given unexpected rewards or no rewards at all. Other studies (Deci, 1975; Staw, 1976) confirm these findings on the effect of extrinsic rewards on intrinsic interest.

Such findings are especially significant because they indicate that what happens in the case of extrinsic rewards may also happen in the case of external evaluation. Diggory (1966), in his review of related studies, suggested that the Zeigarnik-like effect—"return in thought or action to the situation where failure was experienced" (Maehr & Stallings, 1972, p. 178)—occurs most frequently when external evaluation is less pronounced. Diggory (1966) points out that "the relative deficiency in the recall of failures (observed in several of the studies reviewed) is a cognitive withdrawal from facts that might tend to decrease self-evaluation [p. 213]." Moreover, Maehr (1967) showed that optimal performance is obtained through the use of extrinsic rewards only in conditions of assured success. However, with uncertainty of outcome and its implied threat of failure, performance is enhanced when extrinsic rewards are minimized and the primary reward is intrinsic to the task.

Maehr and Stallings (1972) provide other evidence to suggest that external evaluation relates to the continuing interest, or continuing motivation, exhibited by students for a task. Continuing motivation was defined by Maehr (1976) as "the tendency to return to and continue working on tasks away from the instructional context in which they were first confronted [p. 443]." Two experiments were conducted in which children performed "easy" and "hard" tasks under test-like conditions (external evaluation) or internal evaluation conditions in which such external evaluation was minimized and emphasis was placed on performing the task for its own sake. Internal evaluation appeared to encourage a continued interest in returning to work on hard tasks, especially in the case of highly motivated students. Continued motivation was not exhibited for hard tasks after the external evaluation condition. Maehr and Stallings (1972) concluded:

> A clearly practical question emerges from these results... Perhaps external evaluation (and contraint in general?) may at times be followed immediately by higher levels of performance... (however) the present results indicate that external evaluation may eventuate in unfortunate motivational outcomes, particularly in the case of those who are inherently oriented to achievement [pp. 184-185].

These assertions and findings have a familiar ring. Similar predictions have been made concerning anxious children from both the Hill and Atkinson theories (Atkinson & Feather, 1966; Hill, 1972; Maehr & Sjogren, 1971). This has been followed by research which indicates high-anxious children will avoid achievement situations in general, quit in the face of failure, and select easy tasks under evaluation. In view of the high-test-anxious individual's strong motive to avoid failure and criticism, it seems reasonable to believe that the effects generally found in regard to continuing motivation would be exaggerated and that test-anxious students' unwillingness to return to and overcome their failures may play a role in their school performance. In Maehr's external evaluation condition, favorable evaluation is less likely, and negative evaluation is more likely, to follow difficult tasks; therefore, anxious children, especially sensitive to such evaluative conditions, may be even less likely to return to externally evaluated, difficult tasks. Furthermore, since almost all school behavior is externally evaluated to some degree, lower continued motivation among anxious students may cause them to have less exposure to, and active involvement with, school tasks, and this may negatively influence their school performance.

Broad implications seem relatively clear. Teachers and techniques that encourage attention to a task in the classroom might, at the same time, discourage continuing interest outside the teacher's domain. It must be emphasized, however, that this tendency has only been studied in relation to external evaluation incentives that were added to learning tasks already of interest to the child. More research pertaining to other tasks would be valuable to better understand the short- and long-term effects of evaluation. Similarly, anxiety theory might suggest how and when some students might exhibit continuing interest, as well as suggesting possible causal relations of low motivation to performance. Although these perspectives readily come to mind, work in this area has not focused on continuing interest in relation to children's anxiety.

NEED FOR A SCHOOL ECOLOGICAL PERSPECTIVE IN TEST ANXIETY RESEARCH

A final issue that needs discussion concerns the ecological validity of the laboratory type of studies that have been common in test anxiety research. This experimental approach has been effective in investigating a wide range of variables associated with test anxiety. What is lacking, however, is a demonstration of the ecological validity of these results and principles. In particular, researchers have failed up to now to show whether these principles apply to the classroom. This is important because applying a school ecological validity viewpoint to test anxiety research can be useful in pointing out areas in need of further research, plus aiding us in understanding and applying current research results and principles.

As an illustration of this point of view, let us examine some elements of the *experimental* situation, in contrast to the *classroom* situation. In the typical experimental situation used in test anxiety research, the child is confronted by a stranger who invites the child to participate in a novel and frequently interesting activity. In this unfamiliar setting, the child is very dependent on, and looks to, the experimenter for information about what behavior is appropriate in the situation. The experimenter also has a high degree of control over alternate responses in the setting. In contrast, in classroom settings, the child's familiarity with the teacher and the activity and the availability of alternate responses makes school situations quite different.

Ecological analysis, therefore, may yield insights on test anxiety that are quite different from those obtained in laboratory settings.

The inherent complexity of test anxiety phenomena in schools is another reason for more emphasis on school ecologically oriented research. For example, it is important to know what sources of school stress, other than test- and test-like situations, contribute to test anxiety. Few investigators have systematically researched school stress, although research reported by Phillips (1978) has examined sources of school stress at the elementary level, revealing some interesting aspects of stress relevant to test anxiety (see, e.g., pp. 35–48 in Phillips, 1978). Many children, for example, report that those children who do poorly on tests the teacher gives lose the approval of the teacher. This is especially true of Mexican-American and black children. In contrast, significant numbers of children cause stress for themselves, in terms of the "negative" reactions of other students, when they are academically successful in school. Again, this is particularly applicable to minority children. Thus, the role of tests in the teacher's encouragement, and evaluation, of excellence creates a dilemma for some children. If they do poorly on tests, they lose their teacher's approval, but if they do well, they lose the approval of some of their peers. Such conflicts are probably much more common than generally realized, and because conflict is a recognized source of anxiety, the role of such conflicting pressures in test anxiety needs more scrutiny.

Although minority children tend to be more test-anxious in the typical school, there is indirect evidence (see Phillips, 1978, pp. 44–48) that some limitations need to be put on such a generalization. In a study of anxiety in several elementary schools where Mexican-Americans varied from their usual minority status to having status as the majority, it was found that the actual minority, whether Mexican-American or Anglo, was more anxious. That is, Mexican-Americans were more anxious in the elementary school which was predominantly middle-class Anglo in student body and cultural orientation, but Anglo children were more anxious in the school where they were the minority. This suggests that minority status, regardless of racial-ethnic status, may be an important factor in some children's stress and test anxiety in schools. From the same study, it also appears that similar situations may elicit more anxiety in some schools than in others, due to the interdependence of such situations, school practices, and aspects of school culture.

As further evidence of the complexity of test anxiety phenomena in the school environment, school socialization and academic achievement experiences in the early grades have markedly different effects as antecedents to anxiety in later grades. In one such study (Phillips, 1978, pp. 100–103), inappropriate conduct in first grade predicted higher anxiety in fourth grade more accurately for girls than for boys, whereas appropriate conduct predicted lower anxiety more accurately for boys than for girls. That is, inappropriate conduct had little apparent effect on the later anxiety of boys, whereas appropriate conduct had little apparent effect on the later anxiety of girls. In contrast, by third grade, the special effects of inappropriate conduct seemed to have dissipated for girls, while by then, appropriate conduct had greatly increased special effects for boys. Various "explanations" can be offered for such sex differences in the role of early school experience in the development of anxiety. In contrast to boys, girls are expected to do well in school, especially in the early grades, so doing poorly may be more threatening and anxiety-producing for a girl. And because of these expectations, doing well does not lead to increased attention, satisfaction, and self-confidence to the degree that it does when a boy does well. Along the same line, when test anxiety is considered as a predictor of academic achievement, racial-ethnic factors figure prominently in results obtained in a racially-ethnically integrated school environment. For example, using a number of predictors, such as locus of control, intelligence, prior achievement, self-perception, social distance, and anxiety, in a racially-ethnically integrated school environment, anxiety was the *best* predictor of reading and mathematics achievement of Mexican-American females. This was true of none of the other racial-ethnic by sex subgroups, although noncognitive factors were relatively more important overall among black and Mexican-American children than among Anglo children (Phillips, 1978).

In summary, in addition to the point made earlier in this section, the laboratory paradigm has led test anxiety researchers to concentrate on proximal and direct antecedents and consequences of test anxiety. In the context of schooling, however, more emphasis needs to be given to indirect and distal factors or factors that are imbedded in the school environment, and that are opaque to superficial observation and analysis.

SOME SCHOOL POLICY IMPLICATIONS

The lines of research reviewed in this chapter to some extent clarify what appear to be subtle, but powerful, influences exerted by aspects of the school environment on test anxiety. Although the focus has been on evaluative aspects of schooling, a variety of social and achievement factors, as well as wide individual differences, enter into school-anxiety relationships. As noted throughout the chapter, further research is needed on the school-related causes and consequences of test anxiety, and such research may have considerable practical as well as theoretical importance.

The research reviewed does provide some general guidelines as to how school practices, interpersonal relations, tests and testing conditions, and other evaluative practices might be handled to minimize the development of test anxiety, and/or to ameliorate its debilitating and interfering effects. In some cases, such efforts would require fundamental changes in school organization, curricular structure, instructional procedures, and educational philosophy. A case in point is external evaluation, which is widespread in the schools. In general, external evaluation, as in teacher grading, has a number of negative effects, such as on continuing motivation and intrinsic interest, and it appears such effects may be exacerbated for the high-test-anxious child. A major goal of such educational change, therefore, might be to decrease the role of external evaluation, while at the same time creating intrinsic interests in school achievement activities where there are none.

Obviously, there are a number of other situational conditions, particularly those imbedded in the evaluation of student performance, that need to be taken into account. The teacher's response to inadequate performance is, for example, an important consideration, as is the teacher's use of disciplinary techniques. Such efforts, however, would require more than the development of specific teaching components, such as strategies of lesson design. Instead, they would require systematic reprogramming of the school learning environment. In essence, in working with test-anxious children, schools will need to emphasize general cognitive, affective, and behavioral "resocialization," attending to modes of thinking, feeling, and acting that are incompatible with school expectations and achievement demands.

Pursuing this goal short of fundamental changes, a number of school intervention approaches have been identified that have potential value in dealing with test anxiety (Phillips, 1978). One approach is to eliminate or modify school stress conditions that contribute to test anxiety and its interfering consequences. Another is to isolate test-anxious children from such stress conditions, at least temporarily, which is an approach that can be utilized with vulnerable children. At the same time, attempts can be made to build up such children's "resistance" to the debilitating effects of stress and test anxiety. This might involve building up the child's self-esteem, reducing test-anxiety-related conflicts, or increasing the child's tolerance for test-induced stress and anxiety. One can also aim at reducing maladaptive reactions to test anxiety, either through efforts to enhance coping behaviors, or by modifying achievement situations and tasks so that formerly debilitating behavior has a less debilitating impact. A number of specific intervention strategies that are pertinent to the problem of test anxiety are discussed by Phillips (1978, Chapter 5), which the reader should consult for more details.

As S. B. Sarason (1972) has pointed out, however, changing the school setting to control, dilute, or eliminate the debilitating effects of test anxiety requires far more than a strong theoretical and empirical base. Nor is it sufficient to have a number of potentially useful and specific intervention strategies in mind. One needs, in addition, a theory of educational change and an understanding of school culture, in conjunction with an in-depth understanding of how to plan and implement school interventions.

REFERENCES

Atkinson, J. W., & Feather, N. T. *A theory of achievement motivation.* New York: Wiley, 1966.
Bauer, D. H. The effect of test instructions, test anxiety, defensiveness, and confidence in judgment on guessing behavior in multiple-choice test situations. *Psychology in the Schools,* 1971, *8,* 208–215.
Bauer, D. H. The effect of instructions, anxiety, and locus of control on intelligence test scores. *Measurement and Evaluation in Guidance,* 1975, *8,* 12–19.
Caron, A. J. Curiosity, achievement and avoidant motivation as determinants of epistemic behavior. *Journal of Abnormal and Social Psychology,* 1963, *67,* 535–549.
Coates, T. J., & Thoresen, C. E. Teacher anxiety: A review with recommendations. *Review of Educational Research,* 1976, *46,* 159–184.
Cox, F. N. Some effects of test anxiety and presence or absence of other persons on boys' performance on a repetitive motor task. *Journal of Experimental Child Psychology,* 1966, *3,* 100–112.
Cox, F. N. Some relationships between test anxiety, presence or absence of male persons, and boys' performance on a repetitive motor task. *Journal of Experimental Child Psychology,* 1968, *6,* 1–12.
Deci, E. L. *Intrinsic motivation.* New York: Plenum Press, 1975.
Diggory, J. C. *Self-evaluation: Concepts and studies.* New York: Wiley, 1966.
Doyal, G. T., & Forsyth, R. A. The relationship between teacher and student anxiety levels. *Psychology in the Schools,* 1973, *10,* 231–233.
Duffey, J. B., & Martin, R. P. The effects of direct and indirect teacher influence and student trait anxiety on the immediate recall of academic material. *Psychology in the Schools,* 1973, *10,* 233–237.
Dusek, J. B., & Hill, K. T. Probability learning as a function of sex of subject, test anxiety, and percentage of reinforcement. *Developmental Psychology,* 1970, *3,* 195–207.
Dweck, C. S. The role of expectations and attributions in the alleviation of learned helplessness. *Journal of Personality and Social Psychology,* 1975, *31,* 674–685.
Dweck, C. S. Children's interpretations of evaluative feedback: The effect of social cues on learned helplessness. *Merrill-Palmer Quarterly,* 1976, *22,* 105–109.
Dweck, C. S., & Repucci, N. D. Learned helplessness and reinforcement responsibility in children. *Journal of Personality and Social Psychology,* 1973, *25,* 109–116.
Flanders, N. A. *Interaction analysis in the classroom: A manual for observers.* Ann Arbor: University of Michigan Press, 1960.
Flanders, N. A. Some relationships among teacher influence, pupil attitudes and achievement. In E. J. Amidon & J. B. Hough (Eds.), *Interaction analysis: Theory, research, and application.* Reading, Mass.: Addison Wesley, 1967.
Ganzer, V. J. Effects of audience presence and test anxiety on learning and retention in a serial learning situation. *Journal of Personality and Social Psychology,* 1968, *8,* 194–199.
Gaudry, E., & Speilberger, C. D. *Anxiety and educational achievement.* Sydney: J. Wiley and Sons Australasia, 1971.
Geen, R. G. Test anxiety, observation, and range of cue utilization. *British Journal of Social and Clinical Psychology,* 1976, *15,* 253–259.
Hill, K. T. *Social determinants of imitation: The questions of direction and generality of effects.* Paper presented at the biennial meeting of the Society for Research in Child Development, Minneapolis, Minn., April 1971.

Hill, K. T. Anxiety in the evaluative context. In W. W. Hartup (Ed.), *Young Child* (Vol. 2). Washington, D. C.: National Association for the Education of Young Children, 1972.

Hill, K. T. Individual differences in children's response to adult presence and evaluative reactions. *Merrill-Palmer Quarterly*, 1976, *22*, 99–104.

Hill, K. T., Emmerick, H. T., Gelber, E. R., Lazar, M. A., & Schickedanz, D. Children's interpretation of adult non-reaction: A trial-by-trial self-report assessment and evidence for contrast effects in an observational context. *Journal of Experimental Child Psychology*, 1974, *17*, 482–494.

Katz, I., Cole, O. J., & Baron, R. M. Self evaluation, social reinforcement, and academic achievement of black and white schoolchildren. *Child Development*, 1976, *47*, 368–374.

Kestenbaum, J. W., & Weiner, B. Achievement performance related achievement motivation and test anxiety. *Journal of Consulting and Clinical Psychology*, 1970, *34*, 343–344.

Kozma, A. The effects of anxiety, stimulation, and isolation on social reinforcer effectiveness. *Journal of Experimental Child Psychology*, 1969, *8*, 1–8.

Lepper, M. R., & Greene, D. Turning play into work: Effects of adult surveillance and extrinsic rewards on children's intrinsic motivation. *Journal of Personality and Social Psychology*, 1975, *31*, 479–486.

Lepper, M. R., Greene, D., & Nisbett, R. Undermining children's intrinsic interest with extrinsic reward: A test of the "overjustification hypothesis." *Journal of Personality and Social Psychology*, 1973, *28*, 129–137.

Lund, K. W. *Test performance as related to the order of item difficulty, anxiety, and intelligence.* Unpublished doctoral dissertation, Northwestern University, 1953.

Maehr, M. L. *Competence revisited.* Paper presented at American Educational Research Association, New York, 1967.

Maehr, M. L. Continuing motivation: An analysis of a seldom considered educational outcome. *Review of Educational Research*, 1976, *46*, 443–462.

Maehr, M. L., & Sjogren, D. D. Atkinson's theory of achievement motivation: First step toward a theory of academic motivation? *Review of Educational Research*, 1971, *41*, 143–161.

Maehr, M. L., & Stallings, W. M. Freedom from external evaluation. *Child Development*, 1972, *43*, 177–185.

Marlett, N. J., & Watson, D. Test anxiety and immediate or delayed feedback in a test-like avoidance task. *Journal of Personality and Social Psychology*, 1968, *8*, 200–203.

Meddock, T. D., Parsons, J. A., & Hill, K. T. Effects of an adult's presence and praise on young children's performance. *Journal of Experimental Child Psychology*, 1971, *12*, 197–211.

Messer, S. The effect of anxiety over intellectual performance on reflection-impulsivity in children. *Child Development*, 1970, *41*, 723–735.

Nottelmann, E. D., & Hill, K. T. Test anxiety and off-task behavior in evaluative situations. *Child Development*, 1977, *48*, 225–231.

Paris, S. G., & Cairns, R. B. An experimental and ethological analysis of social reinforcement with retarded children. *Child Development*, 1972, *43*, 717–729.

Parke, R. D. Social cues, social control, and ecological validity. *Merrill-Palmer Quarterly*, 1976, *22*, 111–123.

Peterson, R. F., & Whitehurst, G. J. A variable influencing the performance of generalized imitative behaviors. *Journal of Applied Behavioral Analysis*, 1971, *4*, 1–9.

Phillips, B. N. *School stress and anxiety.* New York: Human Sciences Press, 1978.

Phillips, B. N., Martin, R. P., & Meyers, J. School-related interventions with anxious children. In C. D. Spielberger (Ed.), *Anxiety: Current trends in theory and research* (Vol. 2). New York: Academic Press, 1972.

Ruebush, B. K. Interfering and facilitating effects of test anxiety. *Journal of Abnormal and Social Psychology*, 1960, *60*, 205–212.

Ruebush, B. K. Anxiety. In H. W. Stevenson, J. Kagan, & C. Spiker (Eds.), *Sixty-Second Yearbook of the National Society for the Study of Education, Part I: Child Psychology*. Chicago: University of Chicago Press, 1963, 460–517.

Samph, T. *Observer effects on teacher behavior.* Unpublished doctoral dissertation, University of Michigan, 1968.

Sarason, S. B. Anxiety, intervention, and the culture of the school. In C. D. Spielberger (Ed.), *Anxiety: Current trends in theory and research* (Vol. 2). New York: Academic Press, 1972.

Sarason, S. B., Davidson, K. S., Lighthall, F. F., Waite, R. R.,& Ruebush, B. K. *Anxiety in elementary school children: A report of research.* New York: Wiley, 1960.

Sellinger, S. An investigation of the effects of organizational climate and teacher anxiety on test anxiety of elementary school students. (Doctoral dissertation, New York University, 1972). *Dissertation Abstracts International, 1972, 32,* 5515A. (University Microfilms No. 72-11494)

Shelton, J., & Hill, J. P. Effects on cheating of achievement anxiety and knowledge of peer performance. *Developmental Psychology,* 1969, *1,* 449–455.

Sherriffs, A. C., & Boomer, D. S. Who is penalized by the penalty for guessing? *Journal of Educational Psychology,* 1954, *45,* 81–90.

Silverman, I. W., & Waite, S. V. Test anxiety and the effectiveness of social and nonsocial reinforcement in children. *Child Development,* 1969, *40,* 307–314.

Spence, J. T. Verbal discrimination performance as a function of instructions and verbal-reinforcement combinations in normal and retarded children. *Child Development,* 1966, *37,* 269–281.

Stanton, H. E. The relationship between teachers' anxiety levels and the test anxiety level of their students. *Psychology in the Schools,* 1974, *11,* 360–363.

Staw, B. M. *Intrinsic and extrinsic motivation.* (University Programs Modular Series). Morristown, N. J.: General Learning Press, 1976.

Steinke, J. M. Paired associate learning as a function of test anxiety and audience effects. (Doctoral dissertation, Northern Illinois University, 1973). *Dissertation Abstracts International,* 1973, *34,* 1265B. (University Microfilms No. 73-20, 564).

Steinman, W. M. *The effect of instructions, discrimination difficulty and methods of assessment on generalized imitation.* A symposium paper presented at the biennial meetings of the Society for Research in Child Development, Minneapoilis, Minn., 1971.

Weiner, B., Frieze, I., Kukla, A., Reed, L., Rest, S., & Rosenbaum, M. R. Perceiving the causes of success and failure. In E. E. Jones, D. Kanouse, H. H. Kelley, R. E. Nisbett, S. Valins, & B. Weiner (Eds.), *Attribution: Perceiving the causes of behavior.* Morristown, N.J.: McCaleb-Seiler, 1972.

Wine, J. D. Test anxiety and helping behavior. *Canadian Journal of Behavioral Science,* 1975, *7,* 216–222.

Yamamoto, K., & Davis, O. L. Test instructions, test anxiety, and dependence proneness in relation to children's performance on a test of intelligence. *Psychology in the Schools,* 1966, *3,* 167–170.

Zimmerman, B. J. The relationship between teacher class behavior and student school anxiety levels. *Psychology in the Schools,* 1970, *7,* 89–93.

IV OVERVIEW

16 Cognitive-Attentional Theory of Test Anxiety

Jeri Dawn Wine
Ontario Institute for Studies in Education
Toronto, Ontario, Canada

The nature of test anxiety literature has changed markedly in the last decade. In 1971, I reviewed the literature and noted that: (1) the majority of investigators in the area had adopted an emotional reactivity interpretation of test anxiety, an interpretation which had guided most research efforts; and (2) the bulk of the test anxiety literature, with a few notable exceptions, had been devoted to demonstrating the debilitating effects of test anxiety as contrasted with efforts to alleviate these debilitating effects. A good deal of evidence was marshaled in the earlier review to support cognitive and attentional interpretations of the nature and effects of test anxiety. It was recommended that test anxiety research might fruitfully be guided by cognitive analyses in further examination of the concomitants and effects of test anxiety. It was also strongly suggested that test anxiety investigators, in experimental laboratory, educational, and treatment research, turn to a search for means of alleviating the negative effects of test anxiety. The contents of the present volume reflect these caveats with regard to the more recent test anxiety experimental and educational literature, though perhaps less so in the treatment research literature.

Prior to moving into an overview of the recent test anxiety work, which is thoroughly and competently reviewed by the contributors to this volume, several observations are in order regarding the earlier research. The characteristic focus of the early literature on emotional reactivity is due partially to the mechanistic nature of the Hullian drive theory on which the original test anxiety theory was based (Mandler & S. Sarason, 1952; S. Sarason, Mandler, & Craighill, 1952). However, the sophistication of early test anxiety theory as a harbinger of current theoretical constructs in this area should not be minimized. These theorists identified a class of task-irrelevant responses evoked by evaluating conditions as the major characteristic differentiating high- from low-test-anxious persons; these task-irrelevant responses were viewed as elicited by an anxiety drive, and it is this component that has attracted most experimental efforts. The theoretical assumptions that evaluation evoked a high drive level in *both* low- and high-test-anxious individuals and that only the associated response classes differed received surprisingly little research attention. Alpert & Haber's (1960) Facilitating and Debilitating Anxiety constructs were noteworthy exceptions. Early investigators seemed wedded to the assumption, often implicit, that anxiety level was equivalent to emotional arousal.

The second major characteristic of the early research, that of focusing upon the debilitating effects of test anxiety, was a result of the construct validation nature of this work. It was essential in the early research to demonstrate the debilitating effects of test anxiety on cognitive task performance and its interaction with theoretically relevant experimental conditions varying on an evaluative dimension, such as instructional manipulations, feedback conditions, task difficulty, audience presence, etc. Highly test-anxious persons were expected to perform most poorly under conditions of high evaluative stress and at their optimum when evaluation was minimized, whereas the reverse was expected to hold true for low-test-anxious persons. The test anxiety–evaluative-stress interaction has now been amply documented in a large body of research. Indeed, with adolescent and adult populations, it has assumed the status of an empirical generalization. Children are a bit more difficult to deceive with superficial situational manipulations. Children seem to know a test when they see one! (See Phillips, Pitcher, Worsham, & Miller, Chapter 15). At any rate, the test anxiety–evaluative-stress interaction was amply researched in the earlier literature. The present book reflects the changing thrusts of test anxiety research to cognitive interpretations of the nature and effects of test anxiety and to examination of means for alleviating its negative effects.

In providing an overview for this volume, I have not presented a systematic and discrete critique of each chapter. Instead, I have attempted to organize the evidence and observations presented in these review chapters within a framework that I consider reflects the current Zeitgeist of test anxiety theory and research alluded to in the preceding paragraph. The framework reflects, of course, my own theoretical biases, but I'm gratified to find that these have been amply supported by the recent literature. My "current concern" (Klinger, 1977; Meichenbaum, Chapter 9) is for theoretical constructs, experimental conditions, educational and treatment approaches that show promise for alleviating the negative effects of test anxiety. In the context of this overriding "current concern," I am concerned with evidence regarding further delineation of a cognitive interpretation of test anxiety.

The remainder of the chapter is organized as discussions of the following issues: (1) problems involved in the definition and measurement of test anxiety; (2) the cognitive and behavioral concommitants of test anxiety, with emphasis on the former; (3) approaches to alleviating the negative effects of test anxiety, including experimental, educational, and treatment approaches; (4) presentation of a bidirectional model of test anxiety, with suggestions for characteristics of low- as well as high-test-anxious individuals; and (5) implications for further research and theoretical development.

THE TEST ANXIETY CONSTRUCT: DEFINITION AND MEASUREMENT

At the outset, I will make the heretic declaration that I consider the label "test *anxiety*" to be one which has outlived its usefulness; it is a term that should become obsolete with further theoretical and measurement advances in this field. "Anxiety" is an omnibus term, with much surplus meaning, defined quite differently by investigators of varying theoretical persuasions. The common denominator in these definitions, that of emotional or physiological reactivity, does not capture the most outstanding differences between persons who score at extremes on test anxiety measures. These differences lie in the nature of cognitive structures (Meichenbaum, Chapter 9), the phenomenology of consciousness (Sieber, Chapter 2), and the relative presence of worry (Deffenbacher, Chapter 6). As Holroyd and Appel have amply documented (Chapter 7), tonic measures of physiological reactivity are not related to test anxiety level. Though highly test-anxious individuals report that they experience higher levels of physiological reactivity than do low-test-anxious persons, these data reflect differences in "contents of consciousness" rather than actual tonic reactivity. Holroyd makes provocative suggestions regarding possible differences in patterning of physiological reactivity between high- and low-test-anxious individuals, but these suggestions are closely tied to cognitive-attentional analyses. It may be time for test anxiety researchers to attend to Sarbin's (1968) caveat to delete the word "anxiety" from our psychological vocabulary and use more specific descriptive terms such as "worry"—certainly a directive appropriate to test anxiety.

Moreover, "*test* anxiety" is misleading—though not as seriously so as is the case with "anxiety." Persons who score high on measures of test anxiety are ones who typically interpret a wide range of situations as evaluative and react with cognitive concern and performance deficits. Perhaps Rosenberg's (1965) term "evaluation apprehension" is a more accurate label, although there would be problems with its use because it is associated with another research tradition and methodology. I have recently proposed the term, "evaluation anxiety: a cognitive–attentional construct" (Wine, in press-a). This label is, of course, cumbersome and does not escape the most telling criticisms I've mentioned.

Because this is the concluding chapter of a volume on "test anxiety," I will adhere to the traditional label in the remainder of the chapter. The broad operational definition governing my use of the term is that adopted in my 1971 review paper, "...the terms 'high test anxious' and 'low test anxious' refer to persons who score at extremes on measures of debilitating test anxiety...[p. 93]." Characteristics of specific test anxiety measures are discussed later.

There is a bewildering array of measurement devices available to the test anxiety researcher that differs considerably on several dimensions. The following discussion is not intended as an exhaustive delineation of these dimensions and their use in the description of various test anxiety scales, but rather as illustrative of the measurement issues in the area. The first dimension concerns the type of individual reaction that is tapped by a given scale—for example, cognitive reactions and emotional responsivity. As a rule of thumb, the earlier the scale was developed, the more likely it is to be an omnibus measure yielding only total scores, not separate ones for these components. For example, the TASC (S. Sarason, Davidson, Lighthall, Waite, & Ruebush, 1960), the earliest test anxiety measure for children and still the one most widely used, is a multidimensional scale, which typically is used only in terms of its total score (see Dusek, Chapter 5). The TAS (I. Sarason, 1972-a) contains items that might be scored separately for cognitive concern and emotionality, but it has not been scored in this manner. Spielberger, Gorsuch, and Lushene's (1970) Trait Anxiety Inventory (though not strictly a test anxiety questionnaire, it has been frequently used in this fashion) is primarily an emotionality measure but contains a few items which might be scored for cognitive concern. The STABS (Suinn, 1969) and the MARS (Richardson & Suinn, 1972) are both explicit self-reports of emotional arousal in response to specific evaluating situations, an observation to which I return in discussing the test anxiety treatment literature. There is implicit cognitive theory underlying Alpert and Haber's (1960) facilitating and debilitating anxiety scales of the AAT, which might be described as the nature of the interpretation which individuals place on emotional reactivity. Deffenbacher (Chapter 6) describes more recent measures designed explicitly to tap separately the Worry and Emotionality components of test anxiety (Liebert & Morris, 1967; Osterhouse, 1972).

A second major dimension on which test anxiety scales vary considerably is that of the nature and specificity of the evaluating situations to which respondents report their anxiety-related responses. The most general measure, the Trait Anxiety Inventory, (Spielberger et al., 1970) does not refer at all to specific situations. The TASC refers to a wide variety of situations (see Dusek Chapter 5, for specific factors) ranging from items specific to test taking, to anticipatory reactions to examinations expected the next day, to being called upon to recite in class, to *dreaming* about school evaluating situations. Phillips's (chapter 15) School Anxiety Inventory is even more broadly based with regard to school-related stimulus situations. Items of the AAT are very specific to academic examinations, whereas the STABS taps reactions to a wide range of academically related evaluating situations. The MARS assesses anxiety responses specifically to math-related activities, but a wide range of such situations are represented.

Test anxiety inventories also vary in the extent to which they are designed to measure general dispositions versus situational reactions. (I will avoid Spielberger's state–trait terminology because this dimension is one that may be used to describe measures other than those derived from his theoretical position.) Most test anxiety measures are of the general dispositional type. Spielberger's State Anxiety Inventory might be considered a representative of the situational reaction type of inventory, though again it must be noted that the STAI is not strictly a test anxiety measure because it does not refer to evaluative stimulus situations.[1] Perhaps the most outstanding of the situational reactivity measures is Liebert and Morris' Worry-Emotionality questionnaire, (1967) which has contributed so heavily to theoretical advancements in this field (Deffenbacher, Chapter 6).

An obvious dimension, which I will not expand upon, is that of the age group and educational level for which inventories have been designed. The purpose of this brief discussion of dimensions of test anxiety inventories is to alert investigators to issues in choosing instruments for subject selection and assessment. The instrument selected should be appropriate to the sample and to the theoretical and applied issues under examination. The test anxiety researcher should be prepared to define in specific terms what he or she means by the label "test anxiety." The contents of this volume indicate that such definitions, and related measurement devices, are likely to become more cognitive in nature.

The second major purpose of this section is to note the limitations of existing measures of test anxiety. These devices have been designed to measure the relative presence of test anxiety, however that construct may be defined by the originator of each measure. As Meichenbaum has noted (Chapter 9), they tell us virtually nothing about the low-test-anxious individual. Given the purpose of test anxiety questionnaires to measure the *presence* of test anxiety, it seems likely that low-test-anxious persons may differ from each other in many more ways than high-test-anxious persons, e.g., ranging from a total lack of concern or motivation regarding evaluation to supreme self-confidence or very high levels of self-efficacy (see Rosenthal,

---

[1]Spielberger (1978) is developing a measure of test anxiety, the Test Anxiety Inventory.

Chapter 11) regarding evaluating situations. As Tobias (Chapter 13) has noted, test anxiety measures increase in their predictive powers when used in combination with measurement devices which assess positive orientations to evaluation, such as n Ach. A measure recently developed by one of my colleagues, the Measure of Academic Self-Efficacy (Lalonde, 1979) may prove to have similar power in combination with test anxiety devices.

Moreover, as Meichenbaum's provocative theoretical discussion has pointed out, test anxiety measures do not even tell us much about the highly test-anxious individual. Though the evidence indicates that the "contents of consciousness" of high- and low-test-anxious individuals differ and that highly test-anxious persons react with worry and self-reports of high emotional reactivity to evaluating situations, we know little about the nature of the worry or the cognitive structures associated with it. There is a need for measurement devices which provide us with more information with greater specificity regarding the cognitive strategies and structures and the contents of consciousness of high- as well as low-test-anxious persons. I. Sarason and Stoops's (1978) Cognitive Interference Questionnaire (see Chapter 1) shows some promise in this regard, though to date it has yielded only a single global score. In the assertiveness literature, Schwartz and Gottman (1976) have devised a Self-Statement Questionnaire regarding specific situations which might readily be adapted for use by test anxiety researchers. Meichenbaum (1976) has described a variety of cognitive assessment techniques designed to tap thought processes. As a final note of caution, test anxiety researchers should not make the mistake of equating thought with language (Christensen, 1978). Imagery, kinesthetic as well as visual, may reveal major differences between high- and low-test anxious individuals, an observation that I return to in a later section.

COGNITIVE AND BEHAVIORAL CONCOMITANTS OF TEST ANXIETY

In this section, research bearing upon or derived from cognitive-attentional interpretations of test anxiety is discussed. In addition, research on the overt behavioral concomitants of test anxiety is referred to in the context of these data contributing to cognitive interpretations of test anxiety. I have attempted to avoid simply reiterating the conclusions reached by the contributors of the various chapters related to these issues but rather have searched for common theoretical and evidential trends across chapters.

The section is organized in the following fashion:

1. The evidence which bears upon the self-preoccupied direction of attention of highly test-anxious persons in comparison to low-test-anxious

individuals (an hypothesis I advanced in my 1971 review paper) is briefly summarized.

2. The evidence regarding the relationship between test-anxiety level and attention to task-related cues (evidence which is reviewed in detail in Geen's chapter, with additional data presented by Dusek) is summarized. Reference is also made to Mueller's work on memory processes and test anxiety.

3. A similar, though briefer, discussion regarding the differential attention of high- and low-test-anxious individuals to social-evaluative stimuli is presented. Several contributors have discussed evidence bearing on this issue, including Tobias, Geen, Phillips et al., and Dusek.

4. Two chapters have considered attribution theory analyses of differences between high- and low-test-anxious persons (Geen, Phillips et al.). These analyses are summarized, and an additional attribution theory construct, the actor–observer distinction, is proposed as a useful theoretical addition to the analysis of test anxiety.

5. Finally, the evidence regarding overt behavioral differences between high- and low-test-anxious individuals that contributes to the cognitive-attentional framework emerging from the preceding discussion is summarized. This evidence is referred to by Tobias and Dusek in this volume and includes data from two studies I've recently reported (Wine, 1975, in press-b).

The Direction of Attention Hypothesis

Highly test-anxious individuals typically perform more poorly on cognitive tasks than less anxious individuals, especially if the tasks are difficult and are given under situational conditions of evaluative stress. The direction of attention hypothesis states that the explanation for this performance difference lies in the different attentional focuses of high- and low-test-anxious persons in evaluative conditions, with the test-anxious individual dividing attention between self-preoccupied worry and task cues and the less anxious person focusing more fully on task-relevant variables. The research bearing upon this hypothesis was extensively discussed in my earlier review paper (Wine, 1971); additional evidence was presented by I. Sarason (1976); and I have recently presented a thorough update of the most recent research (Wine, in press-a) bearing upon the hypothesis. Consequently, only a brief summary is presented in the following paragraph.

Evidence regarding the self-preoccupation of test-anxious persons is provided by a number of studies. Highly test-anxious individuals tend to be generally negatively self-preoccupied, describing themselves in self-devaluing terms on other paper and pencil measures (I. Sarason, 1960; Many & Many, 1975) as well as in oral interview situations (I. Sarason & Ganzer, 1962, 1963; I. Sarason & Koenig, 1965). When being evaluated while performing tasks, they are likely to report a greater incidence of non-task relevant thoughts than low-test-anxious persons (Mandler & Watson, 1966; Marlett & Watson, 1968; Neale & Katahn, 1968; I. Sarason & Stoops, 1978). They are more likely than low-test-anxious persons to attribute responsibility to themselves for task failure (Doris & S. Sarason, 1955), to set lower levels of aspiration even when actual task performance does not differ (Trapp & Kausler, 1958), and to have less confidence in their perceptual judgments (Meunier & Rule, 1967). Their self-preoccupation during task performance is evidenced by a higher incidence of task-irrelevant comments, mostly of a self-deprecatory nature, when completing an oral verbal learning task (Ganzer, 1968).

The Worry–Emotionality analysis of test anxiety (Liebert & Morris, 1967), though developed independently of the direction of attention hypothesis, is a closely related theoretical development. These authors have analyzed test anxiety into the two components of Worry, defined as cognitive concern over performance, and Emotionality, or the autonomic arousal aspect of anxiety. The research bearing upon the Worry–Emotionality analysis is reviewed in detail by Deffenbacher in Chapter 6. In brief, the evidence indicates that Worry is the more stable, enduring component of test anxiety, whereas self-report of Emotionality has a more transient quality and is confined to evaluating situations. Worry interacts with other cognitive variables and bears a consistent, negative relationship to cognitive performance and to performance expectancies; Emotionality does not relate consistently to these variables. Thus it is the cognitive, self-preoccupied Worry component of test anxiety that interferes most directly with task performance. As Holroyd and Appel (Chapter 7) have noted, the higher self-reported levels of Emotionality on the part of high-test-anxious persons also probably reflect greater attention to internal events as opposed to externally directed task-focused attention.

Test Anxiety and Task-Related Cues

Easterbrook's (1959) arousal–cue-utilization hypothesis, which states, in part, that anxiety reduces the range of task cues utilized in task performance, has been investigated in several test anxiety studies. Geen presents an excellent review of this literature in Chapter 3. In addition, Dusek (Chapter 5) reports several relevant studies. The cue-utilization hypothesis as applied to test anxiety predicts that the range of task cues utilized in performance will become progressively narrower or smaller as the level of test anxiety rises. The evidence from different investigations appears at first blush, to be contradictory.

Geen reviews a number of studies that are clearly supportive of the hypothesis. The methodology used in most of these studies involved embedding cues within task materials that were either directly relevant to effective task performance (i.e., if attended to, they would enhance task performance) or irrelevant to task performance (i.e., if attended to, they would lower task performance). In each of these studies, the performance levels of low-test-anxious subjects reflected the presence of the added task cues more than did the performance levels of high-test-anxious subjects; i.e., the performance of the low-test-anxious persons was facilitated more by the addition of relevant task cues and debilitated more by the addition of irrelevant cues. The performance of the low-test-anxious subjects reflected a wider range of task cue utilization in accordance with the Easterbrook hypothesis.

The evidence contradictory to the cue-utilization hypothesis comes largely from investigations that utilized quite different methodologies, as well as younger samples. In two of these studies discussed in detail by both Dusek and Geen (Dusek, Kermis, & Mergler, 1975; Dusek, Mergler, & Kermis, 1976), measures of incidental learning were intended to reflect range of cue utilization. Children differing in level of test anxiety were instructed to learn the positions of line drawings of animals presented serially on cards—the central task. Each card also contained drawings of figures that the child was not instructed to learn—the incidental task. In general, the low-anxious children performed better on the central task; the high-anxious children scored better on the incidental task. Another study cited as related to the attentional range of children varying in test anxiety (Nottelman & Hill, 1977) reported that high-test-anxious children glanced away from an anagram task that they were working on more frequently than did middle- or low-test-anxious children.

Geen cites Wachtel's (1967) flashlight analogy regarding attention as a possible explanation for these results; i.e., anxiety level may reduce the width of the flashlight beam while simultaneously increasing the range of stimuli scanned. Another reasonable interpretation relates to the contrasting methodologies used in these studies. In those investigations supporting the test anxiety–cue-utilization hypothesis, the additional cues were embedded in the task materials, and thus were likely to be viewed by the subjects as an integral part of the task. In the incidental learning studies and the Nottelman and Hill study, the peripheral cues were not integral to the task that the subjects were performing. Attention to these cues may have represented a general task-avoidant strategy on the part of the high-test-anxious subjects. Moreover, there is some indication that the greater attention to peripheral cues is most likely to occur among younger test-anxious subjects. One is tempted to consider Luria's developmental theory regarding the gradual internalization of behaviors; test anxiety in young children may be associated with overt avoidant behaviors, but with increasing age, these avoidant behaviors may become covert and internalized.

Mueller (Chapter 4) has reported several studies, utilizing memory methodology, that bear upon the specific cognitive-attentional deficiencies associated with test anxiety. He has proposed that highly test-anxious subjects, in comparison to low-test-anxious subjects, utilize fewer stimulus attributes in encoding for memory, a hypothesis closely akin to the cue-utilization hypothesis. In support, he has demonstrated that test anxiety affects organizational processes during free recall, with highly test-anxious subjects clustering less than low-test-anxious subjects across a number of categories as well as showing less subjective organization. They also showed less immediate recall as well as a deficiency in using subtle cues to mediate from one stimulus category to another.

Test Anxiety and Attention to Social-Evaluative Cues

A number of the reviewers in this volume have noted evidence that bears upon the greater attentiveness of highly test-anxious persons as compared to lows with regard to social-evaluative cues (Dusek, Chapter 5; Geen, Chapter 3; Phillips et al., Chapter 15; Tobias, Chapter 13). Most of these reviewers have referred to Hill's (1972) conceptualization as outlined by Phillips et al., Chapter 15 of this volume, as follows:

> that the high anxious child has a stronger motive to avoid criticism than to avoid success, but that both motives are stronger in the high anxious child than the low anxious child . . . Low anxious children are task-oriented, more interested in the adequacy of their performance and less concerned about external evaluation than high anxious individuals, who are more oriented toward, and responsive to, evaluation by others [p. 329].

The nature of the evidence marshaled to support the greater attentiveness to social-evaluative cues associated with high test anxiety is of several kinds, including studies with both children and adults and in both laboratory settings and naturalistic settings. Dependent measures have included cognitive task performance, conformity in perceptual judgments, oral interview behaviors, and observation of visual behavior. The nature of the social-evaluative cues that have been examined are success and failure manipulations, verbal reinforcement, cues presented via models, and the mere presence of other persons.

In brief, the evidence from these studies indicates that both success and failure manipulations have greater impact on the subsequent performance of high-test-anxious subjects that on that of the lows (Weiner, 1966; Weiner & Schneider, 1971). Observation of models performing tasks has more powerful effects on the subsequent task performance of high-test-anxious subjects as compared to low-test-anxious subjects (I. Sarason, 1968, 1972a, 1973, 1975a; I. Sarason, Pederson, & Nyman, 1968). The nature of the impact of modeling on the highly test-anxious person's performance varies with model characteristics. Some of these data are discussed in a subsequent section. Highly test-anxious subjects are very responsive to verbal reinforcement of specific response classes in oral interview situations (I. Sarason & Ganzer, 1962, 1963). The range of task cues utilized in cognitive task performance of highly test-anxious persons has been demonstrated by Geen (1976) to be narrowed by the presence of observers more than that of low-test-anxious individuals. In a subsequent study, Geen (1977) replicated this result but included a condition in which the observer's presence was defined as nonevaluative and "helpful." The performance of the highly test-anxious subjects was superior in the latter condition, suggesting "that highly test-anxious subjects are more sensitive to audience cues in evaluative situations than less test-anxious ones." Tobias (Chapter 13) cites evidence which demonstrates that high-test-anxious subjects conform more to others' opinions than low-anxious ones in making perceptual judgments (Meunier & Rule, 1967) and are more conforming under conditions of public commitment. Finally, in the previously mentioned study by Nottelman and Hill (1977) in which children varying in test anxiety level were observed while working on anagram tasks, it was found that the highly test-anxious children glanced at the experimenter significantly more often than did the middle- and low-test-anxious children. The conclusion seems inescapable that highly test-anxious persons are more attentive to social-evaluative cues than are low-test-anxious persons.

Attribution Theory Analyses and Test Anxiety

Geen and Phillips et al. (Chapters 3 and 15) have discussed analyses of the attributions of causality made by high- and low-test-anxious persons with reference to their cognitive task performance, especially as a function of success and failure experiences. The reader is referred to the appropriate sections of these chapters for further discussion of responsibility attributions. Suffice it to say at this point that the data regarding attribution of responsibility for task failure is fairly clear in its implications for cognitive analyses of differences between persons high and low in test anxiety. The data regarding responsibility attributions for success feedback is less clear-cut. The performance data indicates that following failure, highly test-anxious people are likely to perform more poorly than they did prior to the feedback, while low-test-anxious individuals are likely to perform better. The reverse performance changes are likely to occur following success; i.e., high-anxious persons perform better and low-test-anxious people perform worse after success.

The "pervading assymetry" (see Geen, Chapter 3) of the contrasting effects of success and failure on the cognitive task performance of persons high and low in test anxiety (or resultant achievement motivation) has been a matter for puzzlement among attribution theorists. Attribution analyses of the performance differences following failure suggest that persons high in resultant achievement motivation (low-test-anxious) attribute their failure to an unstable internal factor, lack of effort, and subsequently direct more effort and attention to the task at hand. It is suggested that persons low in resultant achievement motivation (high-test-anxious) attribute their failure to a stable internal factor, lack of ability, and, subsequently, give up and disengage from the task. No adequate attribution analyses of the differential effects of success on the task performance of persons differing in test anxiety have been advanced.

The major problem for attribution theorists appears to lie in the necessity for postulating different responsibility attributions for high- and low-test-anxious persons as a function of failure versus success. It seems likely, however, that, to date, attribution analyses have been too simplistic and nonspecific. First, although it would be parsimonious for persons at a particular level of test anxiety to make similar kinds of responsibility attributions for both their failures and successes, theoretical parsimony does not necessarily lend itself to an adequate understanding of the complexity of human functioning. Second, the nature of the questions that attribution theorists pose regarding causal factors may not be adequate for an understanding of responsibility attribution as related to test anxiety. Specifically, in this area, attribution researchers might fruitfully pose questions regarding self-evaluation factors and attention to task-relevant cues as opposed to social-evaluative cues.

Briefly, I wish to consider a combination of responsibility attribution interpretations, using Meichenbaum and Butler's (Chapter 9) suggestions regarding internal dialogue, and the task, self, and social-evaluative cues attentional analyses, to arrive at an understanding of the differential responses of high- and low-test-anxious persons to failure and success.

For low-anxious persons, success and failure feedback are likely to be interpreted as task-relevant information. Failure informs the low-anxious person that he or she is not investing enough effort and may result in a self-statement to the effect: "I'm not trying hard enough. I'd better pay attention and work harder."—thus, an internal unstable responsibility attribution. Success has the task informational value for the low-anxious person of confirming his or her ability: "I'm doing OK; I'm bright enough to handle this task; I can relax."—a stable internal attribution.

For highly test-anxious persons failure and success feedback provide information regarding social-evaluative cues bearing upon his/her generally negative self-evaluation. In contrast to the low-test-anxious person, their cognitive set, "current concern," is not "How am I doing?" but "How is this person evaluating me? Has he got my number?" In response to failure feedback, the internal dialogue is likely to resemble the following: "This person thinks I'm stupid and he's right."—a stable internal attribution. In response to success, the dialogue is likely: "I'm reassured; this person doesn't think I'm stupid. *Maybe* I'm not. I'll work very hard and not disappoint him or her." In the traditional attribution theory framework, one may consider another person an external factor and that person's evaluation to be unstable. The internal-external, stable-unstable dimensions are clearly not, however, adequate to describe the causal attributions made by high- and low-test-anxious persons for successful and unsuccessful task performance. The specific nature of those factors, i.e., task, self, social-evaluative and their interaction with the negative self-preoccupation of the high-test-anxious person, must be taken into account.

An additional theoretical construct derived from attribution theory may prove useful to an understanding of cognitive differences between high- and low-test-anxious individuals. The actor–observer distinction advanced by Jones and Nisbett (1972) refers to the "pervasive tendency for actors to attribute their actions to situational requirements, whereas observers tend to attribute the same actions to stable dispositions [p. 80]." These authors reviewed studies in which subjects were asked to attribute responsibility for actions, either when they were observing another person's behavior or when they were reporting on the causes of their own behavior. The evidence indicates that observers tend to attribute responsibility for an actor's behavior to stable personal dispositions of the actor, whereas actors are themselves likely to explain their behavior on the basis of the demands of immediate situational circumstances.

Through the use of videotaped feedback, Storms (1973) has demonstrated that individuals' responsibility attributions along this dimension may be affected by altering their physical point of view. Following brief dyadic social interactions, one-half of the interactants subsequently viewed themselves on videotape from the point of view of an observer, whereas the other half did not. The interactants were then asked to complete questionnaires regarding the extent to which their behavior was determined by stable personal characteristics or by characteristics of the situation. Those subjects who observed themselves on videotape were likely to attribute responsibility for their behavior to their own personal dispositions, whereas the subjects who had experienced the discussion only from the viewpoint of an actor attributed their behavior to situational demands.

Attribution theorists have considered the actor–observer distinction to be one dependent upon physical point of view and not an individual difference characteristic. The dimension has some theoretical value, however, for an understanding of cognitive differences between high- and low-test-anxious persons, and perhaps, for means of altering the chronic self-observation of highly test-anxious persons. In brief, it is suggested that highly test-anxious persons are self-observers in evaluating situations, attributing their typically inadequate performance to stable negative dispositions, whereas low-test-anxious persons may be described as actors matching their behavior to shifting situational demands.

One of I. Sarason's (1968) early modeling studies provides evidence bearing upon this proposition. Delinquent boys differing in level of test anxiety were exposed to models of appropriate social behaviors and then role-played similar responses. Higher levels of test anxiety were facilitative of responsiveness to the modeling *except* when the boys viewed videotapes of their own role-played responses. When given such videotape feedback, test anxiety level was negatively related to the effectiveness of the modeling treatment. Within the context of the present discussion, one might surmise that the videotape feedback accentuated the test-anxious boys' negative self-observation and further decreased their attentiveness to cues in the simulated social situations.

Overt Behaviors and Test Anxiety:
Implications for Cognitive Theory

There is a good deal of evidence regarding systematic variations in task performance as a function of test anxiety and evaluative stress. There is, however, surprisingly little information regarding variations in other behaviors. The previously cited study by Nottelman and Hill (1977) is discussed in this volume by Tobias and Dusek (Chapters 13 and 5, respectively). The visual behaviors of children differing in test anxiety level were observed while performing an anagram task in the presence of an experimenter. The results of the study that bear upon a cognitive-attentional analysis showed that high-test-anxious children glanced away from the task more often than low-test-anxious children, and they glanced more frequently at the experimenter, the social-evaluative figure in the situation. A study by Potter (1974) discussed by Tobias, provides evidence on the test-anxious child's orientation to the social-evaluative figure, the teacher, in the classroom. Test-anxiety level predicted to the number of times children raised their hands in class and how often they initiated private conversations at their desks with the teacher.

Two studies that I've recently reported (Wine, 1975, 1979) provide further information regarding variations in overt behaviors as a function of test anxiety level, in interaction with evaluative stress. Children differing in level of test anxiety were given the opportunity to help another child with a paper-sorting task following completion of a cognitive task administered under either evaluatively stressful conditions or nonstressful conditions. The low-test-anxious children's helping behaviors did not vary with evaluation, whereas the high-test-anxious children were significantly less likely to help in the evaluative than the nonevaluative condition. It appears that the self-preoccupation elicited in the highly test-anxious individual by evaluation may interfere with attentiveness to cues bearing upon the needs of other people as well as to task cues.

In the second study, the overt classroom behaviors of children differing in test anxiety level were observed in an art class immediately before they were to take a difficult examination and in an art class when no examination was expected. Though it was not possible to record children's verbal behaviors, other overt observable behaviors were coded. There were several interactions between test anxiety level and examination-expectancy conditions that reflect the effects of the self versus task-attentional focuses of children differing in test anxiety level. In the examination-expected art class, the low-test-anxious children spent more time working quietly on their art tasks and less time sitting idle than in the no-examination-expected class, whereas the reverse was true for the high-test-anxious children. These results may be interpreted as a reflection of the externally task-focused attention of the less anxious children when anticipating evaluation, and the self-preoccupation of the high. In addition, the high-anxious children both initiated and received significantly fewer communications from other children in the examination-expected than the no-examination class—a result again probably reflective of the self-preoccupation elicited by the threat of evaluation in the highly anxious children. There were no communication differences in the no-examination class.

Several results bear upon the cue-utilization hypothesis. A significant main effect for anxiety revealed that the high-anxious children were much less likely than the lows to look at other children's art work—in the context of an art class, an entirely appropriate behavior and a source of task-relevant cues. In addition, though all of the children listened to the teacher's communications to the entire class more in the examination-expected than the no-examination class, the low-anxious children were more likely to listen to the teacher's communications to other childen in the examination-expected than the no-examination class, whereas the reverse was true for the high-anxious children. If teacher's communications to the entire class are interpreted as a central task cue and his or her communications to another child as a peripheral task cue, these results are in support of the cue-utilization hypothesis.

The results of these two studies are evidence for the pervasive effects of test anxiety in evaluatively stressful conditions on behaviors other than those directly involved in cognitive task performance. The self-preoccupation of the highly test-anxious individual appears to be related to behavioral constriction as well as attentional constriction.

APPROACHES TO ALLEVIATING THE
NEGATIVE EFFECTS OF TEST ANXIETY

A major thrust of the recent literature, in contrast to the early work in test anxiety, is a search for means of reducing test anxiety and alleviating its debilitating effects on task performance. Most of the contributions to this volume reflect this general concern. I have not, therefore, simply restated the findings thoroughly discussed by other contributors but rather have selectively summarized those studies which bear upon a cognitive-attentional theory of test anxiety. These investigations may be grouped under the headings of experimental, educational, and treatment approaches.

Experimental Approaches

Geen's chapter is the most complete in its discussion of experimental laboratory manipulations intended to facilitate test-anxious persons' cognitive performance. The reader is referred to his excellent chapter (Chapter 3) for a thorough discussion of this work. Other contributors, including Dusek, Tobias, and Mueller have made briefer reference to this research; in addition, Rosenthal has discussed laboratory studies of modeling effects on test-anxious persons. In this section, the major findings bearing upon a cognitive-attentional analysis are briefly summarized, followed by a description of a study (Crossley, 1977) in which attentional training implications of the direction of attention hypothesis were systematically examined. An overview of I. Sarason's excellent work on laboratory manipulations designed to facilitate test-anxious persons' cognitive performance and a summary of his research on the effects of observation of models on the performance of persons differing in test-anxiety level conclude the section.

It should be noted, initially, that those experimental manipulations showing the greatest applied promise are those which facilitate the highly anxious individual's performance, while simultaneously maintaining the high performance levels of low-test-anxious persons. Although success feedback, discussed in the preceding section, has a facilitating effect on the subsequent performance of highly test-anxious persons, it has a detrimental impact on the performance of low-test-anxious subjects. The same observation holds for the "reassurance" instructional manipulations designed to eliminate evaluative stress, investigated by I. Sarason. Geen (1977) has reported a study in which evaluative stress was manipulated by defining the presence of an observer as helpful and *information giving* versus evaluative. The helpful condition facilitated the cognitive performance of high-test-anxious subjects to a level comparable to that of the low-anxious subjects.

Several studies have demonstrated that attention-directing, task-orienting manipulations have facilitative effects on test-anxious persons' recall and cognitive task performance. Dusek, Kermis, and Mergler (1975) and Dusek, Mergler, and Kermis (1976) reported that labeling of stimuli in a learning task facilitated the recall of high-test-anxious children to a level comparable to that of low-test-anxious children, in comparison to a no-labeling condition. In a provocative study, Edmunsen and Nelson (1976) found that instructions to use mental imagery, in contrast to mere rehearsal, facilitated recall of paired associates for high-A-trait subjects to a recall level comparable to that of low-A-trait subjects. Mueller (1978) investigated the effects of an orienting task designed to focus attention on attributes of verbal lists on the recall of persons differing in level of test anxiety. His findings indicated that a "deep processing" semantic orienting task was facilitative of high-test-anxious persons' recall, resulting in comparable recall to that of the low-test-anxious persons. In a second study Mueller, Bailis, and Goldstein (1978) examined the effects of several orienting tasks on facial recognition. The recognition accuracy of the highly anxious subjects was facilitated by the use of an orienting task which required them to make self-reference judgments regarding each face. However, self-reference judgments hindered the performance of low-anxious subjects. The results of these studies are consistent in indicating that task-attention-directing procedures and procedures that provide specific instructions on appropriate task strategies have beneficial effects on test-anxious persons' cognitive performance while maintaining the high performance levels of low-anxious persons. Removing evaluative stress or suggesting that low-test-anxious persons shift from their typical external task focus to self-reference has detrimental effects on low-anxious subjects' performance; however, high-test-anxious persons' performance is benefited by such manipulations.

O'Neill and Richardson (Chapter 14) and Tobias (Chapter 13) have discussed the results of a number of studies which examined interactions between test anxiety and experimental manipulations in computer-assisted or self-instructional contexts. Though the results of this research are somewhat disappointing in their failure to replicate findings, there is consistent evidence to indicate that the use of "memory supports" (Sieber, 1969), procedures designed to reinstitute previous segments of task input, are beneficial to high-test-anxious students' performance but do not hinder that of low-anxious students. These results again support the use of task-orienting procedures.

In quite a different vein, Weiner and Samuels (1975) investigated the impact of cognitive labeling of affective states on performance. As Holroyd has documented, although highly test-anxious persons do not show higher levels of tonic physiological reactivity than lows, they report greater distressing emotionality. These investigators examined the impact of cognitive reintepretation of affective states, using a misattribution procedure. High- and low-test-anxious subjects completed a difficult anagram task in either a control or a misattribution condition, in which they were instructed that their arousal was a result of a pill they had taken. Attributing arousal to the pill facilitated the performance of high-test-anxious subjects to a performance level comparable to the lows. Most likely, the misattribution procedure directed the high-anxious subjects' attention away from preoccupation with and concern over arousal.

Crossley (1977) reported a carefully controlled experimental analog study that is the most direct existing test of the attentional training implications of the direction of attention hypothesis. The Thurstone Hidden Digits Test (HDT), a task highly reflective of immediate attentiveness to task cues, was used as a dependent measure. The task consists of a number of capital letters concealed in a series of black dots superimposed on a white background, which are presented tachistoscopically via slides in a rapid series of discrete trials. Self-report test anxiety level was a second dependent measure. Following pretesting with these instruments, which revealed that high-test-anxious subjects performed more poorly than the low-anxious on the HDT, all subjects were given three half-hour training sessions in one of three conditions: Task-attentional training, relaxation training, and a placebo condition, all presented via typewritten scripts. The attentional training scripts were based on a test anxiety cognitive-attentional treatment manual devised by this author (1974). The relaxation training scripts were based on sections from Jacobson's (1964) *Anxiety and Tension Control,* whereas the placebo condition scripts consisted of three achievement-oriented autobiographical stories. None of the conditions had significant effects on the test anxiety level or cognitive task performance of low-test-anxious subjects. The high-test-anxious subjects in both the attentional and relaxation training conditions reported significant reductions in test anxiety level. *Only* those highly test-anxious subjects who were given attentional training improved in their performance on the HDT, and they improved to a level comparable to that of the low-test-anxious subjects. These results provide strong support for the task-attentional training implications of the direction of attention hypothesis.

I. Sarason has been a major contributor to the exploration of experimental manipulations beneficial to the performance of test-anxious persons. His investigations of the effects of variations in instructions and exposure to models on performance of a variety of cognitive tasks provide valuable clues for means of reducing the debilitating effects of test anxiety.

As noted earlier, he has investigated "reassurance" instructional manipulations (I.Sarason, 1958, 1972b) with verbal learning tasks. These instructions warned that many people would become tense when performing this kind of task, that progress would be slow, and that the subject should concentrate on the task rather than worrying about performance. The instructions might be described as informative and attention-directing as well as reassuring. In both studies, "reassurance" facilitated the performance of high-test-anxious persons but resulted in performance reductions for low-test-anxious subjects.

In two additional studies, I. Sarason (1972b, 1975b) has explored further the use of informative, attention-directing instructions. In the first of these, five instructional variations were used with a verbal learning task: minimal task instructions, achievement orientation, reassurance, task orientation, and motivating task orientation. The effects of the latter condition are those of most interest in the present context. These instructions informed subjects that the experimenter was interested in the shape of learning curves rather than individual performance. In addition, subjects were told that they would find the task interesting and worthwhile. Highly test-anxious subjects performed best in the motivating task-orienting condition. Consistent with previous research, low-test-anxious subjects performed best in the achievement-orientation condition, but their performance in the motivating task-orientation condition was very nearly as high. The second study investigated instructional manipulations interpolated between two anagram tasks; all subjects were arbitrarily failed on the first task. The interpolated conditions included waiting silently, being reassured by the experimenter, being given specific, useful hints about how to solve anagrams, and being reassured plus being given hints. The latter condition was most conducive to the high-test-anxious subjects' performance on the second anagrams task. The low-anxious subjects performed best in the hints-only condition, but their performance in the reassurance-plus-hints condition followed closely. In brief, these studies indicate that task instructions that direct attention away from self-preoccupied worry, direct attention to tasks, and give information about appropriate problem-solving strategies are helpful to the test-anxious individual's cognitive functioning. They also minimize performance differences between high- and low-test-anxious persons.

Sarason has also made a considerable contribution by investigating the influence of observation of models by persons differing in test-anxiety level on performance of several kinds of tasks. In the first of this series of studies, Sarason, Pederson, and Nyman (1968) found that observation of a task-oriented, businesslike model performing a serial verbal learning task facilitated the subsequent verbal learning of highly test-anxious subjects. Subsequent studies explored the effects of characteristics of models' problem-solving behaviors and feedback to models on high- and low-test-anxious individuals' cognitive performance.

In one of these studies (I. Sarason, 1973), prior to solving anagrams, subjects observed a model either silently solving anagrams, or describing the manipulation of letters while solving the anagrams, or describing principles underlying the successful solution of anagrams while working. The high-test-anxious subjects performed best in the latter condition, again indicating the value of providing the test-anxious person with information regarding cognitive problem-solving principles.

Studies of the effects of exposure to models who succeed, fail, or are self-derogatory are somewhat more difficult to interpret. In one study, I. Sarason (1972b) found that exposure to a model who made self-derogatory comments while performing serial verbal learning tasks had no differential effects on the subsequent performance of high-and low-test-anxious subjects on a similar task. In the same study, the verbal learning of high-test-anxious subjects was detrimentally affected by exposure to a model who received failure feedback on a similar task but was positively affected by exposure to a model who received success feedback. The reverse was true for the low-test-anxious subjects. Similar results were obtained in another study (I. Sarason, 1972b) in which word association test performance was examined, especially with regard to the detrimental effects of observing a failing model on the performance of highly anxious subjects. Clues to the lack of detrimental impact on the high-anxious subjects' performance as a result of exposure to self-derogatory models, whereas exposure to failing models was quite debilitating, are provided by the construct of the "coping model." Meichenbaum has described the coping model as one who experiences problems similar to those of the subject but who actively copes with and overcomes those difficulties in successful goal attainment. It is likely that the self-derogatory model was seen as coping with problems similar to those of the test-anxious subjects and thus did not negatively influence their subsequent performance. Failure feedback, on the other hand, is clear-cut evidence of a failure in coping efforts.

I. Sarason (1975a) has examined this possibility by exposing subjects to a model who admitted experiencing anxiety and described ways of coping with it, or to one who only admitted to the anxiety, versus one who did not admit to anxiety. Exposure to the self-disclosing coping model was highly facilitative of the test-anxious subjects' verbal learning. The results of these studies suggest, in general, that exposure to models who are task-oriented and provide attention-directing cognitive structuring clues is beneficial to the performance of test-anxious persons. Evidence in the behavior of the model that he or she is successfully coping with the worry and tension associated with test anxiety is of additional benefit to the test-anxious person.

The laboratory experimental literature has provided very rich information regarding procedures for improving the test-anxious individual's cognitive functioning while not interfering with the performance of low-anxious persons. These procedures may be described as attention-directing task orientation, cognitive aids to memory, information regarding problem-solving strategies, cognitive reinterpretation of arousal, and exposure to effective coping models.

Educational Approaches

Although the experimental literature is rich in its implications for performance improvement in test-anxious persons and test anxiety reduction, the results of the educational research literature have proven disappointingly meager in this regard. Perhaps the major difficulty involved in achieving beneficial effects with specific manipulations in the school environment is that noted by Phillips et al., in Chapter 15, regarding the pervasive atmosphere of evaluation in the schools. It is extemely difficult to manipulate specific variables intended to alleviate the effects of test anxiety without taking into account the total ecology of the school environment. As Phillips et al., have documented, when tests are administered with instructions varying in evaluative stress, highly test-anxious children are likely to perceive all conditions as evaluative in nature, whereas low-anxious children respond to the essential nature of the task. Therefore, it appears unlikely that weak, localized manipulations will beneficially affect test-anxious children in the traditional classroom setting.

As discussed in the preceding section, research on computer-assisted instruction and individualized programmed instructional approaches has provided some information regarding procedures helpful to test-anxious students. It should be noted at the outset, however, that CAI and individualized instructional formats may have little generalization value for the conventional classroom setting. Typically, these formats are administered without the mediation of a social-evaluative figure in the setting, analogous to a teacher. Feedback, when provided, is usually mediated via the computer or the instructional materials themselves rather than through an evaluating figure. One of I. Sarason's (Sarason & Harmatz, 1965) early studies demonstrated that test anxiety level does not interact with machine-mediated feedback. In order for this research to have direct applied value for the typical educational setting, it may be necessary to have individuals emitting social-evaluative cues present during the instruction. Indeed, the CAI research has reported some difficulties in replicating interactions commonly found in other laboratory research between various evaluative stress manipulations and test anxiety. This failure to replicate may simply reflect the fact that typically the tasks were not completed in the presence of an evaluating observer. Other features of the prototypical individualized instructional format that reduce evaluative stress, such as self-pacing, informational feedback, and the opportunity to branch back to previous task input, also probably water down the effects of additional evaluative-stress manipulations.

I do not wish to imply that I consider the evidence from this literature irrelevant to educational practices. Indeed, the CAI and individualized instructional research have very powerful implications for education; these implications are expanded upon in the concluding section of this chapter. At this point, I will simply describe the major findings of this research that bear examination in the ecology of the school setting. Those variables that have proven beneficial to test-anxious students and that leave the performance level of low-test-anxious students unaffected are procedures which allow self-pacing and give students the opportunity to reinstitute segments of previous task input as well as highly organized, clear instructional materials.

These results have been replicated in classroom settings, where Oosthoek and Ackers (1973) reported that the opportunity to rewind an audiotape presenting task materials facilitated test-anxious students' performance. Two studies (Dowaliby & Schumer, 1973; Domino, 1974) reported that tightly organized instructor-centered classes were beneficial to test-anxious students' achievement, in comparison to more loosely structured, student-centered classes.

Other investigators have examined the interaction between test anxiety and instructional modes, described variously as: highly structured, teacher-oriented, "direct," "conventional" versus loosely structured approaches, student-centered, "indirect," "open," and "individualized" approaches. The combined results of these investigations have been confusing and conflicting. I have not discussed these findings in detail but refer the reader to the appropriate sections of Chapter 13 (Tobias) and Chapter 15 (Phillips et al.). Differing and sometimes directly opposed findings have been reported in this area; test anxiety and instructional format interact with other personality indices, ability level, age, and educational level, and the overall results form no interpretable pattern. It may well be that these studies have examined variables that were too gross, broad in definition, and as Tobias suggests, more "conservative unpacking" of these variables is necessary. In my view, it seems likely that these studies were not directed to the most germane issues that interact with test anxiety in the school environment relating precisely to its "pervading atmosphere of evaluation," or stated differently, evaluative stress versus task-orientation variables.

Treatment Approaches

In broad overview, the treatment research literature has not kept pace with theoretical and laboratory research advancements in the field, though there are pockets of exciting developments. The major reason for the lag in evolution of treatment approaches appropriate to test anxiety lies in an observation which I made in my 1971 review:

> *these studies have evolved from interest in specific treatment techniques, rather than from an analysis of the nature and effects of test anxiety.* Test anxiety has been considered to be a severe problem and thus its treatment is considered a stringent test of systematic desensitization procedures. It has implicitly been

assumed that test anxiety differs only in degree from the specific anxieties dealt with in much of the behavior modification literature [p. 10].

This state of affairs has not changed markedly. Allen, Elias, and Zlotlow (Chapter 8) make very similar observations regarding the very recent test anxiety treatment literature, though they view the situation positively: "...test anxiety is indeed a useful target construct for assessing the efficiency and efficacy of a growing number of therapeutic interventions." "...we must insure that our therapeutic manipulations are construct valid comparisons of competing models of basic behavior change processes."

I view the focus on treatment interventions as contrasted to a focus on the nature of the target problem of test anxiety as an unfortunate one. In my earlier 1971 review paper, it was stated that "...by training test anxious subjects to relax in the presence of progressively more stressful stimuli, a systematic desenitization treatment approach assumes that the emotional arousal component of test anxiety is its defining characteristic [p. 101]," as opposed to its cognitive components. The recent treatment literature continues to reflect the assumption that emotional arousal is the major characteristic of test anxiety and to focus on anxiety or arousal reduction. This state of affairs is due largely to the fact that the traditional behavior therapy methodologies have been concerned with "anxiety reduction," defined as emotionality.

An examination of the 43 studies reviewed by Allen et al. reveals that 26 of them used treatment approaches explicitly and solely designed to reduce emotionality. The nature of these approaches is much more varied than in the earlier treatment literature. In addition to variants of traditional systematic desensitization, implosion, anxiety management, cue-controlled relaxation, active coping relaxation, autogenic training, and biofeedback have been investigated for their impact on test anxiety. All of these approaches assume emotionality to be the major characteristic of test anxiety in spite of mounting evidence to the contrary. Ten studies examined treatment approaches which may be described as explicitly cognitive in nature, either singly or in comparison with emotionality-based approaches. Of these 10 studies, eight provided test-anxious students with study skills training, which may be described as a rather gross, but traditional, therapy intervention which may or may not address the specific cognitive concomitants of test anxiety. That is, a subgroup of test-anxious students may require assistance in this regard, but study skills training does not specifically address the major cognitive characteristics of test-anxious persons, i.e., negative self-preoccupation, and attention to evaluative cues to the detriment of task cues. Only two of the 43 studies focused specifically on cognitive restructuring. The therapy modalities used in the remaining seven studies cannot be readily classified as solely emotionality-based or cognitively based.

The aforementioned remarks are not intended to detract from the excellence of the Allen et al. chapter, which is a very competent methodological overview of the test anxiety behavior therapy research literature. Indeed, Allen (1972) was the earliest reviewer to note that behavior therapy practices focused solely on emotionality reduction, though likely to produce self-reported reductions in test anxiety level, were highly unlikely to effect changes in cognitive performance. The studies he reviewed indicated that it was necessary to combine such approaches with therapy modes focused specifically on cognitive change in order to reliably elicit improvement in cognitive performance. His review has been updated by other reviewers (Wine, 1973; Spielberger, Anton, & Bedell, 1976) who reached the same conclusions. In the present Allen et al. chapter, this point is further emphasized by their observation that "multimodal" treatment packages are most likely to be effective and by their support for the measurement of multiple domains related to test anxiety. The major point I wish to make is that the behavior therapy research literature on test anxiety, as a whole, continues to adopt an emotional reactivity interpretation.

I wish also to note that I do not consider emotionality-based approaches to be entirely misguided. As Deffenbacher and Holroyd and Appel have documented, high-test-anxious persons do typically self-report distressingly high levels of physiological reactivity, though physiological measures do not support their self-report. They are preoccupied with their internal physiological processes as well as with other internally focused cognitions. It may be beneficial, if only for heuristic reasons, to provide test-anxious students with self-control strategies for managing physiological reactivity or reinterpretations of the arousal so that attentional and cognitive processes may be freed to redirect to task cues. However, such procedures may have little or no impact on actual tonic physiological reactivity.

Test anxiety treatment is a major focus of a number of other chapters in this volume, including those of Denney, Deffenbacher, Richardson and Woolfolk, and Rosenthal, all of which have emphasized cognitive self-control or restructuring procedures or the impact of specific therapy practices on cognitive performance. Meichenbaum's and Seiber's provocative suggestions regarding new directions in test anxiety treatment strategies are discussed in the concluding "Implications" section of this chapter.

Denney's insightful review is of a smaller number of treatment studies that were specifically focused on training test-anxious persons in self-control strategies. Prior to examining the conclusions from his review, it is important to observe that, even among researches specifically generated from a self-control perspective, an emotional reactivity interpretation predominates. Of the 20 studies reviewed by Denney, 12 used only treatment approaches addressed to emotionality reduction, i.e., desensitization, relaxation, and anxiety management. Of the remaining eight studies, six compared emotionality reduction procedures to cognitive modification approaches, whereas only two examined cognitive restructuring techniques alone. Clearly, a cognitive-attentional interpretation of test anxiety has not permeated the treatment literature.

In his discussion of these studies, Denney has ordered them on a continuum on which one extreme represents approaches solely focused on emotionality reduction, whereas the other extreme emphasizes cognitive restructuring. The labels used for sections of the continuum are: at the extreme left, "applied relaxation techniques;" in the center, "self-control training techniques"; and at the far right, "cognitive coping techniques." As one moves from left to right on the continuum, there is increasing emphasis on in vivo application training, guided rehearsal, in addition to cognitive restructuring. (See Fig. 10.1, Chapter 10). His analyses of the comparative impact of these treatment strategies on cognitive performance is startling in its clarity. Of the studies categorized under "applied relaxation," only 33% resulted in cognitive performance improvement for test-anxious students. Among those classified as "self-control training," 50% effected cognitive performance improvement, whereas 71% of the studies employing "cognitive coping" techniques demonstrated cognitive improvement. The reader is referred to Denney's excellent chapter for a more detailed discussion of this research.

Deffenbacher's chapter (Chapter 6) reviewing the literature on the Worry–Emotionality analysis of test anxiety contains reference to several treatment studies generated from this framework. His discussion of this work does not refer to cognitive performance changes but rather to the effects of emotionality versus worry-focused treatment approaches on the differential reduction of self-reported emotionality and worry. In general, these studies do not indicate that emotionality-reduction and worry-reduction strategies differentially affect self-reports of emotionality and worry; rather these two kinds of self-report indices tend to co-vary in response to these treatments. One explanation for these results lies in the observation made previously that emotionality self-control procedures, as well as cognitive approaches, likely have impact on cognitive processes, on the "contents of consciousness." Or as Deffenbacher notes: "It may be that relaxation-based interventions reduce worrisome cognitions and that cognitive restructuring reduces physiological arousal or at least the preoccupation with it."

Richardson and Woolfolk (Chapter 12) review research related to mathematics anxiety in which several treatment studies are discussed. The MARS (Richardson & Suinn, 1972), reproduced in Chapter 12, has been used as the major self-report index of treatment effectiveness. The instrument requires respondents to rate their subjectively experienced anxiety levels in response to a wide variety of math-related activities—clearly an emotional reactivity measure. The nature of the math anxiety treatment studies reviewed by Richardson and Woolfolk also reflects an emotionality interpretation. The results of these studies "encouraged the belief that behavior therapy programs of this type have an impact on math anxiety (as assessed by the MARS), but they do not clearly demonstrate effectiveness in improving math performance, in maintaining this improvement, or in modifying other attitudes that may indicate participation and pleasure in mathematics-related activities." Richardson and Woolfolk suggest that future treatment efforts in this area adopt a cognitive-attentional interpretation of math anxiety and employ multifaceted treatment approaches. They describe the work of mathematics clinics at Wellesley and Mills Colleges and their own recent, as yet unassessed treatment efforts that adopt such a multifaceted approach, providing math-anxious students with cognitive restructuring and highly specific task-oriented information on math-related activities as well as techniques for managing emotionality. Perhaps the self-report measurement devices in this area will soon reflect this shift to a concern with cognitive processes, a highly desirable shift in view of the very cognitively demanding nature of mathematics.

Rosenthal's chapter on modeling approaches is a wide-ranging one, reviewing both laboratory and treatment research on modeling approaches to test anxiety and "related performance problems." The construct underlying these performance problems may be labeled "evaluation anxiety" or "evaluation apprehension," as discussed in a preceding section. Unfortunately, there is very little treatment research in contrast to laboratory research on the effects of modeling specifically with test-anxious individuals. Most of the modeling treatment studies that have been reported have adopted an emotionality interpretation of test anxiety and report that vicarious desensitization is as effective in reducing self-report test anxiety level as is direct desensitization. There are two treatment study exceptions to the preoccupation with systematic desensitization in the modeling research reviewed by Rosenthal, though both were based on emotionality interpretations. Horne and Matson (1977) reported that test-anxious students exposed to multiple models learning to face examinations calmly surpassed a number of other treatment strategies in impact, including desensitization. Jaffe and Carlson (1972) found that exposure to a model experiencing but coping with anxiety, in comparison to a mastery model, resulted in improved cognitive performance as measured by an intelligence test and course grades.

Rosenthal's chapter is rich in suggestions for future directions in test anxiety treatment research. He proposes as a unifying construct for the effects of modeling approaches Bandura's (1977) "belief in self-efficacy," the belief that one is capale of performing the actions necessary to achieve desired consequences. Self-efficacy is a very useful theoretical construct in an understanding of test anxiety and is discussed in the following section.

In summary, an overview of the test anxiety treatment literature reveals that researchers in this area, by and large, continue to adhere to an emotional reactivity interpretation of test anxiety. The evidence points to the inescapable conclusion, however, that cognitively based treatment strategies are more powerful in effecting cognitive performance change and as effective in reducing self-report test anxiety level as are emotionality-based approaches. It is hoped that future treatment research efforts in this area will reflect the weight of this evidence. The laboratory experimental literature, the modeling research, and the CAI literature provide abundant suggestions for future treatment efforts.

A BIDIRECTIONAL MODEL OF TEST ANXIETY

At the outset, I must state that I do *not* consider test anxiety to be a unitary dimension. As indicated earlier in this chapter, and as other contributors, including Meichembaum, Dusek, and Seiber have noted in their thoughtful discussions, test anxiety is a multidimensional construct. Highly test-anxious persons are likely to resemble each other on additional dimensions more than do low-test-anxious persons, because test anxiety indices are designed to measure the presence of test anxiety. However, there are probably as many differences within each group as there are similarities. I also wish to note that, though I have used self-efficacy as one unifying theoretical construct in the subsequent discussion, test anxiety and self-efficacy are not identical constructs. The Measure of Academic Self-Efficacy (Lalonde, 1978) referred to earlier, correlated -.36 with the TAS in a sample of 350 adolescents, indicating some overlap but not identity. Combining test anxiety measurement with measures of positive orientations to achievement should improve predictive power in future test anxiety research. Further measurement devices directed toward specific cognitive concomitants of test anxiety are desperately needed.

Having made these comments, I will now proceed to ignore my own warnings by considering test anxiety as a unitary dimension and speculating regarding cognitive-attentional characteristics of individuals scoring at extremes on test anxiety measures. In justification, the extreme scorers whose characteristics are discussed are the "prototypical" or "ideal" high-test-anxious and low-test-anxious individuals. An explicit assumption is that the low-test-anxious persons who are described are that subgroup of extreme low scorers who have positive orientation to achievement. Most of the cognitive-attentional differences between high- and low-test-anxious individuals that have been documented by research have been alluded to earlier in this chapter. In the present section, those differences for which there exists evidence have been combined with a speculative discussion regarding additional possible differences.

The research literature provides more information regarding the contents of consciousness of the highly test-anxious person than of the lows. It is obvious, for example, that highly test-anxious individuals are likely to have a general cognitive set of negative self-preoccupation. They are likely to carry around with them a set of negative self-deprecatory cognitions that are readily elicited by the threat of evaluation. These cognitions may vary across individuals but are probably quite stable within a given individual. Moreover, test-anxious persons are likely to interpret a wide range of situations as evaluative and be tuned to cues from other persons which they interpret as reflecting evaluatively upon them. They are more likely to perceive such cues as negative than positive. Their negative self-preoccupation and characteristic absorption in social-evaluative cues interfere with memory storage of task information, attention to task cues, and with cognitive task performance in general as well as being associated with inaction and behavioral constriction. Their current and constant concern is "How am I being evaluated?"; their expectation is "I'm being negatively evaluated."; and they generate a variety of negative self-statements from these general sets. Their self-statements while performing tasks are likely to be task-irrelevant, to be "out of the situation" cognitions, either global negative self-evaluations or preoccupation with failures in the past or future negative consequences. These cognitions may be viewed as functional in that they protect the individual from action, i. e., by being preoccupied with such cognitions, the test-anxious person avoids those noxious tasks on which he or she anticipates being negatively evaluated. An additional task-avoidant strategy lies in their interpretation of physiological arousal as unpleasant and distressing, and their preoccupation with it.

In order to describe the cognitive-attentional concomitants of low test anxiety, we must fill in holes in the evidence through educated guesswork. The cognitive structures and self-statements of the low-test-anxious individual are not simply the opposite of that of the highs but rather differ qualitatively. For example, whereas high-test-anxious individuals are negatively self-preoccupied, it is highly unlikely that low-test-anxious persons are positively self-preoccupied. Although they have a high generalized belief in their own self-efficacy, they are highly unlikely to be cognitively preoccupied with talking to themselves about how wonderful they are. Indeed, the contents of consciousness of the low-test-anxious individual probably reflect current concerns, such as "What are the demands of this situation?" and "What can I do to meet those demands?" Thus, their self-statements will vary from situation to situation and will reflect their processing of the cues that they perceive as relevant in each situation and the generation of appropriate behaviors for dealing with the specific demands presented to them. In short, cognitions are likely to be situationally specific, and active or problem-solving in nature. Low-test-anxious persons are less likely than high-test-anxious persons to interpret situations as evaluative in nature, but when they do, they are more likely to see the evaluation as positive than negative. When negative evaluation is clear-cut, it is interpreted as a challenge and an opportunity to exercise their problem-solving skills. When physiologically aroused, they are likely to interpret the arousal as energy, alertness, and being "turned on" and to direct that energy to situational demands.

In the preceding discussion, I have referred primarily to the language dimension of cognitions; however, language is not synonymous with thought. It is likely that high- and low-test-anxious individuals differ markedly in imagery as well as in verbalized thoughts. Mahoney and Avener (1977) recently reported highly provocative results regarding differences in cognitions between successful and unsuccessful Olympic athletes; this set of findings bears examination by researchers in evaluation anxiety. One difference between the successful and unsuccessful athletes was their use of kinesthetic versus visual imagery in imagined rehearsal of competitive behavior. According to Mahoney and Avener (1977), the successful athletes used kinesthetic imagery which "requires an approximation of the real-life phenomenology such that the person actually imagines being inside his/her body and experiencing those sensations which might be expected in the actual situation [p. 137]." In contrast, in the same study, the less successful athletes tended to use visual imagery, in which "a person views himself from the perspective of an external observer [p. 137]." These differences are reminiscent of the actor–observer dimension proposed earlier in this chapter as characterizing low- and high-test anxious persons, respectively.

Clearly, the bidirectional cognitive-attentional model presented in this section goes far beyond the existing data and bears detailed research examination. These proposed differences are summarized as follows:

Low-Test-Anxious	High-Test-Anxious
Current concerns—relevant cues in situation and appropriate actions	Current concerns—evaluation of others and anticipation of negative evaluation.
Focused on task or situation	Focused on self and social-evaluative cues
Task-oriented	Task-avoidant
Actor	Observer
Behavioral, problem-solving cognitions	Static cognitions
Active	Inactive

Low-Test-Anxious	High-Test-Anxious
High belief in self-efficacy	Low belief in self-efficacy
In the present	Out of the situation
Cognitions situationally specific (wide range)	Cognitions global and stereotypic (restricted range)
Arousal interpreted as energy (directed to problem-solving)	Arousal interpreted as distress (preoccupied with)
Kinesthetic imagery— rehearsal of problem-solving strategies	Visual imagery-observes self negatively evaluated

FUTURE DIRECTIONS IN TEST ANXIETY THEORY AND RESEARCH

I view this volume as an extremely exciting one. Each contribution is of the highest quality, every chapter reflects concern with the nature and negative effects of test anxiety, and each author suggests means for alleviating those effects. The volume is far from being the "swan song" of test anxiety research. Rather, exciting directions for additional research are evident in each of these reviews and in an overview of them as representative of the best, most recent, and thorough compilation of research findings in test anxiety. As I have strongly suggested earlier, future researchers may generate more appropriate descriptive labels than "test anxiety" and should begin to tease apart the construct into its cognitive, behavioral, and affective components.

Nature and Concomitants of Test Anxiety

It is apparent that a more complex theoretical model of test anxiety is in the offing; indeed, in the preceding section I have presented an informal description of some possible dimensions of such a model. Meichenbaum (Chapter 9) and Sieber (Chapter 2) have also made interesting suggestions that serve to enrich test anxiety theory. It is clear that theoretical advancements will be cognitive in nature, with specification of cognitive structures, internal dialogue, the nature of imagery and fantasy, and of attentional and memory processes. In addition, theoretical constructs are likely to specify overt behavioral concomitants of test anxiety beyond those specifically related to cognitive task performance. Interpretations of physiological reactivity are an important aspect of emerging test anxiety theory. In this context, Alpert and Haber's (1960) intriguing theoretical derivations regarding debilitating versus facilitating anxiety merit further attention. In the context of theoretical development, it is essential that constructs concerned with the development of test anxiety be generated and that hypotheses derived from them be put to empirical test. This concern is expanded upon in the following section.

Development of Test Anxiety

The paucity of research findings in this area is appalling. We know virtually nothing about how children are socialized to differential levels of test anxiety, why some survive the evaluative atmosphere of the school setting with aplomb, or why others succumb to it. Dusek (Chapter 5) has reviewed the few existing studies in this area. The research reported by S. Sarason et al. (1960) remains the most extensive in this area; it concludes that test anxiety is a function of interaction with parents who set unrealistically high levels of expectation for the child, focus on failure, and give a great deal of negative feedback. Examination of problem-solving interactions between parents and children suggest straightforward modeling of behaviors and direct instruction, with the parents of high-test-anxious children engaging in task-irrelevant behaviors and behaving aversively towards their children. Parents of low-anxious children are task-focused, offer effective problem-solving strategies while allowing the child to complete the task. Additional research in this area is sorely needed, especially with regard to parental socialization practices.

Sex Differences

The only chapter in this volume to reflect a concern with sex differences is Chapter 12 by Richardson and Woolfolk on the topic of mathematics anxiety, perhaps because this is a cognitive performance area in which females have been socialized to experience more difficulty than males. Additional research on sex differences is indicated. There is some evidence that females are generally higher in fear of negative evaluation than males, that they are more likely to devalue their cognitive performance, and that they score higher on most test anxiety measures. Many laboratory investigations of test anxiety use only females as subjects. Is this because females tend to respond more in accord with hypotheses derived from test anxiety theory? Further explicit examination of sex differences in test anxiety in interaction with theoretically relevant variables is indicated for laboratory, educational, and treatment research.

Laboratory Experimental Research

The interaction between test anxiety level and evaluative-stress dimensions has been amply researched, except perhaps with children. Test-anxious children interpret a much wider range of situations as evaluative in nature than do test-anxious adults. It is of interest to examine the structures which mediate these differences. Perhaps these findings simply reflect the development with age of discrimination abilities. Perhaps, however, they reflect the continuous exposure on the part of young children to specific evaluating adults, to the single teacher in the traditional classroom, and to deprecatory parents.

Further exploration of task-orienting, attention-directing experimental manipulations is important, building on the already existing excellent work on task instructions, orienting tasks, the use of imagery, attentional training, and memory supports. Memory research is quite rich in methodological suggestions for test anxiety researchers. Memory researchers would also do well to attend to differences that have been identified between high- and low-test-anxious individuals. The *content* of memory materials might be varied e.g., social-evaluative versus task-informational. In examining the use of self-reference orienting tasks, evaluative (smarter, more attractive than me) versus physical dimensions (taller or darker-haired than me) might have differential effects.

The competing models that Geen (Chapter 3), Wachtel (1967), and I have proposed regarding the anxiety–cue-utilization hypothesis merit experimental examination i.e., the flashlight beam analogy, as opposed to cues perceived as task-relevant or task-avoidant, and development of the internalization of task-avoidant behaviors. Holroyd and Appel's (Chapter 7) exciting suggestions regarding differential patterning of physiological responding as a function of test anxiety and internal versus external attention deserve experimental examination.

The actor–observer research alluded to earlier merits examination for means to encourage the test-anxious individual to assume the role of actor as opposed to the typical role of self-observer. In interpersonal evaluative situations, other interactants' behaviors might be videotaped from the visual perspective of the evaluation-anxious person and replayed to accentuate the "actor" role and to alert him or her to the others' behavioral cues. This approach would extend the use of memory supports from cognitive task performance to interpersonal performance.

Educational Applications

Initially, I should note that the following suggestions are highly idealistic and unlikely to be readily adopted by the conventional educational system. In my view, it is precisely the "pervading atmosphere of evaluation" in the schools, which is referred to by Phillips et al., that must be altered in order to elicit reductions in test anxiety and change its accompanying performance decrements and behavioral constrictions.

Specific suggestions for altering the evaluative character of the school are:

1. Redefinition of the teacher and his or her role. Rather than the traditional heavily evaluative character of the teachers' interactions with children, a shift is proposed to a task-oriented, information-giving role model, showing excitement and involvement in specific subject matter.

2. Following directly from the preceding suggestion it is suggested that feedback be informative, immediate, and directed to specific tasks rather than global evaluations. Though Glasser's *Schools Without Failure* (1969) has not gained academic respectability, many schools have adopted his approaches. It would be of interest to examine the test anxiety levels *and* cognitive performance of children in these schools in comparison to conventional schools.

3. More heretic yet, it is suggested that the teacher, as a social-evaluative figure, remove himself or herself as much as possible from the test-anxious child's environment. The CAI and self-instructional literature provide strong support for individualized, well-organized, self-paced, immediate-feedback instructional packages, which provide the opportunity to replay task segments. These require minimal intervention from an evaluating teacher.

4. Finally, task materials should be made as interesting and engaging as possible and should be presented with task-oriented, curiosity- and attention-eliciting instructions, with a minimal evaluative component.

Treatment Research

The treatment literature has, on the whole, lagged far behind in its development in comparison to other areas of test anxiety research. If the emotional reactivity interpretation of test anxiety were dropped and the adherence to traditional therapy approaches that assume such an interpretation were weakened, treatment developments might take place in widely varying directions. Though cognitive-attentional theory is likely to guide new treatment efforts, these efforts may be in a variety of directions, ranging from cognitive modification, self-instructional training, rational restructuring, and attentional training, to "taking responsibility." Meichenbaum, Seiber, and Richardson and Woolfolk present thoughtful discussions of alternative treatment approaches, which are appropriately complex to the intricacy of evaluation anxiety, and which emphasize individualization of treatment and cognitive theory or the phenomenology of consciousness. Rosenthal (Chapter 11) also provides a number of exciting suggestions for the application of modeling approaches derived from social learning theory that are assumed to have direct impact on the level of self-efficacy. Empirical examination of these approaches is essential.

In working with evaluation-anxious clients, I have found a social learning theory approach, developed by Christensen (1974), to be highly effective. The model assumes that emotion is a byproduct of behavior and cognition rather than playing a directive function. The basic components of the treatment approach include:

1. Identification of troublesome social stimuli which are specific behaviors of significant persons in the client's life. These stimuli are typically evaluative in nature.

2. Imaginal kinesthetic exposure to the troublesome stimuli until the client can tolerate the image without becoming tense and experiencing the need to avoid or change it. Seiber's description of "taking responsibility" bears a close similarity to this procedure.

3. Cognitive reappraisal of the troublesome stimuli.

4. Experimentation with alternative behaviors in the presence of the stimuli.

An additional essential component is examination of one's own impact on others. The client is taught to make specific descriptive observations of others' behaviors and his or her own and to check inferences, such as evaluative ones, carefully through observation. Though I have not submitted the model to empirical test specifically in its impact on evaluation-anxious clients, it has been demonstrated in several studies to be highly effective with a variety of populations. It is suggested that more sophisticated cognitively based models of this kind be examined in their impact on test-anxious persons.

This brief summary of possible theoretical and research directions in test anxiety do not, of course, exhaust the possibilities of a cognitive-attentional analysis of test anxiety. It is suggested that the reader direct his or her attention to the task at hand. The possibilities are exciting.

REFERENCES

Alpert, R., & Haber, N. Anxiety in academic achievement situations. *Journal of Abnormal and Social Psychology,* 1960, *61,* 207–215.

Bandura, A. Self-efficacy: Toward a unifying theory of behavioral change. *Psychological Review,* 1977, *84,* 191–215.

Christensen, C. *Development and field testing of an interpersonal coping skills program.* Unpublished manuscript, Ontario Institute for Studies in Education, 1974.

Christensen, C. *An interpersonal coping skills approach to counseling.* Unpublished manuscript, Ontario Institute for Studies in Education, 1978.

Crossley, T. *The examination and validation of attentionally based test anxiety reduction on college freshmen.* Unpublished MA thesis, University of New Brunswick, 1977.

Domino, G. *Aptitude by treatment interaction effects in college instruction.* Paper presented at the American Psychological Association Convention, New Orleans, September, 1974.

Doris, J., & Sarason, S. B. Test anxiety and blame assignment in a failure situation. *Journal of Abnormal and Social Psychology,* 1955, *50,* 335–338.

Dowaliby, F. J. & Schumer, H. Teacher centered vs. student-centered mode of college instruction as related to manifest anxiety. *Journal of Educational Psychology,* 1973, *64,* 115–132.

Dusek, J. B., Kermis, M. D., & Mergler, N. L. Information processing in low- and high-test anxious children as a function of grade level and verbal labeling. *Developmental Psychology,* 1975, *11,* 651–652.

Dusek, J. B., Mergler, N. L., & Kermis, M. D. Attention encoding, and information processing in low- and high-test anxious children. *Child Development,* 1976, *47,* 201–207.

Easterbrook, J. A. The effect of emotion on cue utilization and the organization of behavior. *Psychological Review,* 1959, *66,* 83–201.

Edmunsen, E. D., & Nelson, D. L. Anxiety, imagery and sensory interference. *Bulletin of the Psychonomic Society,* 1976, *8,* 319–322.

Ganzer, V. G. Effects of audience presence and test anxiety on learning and retention in a serial learning situation. *Journal of Personality and Social Psychology,* 1968, *8,* 194–199.

Geen, R. G. Test anxiety, observation, and range of cue utlization, *British Journal of Social and Clinical Psychology,* 1976, *15,* 253–259.

Geen, R. G. The effects of anticipation of positive and negative outcomes on audience anxiety. *Journal of Consulting and Clinical Psychology,* 1977, *45,* 715–716.

Glasser, W. *Schools without failure.* New York: Harper and Row, 1969.

Hill, K. T. Anxiety in the evaluative context. In W. W. Hartup, (Ed.), *The Young Child* (Vol. 2). Washington D.C.: National Association for the Education of Young Children, 1972.

Horne, A. M., & Matson, J. L. A comparison of modeling, desensitization, flooding, study skills and control groups for reducing test anxiety. *Behavior Therapy,* 1977, *8,* 1–8.

Jacobson, E. *Anxiety and tension control.* Montreal: Lippincott, 1964.

Jaffe, P. G., & Carlson, P. M. Modeling therapy for test anxiety: The role of modeled affect and consequences. *Behavior Research and Therapy,* 1972, *10,* 329–339.

Jones, E. E., & Nisbett, R. E. The actor and the observer: Divergent perceptions of the causes of behavior. In E. E. Jones, D. E. Kanouse, H. H. Kelley, R. W. Nisbett, S. Valins, & B. Weiner, (Eds.), *Attribution: Perceiving the causes of behavior.* Morristown, N.J.: General Learning Press, 1972.

Klinger, E. *Meaning and void: Inner experience and the incentives in people's lives.* Minneapolis: University of Minnesota Press, 1977.

Lalonde, B. *The construction and validation of a measure of self-efficacy.* Unpublished PhD. dissertation, Ontario Institute for Studies in Education, 1979.

Liebert, R. M., & Morris, L. W. Cognitive and emotional components of test anxiety: A distinction and some initial data. *Psychological Reports,* 1967, *20,* 975–978.

Mahoney, M. J., & Avener, M. Psychology of the elite athlete: An exploratory study. *Cognitive Therapy and Research,* 1977, *1,* 135–141.

Mandler, G., & Sarason, S. B. A study of anxiety and learning. *Journal of Abnormal and Social Psychology,* 1952, *47,* 166–173.

Mandler, G., & Watson, D. L. Anxiety and the interruption of behavior. In C. D. Spielberger (Ed.), *Anxiety and behavior.* New York: Academic Press Inc., 1966.

Many, M. A., & Many, W. A. The relationship between self-esteem and anxiety in grades four through eight. *Educational and Psychological Measurement,* 1975, *35,* 1017–1021.

Marlett, N. J., & Watson, D. Test anxiety and immediate or delayed feedback in a test-like avoidance task. *Journal of Personality and Social Psychology,* 1968, *8,* 200–203.

Meichenbaum, D. A cognitive-behavior modification approach to assessment. In M. Hersen & A. S. Bellack (Eds.), *Behavioral assessment: A practical handbook.* New York: Pergamon, 1976.

Meunier, C., & Rule, B. G. Anxiety, confidence, and conformity. *Journal of Personality,* 1967, *35,* 498–504.

Mueller, J. H. The effects of individual differences in test anxiety and type of orienting task on levels of organization in free recall. *Journal of Research in Personality,* 1978, *12,* 100–116.

Mueller, J. H., Bailis, K. L., & Goldstein, A. G. *Depth of processing and anxiety in facial recognition.* Paper read at the annual convention of the Midwestern Psychological Association, Chicago, 1978.

Neale, I. M., & Katahn, M. Anxiety, choice, and stimulus uncertainty. *Journal of Personality,* 1968, *36,* 235–245.

Nottleman, E. D., & Hill, K. T. Test anxiety and off-task behavior in evaluative situations. *Child Development,* 1977, *48,* 225–231.

Oosthoek, M., & Ackers, G. The evaluation of an audio-tape mediated course II. *British Journal of Educational Technology,* 1973, *4,* 54–73.

Osterhouse, R. A. Desensitization and study skills training as treatment for two types of test anxious subjects. *Journal of Counseling Psychology,* 1972, *19,* 301–307.

Potter, E. F. *Correlates of oral participation in classrooms.* Unpublished doctoral dissertation, University of Chicago, 1974.

Richardson, F. C., & Suinn, R. M. The Mathematics Anxiety Rating Scale: Psychometric data. *Journal of Counseling Psychology,* 1972, *19,* 551–554.

Rosenberg, M. J. When dissonance fails: On eliminating evaluation apprehension from attitude measurement. *Journal of Personality and Social Psychology,* 1965, *1,* 28–43.

Sarason, I. G. The effects of anxiety, reassurance, and meaningfulness of material to be learned on verbal learning. *Journal of Experimental Psychology,* 1958, *56,* 472–477.

Sarason, I. G. Empirical findings and theoretical problems in the use of anxiety scales. *Psychological Bulletin,* 1960, *57,* 403–415.

Sarason, I. G. Verbal learning, modeling and juvenile delinquency. *American Psychologist,* 1968, *4,* 254–266.

Sarason, I. G. Experimental approaches to test anxiety: Attention and the uses of information. In C. D. Spielberger (Ed.), *Anxiety: Current trends in theory and research,* (Vol. 2). New York: Academic Press, 1972.(a)

Sarason, I. G. Test anxiety and the model who fails. *Journal of Personality and Social Psychology,* 1972, *22,* 410–413.(b)

Sarason, I. G. Test anxiety and cognitive modeling. *Journal of Personality and Social Psychology,* 1973, *28,* 58–61.

Sarason, I. G. Test anxiety and the self-disclosing coping model. *Journal of Consulting and Clinical Psychology,* 1975, *43,* 148–153. (a)

Sarason, I. G. Test anxiety, attention and the general problem of anxiety. In C. D. Spielberger & I. G. Sarason, (Eds.) *Stress and anxiety* (Vol. 1). Washington D.C.: Hemisphere, 1975.(b)

Sarason, I. G. Anxiety and self-preoccupation. In I. G. Sarason & C. D. Spielberger (Eds.), *Stress and anxiety* (Vol.2). Washington, C.D.: Hemisphere, 1976.

Sarason, I. G., & Ganzer, V. J. Anxiety, reinforcement and experimental instructions in a free verbalization situation. *Journal of Abnormal and Social Psychology,* 1962, *65,* 300–307.

Sarason, I. G., & Ganzer, V. J. Effects of test anxiety and reinforcement history on verbal behavior. *Journal of Abnormal and Social Psychology,* 1963, *67,* 513–519.

Sarason, I. G., & Harmatz, M. G. Sex differences in experimental conditions in serial learning. *Journal of Personality and Social Psychology,* 1965, *1,* 521–524.

Sarason, I. G., & Koenig, K. P. The relationship of test anxiety and hostility to description of self and parents. *Journal of Personality and Social Psychology,* 1965, *2,* 617–621.

Sarason, I. G., Pederson, A. M., & Nyman, B. Test anxiety and the observation of models. *Journal of Personality,* 1968, *36,* 493–511.

Sarason, I. G., & Stoops, R. Test anxiety and the passage of time. *Journal of Consulting and Clinical Psychology,* 1978, *46,* 102–109.

Sarason, S. B., Davidson, K. S., Lighthall, F. F., Waite, R. R., & Ruebush, B. K. *Anxiety in elementary school children.* New York: Wiley, 1960.

Sarason, S. B., Mandler, G., & Craighill, P. G. The effect of differential instructions on anxiety and learning. *Journal of Abnormal and Social Psychology,* 1952, *47,* 561–565.

Sarbin, T. R. Ontology recapitulates philology: The mythic nature of anxiety. *American Psychologist,* 1968, *23,* 411–418.

Schwartz, R. M., & Gottman, J. M. Toward a task analysis of assertive behavior. *Journal of Consulting and Clinical Psychology,* 1976, *44,* 910–920.

Sieber, J. E. A paradigm for experimental modification of the effects of test anxiety on cognitive processes. *American Educational Research Journal,* 1969, *6,* 46–61.

Spielberger, C. D., Anton, W. D., & Bedell, J. The nature and treatment of test anxiety. In M. Zuckerman & C. D. Spielberger (Eds.), *Emotions and anxiety: New concepts, methods and applications.* Hillsdale, N.J.: Lawrence Erlbaum Associates, 1976.

Spielberger, C. D., Gonzalez, H. P., Taylor, C. J., Algaze, B., & Anton, W. D. Examination stress and test anxiety. In C. D. Spielberger & I. G. Sarason (Eds.), *Stress and Anxiety* (Vol. 5). Washington, D.C.: Hemisphere Publishing, 1978.

Spielberger, C. D., Gorsuch, R. L., & Lushene, R. E. *Manual for the state–trait anxiety inventory.* Palo Alto, Calif.: Consulting Psychologists Press, 1970.

Storms, M. P. Videotape and the attribution process: Reversing actors' and observers' points of view. *Journal of Personality and Social Psychology,* 1973, *9,* 297–306.

Suinn, R. The STABS, a measure of test anxiety for behavior therapy: Normative data. *Behaviour Research & Therapy,* 1969, *7,* 335–339.

Trapp, E. P., & Kausler, D. H. Test anxiety level and goal-setting behavior. *Journal of Consulting Psychology,* 1958, *22,* 31–34.

Wachtel, P. L. Conceptions of broad and narrow attention. *Psychological Bulletin,* 1967, *68,* 417–429.

Weiner, B. The role of success and failure in the learning of easy and complex tasks. *Journal of Personality and Social Psychology,* 1966, *3,* 339–344.

Weiner, M. J., & Samuels, W. The effects of attributing internal arousal to an external source upon test anxiety and performance. *Journal of Social Psychology,* 1975, *96,* 255–265.

Weiner, B., & Schneider, K. Drive versus cognitive theory: A reply to Boor and Harmon. *Journal of Personality and Social Psychology,* 1971, *18,* 258–262.

Wine, J. D. Test anxiety and direction of attention. *Psychological Bulletin,* 1971, *76,* 92–104.

Wine, J. D. *Cognitive-attentional approaches to test anxiety modification.* Paper presented at the annual conference of the American Psychological Association, Montreal, August, 1973.

Wine, J. D. Counsellor's manual for attentional strategies in evaluation anxiety management. Invited address, the Atlantic Regional Conference of the Canadian University Counseling Association, Halifax, April, 1974.

Wine, J. D. Test anxiety and helping behaviour. *Canadian Journal of Behavioral Science,* 1975, *3,* 216–222.

Wine, J. D. Test anxiety and evaluative stress: Children's behavior in the classroom. *Journal of Abnormal Child Psychology,* 1979, *7,* 45–59.

Wine, J. D. Evaluation anxiety: A cognitive-attentional construct. In H. W. Krohne & L. C. Laux (Eds.) *Achievement, stress and anxiety.* Washington, D.C.: Hemisphere, in press.

Author Index

Numbers in italic indicate the page on which the complete reference appears.

Subject Index

Social interaction,
  preexamination, 192–193
  therapeutic change of, 25–26
  mathematics and, 279
State anxiety, 20
  components of, 112, 123–124
State Anxiety Inventory, 353
State-Trait Anxiety Inventory, 94, 165
State-trait model, 18–21
  components of, 21–24
Stimulus (i), of anxiety, see also Test stimuli
  transpersonal psychology and, 36
Stress, reponses to, 6
Stress-inoculation training, 204–205
Stress management, computer-assisted
    training in, 319–325
Study counseling,
  desensitization with, 192
  effectiveness of, 180
Study habits, 192
  improvement of, 192
Subpoena, of research data, 30
Success,
  attribution of reasons for, 359–362
  etiology of test anxiety and, 91–94
  reactions to, 51–54
Suinn Test Anxiety Behavioral Scale
    (STABS), 165, 274, 352, 353
Systematic rational restructuring, 234–235

T

Task demands, physiological arousal and,
    137–141
Task difficulty, 301
  reactions to success and failure and,
    51–52
Teacher,
  anxiety in, effect on students, 334
  effect on test anxiety, 333
  evaluative responses of, students'
    responses to, 334–336
  expectancies of, 106
Test(s),
  guessing corrections and, 332–333
  instructions for, 331–332
  order of items in, 331
Test anxiety,
  bidirectional model of, 375–378
  concomitants of, 378–379

Test anxiety (cont.)
  definition of, 15–18, 351–352
    operational, 24–26
    state-trait model and, 18–24
  development of, 379
  effects of, 289–290
    on children, 90–94
  etiology of, 88–90, 341–342
  mathematics anxiety and, 274, 278
  measurement of, 94, 352–354
  model of, 189–201
    treatment and, 201–205
  as motive to avoid failure and criticism,
    329–330
  prevalence and significance in school,
    328–329
  study and definition of, ethical
    considerations in, 27–32
Test Anxiety Questionnaire, 94
Test Anxiety Scale (TAS), 94, 165, 352
  cue utilization and, 44–45
  research using, 8–12
Test Anxiety Scale for Children (TASC),
    94–95, 352
  developmental trends in, 97–99
  multidimensionality of, 95–97
Test stimuli, 18–19
  definition of, 21
  interpretation of, 19
    definition of, 21–22
    transpersonal psychology and, 36
Test-taking behavior, 193
Theory, future directions in, 378–382
Therapist specificity, in outcome studies,
    175
Thought see also Cognitive structures;
    Internal dialogue
  attributional, 321
  moralistic, 321
Trait anxiety, 20
  cue utilization and, 44
Trait Anxiety Inventory, 352
Transpersonal psychology, 33–37
Treatment, see also specific approaches
  approaches to, 25–26
  for A-state reactions, 23
  ethical considerations and, 27, 31–32
  instructional, 291–292
    postprocessing effect and, 295
    preprocessing and, 292, 294
    processing effect and, 294